Esther-Maria Guggenmos

"I believe in Buddhism and Travelling"

BEITRÄGE ZUR KULTURWISSENSCHAFTLICHEN SÜD- UND OSTASIENFORSCHUNG

Herausgegeben von

Eva De Clercq, Bart Dessein, Franziska Ehmcke,
Ann Heirman, Andreas Niehaus

Band 7

ERGON VERLAG

Esther-Maria Guggenmos

“I believe in Buddhism and Travelling”

Denoting Oneself a Lay Buddhist in Contemporary Urban Taiwan

ERGON VERLAG

Cover photo:
A lay Buddhist taking a picture at the temple site of an innovative Buddhist movement. Tang style figures, fireworks, an illumined Christmas tree, recitations inside the temple hall, fortune-telling, and a barbeque restaurant provide a rich array of entertainment to be enjoyed under the label of Buddhism.
Photo taken in Taiwan by the author, New Year's Eve, Taipeh county, 2007.

Bibliographic information published by the Deutsche Nationalbibliothek
The Deutsche Nationalbibliothek lists this publication in the Deutsche Nationalbibliografie; detailed bibliographic data are available in the Internet at http://dnb.d-nb.de.

Gedruckt auf alterungsbeständigem Papier.
Satz: Sandra Kloiber, Ergon-Verlag GmbH
Umschlaggestaltung: Jan von Hugo

www.ergon-verlag.de

ISBN 978-3-95650-216-3
ISSN 2195-0962

Dedicated with love to my family
and
in gratitude and respect to all my interviewees

Preface

Historically, Buddhism was studied by Europeans and Americans from a philosophical and philological perspective at first. It were among others Richard Gombrich for the case of South Asian Buddhism (Gombrich 1971) and Holmes Welch with regard to Chinese Buddhism (Welch 1967) who introduced English speaking readers to the field of how we have to imagine daily Buddhist life. Gaining a deeper understanding of Buddhist doctrine and of a professional Buddhist self-understanding and life concepts, naturally the question arises that of what the average lay Buddhist actually believes. What leads an average citizen to state that she or he is a Buddhist? What do people understand by "being a lay Buddhist"? Is "being a Buddhist" socially well recognised? In different ways, these questions were approached with regard to East Asia (esp. China and Taiwan) in research projects in the last ten years–and in one way or another the researchers involved in these projects were all given the chance to learn about each other's work, especially within the frame of the "Buddhism after Mao" project initiated by Ji Zhe, CNRS, Paris ("Le bouddhisme après Mao: religion, politique et société en Chine depuis 1980", Groupe Sociétés, Religions, Laïcités, CNRS-EPHE, Paris, sponsored by Ville de Paris, and follow-up projects). The recent reemergence of Buddhism and the general revival of religion on the mainland is attracting academic attention. Two extensive studies, both concentrating on the Chinese mainland, share the concrete focus on lay Buddhist life with the work presented: Gareth Fisher (*From Comrades to Bodhisattvas*, 2014) focuses in his ethnographical field study on the outer courtyard of the Temple of Universal Rescue in Beijing, while Alison Denton Jones (*A Modern Religion? The State, The People, and the Remaking of Buddhism in Urban China Today*, PhD thesis, 2010) focuses on lay Buddhism in the city of Nanjing. The results of these two works and that presented here enable for the first time a comparison between lay Buddhist belief on the Chinese mainland and in Taiwan. Therefore, while the present book provides an in-depth analysis of lay Buddhist self-denotification in contemporary urban Taiwan, it includes in its final reflections a first comparison between the situation of lay Buddhists in mainland China and Taiwan.

The work on lay Buddhist self-denotification in contemporary Taiwan that is presented here is based on narrative biographical interviews. In the introduction, the leading question of this book is developed with the help of statistical material, the *Taiwan Social Change Survey*, and the methodology is outlined. The statistical finding that the percentage of Buddhists is higher in the urban areas of Taiwan than in rural areas induces the question of why this is so and therefore leads the quantitative approach to a qualitative analysis of the interviews presented in Part I and II. In Part I, full case analyses are given with the aim of analysing the conventional narrative patterns underlying lay Buddhist self-construction. In Part II, intense believers and practitioners exploring new options for living a Buddhist lay life are in the focus. Finally, a reflection on the attractiveness of denoting oneself a Buddhist in the urban spaces of Taiwan compares the findings with the situation in mainland China.

The interviews are analysed with the help of Structural Hermeneutics by Ulrich Oevermann. The methodology itself is explained in the introduction. Its characteristic is that the researcher–deeply familiar with the situation under investigation–takes a step back and goes (with the help of a group of interpreting colleagues), sentence by sentence, into the layers of meaning that the interview text provides in order to build up a structural hypothesis and compare it with other parts of the interview. This procedure takes space and time. The method was originally developed to analyse the mental maps of blue collar workers in Germany and became one of the main methods for qualitative interview analysis in Germany. It has been applied in Anglo-American sociology in single cases only. This is the first time that this method is used in a context which is culturally different from that of the researcher. Therefore, this book takes the freedom to present full-case analyses first, and only in its second part shortens new cases to the form of portraits. The reader who would like to learn more about the analytical method might go more deeply into the methodological chapter and read through the whole case analyses. Anyone who would like to learn more about lay Buddhism in Taiwan might jump directly to the respective case summaries and reflections in the first part and skip the longer analyses.

Finally, a preface offers the precious chance to express one's gratitude. This present monograph results from my PhD thesis that was completed in 2010 at Ghent University and it goes without saying that it is with deep thankfulness that I remember all my teachers, colleagues, and friends who made my time at Ghent a highly academically fruitful, inspiring and joyful time of my life. I am indebted to Ann Heirman, who as my adviser during my PhD research supported me with her profound comments. It was on her initiative that a generous four year scholarship from the Belgium Research Foundation from 2005–2009 enabled me to undertake extensive field research, participate in international conferences, and work as a research assistant at the Department of Eastern Languages and Cultures at Ghent University–four years, for every aspect of which I am deeply grateful. During that time, I also greatly benefited from the extensive guidance of Albrecht Schöll in the field of Structural Hermeneutics, whose methodological advice kept the process on track.

As any field research comes to life through the interaction between its members, my gratitude and respect go to all of the innumerable lay devotees who graciously allowed me to participate in their life experience of "Buddhism", especially all of my interviewees. Not only are these too numerous to be named individually, but my methodological commitment to anonymity also prevents me from mentioning any of them specifically. Still, it was their hospitality, warm-hearted openness without prospect of reward, help and patience that made this study possible. I did my best to try to analyse the concepts of "Buddhism" as they presented them through their narrations. Nevertheless, while I wish to share the credit for this project with everyone who was involved in it, any and all errors of judgement or fact are of course my responsibility alone. Concerning the statistical investigations and other sociological and anthropological questions, I owe a deep debt of gratitude to Chiu Hei-Yuan, Tang Chih-Chieh, Hsin-Huang Michael Hsiao, and Ting Jen-Chieh of the Academia Sinica. Chiu Hei-Yuan not only introduced me to the *Taiwan Social Change Survey*, but also examined my interpretations in detail and graciously discussed subtle questions with me during his stay in Leiden in 2008. Invaluable also was the help of Sun Kuei-Fang, who helped with decoding precisely and conscientiously whatever utterances the interviewee records had caught. She, together with a group of students from the University of Münster, helped enormously by exploring the possible width of associations that the transcriptions hold. The courses and meetings on training methods for qualitative research offered by the Seminary of Religious Studies, University of Münster, with Annette Wilke gave the project a perfect and methodologically concise start.

In the past five years, the unique intellectual *fluidum* at the International Consortium for Research in the Humanities in Erlangen, with its director Michael Lackner, was the solid base for my postdoctoral research after 2009 and gave my intense focus on lay Buddhism a broader perspective. I am grateful to Ji Zhe who invited me to join his "Buddhism after Mao" project (see above, Paris, November 2012 and October 2014) and who managed to assemble nearly all scholars working on contemporary Buddhism in mainland China in Paris so that we could dive freely into an exchange on the latest sociological and anthropological works in progress.

Over the years, many teachers, colleagues, and friends have contributed valuable inspirations and suggestions to this book. The contact with the Chung-Hwa Institute of Buddhist Studies and the exchange that grew out of the highly informed comments I received on several papers at conferences in Oregon, Taipeh, Cambridge, Paris, and at the Chinese Academy of Social Sciences helped to shape and develop further my ideas. I am grateful to my colleagues and all those who helped in various ways to make my numerous stays in Taiwan a success including especially: Marcus Bingenheimer, Adam Yuet Chau, Isabelle Devos, Vincent Goossaert, Friedrich Grohmann, Marcus Günzel, Fabian Heubel, Carys Humphreys, Charles Brewer Jones, Hans-Rudolf Kantor, Barbara Meisterernst, Christian Meyer, Ng Zhiru, Albert Poulet-Mathis†, Hanspeter Rissi, Dan Stevenson, Francesca Tarocco, Stefania Travagnin, Wei Chih-Xian, Robert Weller, the family Züger-Fischer, as well as Mieke Matthyssen and the colleagues in Ghent, who nearly all were working on topics related to Chinese Buddhism. Yü Chün-Fang, Edith Franke, Albrecht Schöll, and Bart Dessein served on the reading committee for the dissertation and their comments and encouragement helped strongly to transfer the manuscript into a book. Sue Casson accepted the challenge of checking my "German English" with enormous reliability and speed. It is due to the high aesthetic sensitivity and design talent of the Sinologist Florian Wagner that the graphics gained their beautiful shape. I am thankful to the Center for the Anthropology of Religions at the Friedrich-Alexander University Erlangen-Nürnberg which financed the correction. My special gratitude goes to the the publisher, Hans-Jürgen Dietrich, and the series editors, who made it possible for the manuscript to become part of a wider discourse in cultural studies in South and East Asia. Their constant exchange, support and certainly also patience brought the project to fruition in this final phase.

Finally, all of this would be unthinkable without the boundless love and support of my family and beloved ones. It is my parents, my brother and his wife, and my husband whose encouragement, patience and understanding saw me through all these years and were of crucial help solving the communicational miracle between necessary deprivation and care. I hope that the times of seclusion serve the pleasure of the readers whose comments are deeply welcomed and appreciated.

Erlangen, March 2016 Esther-Maria Guggenmos

Contents

Tables

Figures

Definitions

Young Buddhist Monasteries

The term indicates Taiwanese monasteries established since the 1960s and includes especially Tzu Chi 慈濟, Foguang Shan 佛光山, Fagu Shan 法鼓山, Zhongtai Shan 中台山, Lingjiu Shan 靈鷲山 and Tianfo Shan 千佛山. They mainly inherited the ideals of Buddhist Modernism, the search for an active role in society and a focus on the involvement of lay people beyond simply giving donations. In order to preserve the anonymity of the interviewees, the monasteries are renamed as Monastery A–F without keeping the above named order. They are randomly but consistently named with their respective abbots as [..., monastery A–F]; [..., abbot A–F].

New Buddhist Organisations

In contrast to the Young Buddhist Monasteries, this term refers to the more recently established Buddhist organisations, some of which are composed wholly of lay people. Their doctrinal development is often still in process and they are less aware of the reformatory monastic tradition of the mainland, but highly influenced by the needs of an urbanised society. They might emphasise international involvement, interreligious openness, ecological sustainability and processual thinking. Examples include Sōka Gakkai 創価学会, Fuzhi 福智, Fosheng Zong 佛乘宗, or Master Xiao Pingshi's 蕭平實 Zhengjue Tongxiu Hui 正覺同修會. These organisations are also kept anonymous for the above mentioned reason.

This twofold structure–for details please refer to ann. 5–especially with its time period connection, helps to provide a rough structure for the broad field of Buddhist organisations in Taiwan, but is of course of a preliminary nature and cannot be applied indiscriminately to all cases.

Conventional Buddhists

Those people who, when asked in the *Taiwan Social Change Survey* 2004.2 about their religious affiliation, chose the option "believing in/venerating Buddha" (*xinfo baifo* 信佛拜佛). The other options offered the possibility to identify with various Buddhist schools like Zen or Pure Land. This definition is further developed through the qualitative approach (see especially pp. 225–226).

Specifying Buddhists

This group is complementary to the group of Conventional Buddhists and refers to all those who opted for a specific Buddhist school in the survey. Other options of intense Buddhist belief are explored in Part II of this book.

A Note on Romanisation

The romanisation of Chinese is marked by italics and presented in *Hanyu Pinyin*. The romanisations of Japanese, Sanskrit, and Pāli are also marked by italics despite certain words which have become common in English usage, such as karma, sūtra, Mahāyāna, Theravāda, etc. The diacritics are preserved. As in general, works and titles (but not beings) are marked in italics, names of people, other beings, and also organisations are not marked by italics (the '*Amitābha Sūtra*', but the bodhisattva 'Amitābha').

Rules and Abbreviations for Transcription and Translation–Interviews

Taiwanese sentences are transcribed as far as they were understood. They are marked by "[tw]". Where they were not understood, the passage is left out and marked by "[…, tw]".

The translations aim to make the structure of spoken Chinese traceable. Aesthetic and literary considerations do not serve this purpose and therefore the translations given cannot be read fluently. Still, in contrast to the transcriptions, the translations have been punctuated for readability.

Quotations are arranged according to interacts and sequences:

(1)	Interact 1, 2, 3, ...	Interacts of the first passage analysed in detail in the interpretation. This is mostly the initial sequence of the interview regarding the answer to the introductory stimulus.
(S1)	Sequence 1, 2, 3, ...	Sequences that were chosen for further analysis. The selected sequences can be found anywhere in the interview besides the initial sequence.
(R1)	Reference 1, 2, 3, ...	Other short interacts from the same interview.

List of Abbreviations

[1.1:00]	title and time of record [title.minute:second]
[…]	omission
[?]	transcription uncertain
[xxx]	Non-verbal events and comments of the author are inserted in square brackets.
[slurred]	expression preceding brackets lacks precise pronunciation, but is understood
[..., slurred]	inaudible, murmured, hastily spoken passages in the text, not transcribed
[sc. xxx]	scilicet: amendation by author
[/xxx]	alternative for translation
[i.e. xxx]	id est: The expression preceding the brackets is explained by the author.
[lit. xxx]	term preceding the brackets means literally "xxx"
[skt. *xxx*]	Sanskrit equivalent "xxx" of the term preceding the brackets
[BT]	Buddhist Terminology
[saying]	a saying in Chinese is translated freely or, if literally, it is put in quotation marks in advance: "xxx" [saying]

[..., names/ places etc.]	Names of persons and places have been anonymised despite the capital Taipeh.

In some transcriptions–especially in the answers to the introductory stimulus–phonological exactness is especially important for the interpretations. The following abbreviations have been used in these passages:

xxx/	A sudden stop in the middle of a sentence, syntagma or word, which is often not recognisable in the melody of the sentence itself.
[b]	The speaker makes a longer break, more than three seconds, taking a breath, etc.
?	rising voice
.	falling voice
↑xxx ↑	passage in significantly higher voice
↓xxx ↓	passage in significantly lower voice
←xxx →	stretched manner of speaking
→xxx ←	accelerated manner of speaking

Terminological Conventions

Some termini are very common in (Buddhist) Chinese, but sound unfamiliar in English. The conventions chosen for translation are given here and the terms are then not further marked in the translations (not [BT] e.g.):

bai	拜	to venerate, to worship
xiu	修	to practise, mostly in the sense of applying the Buddhadharma in everyday life
guiyi	皈依	to take refuge
fofa	佛法	Buddhadharma, Buddha's dharma, the teaching of the Buddha
chujia	出家	to leave home (in order to get a monastic)
fahui	法會	Literally speaking, a "dharma meeting" is a gathering of Buddhists mostly for recitations, but also for preachings or worship. It is translated with "dharma assembly" or in fixed expressions according to its function also with "recitation" or "ceremony".
Shuilu Fahui	水陸法會	Water and Land Ceremony
Hufahui	護法會	Dharma Protection Society, abbrev. DPS

The whole complex of karmic thinking is highly casual in Chinese, but unfamiliar in English. Therefore translations partly indicate the karmic associations, partly give a more casual English pendant.

yuan	緣	In its Buddhist meaning it refers to a causal relationship as any event can be seen as being the result of its conditions and therefore having a karmic relationship–*you yuan* 有緣–with them.
suiyuan	隨緣	following one's karma, i.e. acting according to given conditions
you yuanfen	有緣分	to have a karmic/causal relation with something or someone.
you yuan	有緣	as *you yuanfen*

For a deeper analysis, please refer to chap. 8.1.

Interjections are transcribed as the speaking manner of the interviewee is essential to the analysis. The following interjections were chosen for transcription according to the sound uttered and independently of their meaning and their sometimes partly grammatical function:

a	阿	reproduced in the translation as "a"
ei	欸	reproduced in the translation as "ei"
m	ㄇ	reproduced in the translation as "m"
ne	呢	reproduced in the translation as "ne"
la	啦	reproduced in the translation as "la"
o	哦	reproduced in the translation as "o"
le	了	is grammatically translated otherwise not reproduced
jiu	就	is translated as "just" wherever possible
na	那	reproduced in the translation as "na"

Introduction

1 "I believe in Buddhism and Travelling"

"I think, Buddhist belief influences my life.
In fact, there is another one:
I think, travelling also hugely influences me".
(Interview with Kong Shuqing, Taipeh, 2005)[1]

While enjoying a lovely cup of green tea in an apartment building located in the more industrial suburbs of Taipeh, the author asked one of her early Taiwanese interviewees, Kong Shuqing 孔淑青 (female, age about 45), in spring 2005, about how her Buddhist belief influences her life. At that time, the interviewee showed a perpetual interest in presenting her holiday photographs and stated that she was inspired by "Buddhism" as well as "travelling". Her wish to combine her interests by embarking on a cycling trip to one of the most important Buddhist monasteries in Taiwan made the researcher–eager to get to the core of lay Buddhism in Taiwan–nervous at first. Still, the analysis of a broad range of interviews led the author back to this precise inconspicuous sequence as it illustrates a peculiarity of religious belief in Taiwan: The fields of discourses on "religion" as well as "Buddhism" cannot be seen as separate differential categories, but serve as an integral part of the interviewee's self-concept.

The interviewee agrees that Buddhist belief influences her life.[2] It gives her–she explains a few sentences later–an understanding of her own destiny

1 The name of Kong Shuqing is fictitious as are the names of all other interviewees. The interviews have been recorded under this premise (for details see the methodological explanations in this introduction).

2 The following paragraphs analyse the interviewee's concept of "belief" and her perceptions of "Buddhism" and "religion" in relation to "travelling." Interview passage: "Interviewer: So that belief influences your life? Kong: Yes. In fact, I think, Buddhist belief influences my life. In fact, I have another one: I think, travelling also hugely influences me. Right. When you travel more, for example, like you for a long time/ Taiwan is a small island state. Your life choice is here. But if you are often here, if you don't go wandering around, you will/ you also have no chance to broaden your mind. But if you often go wandering around, when you walk to many places, you/ you will discover/ your mind will be a bit broader, sometimes you will tend not to argue about some problems. Regarding your view on life, you might also be slightly happier. When you encounter problems, you won't feel so frustrated. When you travel a lot, your will/ your view of life will change. Of course, also some belief related views of Buddhism have on us some/ some influence. For example, we say, we humans all carry karma with us. Karma, you know? That karmic retribution of Buddhism. In fact, a lot of this Buddhist karmic retribution, a lot of karma you/ you have to accept yourself. Others cannot accept it in your place. Na, perhaps there is some karma you brought with you from your last life. Na, in this world, if you don't practise well, in the next life, this karma will still follow you. So, in Buddhism, one says, karma is personal. There is also no way that others can help you to accept it. There-

through its karmic concept. The insight, that negative events in her life are a consequence of her bad karma: 1) helps her to face them alone and not expect others to help her out; and 2) equips her with a positive attitude towards life, as she does not think about negative incidents once they are over, because bad fortune decreases one's bad karma and therefore any bad "luck" will end at some point. "Buddhism" is, for the interviewee, radically reduced to a cognitive insight that enables her to cope in a positive way with the ups and downs of life. It is, for her, a resource for coping with life, which can be summed up in a couple of sentences, neither deserving deeper study of Buddhist doctrine nor involving any ritual dimension. Statistical investigations conducted by the *Taiwan Social Change Survey* show that the belief in karmic retribution is widespread in Taiwan.[3] In 2004, 75.5% (1420/1881) of the population accepted the concept of karmic retribution in general (TSCS 2004.2), although only a quarter of the population defined themselves as "Buddhists" on the same questionnaire (453/1881), and merely 4.4% (83/1881) stated that they had undergone a formal Buddhist initiation process, such as taking refuge. Regarding "Buddhist orthodoxy", one might, from a

fore, only you yourself can change your karma. You have to rely upon your own practice, on your practice in your everyday life, to change your karma. Na, sometimes when karma appears in front of your eyes, sometimes it gives you a concept. That is, also, when you accept your karma, na, perhaps it just lessens, lessens each time, diminishes some [karma], diminishes some, diminishes some. Lets you lighten your karma. So, sometimes I think: Ei, when [your karma] lets you encounter some whatever kind of problems, you want to have some more happy thoughts or some more right thoughts, or some more not pessimistic thoughts. A. When I now encounter this kind of situation, [I think], it's over, just forget it. It just diminished one karma. You will simply engage in less pessimistic thinking when you do something."
(Orig.: Interviewer: 所以那個信仰對你的生活有影響 Kong: 對. 其實我覺得佛教的信仰對我的生活有影響 其實我還有一個 我覺得旅行對我也有 很大影響. 對 當你旅行更多的時候 比如說 像你 長時間/ 台灣是一個小島國家 你的生活選擇在這邊 但是你經常在這裡的話 你沒有 出去走的時候 你會 你也沒辦法把你的心胸擴大 但是你常常出去走一走 你走了很多 地方的時候 你/ 你會發現/ 你的心胸會比較寬一點 有時候你比較不會計較一些問題 在你人生觀上也可能比較樂觀一點 當你碰到問題的時候 你比較不會的那麼深的挫折感當旅行多的時候 你會 對你人生觀會改變 當然佛教的一些信仰的觀點 對我們也有一些/ 一些影響 比如說我們說 我們人都是帶業的 業 你知道嗎 佛教那個業報 其實很多的 那個佛教的業報 很多的業是你自己 你是要去承擔 別人沒有辦法替你承擔 那可能有 一些業 是你前世你帶過來的 那你這一世 你如果沒有好好去修的話 你下輩子 你這個 業 還是會跟著你走 所以在佛教裡頭 是講 業是個人的 也是沒辦法別人去幫你承受 所以只有你自己可以去轉你的業 你要靠你自己的修行 日常生活的修行 去轉你的業 那 有時候業報呈現在你的眼前的時候 有時候是給你的一種理念 那也是 你業你承受的 時候 那可能 就是花掉 花掉每次 消到一些 消到一些 消到一些 讓你減輕你的業 所以 有時候 我會想說 欸 讓你碰到 一些甚麼樣問題的時候 你要有一些比較樂觀的想法 或者 比較正面的一些想法 比較沒悲觀的想法 阿 我現在碰到的這一種狀況 過了就算 了 就少了一個業 就是你會用一個 比較不會很悲觀的想法做一件事情).

3 A more detailed introduction to the *Taiwan Social Change Survey*, TSCS 2004.2, is provided in chap. 4. Karmic concepts are explained further in chap. 8.1.

buddhological perspective, be tempted to establish formal criteria, such as holding the "Five Precepts", taking refuge, affiliating oneself with a Buddhist organisation, etc., for "defining" the field of lay Buddhist believers. The disadvantage of any definition of "lay Buddhist" *a priori* is that it cannot trace the characteristic of the phenomenon: the grey zone of Buddhist believers is far larger than the number of "Buddhists" in any narrower sense. Any definition and deductive approach might therefore serve to refine the search for a certain kind of Buddhism in Taiwan, but the research setting as such would hinder a view about *how "Buddhism" is referred to as a social, cultural, political, organisational, economical, or doctrinal resource by people denoting themselves as Buddhists.* Therefore, the aim of this study is to elucidate the role that Buddhist resources play in the lives of urban Taiwanese citizens who refer to themselves as Buddhists.

Historically speaking, the image of Buddhist "orthodoxy" and the aspirations of professional, especially monastic, Buddhists underwent a radical change in 20th century Taiwan. Buddhist reformist movements, propagating a socially Engaged Buddhism, evolved during the Republican Era in China (1912–1949) and proved highly successful in Taiwan after World War II, winning huge support among lay followers, although not only do the Buddhist agents today follow a different agenda, but also Taiwan's sociocultural climate has changed dramatically during the last few decades. The basis for the dynamics and diversity of Taiwan's cultural life today is, on the one hand, its developed economy–because of its dynamic economic growth from the early 1960s until the 90s, Taiwan is counted among one of the so-called "Four Asian Tigers". This industrial development led to rapid urbanisation, and especially the Northern region, with the capital, Taipeh, as its centre, has expanded into a bustling metropolitan area. On the other hand, Taiwan witnessed a process of democratisation that was marked by the abolishment of martial law in 1989. In 1987, freedom of association was granted–also to religious organisations–and, as a consequence, religiously motivated groups mushroomed all over the island.

The newly emerging Taiwanese Buddhist monasteries and organisations attracted academic attention and the international spread of Taiwanese Buddhist organisations worldwide has been documented.[4] Well-known Taiwanese

4 There exist in-depth studies in English about single Buddhist organisations: Huang (2009) on Tzu Chi, Chandler (2004) on Foguang Shan, Guggenmos (in preparation) delivers an ethnographic study of Lingjiu Mountain. For an overview of the organisational dimensions of contemporary Taiwanese Buddhism and a discussion on how far the Taiwanese Buddhist movement of a *renjian fojiao* is comparable with the international and Western version of Engaged Buddhism, see chap. 12.6 and Guggenmos (2006 and 2012). Regarding the international spread, see in Learman (2005) the contributions of Chandler (2005) and Huang (2005).

Buddhist Monasteries, established around the world, called here the *Young Buddhist Monasteries*,[5] such as Foguang Shan, Fagu Shan, the Tzu Chi Buddhist Compassion Association, Chungtai Shan, or even Lingjiu Mountain, have built up an island-wide and international network of branches, employing the slogan of "Engaged Buddhism" (*renjian fojiao* 人間佛教). While the organisational dimensions of Taiwanese Buddhism are comparatively well-documented, this study puts aside organisational affiliations. The intention of this book is to observe, how far Buddhist social resources, in the form of argumentative patterns, structures of life conduct and concrete activities, are affecting the actual biographical self-construction of lay Buddhists. In consequence, this study is based on an analysis of about 30 biographical narrative interviews conducted between 2005 and 2007 (details see chap. 4). In these interviews, lay Buddhists enlarge on how they first encountered Buddhism and what role it plays in their life. Nine interviews have been chosen for an in-depth analysis.

An additional characteristic of the interviews is that the interviewees are all urban citizens. This decision has been made on the basis of the statistical observation that Buddhism is more frequent in the cities than in rural areas. The statistical findings allow the hypothesis that a self-delineation as an adherent of "Buddhism"–especially in its intense forms–as well as selecting the option "no religion acknowledged" are more attractive to urban citizens than rural dwellers. Buddhism seems to be an attractive option when living in the city. This study is particularly interested in revealing how "Buddhism"

5 The term "Young Buddhist Monasteries" indicates those established since the 1960s, like Tzu Chi, Foguang Shan, Fagu Shan, Zhongtai Shan, Lingjiu Mountain and Tianfo Shan. They mainly inherited the ideals of Buddhist Modernism, the search for an active role in society and a focus on the involvement of lay people beyond simply giving donations. They hold a multitude of activities, like singing classes or special offers for young families, as well as ritual events. Activities are often organised by the lay people themselves. Still, the *saṃgha* plays a decisive role, is present at the rituals and is often responsible for organisational matters. These monasteries are usually founded or inspired by the highly acknowledged traditions of the mainland and seek to put into practice visions that first evolved during the Buddhist Reformatory Phase of Republican China. The Young Buddhist Monasteries are in this work separated from some of the more recently established Buddhist organisations, which in the following are called *New Buddhist Organisations*, some of which are composed wholly of lay people. Their doctrinal development is often incomplete and they are less aware of the reformatory monastic tradition of the mainland, but highly influenced by the needs of an urbanised society. They emphasise international involvement, interreligious openness, ecological sustainability and processual thinking. Examples include Sōka Gakkai, Fuzhi 福智, Fosheng Zong 佛乘宗, or Master Xiao Pingshi's 蕭平實 Zhengjue Tongxiu Hui 正覺同修會 (for details and a broader picture of these organisations, see Guggenmos 2006, 2012, and chap. 12.6). This twofold structure, especially with its time period connection, helps to provide a rough structure for the broad field of Buddhist organisations in Taiwan, but is of course of a preliminary nature and cannot be applied indiscriminately to all cases.

matches the sociocultural dimensions of urban life in Taiwan and in how far "Buddhism" serves urban citizens as a *Lebensbewältigungsressource*–a resource for coping with life.

The book therefore intends, by undertaking a case analysis, to explore the profile of Buddhism, together with the reasons for its attractiveness in Taiwan's urban sphere. In the *first* part, whole cases are analysed to reveal how popular religion, as well as the long-established Buddhist tradition, are shaping people's biographical self-understanding. To illustrate these general connotations underlying Buddhism, Buddhists have been chosen who hold a more conventional concept of Buddhism. The selective criterion for choosing the interviewees was that they would not specify their belief, but might say that it is characterised by "believing in" and "venerating Buddha" (*xinfo/baifo*).[6] The *sec-*

6 The fields of "Buddhism", "Daoism", and "popular religion" overlap in a huge grey zone, making any sharp separation of religious beliefs and traditions unreasonable. The belonging to distinct "religions" is a young differential concept in East Asia, as will be explained below. Analysing general connotations underlying Buddhism therefore requires us to reconsider the expressions of popular beliefs and practices. The distinct terminology does not intend to claim invalid divisions, but will sharpen the view that there is a spectrum of Buddhist believers that includes people denoting themselves as Buddhists while following a common veneration behaviour. These common religious beliefs and practices are referred to in the following as "popular religion." The previously more common term of "folk religion" was probably inspired by works about "religiöse Volkskunde" in early 20th century Germany (see Yoder 1974) and "is a contested category within the study of religions, with scholars increasingly advocating its abandonment" (Kapaló 2013, 3; this article develops its own approach to research on "folk religion" and reviews previous attempts to redefine "folk religion", including the discussion on "vernacular religion"). A valid alternative to the term "popular religion" is, especially for the Japanese case, the expression "Common Religion" (see Reader and Tanabe 1998, 23–32), while "traditional" religion (see Reader and Tanabe 1998, 27f.) insinuates a social change, which leads away from the "original" tradition. Talking of a "primal" religion, as Michael Pye does with regard to Japan (Pye 1996, 261–270), might hint at the fact that popular religion also in Taiwan appears to the majority of people as a kind of primary religious socialisation, but could be understood pejoratively. Applying the term "popular religion" in the following shall by no means impose a false picture of unity on a highly-diverse phenomenon. By the expression "popular religion", the author does not wish to imply that the religious beliefs and practices are bound to a particular social stratum, nor does she suppose that "popular religion" is more doctrinally "pure" or "corrupt" than any other religious tradition. Helpful for a deeper understanding of the concept of "popular religion" as it is applied in this book is the approach by the sociologist Hubert Knoblauch who distinguishes between "populare" and "populäre Religion" (Knoblauch 2009): this suggests that "populare Religion" might imply a concept of heterodoxy that is close to what was historically pejoratively denoted as "Aberglaube" (superstition) in Germany. Turning towards the concept of "populäre Religion", Knoblauch describes a historical transformation and develops an analytical tool to describe adequately the function of religious practices in contemporary German society. Taiwan's processes of modernisation are multilayered and therefore the author will apply in the following the term "popular religion" in its broadest sense to encompass

ond part goes beyond the underlying, general perception of "Buddhism", aiming to demonstrate its possible width of variety in contemporary Taiwan. The urban climate allows people to invent and consume new forms of "Buddhist" resources. Therefore, in the second part, the focus is on differentiating specific, and intense ways of living a Buddhist lay life, while the mode of presentation changes from detailed, whole case analyses to brief portraits, delineating the specific situation and concept of the respective case.

Returning to the initially-cited statement of the interviewee, Kong Shuqing, it exactly mirrors how distorting it might be to portray "Buddhism" as a "religion" in contemporary Taiwan, delivering a meaning of life in contrast to the secular field, where this "belief" might come into use. It is significant how the interviewee juxtaposes "Buddhism" with her hobby of "travelling". Explaining the functions of travel and Buddhism in her life, it turns out that both fulfil the same purpose for her: they enable her to cope more positively with the everyday occurrences of her life. Her view of karmic retribution enables her to regard negative incidences as a chance to diminish her bad karma and reassures her that bad fortune can even be seen as an opportunity to diminish her bad karma. Bad luck does not happen accidentally, but future bad luck becomes more unlikely if she copes well with her present challenges. Her concentration upon her personal condition is complemented by her enthusiasm for travel, which helps her, in her words, to "broaden her mind" (lit. "widen her bosom", *ba ni de xinxiong kuangda* 把你的心胸擴大). Her "view of life" changes as a result, and she is less inclined to "argue about problems" and is "happier". Travel puts her personal experience into a broader context, enabling her to relativise events from a broader perspective. Within this construction, "Buddhism" is not regarded as a "religion", separate from her travelling, but karmic understanding and travel experiences are revealed as Kong Shuqing's main *complementary cultural resources*, enabling her to face life positively by managing negative circumstances through the concept of karma, while seeing them in a broader perspective by experiencing other ways of life through travelling.

both, "populare" and "populäre Religion." Still, it should be noted that the aspect of "heterodoxy" as opposed to "orthodoxy" is especially valid for the case of popular religion in Chinese history (see Seiwert 2003, 485–501). Following the pragmatic approach of Seiwert, by "popular religion", the author refers to common religious behaviour in Taiwan, which certainly includes the veneration of gods and ancestors in the social sphere of temples as well as within the family. Veneration can be linked with retributionary thinking and can serve as very concrete means, like asking the gods for success in business or family matters and preventing negative events. The addressees of the veneration, as well as the rituals and doctrines connected to it, can vary locally.

Such a parallelisation sheds light upon: 1) the socio-geographical location of Taiwan; and 2) the construction of "Buddhism" as a "religion" in Chinese culture. As Kong herself recognises, Taiwan is a "small island" which was, moreover, over the centuries under the continuous influence of other cultures. While the Austronesian immigrants seem to belong to the first settlers in Taiwan and today are regarded as "aborigines", consisting of a small minority of about 450,000 people (Taiwan total: 23 mil.), Taiwan welcomed, especially after Koxinga's defeat of the Dutch colonialists in 1662, several waves of refugees from the neighbouring provinces on the Chinese mainland, who brought with them their cultural and religious habits and also their Fujianese or Cantonese dialects. During the Qing dynasty (1644–1911), Taiwan belonged officially to the Chinese empire, albeit it clearly lay at the periphery of the mainlanders' attention. This situation changed drastically during the Japanese colonial period (1895–1945). Taiwan's population was indoctrinated by the Japanese–including Japanese Buddhist missionaries–with the aim of encouraging Taiwanese compatriots to wage war against China. Taiwan's infrastructure and public administration developed rapidly during that period and laid the basis for its later economic prosperity. When Chiang Kai-Shek fled to Taiwan after World War II, he took with him the Nationalist army and a wave of new mainland immigrants. The Nationalist party first ruled Taiwan rigidly, suppressing any longing for a Taiwanese identity. The United States granted the Nationalists protection against the communist mainland. A generation of young, ambitious Chinese intellectuals was educated abroad and equipped with–besides the well-established Japanese influences–a pro-American cultural orientation. The fight to restore the Chinese mainland under Nationalist control has faced, over the decades, a decreasing chance of success. A new generation of Taiwanese, significantly better-educated than previous generations and often economically more independent, began to develop their own vision of private happiness and the search for a Taiwanese identity began. With the democratisation of the island, the direct opposition to the mainland attracted diminishing public interest, but opened up for many Taiwanese the freedom to explore a huge variety of personal interests. This was expressed through the rapid sociocultural pluralisation, within which the Chinese mainland was also rediscovered by the younger generation, while the Japanese and "Western" influences were simultaneously widely positively perceived.

Located at the periphery of China and Japan, with a growing working class from Indonesia and an openness towards America, Taiwan remains ethnically mainly Chinese, but has become extremely culturally hybridised over the centuries, creating a unique contemporary ethnoscape. On the island, the histories of different countries "connect" with each other.[7] This multitude of influences combines into a picture of "Taiwanese modernity" that often reveals the striving of Taiwan's urban citizens to catch up with a, mainly "Western" perceived, modernisation process.[8] Thus, the interviewee's ambition to "travel" certainly fits into contemporary Taiwan's sociocultural climate. Taiwan's urban citizens tend to be strongly aware of the rest of the world. Their income often enables them to travel and sometimes send their children to study abroad, while Taiwanese companies participate in trade fairs worldwide. The religious sector is no exception regarding Taiwanese people's international ambitions. Religious, especially Buddhist, networks are spreading their branches from Taiwan worldwide, celebrate the growing monastic community in Africa, maintain contact with overseas Chinese in America and Europe, and recently discover the Chinese mainland as a field ready to be re-proselytised with its own cultural heritage, Buddhism.[9]

When an interviewee does not regard "Buddhism" as a distinct "religion" in contrast to the secular field of its application this may not merely hint at the hybridity of "Taiwanese" culture, as the notion of "Buddhism" and "religion" within Chinese culture has its own history. Bearing this concept in mind is an essential precondition for acquiring an appropriate understanding of the impact of "Buddhism" as a cultural resource on the biographies of Taiwanese lay people. It is a commonly assumed that the Chinese term "religion" (*zongjiao* 宗教) is a neologism that was taken from the Japanese "*shūkyō*". While Rebecca Nedostup and Vincent Goossaert analysed in greater detail the emergence of the term "religion" in its sociopolitical relevance,[10]

---

7 Gurminder Bhambra (Bhambra 2007), a postcolonial historian, established the term "connected histories" as a model to describe the interdependence of historical development. In Taiwan, this transnational embeddedness is a defining moment in its development.

8 Taiwanese urban citizens' personal perception of their life mirrors less an independent variation of modernity, but combines well with critiques of the "multiple modernities" approach, such as that formulated by Peter van der Veer (van der Veer 2002), who stresses the importance of acknowledging the imperial influences in order to acquire an appropriate understanding of colonial modernity in South Asia.

9 The recent re-emergence of Buddhism on the mainland is analysed by the research project under the guidance of Ji Zhe "Le bouddhisme après Mao: religion, politique et société en Chine depuis 1980", Groupe Sociétés, Religions, Laïcités (CNRS-EPHE, Paris), sponsored by Ville de Paris (2010–2013) and follow-up projects. Relevant recent publications in this field include Ji/Goossaert (2011), Chao (2011), Fisher (2014), and Jones (2010).

10 See Nedostup 2009, esp. 6–11, who worked on the role of religion in the context of secular nationalism during the Nanjing Decade (1927–1937) of Nationalist rule in China. The upcoming idea of the nation state and the nationalist agenda shaped at the end of the 19th and first half of the 20th century in China a major shift from the distinction between "orthodoxy" (*zheng* 正) and "heresy" (*xie* 邪) to "religion" (*zongjiao* 宗教) and "superstition" (*mixin* 迷信; see Goossaert 2005 and Goossaert and Palmer

detailed terminological investigations into the usage of single expressions in the second half of the 19th century led Frederico Masini to conclude that works, such as the "History of Japan" (*Riben Guozhi* 日本國志; around 1890) by Huang Zunxian 黃遵憲, had a "certain lexical influence on [the well-known journalist] Liang Qichao" (梁啟超, 1873–1929; Masini 1993, 101), and hence the term *zongjiao* found its way from Japanese into Chinese common usage.[11] The straightforwardness of this argument has recently been challenged and first observations (Barrett and Tarocco 2006, English version 2012) led Tarocco to the conclusion that "'religion' was established in China through the concurrent efforts of Buddhists and Christians and to the exclusion of the daily practices of the many" (Tarocco 2008, 45). She traces Christian (Manichaic) and especially Buddhist attempts to classify their schools and teaching, and finds that certain expressions, dating back as far as Fazang (642–712 AD) and the later famous Zen-Masters, were already intending to structure the religious field.

Still, Tarocco also admits: "In fact, premodern China lacked both a lexical equivalent of the English term religion and the current notion of 'religion' as a discrete feature of culture and matter of individual belief" (Tarocco 2008, 43). This is supported by the fact that, for example, the Chinese Emperor fulfilled important religio-ritual functions, while single individuals performed rites within the family and community contexts. Religion as an individual belief therefore "must have been alien to the experience of any lettered or indeed illiterate person born in late imperial China" (Tarocco 2008, 43). The "religious sphere" was–as in pre-enlightened Europe–not separated from the state and the secular sphere, but the state recognised and registered orthodox religious behaviour, while heresy and superstition (*mixin* 迷信) are still prosecuted even today by the Chinese state as endangering public security. In seeking an appropriate understanding of "religion" in the Chinese context, Robert F. Campany (Campany 2003, 287–319) searches for earlier, Chinese ways to describe "religion". His outline of emic categories delivers a historically rooted, lexicographical background for the conceptual field of "religion" in China. Campany differentiates between four ways of referring to Buddhism in medieval Buddhist texts: Firstly, he explores the references to founders and paradigmatic figures–terms which can be synecdochally employed to refer to a whole religious tradition. Secondly, the term "*dao*" 道, a "way" or "path", can be used in compounds: "People see, travel, follow, abandon, or

2011, esp. 50–51). Goossaert (2005) outlines the massive socio-political implications for religious belief and popular religion the introduction of "religion" in contrast to "superstition" had and continues to have.

11 Masini cites three authors (Gao Mingkai, Wang Lida and Zhou Zhenhe) and one further source as stating that the word *zongjiao* is an "original loan from Japanese" (Masini 1993, 222).

deviate from *dao*s, rather than simply being contained in them; the verbs are verbs of doing, not copulae" (Campany 2003, 305). "Buddhism" in this variant is referred to as the "way of Buddha" (*fodao* 佛道). A third way is to specify Buddhist teachings as "law", "method(s)", or "regulations" (*fa* 法 in *fofa* 佛法). This term includes a "praxeological" meaning as "a set of norms or regulations–implying, first and foremost, regulations concerning what to do" (Campany 2003, 306). As a fourth variant, to refer to religion in general and the Buddhist tradition in particular, a combination with *jiao* 教, "teaching", is used also today. While the usage of "*fojiao*" as a reference to "Buddhism" is according to Campany imported from the Japanese, Campany asserts that its usage in the Buddhist canon emphasises the source of the teaching rather than the attitude of the "believer" (see Campany 2003, 307). Campany points out that "belief" (*xin* 信) is not "an inward assent to doctrinal propositions or else lists of such propositions themselves", but instead connotes "not assent to propositions but trust or confidence in a teaching, method, or path" (Campany 2003, 310). He concludes: "In sum, the language tends to emphasize practice or some mode of active participation rather than either simple membership in container-like set or assent to a set of core doctrines" (Campany 2003, 311). Therefore it often makes sense to talk of a "believer" as a "practitioner". In the following, both terms are applied to hint at the peculiarity of the Chinese concept of "belief".

Although Campany's construction of "religion" in the "West" as "static", "container-like", and doctrinally based, is certainly roughly carved, his description of the construction of "Buddhism" as teaching helps to elucidate the situation in Taiwan. Throughout the colonial occupation and also the period following 1917, the influential first statistical investigation into religious associations and temples in Taiwan shows that Japan's impact was probably even more direct than on the mainland. Still–possibly even due to the later immigration of mainlanders after World War II–this Japanese impact does not seem to have completely transformed the notion of "religion" in Taiwanese society. In Taiwan, "Buddhism" and "religion" are generally recognised as underlying concepts, and "religion" is not perceived as a separate "identity", central to any individual and the meaning of life in general. To the interviewee Kong Shuqing, in consequence, the question about the influence of her "belief" upon her life might be more closely associated with questions about what she "trusts", and so might feel far less separated from the other sources of inspiration in her life. In consequence, she can switch between "Buddhism" and "travel" with ease. Indeed, the belief she describes is designed to give her a more positive outlook on life and has, in that sense, a highly "praxeological" focus.

Buddhism, according to the semantic historical outline presented here, is far less a category that constitutes religious "belonging", and indeed most "believers" in Taiwanese "Buddhism" do not have a clear mental concept of what being a "Buddhist" means. "Buddhism" is not central in their life as a texturing creed or "pole" of orientation. Bearing this peculiarity of "Buddhism" in mind, this book is unconcerned with the invention of a lay Buddhist community which is characterised by a certain set of types. In contrast, it adopts as its basic selective criterion for the interviews the fact that the interviewees consider themselves, in some sense, to be a Buddhist. This can be extended to Zhang Yimin's case (see chap. 12.4), who has neither taken refuge nor had any contact with a Buddhist organisation, but feels inspired by Buddhist views about life and frequently reads American Buddhist publications. Apart from that, the interviewees themselves recognise the process whereby "religion" is increasingly becoming established in Taiwan as a differential category. In describing her struggle over whether to define herself as a Daoist or a Buddhist, Luo Peirong states that, in the past, one simply referred to single gods whom one venerated. Buddhism did not exist as a distinct belief and was less flourishing (*xingwang* 興旺). She comments, "At that time, there was no Buddhism, so one said this or that god. [...] only now, as there is Buddhism, do we separate between Buddhism and Daoism [...]" (Luo S7, see below, chap. 7.2). Elements of Buddhist belief are intermingled with the popular religious tradition and Buddhas or bodhisattvas have become integrated into the pantheon that is venerated in the temples. "Buddhism" was, organisationally speaking, but probably also in the public consciousness, mainly promiment during burial rites, during which recitations are commonly undertaken by monks to accompany individuals' souls for a period of 49 days after death. Religious experts like priests or ritual specialists were, therefore, in contrast to the general public, the only people who held a consciously exclusive religious belonging.

2 Who is a "Lay Buddhist"?

The hermeneutical principle of this study is to assess the interviewees' narrations right down to the subtleties of their language behaviour in order to discover how *they* interpret the expression "being a lay Buddhist". To understand the interviewees' narrations, it is important to: a) be aware of the basic structure of the Buddhist community as it is transmitted, especially through the early Indian scriptures that influenced Chinese Buddhism; and b) recognise the Chinese semantics that are at the interviewees' disposal in order to refer to themselves as a "lay Buddhist".

a) The contemporary "grey zone" phenomenon of lay Buddhists is already a characteristic of the earliest Indian Buddhist sources: even from this earliest stage, the definitions of lay devotees are multilayered. Already in the Pāli canon, the distinct boundaries of the lay Buddhist group are in flux. Jeffrey Samuels argues, in his article entitled "Views of Householders and Lay Disciples in the *Sutta Piṭaka*: A Reconsideration of the Lay/Monastic Opposition", that "the Pāli canon contains a historically diverse group of viewpoints and attitudes towards religious practice and that the complexity of views contained in the canon actually undermines, to a large degree, the absoluteness of the categories of 'monastic' and 'laity'" (Samuels 1999, 232). Also, Gregory Schopen describes, in an analysis of early inscriptions, similar activities being undertaken by both laypeople and monks (Schopen 1997). Freiberger resumes, in an in-depth investigation into the Pāli canon:

> Die Erweiterung des Begriffs ‚Laienanhänger' könnte nicht nur für die Erforschung der Lehrkonzeptionen, sondern auch für die Betrachtung der historischen Realität angemessener sein als die auf die Wiedergabe von *upāsaka* und *upāsikā* beschränkte Verwendung. Auch könnte dieser erweiterte Begriff als historischer Oberbegriff dienen, der einen Gegenstandsbereich umfaßt, dessen Abgrenzung in Händen nicht der buddhistischen Tradition, sondern der historischen Forschung liegt.[12]

This recent tendency towards differentiating the picture of lay people within the Buddhist community transcends the well-established patterns of argumentation.

The *saṃgha* (skt., pāli: *saṅgha*), the Buddhist community, appears to be most commonly defined as a fourfold community. It is usually described as

12 "The extension of the term 'lay follower' could be more appropriate than a usage restricted to the rendering of *upāsaka* and *upāsikā*, not only in revealing the teaching concepts, but also in examining the historical reality. In addition, this enlarged term could serve as an historical generic term that encompasses an area of objects, the borderlines of which lie in the hands not of the Buddhist tradition but of historical research" (translated by the author from Freiberger 2000, 146, ann. 402).

consisting of *bhikṣus* (monks), *bhikṣunīs* (nuns), *upāsakas* (laymen) and *upāsikās* (laywomen).[13] While the first two receive alms, as they are "begging" (skt. √*bhikṣ*), the "lay" people are constructed as those who "sit close" (skt. √*as* with *upa-* as prefix) to the monastics, serving them. Nalinaksha Dutt describes householders' duties according to the *Mahāparinibbana-Sutta* (pāli, skt.: *Mahāparinirvāṇa Sūtra*): they take refuge in the Three Jewels (*trisaraṇa*), listen to religious discourses on *uposatha* days, observe the eight *sīlas* occasionally, and offer robes to the monks on certain occasions, especially at the end of the rainy season retreat. They further go on pilgrimage and visit the Buddha's relics (see Dutt 1945, 164). Although Dutt searches for clear boundaries to demark a Buddhist believer and practitioner, he concludes that the initiation, the act of taking refuge, "should not however be taken as indicative of a person's actually changing his creed and becoming an upāsaka". Also, in the Mahāyāna tradition in Taiwan today, it is common for lay devotees to take refuge several times. Some of the Buddhists whom the author met were convinced that one should only take refuge once, yet most of them had done so several times, as well as visiting monasteries not only for religious reasons but simply for pleasure (*qu wan* 去玩). Also, on the mainland, this seems to have been common practice. In his seminal study entitled "The Practice of Chinese Buddhism", Welch describes the mainland Buddhist practices in the first half of the 20th century as follows: "Unlike tonsure, however, the Refuges could be taken over and ove[r] again with different masters or with the same master. Like most master-disciple relationships, it was not exclusive" (Welch 1967, 359).

With regard to the question of how to identify a lay follower terminologically, Dutt introduces into the discourse, besides the term "*upāsaka*" (pāli/skt.) mentioned above, the term "Gahapatis" (pāli: *gahapati*, skt.: *gṛhapati*) the former followers being regarded as more earnest than the latter in the

13 There are also other, parallel groupings of the Buddhist community into seven or eight subgroups. Sevenfold: monk, nun, male novice, female novice, female probationer, layman, and laywoman; Ninefold: adding to the seven groups male and female laypeople, who have taken the Eight Upavastha Vows for a short time. See FBD (2000), 5718 (entry "*sengjia* 僧伽"). The fourfold structure is the most common and is, for example, explained in the Mahāparinibbāna-Sutta: "I will not go into the parinibbāna as long [...] as my bhikkus, bhikkunis, upāsakas, (and) upāsikas did not become male (respectively) female students who are literate, practised, wise and educated–carriers of the dhamma, who follow the truth of the dhamma and the right and who live according to the dhamma" ("Ich werde so lange nicht ins Parinibbāna eingehen, […], wie meine Bhikkus, Bhikkunis, Upāsakas (und) Upāsikas nicht Schüler (bzw.) Schülerinnen geworden sind, die gelehrt, geübt, weise und gebildet sind–Träger des Dhamma, die der Wahrheit des Dhamma und dem Richtigen folgen und dem Dhamma gemäß leben", translation given in Freiberger 2000, 141–142 with reference to the *Dīghanikāya* (Rhys Davids and J.E. Carpenter 1890–1911, here vol. II, 112,30f.; English by author).

early Indian context. Gahapatis, "home dwellers", he connects with the Indian caste system, describing them as being involved in trade and the biggest group of followers: "The Gahapatis [...] were more or less devout listeners to the moral or religious discourses delivered by the monks. They offered food, clothing and other necessaries of life to the monks. Occasionally, at the end of a discourse, they signified their appreciation by saying that they would take Trisaraṇa and become Upāsakas till the end of their lives" (Dutt 1945, 171). Dutt continues: "Out of this body of lay supporters appeared a group of persons who were more earnest in their devotion to Buddhism, and naturally tried to follow the principles of Buddhism as far as compatible with their life as a householder". Regarding the characteristics of these Upāsakas, he states: "[...] that [they] must have not only faith in the Triratna, observe moral precepts, and do good to people in return but also not resort to auspicious rites, and offer gifts to persons outside the Buddhist Saṅgha" (Dutt 1945, 172). The Upāsakas are described as having five moral duties: *saddhā* (faith), *sīla* (observance of moral precepts), *cāga* (charity: providing monks with food, robes, beds and medicine; being open-handed and prone to giving gifts to the needy), *suta* (listening to religious discourses) and *paññā* (comprehending the higher truths) (Dutt 1945, 173). Regarding the monastic regulations, Dutt also mentions five advantages that may be obtained by a householder through observing the moral precepts: "He (i) gains immense wealth and property; (ii) acquires fame; (iii) can appear boldly before any social congregation; (iv) dies consciously and (v) goes to heaven" (Dutt 1945, 175).

This textual evidence of the early attempts to give the lay Buddhist community ideals for moral orientation and life conduct reflect a need to centre the Buddhist community, not necessarily via a clear boundary distinguishing them from others, but via orienting them towards a shared aim and set of ideals. This can be described as the tendency among the lay Buddhist community to adopt a *concentric structure*. The various stages of lay Buddhists are not necessarily divided from each other. Attempts such as that of Harrison[14] to describe the lay Buddhist community as a fourfold structure (1. intense believers, called "semi-ordained lay practitioners"; 2. exclusive supporters; 3. loosely-connected supporters; and 4. Buddhists without any close connection to Buddhism at all)–due to the scarce number of sources–of course cannot guarantee an appropriate description of the actual social differentiation between the lay believers and practitioners at that time, but nevertheless demonstrate that the Buddhist community was, through the impact of its intellectual leaders, from the outset centred on certain ideals, which seek to

14 Paul Harrison (also quoted in Freiberger 2000, 144–145): Harrison (1995).

define a lay Buddhist self-identification through its degree of engagement, while also allowing a smooth entry into the field.

The concentric structure of the Buddhist community is, even today, a powerful narrative in contemporary Taiwanese Buddhism, which structures, for example, the seating arrangements during rituals. Jones analysed the initiation rituals during large Dharma-meetings in Taiwan in the 1990s, suggesting also a structure for increasing Buddhist commitment within the lay Buddhist community: the various degrees of initiation serve as status markers regarding proximity to the ritual centre. The recipients of the lay bodhisattva precepts sit closest to the centre, followed by the five lay precepts' recipients, the three refuges disciples and finally the least closely-connected people, the neophytes (Jones 1997). The ritual arrangement therefore acknowledges to the degree of initiation, reminding the participants that they form part of a hierarchically-structured community, within which higher obligations also imply higher status.

b) Not only has the concentric construction remained a dominant element since early Buddhist times, but Buddhist terminology has also made its way from Indian sources into Chinese ones. During the transmission process, Sanskrit terms, on the one hand, have been translated as phonetic imitations of the original sounds. On the other hand, terms that were already well-established in Chinese society were adopted and reinterpreted. As a result of this process, the Chinese terminology has a variety of terms for denoting "lay Buddhist believers". The aforementioned terms, *upāsakas* and *upāsikās*, were directly transcribed as *youposa* 優婆塞 and *youpoyi* 優婆夷.[15] These are commonly known in Buddhist circles today, but rarely used to refer to concrete lay Buddhist believers or groups of believers in daily life. Through the growing awareness of Buddhism as a religion, the term "follower/adherent of Buddhism" (*fojiaotu* 佛教徒) –a parallel construction to the term "*jidutu* 基督徒", "Christian"[16] –is becoming increasingly common and is easily recognised in conversation. I found that some of the interviewees appeared comfortable identifying themselves as a "*fojiaotu*", while others, inspired by Buddhism to varying degrees, felt an immediate need to specify their being a "*fojiaotu*" further and tended to feel slightly

15 Translations can vary and some refer to the semantic meaning of the words, but the two mentioned are the most common usages. Other translations are: For *upāsakas*: phonetic 烏波索迦, 優波娑迦, 伊蒲塞. Semantic: 意譯為近事, 近事男, 近善男, 信士, 信男, 清信士 (FBD 2000, 6409). For *upāsikās:* phonetic: 優婆私訶, 優婆斯, 優波賜迦. Semantic: 譯為清信女, 近善女, 近事女, 近宿女, 信女 (FBD 2000, 6407).

16 This process should be verified further, but has been used as a common argument for a long time. See Welch 1967, 512, first annotation: "*Fo-chiao t'u* is apparently copied from Christian usage. It implies a formal adherence to Buddhism just as *chi-tu t'u* implies formal membership of a Christian church, whereas the traditional phrase 'to believe in the buddha' has no such implication."

uncomfortable about such a distinction making them a religious adherent. While the term *fojiaotu* clearly sounded slightly stiff and artificial to many, most of my interviewees were very comfortable using the term "householder", a *zaijia xintu* 在家信徒–a construction that parallels the Sanskrit "gṛhapati". Constructed in opposition to the monastics, people who "left home" (*chujia ren* 出家人), people from a Buddhist background could argue well, based on their role and life decision, that they are "householders". At the beginning of the research process, it also became obvious that "householders" were rarely identified as being part of the *saṃgha*, *sengjia* 僧伽,[17] but that the "*sengren* 僧人" were mostly paralleled with the monastics.

Another term denoting a householder in Chinese is "*jushi* 居士", a home-dwelling, respected person. This seems to parallel the aforementioned term "gahapati" (skt. *gṛhapati*).[18] The Chinese term is far less common in daily discourse in Taiwan and usually used to refer to well-acknowledged and respected, not even necessarily Buddhist, intellectuals. In a Buddhist context, this word would be used to refer to a person who has made an outstanding contribution to the development of (Taiwanese) Buddhism. It is therefore unsurprising that, when asked if they regard themselves as a "*jushi*", most of the interviewees humbly denied this, as if it were too great an honour. In addition, the term *jushi* could also be used in a secular context in Late Imperial China, as it is also applied to a retired scholar or an official who has left office (see e.g. Mathews' Dictionary 1975, p. 219, no. 1535[19]).[20]

---

17 Combining Sanskrit and Chinese usages to describe a Buddhist community as *senglü* 僧侶 is also possible. On the various historical attempts to structure the Buddhist community, see Sparham (2004) and FBD 2000, 5718 (entry "*sengjia* 僧伽"), where the different structures of the *sengjia* are enumerated.

18 Parallel expressions are also employed in Pāli/Sanskrit.

19 Mathews' Dictionary has now been surpassed by newer, more detailed and accurate dictionaries. Based on Baller's Analytical Chinese-English Dictionary, it first appeared in 1931, followed by numerous new editions with revisions and supplements. Mathews' selections and translations are close to the usage of the upper literati around 1900. In Taiwan, the Nationalists and, with them, many of the classical literate, conservatively-oriented people took refuge and their mental heritage had an impact on Taiwan. It is therefore reasonable to assume that the associations evoked when hearing the word "*jushi*" might be connected in some sense to the interpretations provided in Mathews' Dictionary.

20 The fact of addressing with this term respected people is, for example, clearly expressed in the Continued Tripiṭaka Edition (*Zokuzōkyō* 續藏經, first printed from 1905-1912), where biographies of lay people are found to be narrated by Peng Jijing 彭際清 (1740–1796) under the title "*Jushi zhuan* 居士傳" (X.1646). This notion of the term is, similarly, recognised by Holmes Welch in his "Practice of Chinese Buddhism": "A somewhat broader term is 'devotee' (chü-shih), literally 'a person who resides (at home)'. 'Devotees' include not only devout laymen who have taken the Refuges or Five Vows, but those who are merely scholars and friends of Buddhism. Indeed it can be loosely applied as a title of courtesy to anyone who has any interest in Buddhism whatever. But it would not be applied to the peasant woman who offers

Summing up, it appears that one may employ several terms to refer to oneself as a lay Buddhist in the Chinese and Taiwanese context. These do not enjoy a clear systematic relation with each other. The most accurate buddhological terms for lay devotees ("*upāsaka*" [layman] and "*upāsikā*" [laywoman]) which were directly transcribed into Chinese, as well as the semantically meaningful construction of a "house-dweller" (*jushi*, skt. *gṛhapati*), are rarely applied by contemporary Taiwanese lay Buddhists in their self-denoting practices. For them, the most common term for the inner-Buddhist denoting practice is a "home believer", *zaijia xintu*. Compared with other religious believers, the parallel construction of a "Buddhist believer" (*fojiaotu*) is also reasonably well-established but seems to be associated with a more formal affiliation.

In the traditional textual sources, the relationship between the lay followers and the monastic community is described as one of mutual reliance. The lay community is generally characterised as supporters of the *saṃgha*. Through donations, they gain merit. They are also reminded to live a virtuous life. Concerning their salvatory status, it is less clear whether their virtuous deeds bring them closer to attaining *nirvāṇa* or rebirth in heaven. Still, the textual evidence of the early expectations of Buddhist lay believers offers a broad picture, suggesting that they were more than the mere providers of food, shelter, clothing and medical treatment for the *saṃgha*. They practised Buddhist teachings, taught them, were acquainted with meditation, and their spiritual attainment was widely discussed. As in the early Buddhist period, so today it is possible for lay Buddhist believers gradually to engage with the Buddhist community. They can be involved in Buddhist practice and doctrine to varying degrees of intensity, and may mark their involvement and obligation through ritual initiations, such as taking refuge, holding the Five Precepts or committing themselves to the bodhisattva vows. Buddhism is already, in its early sources, marked as having a concentric dynamic, loose boundaries and a huge grey zone. Buddhist ideas penetrate society as well, as people without any Buddhist affiliation can, for example, support monastics.

incense to Kuan-yin in hopes of bearing a son. This would be because, although she might be more devout than most devotees, she does not distinguish the Buddhist religion from any other. She has no affiliation with it" (Welch 1967, 357).

3 The Research Question

As stated above, the aim of this study is to analyse how the social practice of Buddhism can be used as a resource for coping with life in contemporary urban Taiwan. Why might there be more Buddhists living in urban Taiwan than in the countryside? Which ways of employing Buddhist resources are arising and becoming established in this rapidly-transforming country? Following up the statistical result that Buddhists seem to be more common in the cities than in the countryside in Taiwan, narrative interviews with urban dwellers who denote themselves as "lay Buddhists" have been conducted. The analysis through the method of Structural Hermeneutics intends to elucidate why Buddhism seems to be an attractive option for Taiwanese urbanites. The results show how "Buddhism" is referred to as a social, cultural, political, organisational, economical or doctrinal resource and thereby present an overview of the possible reasons why Buddhism is an attractive option in urban Taiwan. Recent studies of lay Buddhism on the mainland form the basis for the comparative approach (chap. 17).

This study lays aside the emic Buddhist attempts to classify lay Buddhists, taking as its starting point an integrative, broad selection of self-denoting lay Buddhists in order to reveal how far Buddhism serves as an actual source in the life-management and self-imagining of lay Buddhists in contemporary urban Taiwan. Being interested in daily life and biographical structures, the study is in line with the German as well as Western flourishing interest in daily life practices and the "Life Story Approach". The latter was already prominent before World War II in the US and Poland while, after the war, the interest in biographical research increased. Germany is still witnessing even today a "biographical movement" with a high degree of methodological reflection, resulting in a huge number of publications, in its own section within the German Association of Sociology, and in journals like BIOS (BIOS Zeitschrift für Biographieforschung, oral history and Lebensverlaufsanalysen), which tackles topics ranging from methodological questions about oral history in Chinese villages up to German history's peculiarities, such as the phenomenon of National Socialism.[21]

The process of mass urbanisation is one of the biggest changes that has occurred in contemporary Taiwan, and social change is suspected to be at its

21 BIOS 1/2007 (20th year) is here taken as an example. A first English overview of the biographical research according to country was presented by Daniel Bertaux and Martin Kohli in 1984 (Bertaux and Kohli 1984). Recently published works on biographical research include, for example: Kluge and Kelle (2001); Lucius-Hoene and Deppermann (2002); Lutz, Dausien, Völter, and Rosenthal (2009).

most intense in the urbanised regions of the island. Since more urban citizens than rural dwellers denote themselves as Buddhists, the study conducts case analyses of urban Buddhists and reflects on the usage of Buddhist resources in the light of the effects of urbanisation upon people's lives. With this approach, this study seeks to transcend the wearisome, oft-repeated dichotomy of lay Buddhists as the traditional supporters of the monastic community and modern social activists. It lays aside the emic Buddhist attempts to classify lay Buddhists, taking as its starting point an integrative, broad selection of self-denoting lay Buddhists in order to reveal how far Buddhism serves as an actual source in the life-management and self-imagining of lay Buddhists in contemporary Taiwan under the aspect of urbanisation.

It is important to note that this book goes beyond a study of so-called "Engaged Buddhism". Buddhist movements who identify with the slogan of an "Engaged Buddhism" are dominant players in the contemporary Buddhist discourse in Taiwan which can be traced to the end of the 19th century: Heinz Bechert, in his groundbreaking work on Theravāda Buddhism in Sri Lanka, pointed out the fundamental changes in the modernised Buddhism in Sri Lanka at that time, which Gananath Obeyesekere and Richard Gombrich called "Protestant Buddhism" (Obeyesekere and Gombrich 1988). Regarding its characteristics, Bechert suggested, among other things, that the increasingly active involvement of lay people is to be seen as one of the major shifts in 20th century Buddhism.[22] The fact that the descriptions of the early lay Buddhists as passive, devout listeners to the teaching and mere supporters of the *saṃgha* have been challenged in recent buddhological works (see above Freiberger 2000 and others) mirrors the new self-awareness of the laity in the Buddhist community. Lay people's increased activity and self-awareness is not only a characteristic of Theravāda Buddhism, but seems to have affected the whole Buddhist world. Under the aforementioned slogan of "Engaged Buddhism", this movement is, today, predominantly driven by lay people in the West, especially North America. Also, in China, it took

22 The characteristics, according to Bechert, are: an emphasis on rational elements, an accordance with exact sciences, an increased independent organisation of lay people, an increase in the number of Buddhist educational organisations, the creation of a pan-Buddhist consciousness, prozelytising activities, a will to influence the social world, and a search for the correct understanding of karma; see: Bechert (1966), I, 37–42. The change from a monastic Buddhism towards lay people's involvement is also stated without further reasoning by Welch: "Modern forms of charity did not appear on a large scale before 1912. Soon thereafter Buddhists began to organize orphanages, schools, and relief work" (Welch 1967, 377). Welch follows throughout his description of Buddhism an approach which is restricted to a very selective perception of lay Buddhist believers, as he is, in his own words, interested only in the "seriously religious devotee" who does not use his belief merely as he would "use a gas station", i.e. without any "special commitment" (Welch 1967, 387).

root and the works of one of its driving forces, the monk Taixu 太虛 (1890–1947), spread quickly in East Asia, suggesting a "Buddhism in the Human Realm" (*renjian fojiao*), which implied a stronger social engagement of the Buddhist community and emphasised the relevance of Buddhism in its lay followers' daily life.[23]

This programme of a socially-engaged form of Buddhism makes up the basis of the young Buddhist monastic communities in Taiwan today, especially the few aforementioned Young Buddhist Monasteries that were founded in the second half of the 20th century, which nowadays attract a mass lay following in Taiwan. Over a decade ago, while going for an ethnographical study of a Buddhist monastery in Taiwan the author encountered many of the monastery's lay followers. While discussing with them their motives for visiting and supporting "their" monastery, it was fascinating to witness the broad range of interests that led people to claim to be a "lay Buddhist". It was clear that this monastery was also proclaiming a socially Engaged Buddhism that was explicated in practical applicable wisdom aphorisms and in terms of "Zen for Life" (*shenghuo chan* 生活禪) or "A Bodhisattva living in the Human Realm" (*pusa huo zai renjian* 菩薩活在人間). At that moment, the initial research question arose: Is this terminology simply eye-catching, simply employing the modern sounding slang of contemporary society to attract people and therefore one of the main reasons for the growth of this monastery–in economic terms: as all big monasteries claim to be in some sense socially engaged, this obviously constitutes a strong source of financial income–or does this form of Engaged Buddhism also reach the people it addresses? Does it become an integral part of their life? Does it serve them by building up a modernity-compatible self-concept under the rapid changes of a modernising country or is it rather an intelligent rhetoric of the major monasteries? Are the processes of increasing Taiwanese urban modernity–in terms of functional differentiation, individually-centred careers and internationalisation–and a self-definition as a lay Buddhist really linked via "Engaged Buddhist" concepts?

The starting point for the further field research was, therefore, those people with some connection to the Buddhist monasteries. The search for Buddhist self-denotification beyond the rhetorical patterns of "Engaged Buddhism" quickly led to the discovery that Buddhism, as well as lay Buddhists, extend far beyond a Buddhist monastery's regular visitors. In contrast, the followers whom the monasteries themselves suggested as interviewees often proved to be their community's flagships, eloquently illustrating the monastery's principles using their own life. It turned out that the stereotypes of the

23 On the concept of "Engaged Buddhism" and the role of the monk Taixu within its development see chapters 8.2 and 12.6 as well as Guggenmos (2012).

lay Buddhist self-descriptions' long-established doctrinal patterns were fascinating, but provided little insight into Buddhist resources' actual application in daily life. Regarding the roles that Buddhism can play in Taiwanese citizens' life, it proved more rewarding to contact lay people who had not undergone a monastically-triggered process of re-constructing themselves as an ideal lay person, but still saw themselves as lay Buddhists. Although these people were often far less confident about discussing their beliefs and life, their narrations revealed a spontaneous depth which offers insights into the leading question of this book of how Buddhism features in individuals' attempts to respond to the needs of modernity. Engaged Buddhist concepts might play a role in this process, but are neither the sole focus of this study nor considered to be an appropriate analytical tool for understanding why Buddhism is attractive to urban dwellers in Taiwan.

4 Methodological Considerations

The Cultural Theoretical Approach

The question of how Buddhism is referred to by urban citizens as a resource for coping with life implies a perception of the social world in which the classic opposition between structure and agency is dissolved. Neither are humans described as acting totally independently from the ideas or structures of their social environment nor is every action of an individual seen as being completely determined by the structure of a field. For example, Taiwanese lay Buddhists would generally feel reluctant to describe their life as the imitation of the life of the Buddha and, if they were to do so, they might have to argue this during their social encounters in Taiwan. In Tibet, in contrast, it would be far more acceptable to describe oneself as following in the footsteps of the Buddha, not only as a monk but even as a lay follower.[24] Certain attitudes were, at the time of field research undertaken between 2005 and 2007, respected and well-established in Taiwan, while others were not. This does not imply that it is impossible to describe oneself as imitating the life of the Buddha in Taiwan (to extend the example), but simply that it would presumably be likely to attract the listener's attention if one were to do so. Looking closely at a single interview, one can discover how the interviewees perceive their arguments as relating to their environment. Therefore, without interviewing a huge number of Buddhists in Taiwan, but merely a small number of very different believers, one is in a position to distinguish between which are the acknowledged patterns of argumentation and which are not. Still, cultural habits are constantly in flux and each utterance has an influence on the system itself. The individual and society stand in a dialectical, mutually-influential relationship, which transgresses any dualistic construction. The social reality must be described as a communicative sphere that is being permanently transformed as well as constructed through its agents. This perception of the social world is the main concern of the cultural theoretical approaches. As Reckwitz puts it: "The central idea of the cultural theoretical perspective is simple as well as most consequential: The daily social practices of people–of communicative or non-communicative nature–get enabled as well as restricted through collective patterns of meaning, through mostly implicit staying structures of knowledge, which get ap-

---

24 Monks in Taiwan do this sometimes. See the biographical description in the author's book in preparation "Auf dem Weg zu einem globalisierten Regionalbuddhismus." The information about Tibet and the stimulating idea to search for Taiwanese adequacies I owe to an informal discussion with Hildegard Diemberger in July 2008.

plied in social practice and guide it".[25] Anthony Giddens, who is, together with Pierre Bourdieu, one of the main representatives of the cultural theoretical approach, describes structure through a duality, "as the medium and outcome of the conduct it recursively organizes"; he continues: "the structural properties of social systems do not exist outside of action but are chronically implicated in its production and reproduction" (Giddens 1986, 374). Social agency is reflected in the perspective of structure, which "exists only as memory traces, the organic basis of human knowledgeability, and as instantiated in action" (Giddens 1986, 377).

Adopting the perspective of the individual–as this study is about analysing individuals' narrations, one must situate oneself in a field of action which has its own principles and logic. When an individual makes a choice or has a preference for something, one automatically positions oneself within the field. This is the process of constant positioning which causes individuals to acquire dispositions, or a "habitus", that makes an action more or less likely in its context and gives it its specific meaning. In the process of socialisation, the individual constantly builds up a "tacit knowledge", which is the active and unconscious presence of previous experiences. The concept of "habitus" is today mainly associated with the works of Bourdieu. Again, as in other cultural theories, it is important to recognise the dynamic of the concept: the habitus is in constant transformation; it is a "structuring" as well as a "structured" structure; and it is a *modus operandi* as well as an *opus operatum*:

> The conditionings associated with a particular class of conditions of existence produce habitus, systems of durable, transposable dispositions, structured structures predisposed to function as structuring structures, that is, as principles which generate and organize practices and representations that can be objectively adapted to their outcomes without presupposing a conscious aiming at ends or an express mastery of the operations necessary to attain them. Objectively "regulated" and "regular" without being in any way the product of obedience to rules, they can be collectively orchestrated without being the product of the organizing action of a conductor (Bourdieu 1990, 53).[26]

---

25 Translated by the author. German original: "Der Kerngedanke der kulturtheoretischen Perspektive ist ebenso einfach wie folgenreich: Die alltäglichen sozialen Praktiken des Menschen–kommunikativer und nicht-kommunikativer Art–werden ermöglicht und eingeschränkt durch kollektive Sinnmuster, durch meist implizit bleibende Wissensstrukturen, die in der sozialen Praxis eingesetzt werden und diese leiten" (Reckwitz 1997, 319).

26 "Les conditionnements associés à une classe particulière de conditions d'existence produisent des *habitus*, systèmes de *dispositions* durables et transportables, structures structurées prédisposées à fonctionner comme structures structurantes, c'est-à-dire en tant que principes générateurs et organisateurs de pratiques et de représentations qui peuvent être objectivement adaptées à leur but sans supposer la visée consciente de fins et la maîtrise expresse des opérations nécessaires pour les atteindre, objectivement 'réglées' et 'régulières' sans être en rien le produit de l'obéissance à des règles, et, étant

Bourdieu first described the concept of habitus at length when he translated a work on architecture by Erwin Panofsky into French (Panofsky 1967). What fascinated Bourdieu about this approach was that Panofsky saw Gothic architecture in connection with scholastic literature and the use of the iconographical style in manuscripts. Bourdieu illustrates, by intuitive understanding, the idea of habitus in the example of an artist: "The habitus [connects] the artist with the collectivity and his time and gives its apparently unique project a direction and an aim without him taking notice of that".[27] The habitus includes the sensual perception of the environment, the understanding of daily life, the classifications, ethical norms, and aesthetical criteria that a person holds, as well as which individual and collective activities the agent finally produces. It comprises an individual's schemes of perception, thought and action and is significantly historically constituted ("produit de l'histoire", Bourdieu 1980, 91) through personal and collectively transmitted experiences.[28]

Habitus and "Deutungsmuster" (Patterns of Meaning)

The task of analysing how people use Buddhism as a resource in their daily lives equals a habitus analysis focusing on the (not exclusivisticly defined) Buddhist field. The methodology followed in the analyses exactly matches this need. Developed since the 1970s by Ulrich Oevermann (Frankfurt), the approach of "Structural Hermeneutics" is today widespread in German qualitative social research and has also been internationally applied. Jo Reichertz, presenting as Uwe Flick German methodological developments and Structural Hermeneutics in an international frame, concludes: "The concept of Objective [i.e. Structural; EMG] Hermeneutics is currently one of the most prominent approaches in qualitative research in German-speaking countries, including Austria and Switzerland, and it figures in all of the more recent

tout cela, collectivement orchestrées sans être le produit de l'action organisatrice d'un chef d'orchestre." (Bourdieu 1980, 88–89)

27 "[...] l'habitus par lequel le créateur participe de sa collectivité et de son époque et qui oriente et dirige, à son insu, ses actes de création les plus uniques en apparance." (Bourdieu 1967, 142; translation by the author)

28 For a concise outline of the understanding of "Habitus" by Bourdieu see, for example, Krais and Gebauer (2002). Bourdieu himself refers in a couple of articles and book chapters to his understanding of the habitus concept and develops it over the years: the afterword to his translation of the work of Panofsky (Bourdieu 1967) became well-known, and was translated (German: Bourdieu 1974). In his works "La distinction" and "La sens pratique" (English: The Logic of Practice, Bourdieu 1990), he also refers to the habitus concept in single chapters (Bourdieu 1979 and Bourdieu 1980) while he also presents an overview of his understanding of habitus in an interview (Bourdieu 1992).

methodological handbooks on qualitative research" (Reichertz 2004, 291).[29] Besides the "Institut für hermeneutische Sozial- und Kulturforschung" (Frankfurt, Institute's website: www.ihsk.de, accessed January 6, 2016), which addresses the development of the methodology and lends its analysis services to the public, mainly the economic field, the association "Arbeitsgemeinschaft für Objektive Hermeneutik" is an association that actively links researchers who are working with the method in various fields.[30]

Central to the method is the concept of "patterns of meaning" (*Deutungsmuster*), which are regarded as equivalent to Bourdieu's habitus concept. Oevermann states:

> Similar to Bourdieu, I subsume under the term of "Habitusformation" those deep-lying programs of action operating and running as automatism beyond the conscious controllability, which characterise and determine like a formation of character the behaviour and practice of individuals. [...] Like that, those habitus formations, which determine life practice, are especially acquired in the ontogenetic crisis of milieu determined socialisation and are deeply rooted in the repertoire of

29 As examples, Reichertz (2004) mentions the standard works: Bohnsack (1999): *Rekonstruktive Sozialforschung.*; Hitzler and Honer (1997): *Sozialwissenschaftliche Hermeneutik*; Lamnek (1995): *Qualitative Sozialforschung*. In Germany, qualitative methods are a vibrant field of research. The "Berliner Methodentreffen" is an annual symposium that hosts workshops during which the current developments within qualitative social research are presented. It is attended by several hundred students from different fields within the social sciences (see http://www.qualitative-forschung.de/methodentreffen/, accessed January 6, 2016).

30 In English, there have been several attempts to present Structural Hermeneutics as well as applications of the method. The association "Arbeitsgemeinschaft für Objektive Hermeneutik" (AGOH, www.agoh.de, accessed January 6, 2016) collects at http://www.objective-hermeneutics.com/bibliographic-database.html (accessed January 6, 2016) an English bibliographic database. Axel Jansen is publishing in English applying Structural Hermeneutics and is also co-author of a German introduction to Structural Hermeneutics: Jansen (2016): *Die Methodenschule der Objektiven Hermeneutik.* The author's own selected bibliographic overview includes: Wernet (2014): "Hermeneutics and Objective Hermeneutics"; Jindra and Jindra (2003): "Structural ('Objective') Hermeneutics and the Sociology of Religion"; Oberlaender (1997): "My God, They Just Have Other Interests"; Mann (2007): "Understanding Farm Succession by the Objective Hermeneutics Method"; Reichertz (2004): "Objective Hermeneutics and Hermeneutic Sociology of Knowledge". Wohlrab-Sahr has written a habilitation following the method of Objective Hermeneutics (Wohlrab-Sahr 1998). In English, she summarises the results within the articles: Wohlrab-Sahr (1999): "Conversion to Islam between Syncretism and Symbolic Battle"; Wohlrab-Sahr (2006): "Symbolizing Distance: Conversion to Islam in Germany and the United States". Methodological overviews in which the method of Objective Hermeneutics is mentioned: Bertaux and Kohli (1984): "The Life Story Approach: A Continental View"; Flick (2002): "Qualitative Research–State of the Art"; Gebhardt, Uta (1988): "Qualitative Sociology in the Federal Republic of Germany"; Meja, Misgeld, and Steht (1987): "Modern German Sociology".

behaviour, that much deeply, that a complete renunciation from them is as good as impossible.[31]

To mark clearly the independence of the "habitus formations", or–as Oevermann also calls it–"*Deutungsmuster*" (patterns of meaning) from individual subjective attitudes, Structural Hermeneutics are often called "Objective Hermeneutics".[32]

The Procedure of Structural Hermeneutics

The habitus analysis is reached in Structural Hermeneutics through a given structured procedure which does not take any theoretical assumptions in advance but derives in an inductive manner a hypothesis in a methodologically-controlled way. The attempt to avoid any logic of subsumption is shared with the, in the Anglo-Saxon discussion, widespread method of Grounded Theory (Glaser and Strauss). The concrete procedure of analysis differs from Grounded Theory mainly with regard to its strict sequential approach, which contributes to the strength of Structural Hermeneutics as well

---

31 "Ähnlich wie Bourdieu fasse ich unter dem Begriff der Habitusformation jene tiefliegenden, als Automatismus außerhalb der bewußten Kontrollierbarkeit operierenden und ablaufenden Handlungsprogrammierungen zusammen, die wie eine Charakterformation das Verhalten und Handeln von Individuen kennzeichnen und bestimmen. […] So werden lebenspraxisbestimmende Habitusformationen vor allem in den ontogenetischen Krisen der milieugebundenen Sozialisation erworben und tief im Verhaltensrepertoire verankert, so tief, daß eine vollständige Abkehr von ihnen so gut wie unmöglich ist." (Oevermann 2001, 46; translation by author). Oevermann tries in the following to distinguish between Bourdieu's "Handlungsformationen" and his own concept of "Deutungsmuster." He admits that the distinction between the two will remain problematic, but that "Handlungsformationen" would have a stronger psychological aspect while "Deutungsmuster" would be more milieu-specific, see Oevermann 2001, 45–47.

32 The author prefers in her own usage the expression "Structural Hermeneutics", as the term "objective" evokes a multitude of epistemological implications, which might prove misleading. The successful application of Structural Hermeneutics is basically independent of one's agreement with the philosophical approaches to cognitive science and language philosophy of Noam Chomsky or Charles S. Peirce, which inspired this methodology initially. The claims of Oevermann in defending qualitative against quantitative methods and highlighting the closeness of the method to the exactness of the natural sciences neglect, in the author's humble opinion, to a certain degree, the fact that, especially in the so-called "exact sciences", the role of models for appropriate understanding and the fragility of anything like an "objectivity" (there is no such thing as the "unobserved observer", etc.) are well-known to natural scientists. Still, the in-depth reflections show the benefits of the method as a microanalytical approach, revealing precise insights. In the spectrum of the available qualitative methods, it lies at the outer extreme of what can be reached in terms of precision and depth through an analytical approach, revealing the latent structures of meaning and habitus. For details, see Oevermann (2004).

as being the reason for its time-consuming nature. A detailed description of the method cannot be the aim of this study,[33] although some focal points within the interpretation procedure should be highlighted:

At the beginning of the analysis, contextual knowledge is set aside and the text is followed line-by-line. The analysis usually starts, in the case of interviews, with the opening sequence. These have proven to be most elucidating with regard to the self-representation of the interviewee.[34] In general, the sequential reading is performed by a team of researchers (see below), who attempt to find as many ways of reading (*Lesarten*) the sequence as possible. Attention is paid not only to the subjective meaning of the passage but especially to its "latent structures of meaning" (*latente Sinnstrukturen*), which are the concrete underlying patterns of argumentation and orientation that motivate and form the background of the respective sequence. In the case of an interview, for example, the interviewee does not necessarily have to be conscious about them, but they will structure his/her narration, as they enable the interviewee to provide an indirect picture of the self-evidencies and orientations of the social world in which he/she lives.[35] The search for as many ways of reading as possible is conducted with particular care. "In each shape of expression one can trace back–following the sequence-analytical basics of objective hermeneutics–what could have been (but in fact did not get) the case respectively the practice at a certain point of the narration. [This means one can trace back] how an immanently statable, i.e. an (according to the self-operating rule generating the valid material) inconsistency could have

33 The method developed over time. Groundbreaking was the article of Oevermann (1979). A fully-fledged argumentation about the methodology can be found in Oevermann's (2000) article. The basic texts are also available online: Oevermann, U. (2002); Oevermann, U. (1981). An exemplary application of the analysis method is the research project on the self-concept and pedagogic aims of teachers of religion in Germany: Feige, Dressler, Lukatis, and Schöll (2000).

34 In principle, one can start with any sequence of the interview and, according to this method, should achieve the same result at the end: "man [kann] mit der Sequenzanalyse im Prinzip an irgendeiner Stelle in einem Protokoll beginnen, denn eine Fallstruktur befindet sich permanent im Prozeß ihrer Reproduktion" (Oevermann 2000, 75), although interpretation experience tells us that, especially in the initial sequence, mostly within a short time, the habitus of the person and, through his/her general reaction to the question, the concept of self-representation become evident. This is reasonable, because any concrete action requires an opening and an ending, which set its frame for structured reliable actions.

35 Oevermann defines the latent structures of meaning as: "Der Begriff der latenten Sinnstruktur ist ausschließlich methodologisch zugerichtet und bezieht sich auf die durch Regeln erzeugten objektiven Bedeutungen einer Sequenz von sinntragenden Elementen einer Ausdrucksgestalt, in der alle nur denkbaren konkreten (Lebens-) Äußerungen von Lebenspraxis-Formen verkörpert sein können. Dieser Begriff bezieht sich also ausdrücklich nicht auf gegenstandtheoretische Inhalte, meint nicht irgendwelche in Gegenstandtheorien thematischen Gebilde" (Oevermann 2001, 39).

been abolished or differently been handled".[36] Due to impatience, interpreters often like to jump into the text before building up a profound structural hypothesis. This is prohibited, because it hinders the recognition of the process whereby the structure of the text can establish itself. The text accumulates step by step and tracing this structure not only reveals the possibilities that the interviewee would have had–for example, the breadth of options about being a Buddhist–but also proves more than is possible by jumping around in the text: being selective destroys confidence in the hypothesis, because one might argue that suitable arguments are merely selected from the text, while the rest of the interview is neglected. In the words of Oevermann, reality receives its "maximal chance" through the method.[37] To guarantee this chance, the interpretation team follows a twofold strategy, the principle of "totality" that attempts to be as extensive as possible ("*Totalitätsprinzip*"), and the principal of being literal, restricting the ways of reading by grounding them with reason in the sequence ("*Wörtlichkeitsprinzip*").[38]

After the first sequence, the following sequence is analysed, excluding the ways of reading the first sequence by extracting the "wohlgeformte Anschlußmöglichkeiten" (well-formed possibilities to continue, Oevermann 2000, 64). Sequence after sequence follows until a structural hypothesis of the case develops. The hypothesis is differentiated by contrasting or supporting it with other sequences. The whole process, and especially the structural hypothesis, underlies the principle of fallibility. The hypothesis developed can be rejected and replaced by a new hypothesis through the contrasting sequences. Step by step, the "case structure" (*Fallstruktur*) takes shape through the saturation and testing of the hypothesis and is finally formulated. A second look at the case structure and a comparison of the differing case structures following the theorising interests leads, in the last phase of the research

---

36 "An jeder Ausdrucksgestalt läßt sich nämlich gemäß der sequenzanalytischen Grundsätze der objektiven Hermeneutik ablesen, was der Fall bzw. die Praxis an einer bestimmten Stelle hätte werden können, aber nicht geworden ist, wie also eine immanent feststellbare, d.h. nach den in der Generierung des Materials selbst operierenden Regeln geltende Inkonsistenz hätte beseitigt bzw. auch anders bearbeitet werden können." (Oevermann 2001, 67; English by the author)

37 See Oevermann 2001, 65: "Im Unterschied zum subsumptionslogischen Vorgehen haben diese Verfahren den fallibilistischen Vorzug, daß in ihnen gemäß des Totalitätsprinzips der Auswertung alle Details der auszuwertenden Ausdrucksgestalt (Text bzw. Protokoll) beachtet werden müssen und so die Realität eine maximale Chance erhält, Konjekturen zu Fall zu bringen [...]."

38 Andreas Wernet, in his very instructive introduction for beginners, sums up the principles of Structural Hermeneutics: 1. exclude the context, 2. take the literal meaning of a text seriously: The text at hand is the only counting base of interpretation, not what the interviewee "may have meant", 3. sequentiality, 4. extensivity, and 5. (in the German version only) being economical: no far-fetched interpretations are allowed (Wernet 2014, 238–244, and Wernet 2000, 21–38).

process, to a theoretisation and abstraction according to the specific interest of the researcher; this being, in the current case, how Buddhism is referred to in the urban climate of Taiwan.

In principle, any kind of material suits Structural Hermeneutics, as long as social life is expressed through it, like publications, writings, audio-visual material, and even paintings. Secondary sources, such as the recordings of ceremonies, etc., are also acceptable, but the researcher should ensure that his material is as non-selective as possible and that the natural flow of the field has a chance to "exemplify". Therefore, conducting an interview with a person in the field is feasible, provided that this factor does not persistently restrict the interviewee's narration. In fact, narrative interviews, that are often biographically-oriented, are the most common form employed with Structural Hermeneutics. The material for a habitus analysis following Structural Hermeneutics, with the aim of understanding how the interviewees see themselves as Buddhists in their environment, should therefore aim to be a natural, non-standardised narration in which the interviewer hands over the task of structuring the thoughts to the interviewee. Standardised interviews or even questionnaires are, therefore, unsuited to the analysis method.

It is worth bearing in mind that the interviews are conducted according to the methodological necessity of evoking a free biographical narration. They are not performed in order to collect entertaining or outstanding lay stories, and the cases are not intended to represent an illustrative collection of devoted Buddhists. Also, the interviews analysed were conducted neither to compensate for the researcher's lack of knowledge about the Buddhist field nor to reconstruct a complete life-story. The interview situation is regarded as a whole as social interaction, within which the observed field reproduces its interaction patterns. Through the interview, it becomes clear how the interviewees create their habitus in each specific situation. The aim is to observe the natural interaction behaviour of the interviewees in combination with the world view on which they are enlarging.

Structural Hermeneutics have tended, in the past, to be conducted in a cultural context that is related to that of the researcher and it is self-evident that only a researcher who is fully immersed in his/her field of study will be able to imagine the width of possible associations as they are reflected in the interviews. With the study presented here, it is therefore also intended to take the methodology a step further and test its applicability across cultural boundaries. Reflecting on the challenges, dangers and opportunities associated with such an approach is, in consequence, indispensable (see below, "Contextual Considerations").

Data Assessment

a) Interviewing Methodology: Narrative-biographical Interviews following F. Schütze

Fritz Schütze developed a widely-applied methodology for conducting narrative, biographical interviews,[39] consisting of three phases: firstly, an initial stimulus is provided, a question, which focuses on the researcher's interest. Normally, this will be a request for an autobiographic narration, which can encompass the interviewee's whole life or phases that represent aspects of it. The stimulus intends to evoke a self-developing narration from the interviewee and emphasises radical non-interference. Only after the narration ceases by itself during a break (*Erzählkoda*) does the researcher begin to ask questions. In the second part of the interview, the researcher focuses on the narration's tangential potential (*tangentiales Erzählpotential*), which refers to text immanent questions, that arise out of the first part: breaks in the narration, side narrations, rough summaries, illogical or incomprehensible passages, etc., attract the researcher's interest, who should ask for specifications in a narrative way, reviewing the narration and inserting the question into the context, thus enabling the interviewees to develop their own argumentation. The third phase of the interview makes the interviewees experts in their own field. They will abstract situations and developments and can also be asked theoretical questions. The informant is addressed as an "expert and theorist of himself" ("Experte und Theoretiker seiner selbst", Schütze 1983, 285). The third part especially explores therefore the self-reflective habitus of the interviewee. The result will be a narrative text, which reveals the social process of the development and change of a biographical identity with as few interventions as possible, while allowing the narration to build up a continuity and inner logic by itself. Schütze states: "The autobiographical narrative interview generates data texts, which reproduce as much consistently the ensnarement of events and the up-piling of life experiences of the biography-carrier as this is possible within the frame of systematic sociological research at all".[40]

---

39 Schütze's manner of conducting biographical-narrative interviews became well-established in the qualitative research field in Germany, due to his active influence within the field of biographical research and life-world analysis (*Lebensweltanalyse*). The formally-published small amount of works stands in no relation to the wide influence of the method. Descriptions of the outline of the interview methodology are sketched in: Schütze (1983 and 1984).

40 English by the author, German original: "Das autobiographische narrative Interview erzeugt Datentexte, welche die Ereignisverstrickungen und die lebensgeschichtliche Erfahrungsaufschichtung des Biographieträgers so lückenlos reproduzieren, wie das im Rahmen systematischer sozialwissenschaftlicher Forschung überhaupt nur möglich ist" (Schütze 1983, 285).

In the initial phase of the research, the author tried several introductory stimuli that might evoke a narration that would illustrate the role of Buddhism as a resource for daily life. While questions like "What role do you think Buddhism has played in your life so far?" led to relatively short answers, which skimmed over the concrete situations and biographical aspects, the finally chosen stimulus led in general to detailed narrations and the question as such was normally perceived by the interviewee positively, as an acceptable and understandable research interest. The stimulus, developed during an introductory chat with the interviewee, is not read out, but should be formulated in a casual, non-artificial way, in accordance with the situation. The topic addressed was how the interviewee had first encountered Buddhism or the organisation that he attended at the time of the interview and how his being a Buddhist had developed out of this initial contact. In preparing for the interviews, the question was noted down: "[Can you recall] how initially you came into contact with Buddhism / this monastery / how you joined this organisation? How did that develop?" (*[Ni ke bu keyi huiyi/ ni jide… ma] nin dangchu ruhe gen fofa (/zhe ge daochang) jieyuan/jinru zhe ge zuzhi? Yihou you zenme yang fazhan de?* [你可不可以回憶/你記得...嗎] 您當初如何跟佛法(/這個道場)結緣/進入這個組織? 以後有怎麼樣發展的?). To enable the interviewee to narrate freely and furnish the same basic circumstances for each interview, the author introduced herself and her research in advance. The interviewees' permission to record the interview was requested, and they were informed that their anonymity would be respected. It also proved helpful to explain the method of free narration, as the interviewees often assumed that participating in "research" involved them giving short, precise answers about the data and information and not wasting the interviewer's time. Having learnt about the nature of the interviews, some of the interviewees were astonished, that "this will be research" and, in general, could not imagine what the author would do with "such normal" life-stories. Having been introduced to the task of narrating freely, the interviewees responded positively, seeing it as generally "easy" "simply to state how they first encountered Buddhism". They showed a natural acquaintance with telling stories about their life experience, which mirrors the fact that, as a Buddhist, narrating how one became a Buddhist is not an unusual mode of self-presentation in Taiwanese society.[41] The questions in the second part of the interview could hardly be

41 After a first screening through Foguang Shan's collected Buddhist magazines that goes back to the 1950s and a look into the MFQWJ (2006) and MFQWJB (2007), the author entertains the hypothesis that the genre of conversion stories of ordinary lay Buddhists accompanied the emergence of the Buddhist periodical press. While, initially, only single, short narrations can be found in Chinese Buddhist magazines published since the late 19th century, the genre flourished after World War II. Even today, the printed narrations are highly stereotyped. A comparison between the established

anticipated, as they depended on the interviewee's preceding narration. Often, the interviewees' childhood was omitted from their narrations, and their current Buddhist practice was also rarely mentioned. The intensity of identifying with the Buddhist community, however, was frequently recalled as well as the importance of the choice of the specific Buddhist organisation.

The last part of the interview resulted from the previous narration, but some questions were asked in each case: the self-awareness of the interviewees as lay Buddhists in Taiwan and their awareness of playing a certain role within this field were addressed. Their perceptions of lay Buddhists in Taiwan in general and of the relation and differences between lay people and monastics were tackled because of the interviewer's interest in the lay monastic relationship. Personal motives for not being a monastic rounded off the opinion about this relationship. The interviewee's historical consciousness of the development of lay Buddhism in Taiwan during the last century and an outlook on its future were always included. This topic was also handled on a personal level by asking the interviewees to comment upon their personal future as lay Buddhists. Finally, the interviewees were always given the chance to add anything they wished, to explain what was important to them, and to express whether they had felt able to express themselves adequately during the interview. After the interview, the researcher always wrote down minutes including general impressions about the case, self-observations, theoretical expectations and personal impressions about the interviewees and their relationship with the interviewer.

b) *Transcription and Translation Principles*

Having completed an interview, the next step was the transcription process. For a correct case reconstruction, it is important to obtain a meticulous, detailed transcript of the material analysed. This necessity arises out of the methodological consideration that the protocol–i.e. the record which is interpreted with the help of the transcript–is the only basis for interpretation. Aberrations from the protocol, in the sense of "I knew the interviewee did not mean that, but wanted to say…", leading to hypotheses that are not rooted in the text, fail to respect the objectivity of the protocol ("Achtung vor der Objektivität des Protokolls"; Oevermann 2004, 333). Methodologically speaking, beyond the protocol, there is no access to reality. This is why the transcript, especially the analysed sequences, should aim to illustrate the complexity of the interview, and why a detailed legend to the transcriptions

stereotypes, their development and the biographical spontaneous narrations in contrast to them would be an interesting follow-up research topic, but goes beyond the limits of the research presented.

is given at the beginning of this book. The protocol, therefore, includes all kinds of utterances of the record, even those without any semantic meaning. In extreme cases, the tone and speed of voice is indicated. As is usual for such descriptions, there is no punctuation in the traditional sense, although interruptions and breaks are marked.

Although Chinese characters often contain phonetic elements and are composites of phonetic components and semantic radicals, Chinese characters are morphemes, independent of phonetic changes. This makes Chinese interview transcription distinct from those in other languages. A proficient transcription will generally convey the dialect and individual pronunciation of the interviewee. With Chinese characters, this is impossible. The relationship between spoken and written Chinese is more complex than that of any language that uses a phonetic script. The romanisation of the text–such as via the commonly-applied Pinyin-system, which is used in this book to refer to names, etc.–would make the transcript barely readable, and marking special pronunciations would make it even worse. The most precise solution would be to use the International Phonetic Alphabet but, for the researcher and the interpretation team, this transcript would be unmanageable in the time available. Therefore, it was decided to take as the basis a transcription method that employs Chinese characters and try to imitate the interjections and all other kinds of non-semantic utterances through these. The wide range of interpretations of exclamations of this kind cannot be reflected adequately by a variety of characters and should be open to discussion by the interpretation team. In case of the upcoming questions about the concrete pronunciation, the researcher had to return to the record itself.

By laying such emphasis on the rules of transcription, the role of the translation provided is obvious: it is purely functional, seeking to assist those who cannot read the Chinese version to reconstruct for themselves the Chinese original as far as possible. With the aim of following the original texts as closely as possible, the translations are not meant to be easily readable and certainly do not intend to be of any value in the traditional sense of providing a good translation. For the case analysis, the Chinese text is the only basis for the argumentation.

c) Theoretical Sampling and Research Process

Ideally, each interview should be transcribed immediately after it has been completed. The results of the analysis will lead to new questions about the field and the topic under investigation. Normally, one would search for the maximal contrasts in mapping out the field and the minimal contrasts for more narrow differentiations. The process of moving from the data gathering to analysis which leads back to the field is shared with the process of "theoretical sampling" in Grounded Theory, in which "theoretical sampling" is a method of data collection that focuses on gaining concepts which derive from the data:

> Unlike conventional methods of sampling, the researcher does not go out and collect the entire set of data before beginning the analysis. Analysis begins after the first day of data gathering. Data collection leads to analysis. Analysis leads to concepts. Concepts generate questions. Questions lead to more data collection so that the researcher might learn more about those concepts. This circular process continues until the research reaches the point of saturation; that is, the point in the research when all the concepts are well defined and explained (Corbin and Strauss 2008, 144–145).

Still, every data collection process, and especially those involving field research overseas, faces practical organisational limits. The group in question–in this case, those who term themselves Buddhists–must be theoretically chosen and the method of data collection must be fixed–in this case, narrative biographical interviews. An in-depth analysis after every interview cannot be achieved with a team of interpreters while in the field. Therefore, the field research was conducted in several phases and a preliminary analysis was performed directly after each interview by the researcher herself. The preliminary results made it possible to search for the following interviewee, pursuing the aim of creating minimal and maximal contrasts. The criteria for choosing the next interviewee were developed out of the material.

The interviews were conducted during two field trips to Taiwan in spring 2005 and winter 2006/07. The author had studied Taiwanese Buddhism since her year-long stay in Taiwan in 2000/2001, followed by field trips there in 2002, 2005, 2006/07, and 2008. Between 2000 and 2005 she collected material for an ethnographic description of a Young Buddhist Monastery (see the monograph in preparation by the author). After gaining insights into the organisational structure of Buddhism and contacting members of Buddhist organisations in Taiwan, a first round of interviews, focusing on the self-concepts of Buddhist lay people, was conducted. Initially, the interviewer accepted interviewees very openly. The field showed a certain dynamic, which made it necessary to accept several interviewees before less open personalities felt encouraged to agree to be interviewed. Also, it proved easier to contact young Buddhists, some of whom belonged to a Buddhist youth club. The acquaintance and sensibility of the interviewer grew throughout this initial phase, but these interviews were not chosen for transcription. Some of them would be more suitable for a study on the formative role of Buddhism during adolescence in Taiwan. After a period of evaluation and building up a preliminary description of the options for lay Buddhists' self-construction out of the more settled interviews in the first phase, a second period of field investigation followed in winter 2006/2007, leading to six additional interviews. In summer 2008, a final, three-week visit helped to round off the investigation by pursuing single remaining questions. Naturally, the field visits were used not only to find suitable interviewees, but also to become better acquainted with the Buddhist field itself, especially the newly arising organisations, and the fresh publications about Taiwanese Buddhism. The author is grateful for the fruitful contact with the Institute of Sociology of the Academia Sinica, whose *Taiwan Social Change Survey* (see below) granted the qualitative study a contextualisation through its highly-reliable statistics.

	Field Stay I	*Field Stay II*
Time Period	January to March 2005 (Interviews conducted in February and March)	October 2006 to January 2007 (Interviews conducted throughout the field stay)
Number of interviews	22	6
Gender (m/f)	(7/12), 3 mixed groups	(3/3)
Age *Age Average*	youngest 20, oldest about 60, arithmetic mean 40.4 years.	youngest 40, oldest about 70, arithmetic mean 55.2 years.
Living Area *Place of Interview*	All of them live either in the larger area of Taipeh (20 cases) or spend, at the time of or shortly before the interview, most of their time in Taipeh (2 cases). The interviews were mostly conducted in Taipeh.	Four live in Taipeh County, one in Taipeh City, and one in southern Taiwan, but works in Taipeh.
Buddhist affiliation	18 have some kind of connection with the Young Buddhist Monasteries, 2 are from New Buddhist Organisations, 1 is a lay follower of a traditionally established monastery, and 1 is a lay follower, living in a Buddhist lay community.	(1) Independent, with Buddhist interests. (2) Temple community member. (3) Member of a new Buddhist lay movement. (4) Buddhist publisher. (5) Follower of a well-known Young Buddhist Monastery. (6) Buddhist TV moderator. Active member of a well-known Young Buddhist Monastery.
Presented in Part I and II	4 cases Luo Peirong (chap. 7.2) Xu Wenhua (chap. 12.2) Cai Chenhao (chap. 7.3) Li Zhiqiang (chap. 7.4) (Except for one, they were interviewed in the second half of this research period.)	5 cases Zhang Yimin (chap. 12.4) Lin Yongfu (chap. 7.1) Meng Fanyi (chap. 12.5) Gu Puzhong (chap. 7.5) Ma Fengling (chap. 12.1)

Table 1: Overview of the conducted interviews.

The final sampling of the narrative interviews consists of 28 cases (22 field research I and 6 during field research II) conducted in Chinese. Each interview lasted at least an hour but none exceeded three hours. They were conducted with people of both sexes (f: 10; m: 15; and three mixed group interviews), aged from 20 to nearly 70 years old. People from middle class families are as well represented as independent entrepreneurs, intellectuals and housewives. Still, socio-structural criteria were not employed to obtain the data, but criteria developed from the interview analyses. Any factors relating to gender, age, social stratification, etc. have to reveal their relevance through the material. The described options make, therefore, no statement about the statistical probability of such an option occurring, but explore *how* people resort to Buddhist patterns, i.e. how far the portrayed habitus takes concrete shape in their environment (*modus operandi*) and how far they are an exemplary realisation among more or less likely options and can show the embedding of the case within its social field (*opus operatum*). The sample seeks to present the options representatively rather than the society with its socio-structural characteristics. In contrast, following any socio-structural pattern would presume that the habitus to be reconstructed mirrors the socio-structural characteristics of society. For example, options taken only by very few people can have an important impact on society (see chap. 7.5 on the Buddhist publisher, Gu Puzhong).

Still, after conducting the interviews, it was helpful to examine the teristics of the sample in order to discover the limits and possible blind spots of the investigation. The interviews were conducted over a two-year period, between spring 2005 and winter 06/07. Those conducted during the second field visit were selected very carefully after the year of team analysis in 2005/06, which is why they were spread throughout the whole field visit and nearly all of them were chosen for analysis. The interviewees were, on average, older (general average 55.2 [field stay II] compared with 40.4 years [field stay I]; range of age in field research II: 40 to 70; in field research I: 20 to 60), as the researcher focused on those whose religious development was not part of their adolescent search. During the first field visit, many of the interviewees were connected with the Young Buddhist Monasteries, which helped the researcher to arrange the interviews in some cases–see the case of Ma Fengling, chap. 12.1. In the second research phase, the interviewer used primarily non-organisational contacts to access interviewees. The advantage of this was obvious, as the interviewees did not feel that they had to represent their organisation so their narrations were far more concentrated on their own life stories. Still, some interviewees like to hide behind their organisation and, to many, it was also more understandable to discuss their organisation rather than their own "unimportant" life. The interviews in the second research phase showed, as a consequence, in the analysis, the options of Buddhist self-understanding beyond a primary organisational self-understanding. Still, organisational binding is just one of a multitude of aspects that appear in the biographies, and one should not oversimplify lay Buddhist believers in terms of their organisational (non-)affiliation. Finally, four interviews from the first research phase are presented here, while five were selected from the second phase. What unites these cases is that the interviews were conducted within an urban context with those living mostly in the northern region of Taiwan, Taipeh or its suburbs. The sample reached a degree of saturation within this chosen limit. The study, therefore, makes a statement about lay Buddhists living in the Taipeh area who might be very similar to lay Buddhists living in other urban areas of Taiwan, but may be less relevant to Buddhists living in other, more rural areas of Taiwan. Moreover, from an international comparative perspective, differences will arise especially in comparison with lay Buddhism on the mainland (see chap. 17).

Given that the researcher speaks Mandarin only and not Taiwanese, the restriction to Taipeh-related, urban Buddhists was a reasonable choice that secured the validity of the study. The interviewees normally spoke Mandarin in their daily life but, during the interviews, occasionally included Taiwanese expressions, which still could be transcribed successfully. Especially when discussing their primary religious socialisation via popular religion during their youth, Taiwanese expressions slipped in to compensate for their lack of Mandarin. This was encouraged by the interviewer as, otherwise, the results would have been distorted. Still, all of the interviewees were, in general, able to express themselves naturally in Mandarin and, in the author's view, no potential interviewees refused to participate for the (hidden) reason that they felt uncomfortable using Mandarin to discuss being a Buddhist. In the area of Taipeh, Standard Chinese is the dominant dialect, although many people come from a background where Taiwanese is the daily language. Other urban areas of Taiwan might be slightly more rooted in Taiwanese language and, in the rural regions, it would definitely be necessary to conduct the interviews in Taiwanese in order to obtain any valid results. The study, therefore, could not have claimed any validity if the interviews had been conducted in Chinese in the rural areas of Taiwan.

Extending the Methodology beyond its Boundaries

The study of lay Buddhists in Taiwan, on the one hand, fills a gap in the sociological description of Taiwanese Buddhism, which concentrates mainly on its organisational development. On the other hand, it is innovative in challenging and broadening the methodological approach to Taiwanese Buddhism. Structural Hermeneutics was a method developed by Oevermann within an inner-German context after the 1960s. The motivation to understand the barriers that the less privileged classes were facing in society led to milieu-studies that sought to work out the patterns of meaning that constitute these social milieus.[42] Structural Hermeneutics was therefore well-situated in the German context and became part of the standard curriculum of qualitative social research, although it showed little interest in establishing itself as an internationally-recognised methodological approach. In this situation, the researchers naturally assumed that they speak the same language as the interviewees. Oevermann stated in 1979 that the demand that the researchers should be as well-acquainted as possible with the environment from which the material stems is "trivial".[43] What might be "trivial" in an inner German context is revealed to be a huge challenge in cases where the researcher must overcome cultural and communicational barriers.

On the question of contextualisation, Oevermann mentions the division between case-specific knowledge ("fallspezifisches Vorwissen") and general knowledge with regard to rules and the world ("allgemeines Regel- und Weltwissen"; Oevermann 2000, 104), the former of which is neglected in the interpretation of the initial sequence, while the latter most welcome. Oevermann illustrates his understanding of a "general knowledge about rules and the world" by the gesture of greeting: "The meaning of not greeting back [if someone greets you] is objectively already always determined as the non-closure of an offered opening of a common practice that in concrete obliges to mutuality through valid rules, independently of the question, in which concrete context it was performed".[44] In a German context, a greeting is certainly a casual, mutual gesture but, in a different cultural context, German greeting habits might appear quite different and even the mutuality of the gesture cannot be presumed. Through being a stranger in the context, the researcher will recognise the normality of others as already noteworthy, which can be of value, as it might lead to sharper descriptions. Knowledge about contextual normality needs to be paid, as a consequence, far more attention by the researcher. To stay within the example,

42 Oevermann resumes: "Damals suchte ich nach Deutungsmustern vor allem in zwei Richtungen: zum einen im Zusammenhang mit der Rekonstruktion von gegeneinander abgrenzbaren subkulturellen Milieus, die die letztlich bloß als statistische Größen oder Aggregate abgrenzbaren sozialen Schichten material füllen konnten– und dies nicht nur eindimensional vertikal, sondern mehrdimensional differenzierend–und zum anderen, um die kaum merklich sich in ständiger Transformation befindenden, den 'Zeitgeist' ausmachenden 'kollektiven Haltungen' zu identifizieren" (Oevermann 2001, 37).

43 "Ebenso trivial ist die Forderung, daß die Interpreten mit der Lebenswelt, aus der das Datenmaterial stammt, möglichst gut vertraut sein sollten." (Oevermann 1979, 392)

44 "Die Bedeutung des Nicht-Zurückgrüßens liegt objektiv als Nicht-Schließung einer angebotenen Eröffnung einer gemeinsamen, zur Wechselseitigkeit konkret bindenden Praxis durch geltende Regeln schon immer fest, unabhängig davon, in welchem konkreten Kontext es erfolgte" (Oevermann 2000, 105).

researchers must know that depending on the situation the English "to greet" is to assume more mutuality than the Chinese *yingjie* 迎接, "to welcome someone", and more intimacy than the Chinese *zhaohu* 招呼, "to call someone, to say hello to someone", and is not necessarily an act of courtesy, as implied by *wenhou* 問候, "to send one's regards to someone". One then, of course, needs to know how the language forms part of daily behaviour, how and when people greet and what they assume by it. The extent to which foreign researchers have a "feeling" for situations depends on their degree of immersion. Still, any culture with which one did not grow up will always be more closely linked to single experiences and situations than one's primary socialisation. "General knowledge about rules and the world" seems at least partly to be a culturally specific acquired knowledge.

Dealing with a non-native, though well acquainted cultural context, the author took time to frame the research question. Within the field observations and during the initial interviews, she worked out how the field operates. Is religion a sensitive topic? Is one's Buddhist life story an intimate, private matter, or are life stories commonly shared? How does one react to foreigners? It became clear that, for most of the interviewees, "becoming a Buddhist" was a positive experience, which they wished to share. The intimacy of their personal story seemed to constitute no hindrance to telling it. Being a foreigner had, in this respect, a positive effect: The interviewees felt that the interviewer was not part of their context, so discussing sensitive topics could not cause problems in their environment. They sometimes felt as if they were representing "Taiwan". The presence of the researcher is obviously associated with the need for a rational rectification. Often, the awareness that the interviewer is a foreigner led the interviewees to explain issues in more detail and consider more deeply experiences that would not have needed any explanation in a Taiwanese context. Being a foreigner had a positive effect in enabling the researcher to question the basic attitudes of the interviewees without causing offence. The author being a foreigner meant that she was perceived as a "Westerner". Westerners are normally warmly welcomed in Taiwan, and not necessarily expected to be fluent in Chinese. During the narrations, it turned out that especially those interviewees who considered themselves to be representatives of Taiwan found in the interviewer a representative of the West. For example, the publisher, Gu Puzhong, was so delighted and excited that a Westerner had requested an interview with him, who had lived for ten years in Canada, that his message as a publisher became structured within the West-East dichotomy. Contextual knowledge that ascertains West-East modes of talking as common outside the specific interview context in Taiwan helps to rehabilitate the value of the interview, also revealing the importance of reflecting on the interviewer's impact on the situation. Stating plainly that Gu's world view is solely dominated by the East-West conflict would simply be a wrong hypothesis. Still, the fact that Gu responded enthusiastically to the situation was also not without cause: he was able to enlarge on the East-West dichotomy, in which, for him, Buddhism plays a crucial role in his own and other "Easterners'" positive self-reconstruction, assuming that the interviewer can understand his conflict. Within the interview, he, therefore, presents one option for making use of Buddhism. This is not the only option for him certainly and also, during the analysis, further elements surface, but it is nevertheless a valid one. This example illustrates nicely the basic idea of Structural Hermeneutics that the presented case analyses are not to be misunderstood as being the full representations of the interviewee. In the display of presentations, the cases do not stand side by side like disparate types, but each narration illuminates, from a different angle, the array of possibilities related to employing Buddhist sources within one's life in Taiwan. The East-West dichotomy is one (well-presented by one interviewee) of these, but certainly not the only one. The slight over-representation of the East-West scheme can be attributed to the interviewee's reaction to the interviewer, and a study by a Taiwanese citizen would face other peculiarities. It is important to note that the role of the interviewer can never be eliminated, but that an interpretation becomes valid through a careful consideration of all of the elements that shape the interview. The importance of recognising the impact of researchers upon their field and making it fruitful within the interpretation is central to the validity of the results. The method of Structural Hermeneutics is, due to its microanalytical approach, especially sensitive to this.

How can the project deal with the challenge of being conducted in a foreign cultural context? Firstly, as already mentioned, the researcher has worked on Taiwanese Buddhism since the year 2000 in an attempt to become as closely acquainted with the context as possible by engaging in participatory observation and undergoing a "second socialisation". Structural Hermeneutics to consider and evaluate as far as possible, all of the existing resources, including all the kinds of material in the field.[45]

Secondly, a comparatively high number of 28 interviews was conducted. Milieu-studies with Structural Hermeneutics in Germany are normally based on fewer than 15 interviews. Not only did the researcher go deeper into the field through the initial interviews, but she also had to be sensitive to the fact that the context of an "interview" in Taiwan is different from that in Germany, as giving an "interview" has been relatively more recently-established as a cultural tool and was often connected to other expectations.

45 "Generell sieht die objektive Hermeneutik vor, daß man bei Fallrekonstruktionen zunächst so weit wie möglich recherchierbare, schon vorhandene Ausdrucksgestalten wie z.B. Briefe, Tagebücher, Dokumente, Fotos, Bauten, Appelle, Flugblätter, etc. auswertet und erst dann weitere Befragungen selbst durchführt." (Oevermann 2001, 62)

Of invaluable assistance for the cases' interpretation was, thirdly, the exchange with other researchers and the–methodologically requested–interpretation team. The team is essential for Structural Hermeneutics, as the rational discourse enables the possible structured features of a case to surface. It reduces the likelihood of the structural hypothesis being biased. In the case of the present study, a group of young researchers, receiving training in the qualitative methods of social research within religious studies at the University of Muenster (Germany), analysed, following the field trip in 2005, the initial interview sequences. The line-by-line analyses by the group were recorded and later summarised by a team member. Over several sessions, a structural hypothesis for each case was developed. Within the discussions, it quickly became obvious how important contextual knowledge was for an appropriate understanding. The participation of a Chinese student and the researcher herself in the group revealed: a) discrepancies with the German students' interpretations; and b) discrepancies between religious life on the mainland and in Taiwan. Besides the interpretation team, the assistance of a Taiwanese friend proved invaluable. She not only went through the transcriptions with the author and was able to understand the Taiwanese phrases but the author could also discuss some of her analytical results and align them with the frame set of what would be perceived as culturally "normal". In the experience of the author, it is tempting to establish one's impression of an interview prematurely as a "case structure", and search for appropriate sequences within that interview. This is especially dangerous when working in a foreign language, because one tends to focus on the well understood parts of the interview. Complete transcriptions and also corrections of the parts which seemed to be less important were necessary to differentiate the impressions of each case. It is also due to the regular feedback of Albrecht Schoell who has worked for many years with the method of Structural Hermeneutics who listened carefully to the interpretations, encouraged the researcher to trust the method and helped to concentrate on the cases, putting aside the pressures of time management and content-wise expectations.

Fourthly, the contextual question was greatly helped by the precise statistics of the *Taiwan Social Change Survey*. As the data of the survey itself were at hand for my own investigations and the outcomes are presented in the following, the statistical sources shall be briefly introduced:

The Role of Statistical Material

Statistical data are, in the case of Taiwan, available in uniquely precise and high-standard ways. Historically speaking, the first in-depth survey about religion in Taiwan was conducted during the Japanese colonial period (Taiwan Sōtokufu and Keijirō Marui 1919). Consisting of an initial descriptive part and a second part that states the frequencies of the religious organisations, especially the temples and vegetarian halls (*zhaitang* 齋堂), and religious professionals, this survey provides, with reference to the provinces of Taiwan, extraordinary insights into religious life around 1900 and assists our historical understanding of popular religion. To the options of lay Buddhists' self-construction, however, it can contribute only indirectly.

The tradition of conducting full inventory counts was continued by the Taiwanese government. Even today, Taiwan is, together with Japan, one of the few states to publish regular, full inventory counts by maintaining a detailed household registry. These data are available online.[46] They assist our understanding of the sociocultural situation in Taiwan and the available statistics have been used in this study for this purpose (see chap. 10). Religious affiliation was the focus of a large survey by the Ministry of the Interior in 1991–2, which aimed to continue the tradition begun by the Japanese, mainly concentrating on the religious organisations and their professionals.[47]

A whole new dimension of sociological in-depth investigation concerning religious affiliation, behaviour, and attitudes is revealed by the *Taiwan Social Change Survey* (TSCS), which is conducted annually by the Academia Sinica. First carried out in 1985 and annually after 1990, it follows a five-yearly rhythm, repeating modules that allow longitudinal studies. Every year, two parallel investigations are conducted on various topics so that, in total, about ten modules can be handled. Some of the topics have been replaced over time or switched to different units but, in the first year, there is always a mixed investigation, and topics, such as social stratification, family, communication behaviour, religion, cultural values, political culture, work, and topics related to leisure time, are regularly thematised. For the present evaluation, the author relied especially on the surveys about religion for 1994, 1999, 2004, 2009, and 2014. As the interviews were conducted between 2005 and 2007, the survey of 2004, closest to the interviews, provides the main basis for statistical investigations.[48] For historical comparison, additional material for 1985 and 1990 was also partly evaluated.

46 *Zhonghua Minguo Tongji Xunwang* 中華民國統計資訊網, http://www.stat.gov.tw, last accessed January 6, 2016.

47 The report extends over three years, from 1991–1993 (*Zhonghua minguo bashi/-yi/-er nian Taiwan Diqu: Zongjiao tuanti diaocha baogao* 1992–1995).

48 The abbreviation TSCS 2004.2 refers to the module for religion, i.e. the second questionnaire within the 2004 survey of the research project (台灣社會變遷調查, 2004, fourth phase, fifth round, 第四期第五次). The project was conducted by the Institute of Sociology, Academia Sinica, Republic of China, Taiwan, and sponsored by the National Science Council 行政院國家科學委員會, Republic of China, Taiwan. Dres. Zhang Yinghua 章英華 and Zhuan Yingzhi 傅仰止 were responsible for the report. The data were generously provided by the Academia Sinica. For their interpretations,

The Taiwan Social Change Survey *(TSCS) 2004.2*

Regarding the quality of the *Taiwan Social Change Survey*, especially the 2004 one about religion, it can be stated that, in general, it attempts to reach the limits of what is practicably feasible in Taiwan. The TSCS counts as a representative quantitative survey of high reliability, meeting and even exceeding the international standards. The selection process, the realisation of the interviews, the data collection procedures and the weighting all lead to high standards of sociological quantitative research.[49]

The selection of interviewees for the survey in 2004 was performed on three levels–provinces/townships, cities, individuals–each on the basis of probabilities proportional to size (PPS). The basis was the household registry and the potential interviewees were Taiwanese citizens over 18 years old. The choice of the provinces depended on a stratification of Taiwan into seven clusters performed by Luo Qihong 羅啟宏 in 1993 according to socio-geographical criteria (see below). The goodness of fit of the random choice sample can be seen as sufficient considering the gender-, age-, and gender-cross-age-distribution via the corresponding k-/p-values. The survey process was very carefully planned and documented. After training the interviewers, the interviews were conducted first via telephone to assist the subsequent re-design of the questionnaire and finally carried out face to face in spring 2004. Of the 3,955 chosen individuals, complete interviews with 1,881 of them were realised.[50] Failed interviews were mainly due to the fact, that there was no-one at home or the individual was inaccessible; the reasons are listed in detail in the survey report. Also, 406 people refused to be interviewed.

The questions were very detailed, and the answers to them considered "other" (*qi ta* 其他) possibilities and difficulties in answering, such as not understanding the question (*bu liaojie wenti* 不瞭解題意), a missing value (*yilou zhi* 遺漏值), not knowing or having forgotten the answer (*bu zhidao huo wangji* 不知道或忘記), and being unwilling to answer (*bu yuanyi huida* 不願意回答). The questionnaire was geared to the International Social Survey Program (ISSP). The demographical questions in the introduction are in accordance with international standards.[51] At the end of the questionnaire, the inter-

the author is fully responsible. Further information can be found at http://www.ios.sinica.edu.tw/sc/en/home2.php, accessed January 6, 2016.

49 For details about the selection process, the survey and considerations about the goodness of fit, one may consult the survey report: Zhang Yinghua and Zhuan Yingzhi 2007, 18–36.

50 The number of valid cases for the other religion surveys was, for 1999, 1,925 cases and, for 1994, 1,862 cases.

51 The questionnaire is given in Chinese to the interviewees. An additional English translation is provided by Academia Sinica. In the initial interview phase, questions

viewer has the opportunity to reflect on the value of the interview and a secondary corrector, who collected the interviews, was invited to comment.[52]

In the SPSS-dataset, which was collected by a private company, one finds the subsequently added variable "weight", which is–following oral information–intended to redress factors of age, gender and the ten regions. It weighs the age- and gender-distribution within the 10 different regions. All of the author's investigations were repeated, once with and once without the weight factor. It turned out that the sample never exceeded an aberrance of more than two percent. It can be concluded that the TSCS is a remarkably representative study, due to its careful selection process, made possible by the detailed household registry of Taiwan. This allows the random but concrete selection of single individuals in certain areas. Most current surveys simply cannot provide this degree of reliability because most modern states do not keep such a detailed household registry. In high standard European investigations, like the Shell study or the ALLBUS, the interviewees are chosen through iteration principles after choosing a region. In Taiwan, people can, in contrast, be chosen by name and, if the interview fails, the iteration principle leads to the next interviewee–even this choice can be made according to the household registry.

The design of the study is not only extremely reliable, but also highly multifaceted. The survey about religion poses 93 questions, often with a multiplicity of possible answers, divided into 15 sections. After collecting basic data about the person and their religious self-acknowledgement, certain topics are explored, such as religious attitudes and behaviour, numerology and magic, outstanding religious experiences, behaviour regarding charitable organisations, the usage of religious mass media, their socio-psychological well-being, their attitudes towards cultural values, religion and politics, and charitable organisations, their perceptions of the value of a multicultural society, their daily routine and their personal and family income.

---

are asked about gender, residence and birth place and time, marital status, father's ethnic origin and educational level, own educational level, completed education, name of high school and college, main occupation, whether independent or employed, spouse's occupation and whether one's spouse is independent or employed.

52 The interviewer notes down the telephone number of the interviewee, the start and end time of the interview, the number of attempts and subsequent interviews, the language ability of the interviewee, who filled in the questionnaire, the attitude of the interviewee towards the interview, the degree of annoyance, the credibility, whether he/she could deal with it, cooperation, reliability, language, whether answered alone or not, appointment, the place of the interview, and if anyone else was present during the interview. The secondary corrector can write down any complaints, and counts the mistakes and the answers that lead to no result. On this basis, it is decided whether the questionnaire is complete or not.

A.	Demographics (基本狀況)
B.	Religious beliefs (宗教信仰)
C.	Religious attitudes (個人的宗教行為)
D.	Personal religious behaviour (度宗教態)
E.	Numerology and magic (術數與法術)
F.	Special religious experience (特殊的宗教經驗)
G.	Behaviours concerning charitable organisations (慈善團體的行為)
H.	Exposure to religious programs in mass media 接觸宗教傳播行為
I.	Personal and social situations (個人與社會情勢)
J.	Cultural values (文化價值取向)
K.	Views on religion and politics (對宗教和政治等看法)
L.	Concepts concerning charitable organisations (慈善觀念)
M.	Perceptions and evaluations of different cultures (對各類文化的認知與評估)
N.	Daily life (日常生活)
O.	Personal and family income (個人及家庭收入)

Table 2: Topics of the *Taiwan Social Change Survey* 2004.2 on religion and cultural values.

In the course of the present analysis, variable v15b[53], asking about self-acknowledged religious affiliation, was selected and crossed with the rest of variables in order to obtain an overview about the attitudes and religious behaviour of people denoting themselves as Buddhists in Taiwan. Within this group of Buddhist believers, a differentiation was made between those who consider themselves as "believing in/venerating Buddha" and those who specialise in their belief and claim to belong to a specific Buddhist school such as Pure Land or Zen. The majority of Buddhists belong to the former, non-specifying group. By going through the survey and looking at these Buddhists, who made the conventional choice "believing in/venerating Buddha", the characteristics of the average Taiwanese people who call themselves Buddhists when asked for a religious affiliation became clear. These were given the preliminary name of "Conventional Buddhists", a definition that was later differentiated through the qualitative approach. Going through the data, questions were particularly considered that provide insights into the beliefs, attitudes and behaviour of Conventional Buddhists (v15a venerating ancestors and gods, v23 personal spiritual practice, v26 organisational affiliation, v26 cultural attitudes, including karmic thinking, v29 reasons for believing, v31 visiting temples and shrines, v32 motivation for going there, v55 donative behaviour, v74.5 belief in rebirth and karma, v83 transmittance of fair social behaviour within the family). The other Buddhists who were affiliating with a specific Buddhist school were compared with groups that practise other forms of intense Buddhist be-

53 Varaiables of the TSCS are in general abbreviated by "v" followed by the number of the variable. They are named in accordance with the dataset provided by Academia Sinica.

lief, such as seeing themselves as devoted (v22), having undergone ritual initiation (v19), having taken refuge (v20), following personal spiritual practices (v29), wearing Buddhist beads (v47) or holding a different belief to their parents (i.e. conversion, v16a,b). Before choosing the variables for presentation, the answers of Buddhists were compared to the answers of the rest of the population and other religious affiliations.

The Function of the Statistical Material in Relation to Structural Hermeneutics

What function does the statistical material fulfil in an investigation that is predominantly based on Structural Hermeneutics? Above, the special challenge of obtaining a detailed contextualisation when interpreting cases was mentioned, and the usage of statistics has been introduced in this context. During the research process, the author was firstly not seeking quantitative material, but was introduced to the TSCS by Chiu Hei-Yuan and Tang Chih-Chieh (Academia Sinica).[54] After investigating the survey for a year, the preliminary results proved interesting from a double perspective:

In the beginning stood the discovery that "Buddhists" are more frequent in the urban areas of Taiwan. As the narrative interviews concentrated on urban dwellers, both results naturally combined into an argumentation for this book, finding reasons for supporting the statistical results through the interviews.

The survey also provided a lot of detail on the various specialties of Taiwanese religious practices and helped to gain a deeper understanding of the sociocultural background. Different to the interviews, the TSCS also includes people who would have problems expressing themselves in Mandarin. The population only able to communicate in Taiwanese is not frequent in Taipeh or the urban areas of Taiwan, but they are included in the statistical material. The statistical material, therefore, also serves the function of buffering the other material.

It is currently under discussion in the field of German qualitative social research whether it is better to employ qualitative investigations as preparation for quantitative studies or to decide on a strict separation between the qualitative and quantitative approaches. There have been attempts to analyse systematically the possible relationship between statistical and qualitative data by adopting mixed method designs,[55] but the combination of qualitative and

---

54 Chiu Hei-Yuan's support during the evaluation period was particularly invaluable, as he initiated the TSCS and is familiar with the survey process at first hand. His profound insight into Taiwanese society was precious for reviewing the author's results.

55 For a systematic approach that reflects the methodological designs which mix quantitative and qualitative approaches within empirical social research, see Kelle 2007, here esp. chap. 10–11, 227–292.

quantitative research in this current case takes the unusual step of using statistical material as complementary to the qualitative-centred research. This is a consequence of the concrete results of the survey and might not necessarily be formulated in terms of a general relation between the qualitative and quantitative methods.

Summing up, the statistical overview marks the borders and single characteristics of the conventional perception of Buddhism in Taiwan and is intended to deliver a flexible folio for contextualizing the search for Buddhist life options.

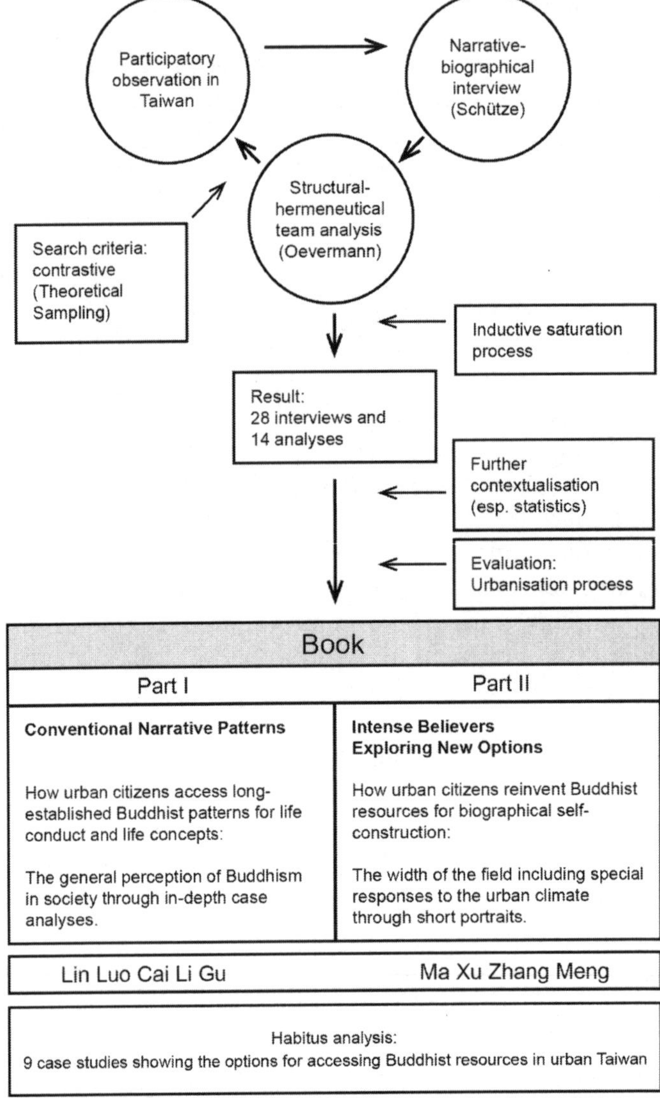

Figure 1: Methodological design of the research process.

Evaluation

The study investigates how urban dwellers in Taiwan make Buddhism a resource in their daily life. This question is not primarily asked from the organisational perspective of Taiwanese Buddhism, but goes for a habitus-analysis by applying the method of Structural Hermeneutics to deliver an in-depth sequential analysis of narrative interviews with people who denote themselves as lay Buddhists. The time-consuming nature of the method results in concisely statable patterns of meaning. The clear separation between the data and the interpretation enabled the researcher to become aware of her own expectations regarding the field, while the line-by-line procedure guarantees the flexibility of the method and the fallibility of any potential structural hypothesis. The extensive but concrete interpretation is able to deliver results that show how the interviewees situate themselves within their social field. By these means, the analysis transcends the dimensions of a content analysis and intends to overcome pre-categorisations.

The analyses are based on interview material consisting of free, but guided biographical narrations which follow the interview technique developed by Fritz Schütze. The interview sample was created through a circular procedure between field research and analysis, which searched for interviewees up to a point of theoretical saturation, guided by contrastive criteria. Through theoretical sampling an array of interviews is obtained which aims to represent, with gradual proximity, the options of Buddhist self-interpretation in urban Taiwan, especially its northern region.

Innovative is the application of Structural Hermeneutics to a cultural context different from that of the researchers. A method well established in German sociological research is tested in an international context. Within such a setting, the group of scholars assisting the interpretation process of the interviews cannot necessarily bring in its natural acquaintance with the cultural context of the interviewee. On the one hand, this creates a clear barrier to understanding and, on the other, the group does not need to seek an "artificial naïveté" (Jindra and Jindra 2003, 262). Daily and scientific knowledge do not mingle in the interpretation process. The interpreters' biases, expectations and general assumptions about daily life do not slip into the sociological interpretation and, therefore, sharpen the view of the peculiarity of the case and its cultural background.

Still, the "natural" acquaintance had to be sublimated through participatory observation, a high number of interviews, cooperation with other researchers and a transcultural interpretation team, as well as statistical investigations. The latter are outstanding in Taiwan regarding their reliability and also consider cultural values and socio-psychological questions. The statistical results complement the qualitative approach by stating the attractiveness of Buddhism in urban in contrast to rural areas.

Therefore, I would venture to state that this explorative attempt to apply the methodology of Structural Hermeneutics has proven successful in a transcultural context. It sharpened the observations of the interpreters. This might also be due to the fairly modernised and open society of urban Taiwan and to the nature of the question, with its inner-Taiwanese sensitivity. The concrete interplay between the qualitative and quantitative approaches could, in the concrete case, show how a mixed method design can lead to complementary results and could provide a helpful basis for further methodological elaborations.

Part I
Conventional Narrative Patterns Underlying Lay Buddhist Self-construction

5 "Buddhism" in Taiwanese Society

Interviewing those who label themselves "Buddhists" in contemporary Taiwan, revealed an inspiring spectrum of experience ranging between two extremes. Some people almost chased after the author in order to be interviewed in their eagerness to talk about themselves, their mission or their "Buddhist" organisations. They saw the interviews as an opportunity to become socially-recognised and acknowledged. Content-wise, they tended to distance themselves from the beliefs of their parents' generation as well as from popular religion–two tropes, which often accompanied each other. On the other side of the spectrum–and this is more the focus of this section–others hid themselves away, refusing to be interviewed or pretending to wish to be interviewed but then constantly inventing excuses to avoid it. With these people, sometimes, informal chats were possible, which gave the author the impression that these potential but unwilling interviewees sometimes lacked the appropriate vocabulary through which to express their beliefs, felt uncomfortable about them, thought that they would immediately be judged as superstitious, had not deeply reflected about their behaviour or had a problem expressing their beliefs in Mandarin. Sometimes, they also felt that their privacy was under attack and hinted at tragic events that had happened in their life. There are self-acknowledged "Buddhists" who are not in the habit of justifying and explaining their beliefs, but follow their parents' ritual practice and religious behaviour. For them, being "Buddhist", "Daoist", or "religious" are terms which do not arise in their daily life, but their religious behaviour centres around worship and veneration, which is less a doctrinal or intellectual matter than a practice–a practice which is normally neither discussed nor questioned by their environment.

In this first part, on coping with the conventional orientations within Buddhist belief, the author will analyse how popular religious as well as long-established Buddhist traditions shape people's biographical self-understanding. As it concerns more those from whom it was more difficult to obtain valid interview material due to the lack of cooperation and language barriers, this part will complement the interviews with statistical investigations. Through an initial overview of the spread of Buddhist ideas in Taiwanese society, it becomes clear that the spread of Buddhism in Taiwan is not merely a question of religious belonging, but far more one of the diffusion of Buddhist doctrinal and social resources throughout society. A closer look at those who claim to be Buddhists reveals that the majority shows a loose commitment and is unaware of belonging to a certain Buddhist school, but state that they "venerate/believe in Buddha". The author will adopt the criterion of school-awareness as an exemplary hint at a differentiated belief. In the following, "Conventional Buddhists" are called those, who do not consider themselves as being school-affiliated (details see above, pp. XXI-XXII definitions). An initial statistical investigation helped to produce an outline profile of these so-called "Conventional Buddhists", which can mark the borders and single characteristics of the conventional perceptions of Buddhism in Taiwan and is intended to deliver a flexible folio for contextualising the search for Buddhist life options. Through analysing the interviews, this preliminary, statistical outline and definition become differentiated and, at the end of the first part, the field of "conventional" belonging can be sketched.

The statistical investigations into Buddhists and Buddhism are based on the *Taiwan Social Change Survey* of 2004 (TSCS 2004.2, see chap. 4). Applying international survey standards, this survey is conducted annually by the Academia Sinica, Taiwan, and provides a representative quantitative survey of the highest reliability. Within its five year cycle, the topic of religion is tackled regularly, occupying a whole questionnaire of its own. This goes far beyond investigating people's formal religious affiliations to explore concrete facets of their religious life, their patterns of religio-cultural reproduction and their ethical values.

Single biographical narrative interviews follow the statistical outline and demonstrate the range of options for constructing a Buddhist belief that is in accordance with the Taiwanese and Chinese Buddhist traditions. Lin Yongfu's narration mirrors the first step of testing a purely terminological application of Buddhism in a popular religious context. Luo Peirong's belief is structured very similarly to that of Lin Yongfu, although she is less integrated into a popular religious community. Luo challenges the reciprocal relationship with "gods and Buddhas" by trying to "accept" her own fate. Cai Chenhao differs from both of the above: he does not perceive Buddhism as a part of or addition to popular religion, but is fully-integrated into a traditional, closed Buddhist group, with whom he lives and which oversees his living arrangements. Li Zhiqiang does not see–especially in contrast to Cai Chenhao, but also unlike Lin Yongfu and Luo Peirong–himself as participating in a Buddhist organisation, but he is in a personal relationship with the abbot, whose secular adviser and whose monastery's donor he is. Finally, the Buddhist intellectual, Gu Puzhong, was brought up by his grandmother, a Buddhist rooted in a Fujianese, mainland Chinese tradition. Gu Puzhong has transformed during his life the Buddhism that he perceived in his childhood into a practice that is compatible with "modern life". In this process, he has developed a message, which he seeks to spread through his publishing activities.

Looking for "Buddhist" thoughts as expressed on the questionnaire of the TSCS 2004.2, one finds repeated mention especially of the concept of "karmic connections". Among the 18 wide-ranging statements relating to attitudes about the basic cultural concepts of human existence (TSCS 2004.2, v27), there seem to be four related to the idea of karmic retribution: 1. "Do you believe in karmic retribution and reincarnation?" (v27.5; chin.: 相信因果輪迴的說法); 2. "[Whether one has] a karmic relation (*yuanfen*) has been decided in a previous life" (v27.8; chin.: 緣份是上輩子甚至是幾世前就決定的); 3. "Marrying the wrong person is settling a debt from a previous life" (v27.9; chin.: 娶錯妻、嫁錯郎都是前世欠的); and 4. "Working like a dog for the children is settling a debt from a previous life" (v27.10; chin.: 為子女做牛做馬都是上輩子欠的債).

With the explicit question, "Do you believe in karmic retribution and reincarnation?" (v27.5), the karmic concept is directly addressed. The terms "*yinguo* 因果" and "*lunhui* 輪迴" are both commonly used in contemporary Taiwanese Buddhism and are also the standard Chinese Buddhist expressions for "cause-and-effect" (*hetu-phala*) and transmigration/reincarnation (*saṃsāra*).[56] Although it is common in Taiwan to combine these two thoughts together, the combination of them into one question is regrettable: one might guess that the affirmation of the idea of rebirth implies a "metaphysical" concept, being rich in doctrinal assumptions, while the idea of karmic retribution can also be detected in the sense of a non-religious but daily life-based human experience that events generally stand in a causal relationship with each other. When asked whether they accept these two concepts, about a third of the sample population stated that they "believe" (*xiangxin* 相信) in retribution and rebirth, while a further over 40% believe in them "somewhat" (*youdian xiangxin* 有點相信). Taking these two results together, one can state that up to about three quarters of the population explain their life experiences through general patterns of retribution and rebirth. As far fewer than that claim to be Buddhist (24.1%, see below), this shows that a belief in concepts like transmigration and karmic connections is not a sufficient criterion for holding a Buddhist identity. The combination of Buddhist monastic centres with a society which cherishes some basic Buddhist views of life without

[56] These terms are, in the following, translated also as "retribution" and "reincarnation." It is clear to the author that this terminology does not correspond exactly to the original Buddhist concepts. Still, how the survey participants define these concepts has not been examined, although their widespread use suggests their familiarity with them. Therefore, it might be more appropriate, in the current context, to apply terms also common in English, than to search for a socially not necessarily relevant orthodox Buddhist terminology.

establishing necessarily a formal affiliation or a distinct Buddhist identity helps us to acquire an appropriate understanding of "Buddhism" as a "religion" in the East-Asian context. Taiwanese culture is a "Buddhist culture" insofar as at least the basic Buddhist–or perhaps just Indian–concepts centring on retribution and rebirth are widely-accepted in society through the daily application of terms that arose originally within a Chinese Buddhist context.

Also, the remaining three statements can be seen from the perspective of karmic retribution. The first statement–"[Whether one has] a karmic relation (*yuanfen*) [which often refers to one's casual relationships with others or the situational developments of one's life course] has been decided in a previous life" (v27.8)–attracts around a 10% less "strong affirmation" than the belief in karmic connectedness and transmigration (v27.8: 23.9%; v27.9: 32.2%). In contrast to the first question, the idea of karmic relations as depending upon previous lives assumes less personal freedom for the individual and is a strong interpretation of a belief in retribution and reincarnation. The two further statements connected to karmic retribution also hint that this idea might be common in Taiwanese society, especially for explaining hardship. There is less affirmation of it than of the other statement, but about 50% of the respondents express a general agreement that "Marrying the person is settling a debt from a previous life" and "Working like a dog for the children is settling a debt from a previous life" (20.8% and 33.4% for v27.9; 19.5% and 32.9% for v27.10). It is obviously a widespread belief that working for one's children is a karmic burden and that a marriage that is perceived as "wrong" must be endured, as it is caused by karmic conditioning in previous lives. Both sentences encourage the bearing of hardships in family life.

v27–Selection	(5) Belief in the concepts of karmic retribution and reincarnation (相信因果輪迴的說法)	(8) *Yuanfen* has been decided in a previous life (緣份是上輩子至是幾世前就決定的)	(9) Marrying the wrong partner is settling a debt from a previous life (娶錯妻, 嫁錯郎都是前世欠的)	(10) Working like a dog for the children is settling a debt from a previous life (為子女做牛做馬都是上輩子欠的債)
Yes, very much	32.2% (605)	23.9% (449)	20.8% (392)	19.5% (367)
Yes, somewhat	43.3% (815)	43.2% (812)	33.4% (629)	32.9% (619)
No, not really	14.0% (264)	22.2% (418)	30.1 (566)	31.0% (583)
No, not at all	6.4% (120)	7.8% (146)	12.7% (239)	14.4% (270)
No opinion	0.3% (6)	0.3% (6)	0.4% (7)	0.3% (5)
Don't understand	0.4% (8)	0.3% (6)	0.4% (7)	0.4% (8)
Don't know/forgot	3.2% (60)	2.2% (41)	2.0% (38)	1.3% (25)
Don't want to answer	0.2% (3)	0.2% (3)	0.2% (3)	0.2% (4)
Total	100.0% (1881)	100.0% (1881)	100.0% (1881)	100.0% (1881)

Table 3: Spread of "Buddhist" ideas in Taiwanese society (TSCS 2004.2, v27, percentage and frequency).

Religious Self-Acknowledgement–"Buddhists" in Taiwan

In contrast to those who have a broad awareness of karmic ideas and the concept of rebirth, the number of self-acknowledged Buddhists in society is–as mentioned above–significantly less. The biggest group of believers in the sample population are popular religious adherents (30.6%), and only 24.1% are Buddhists. People claiming not to hold any religious belief make up a fifth of the population (20.7%). Daoism is also a major group, with 15.3% of the total, while Christianity, other religions, and syncretistic groups play a subordinate role. 2.8% claim that they follow Daoism as well as Buddhism:

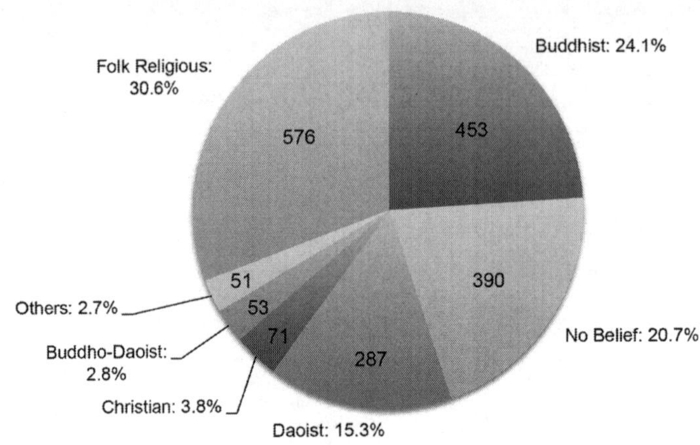

Figure 2: Religious Self-Acknowledgement in Taiwan (TSCS 2004.2, v15b).

v15b	Percentage (Frequ)
I have no religious belief	20.7% (390)
Popular religion–Self-identified	2.2% (41)
Popular religion–One that worships the gods	25.6% (481)
Popular religion–Not clearly specified as such	2.5% (47)
Popular religion–Other	0.4% (7)
Popular Religion	Subtotal: 30.6% (576)
Conventional Buddhists	21.0% (395)
Specifying Buddhist	2.4% (45)
(incl. Japanese religions: Sōka Gakkai 創價佛學會)	(incl. 3)
Buddhist: don't know	0.7% (13)
Buddhism	Subtotal: 24.1% (453)
Taoism	15.3% (287)
Catholicism	0.6% (10)
Protestant Christianity	3.2% (61)
Both Buddhism and Daoism	2.8% (53)
Other indigenous religions: Yiguan Dao 一貫道	2.0% (37)
Other indigenous religions: Tiandejiao 天德教	0.0% (1)
Japanese religions: other	0.0% (1)
Three religions (Buddhism, Taoism and Confucianism) amalgamated into one (三教合一)	0.0% (1)
Other	0.3% (3)
Other, unnamed	0.4% (8)
Total	100.0% (1881)

Table 4: Which religion do you follow? (TSCS 2004.2, v15b).

A quick glance through the survey also reveals that the role of religion in Taiwan is not necessarily connected to ethical and moral values. Instead, values are often passed down within the family context and are not regarded as connected to religion (v83; for details see below, chap. 8). Certain social behaviour which might be deemed religious on subsequent reflection is widespread. For example, the lunar calendar and its usage to determine auspicious dates for central events is widely acknowledged as important in Taiwan. About 80% of the population arranged in 1994 (TSCS 1994.2) their marriage, moving house, and starting a business according to it.[57] The veneration of ancestors is very common: 84.8% (1595/1881) of the population engages in it (TSCS 2004.2, v15a). Also, the general attitude of being "devoted" (*qiancheng* 虔誠) 41.3% (777/1881) of the population ascribe to themselves (TSCS 2004.2, v22). When the questionnaire asks about their reasons for choosing a particular religion, people usually cite the fact that they are following their parents' beliefs (v29.16, 54.7%, 1029/1881) or are in search of peace (v29.4; 37.3%, 701/1881), and only 7.1% (134/1881) mention that they are searching for truth (TSCS 2004.2, v29.3). The concept of retribution, the idea of do-ut-des (see below) towards the gods, is common. About 55% agree with the statement that an intense veneration of the gods will lead to protection (TSCS 2004.2, v50: strong agreement 10.4%, 196/1881, somewhat agree: 44.1%, 829/1881). The gods seem able to compensate for the lack of power among humans; about 80% think that those

57 57 No data on this question has recently been collected. The TSCS of 1994 posed the question "Is it necessary to choose a special day (according to the lunar calendar) for the following events?" (做下列事情是否要選日子, TSCS 1994.2, v54, percentage and frequency):

v54–Selection	v54.1 Marriage	v54.2 Moving house	v54.3 Starting a business
Not possible without it	53.9% (1003)	47.9% (891)	48.9% (910)
Doing it is better than not doing it	30.6% (569)	31.9% (594)	32.4% (604)
Does not matter if yes or no	8.2% (152)	10.6% (198)	7.1% (133)
One does not have to do it	6.3% (117)	8.2% (153)	6.4% (120)
Don't know	0.9% (17)	1.2% (23)	4.8% (90)
Don't understand the question	0.0% (0)	0.0% (0)	0.1% (1)
Don't want to answer	0.2% (4)	0.2% (3)	0.2% (4)
Total	100.0% (1862)	100.0% (1862)	100.0% (1862)

who make efforts by themselves will not need the gods (TSCS 2004.2, v28.1: strong agreement (56.7%, 1066/1881, somewhat agree (31.5%, 592/1881)).

We do not know about the process of discussion which led to the choice of questions for the questionnaire. The degree to which the questionnaire poses questions which exactly mirror the set of common assumptions that appropriately reflect the structures of belief in Taiwan is, of course, unknown. Still, reading through the following statements, which all attracted a high consensus, may give a first impression, in which Buddhist ideas and communities can locate and re-locate themselves:

v27–Selection	Strong agreement	Agreement
(15) To be healthy physically and psychologically, we have to maintain a balance and blending between *yin* and *yang* (要維持陰陽平衡與調和,身心才會健康).	31.4% (590)	44.4% (835)
(4) After a person passes away, his/her spirit and soul still exist (人死後靈魂仍然存在).	27.1 (509)	45.3% (852)
(14) In a place where *qi* is abundant, trees and plants will grow well, and that place will also prosper (地氣盛的地方,樹木花草會長得很好,地方也都會興旺).	24.7% (465)	43.1% (811)
(3) It must be ordained by fate that a person can become president (一個人能做總統一定是有天命的).	24.2% (455)	34.3% (646)
(12) A person's *qi* can be strengthened through cultivation (人的氣可經由修練而加強).	22.0% (414)	45.6% (857)
(2) Heaven and hell certainly exist (確實有天堂及地獄).	21.3% (400)	43.4% (817)
(6) Spirits who are not offered any worship will wander around (無人祭拜的孤魂會四處飄蕩).	19.0% (357)	40.6% (764)
(13) If a person's *qi* is very strong, nothing can harm him or her (一個人的氣很旺,就能夠百邪不侵).	16.9% (318)	32.0% (601)
(7) I believe that demons possess bodies and these kind of things (相信靈魂附身這樣的事).	16.6% (313)	37.9% (712)
(11) Qigong can help to cure diseases (氣功可以幫助人治病).	15.8% (298)	41.1% (774)
(1) There is a supreme god in this universe (宇宙有一個至高無上的神).	14.6% (275)	39.2% (737)
(16) A person is the small magnetic field and the cosmos is the big magnetic field. When a human becomes ill, the small and big magnetic fields are uncoordinated (個人是小磁場,宇宙是大磁場,人會生病是因為大小磁場沒有協調的緣故).	13.1% (246)	35.1% (660)
(17) Science can prove the existence of the spirit and the soul (科學可以證明靈魂的存在).	8.4% (158)	24.3% (457)
(18) Science can prove that some people have supernatural powers (科學可證明有些人確實有特異功能).	8.1% (153)	31.2% (586)

Table 5: Do you believe in the following sayings? (TSCS 2004.2, v27 selection, percentage and frequency, in order of frequency, n=1881).

This overview of Taiwanese religious concepts shall serve as a preliminary orientation only. Further statistical investigations into the easily-recognised characteristics of Conventional Buddhists will, in the following, deepen these first impressions of the religious landscape of Taiwan. The qualitative analysis of the interviews will contextualise the statistical observations and reveal more about the mental maps of Conventional Buddhists.

6 *Conventional Buddhists*? –A First Statistical Investigation

When asked about their religious affiliation (v15b), 453 people identified as Buddhists and 395 (87.2%) of them chose the specification "believe in/venerate Buddha" (*xinfo, baifo* 信佛, 拜佛). The various other possible answers account jointly for the remaining 12.8% of the choices. "Believing in/venerating Buddha" seems to be people's conventional answer, when asked to specify whether they adhere to a specific Buddhist school or are less distinct about their school affiliation. Can one gain, through the statistical results of the TSCS 2004.2, an impression of some of the characteristics of this major group of Buddhists, the "Conventional Buddhists" (CB)?

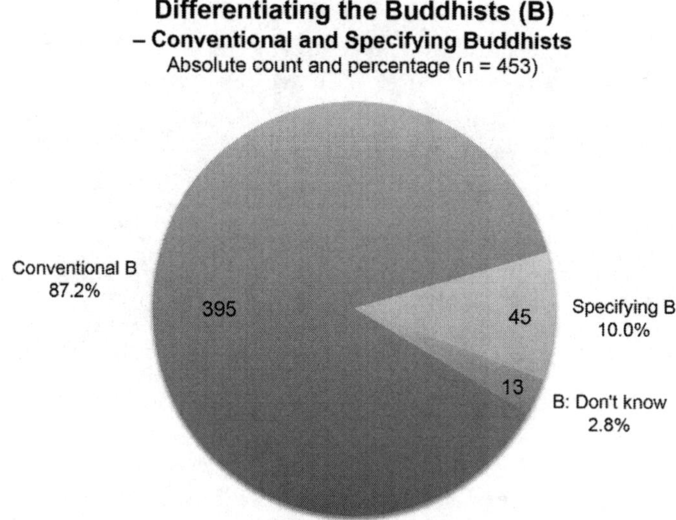

Figure 3: Conventional and Specifying Buddhists (TSCS 2004.2, v15b).

Being conscious that one belongs to a specific Buddhist school, like the Pure Land or Zen, is obviously irrelevant to the majority of those who call themselves Buddhists. Firstly, one might ask whether this is a sign that either: 1) these people have a less differentiated belief, are–as Welch might put it (Welch 1967, 387ff, see chap. 8.3)–more like "occasional Buddhists"; or 2) that their belief is structured according to different criteria and that the differential category "school-awareness" is simply not the most appropriate one for defining Buddhist belief in Taiwan. The author, therefore, searched for other indicators that might give an insight into how seriously the answer "I am a Buddhist as I believe in/venerate Buddha" should be taken.

As a *marker of the decisiveness and intensity* of belief, we could take the question "Do you view yourself as a devout believer?" (v22: 請問您認為自己是不是一個虔誠的宗教信徒?) In the interviewer guidelines, we find the comment that, if the interviewee does not understand the word "*qiancheng* 虔誠" ("sincere and devout"), it can be replaced by the term "*chengxin* 誠心" ("true-hearted").[57] Indeed, the first word is less frequently used in Taiwan today than the second, more casual one, but both ways of asking this question appear to probe into the concept of a person's intense, sincere belief. One observes that over half of the Conventional Buddhists see themselves as devout believers according to that question (53.9%, 213/395), which indicates that their belief is not just a habit to them; though it may not even be reflected in terms of rational verbalisation (no school-differentiation), more than half of them might feel a pious closeness with aspects of life that they link to "Buddhism".

In search of other factors that may indicate the intensity of their belief, they could be asked whether they have undergone any form of *ritual initiation*, such as taking refuge (v19 and v20). We can state that only 58 of the 395 Conventional Buddhists (14.7%) had undergone any initiation ritual, while the majority (84.3%, 333/395) had not.[58]

Another variable, the question about *personal spiritual practice* (*geren lingxiu huodong* 個人靈修活動, v23), hints that the Conventional Buddhists, although often devout, do not seem to express their belief through adopting an individual practice that separates them from the rest of their community: 72.7% (287/395) of the respondents claim that they do not engage in any personal spiritual practice.[59] The supposition that Conventional Buddhism is mainly lived in the sphere of established family and community life is supported by the observation that a high percentage of Conventional Buddhists do not have any experience of conversion. 82.8% of the Conventional Buddhists think that they, in their previous life, followed the same belief as at the time of the interview (v18: 327/395). Even 67.1% (265/395) of the Conventional Buddhists give as a reason for their belief (v29) the fact that they are following the

57 Here according to Mathews 1975, p. 123, no. 894 and p. 49, no. 381. The Grand dictionnaire Ricci de la langue chinoise gives: 誠心 chengxin: 1. Sincérité. 2. Sincère. Sincèrement; de tout coeur. 3. Intentionnellement; exprès; à dessein (Grand Ricci 2001, vol. I, p. 417, no. 740); 虔誠 qiancheng: 1. Respectueux; dévôt; pieux; fervent; sincère. 2. (*Cathol.*) Piété; dévotion; ferveur (Grand Ricci 2001, vol. I, p. 891, no. 1672).

58 Both variables can be seen as qualifiers of the intensity of belief. They are (one-sidedly) interdependent: approximately 4 out of 5 people who underwent a ritual initiation claim to be devout believers.

59 In the same way as ritual initiation and devout belief seem to be interconnected, so do ritual initiation and personal spiritual practice. 77.6% of the Conventional Buddhists who have undergone a ritual initiation follow a personal spiritual practice.

belief of their parents. Also, the perception of their parents' generation matches this observation: Around 80% of the parents of the Conventional Buddhists–in the opinion of their children–are/were also Buddhists.[60]

Conventional Believers tend to wear *Buddhist beads* (v47) more frequently than the rest of the population, but it is not a characteristic of the Conventional Buddhists, as only 1 out of 5 of them does so (19.7%, 78/395). Also, it does not seem to be a strong indicator of intense belief, as all cross-comparisons with the layers of devoutness, ritual initiation and personal spiritual practice lead to the result that never more than approximately a third of the devout, initiated or personally-practising Conventional Buddhists wear Buddhist beads.

We can *summarise* that Conventional Buddhists often regard themselves as devout believers, but have not necessarily undergone a ritual initiation, nor do the majority of them follow any personal spiritual practice, nor in general wear any attribute that makes them recognisable as Buddhists by the public (Buddhist beads), although the majority (80%) do see themselves as continuing the religious tradition of their parents.

What does it mean for Conventional Buddhists to follow their parental tradition? Firstly, this belief is not to be understood as a search for orientation through ethical values, nor is it primarily philosophically-oriented.

We can see from the table below that people are often seeking peace, self-cultivation and spiritual sustenance, while choices such as "seeking wisdom", "understanding the meaning of life" and "seeking the truth" are only made by around 15% of the Conventional Buddhists. It is remarkable that none of the provided choices attracts widespread agreement among the group members.[61] Fair social behaviour (v83.1–4)–not bullying others, not lying, not jumping queues, helping the unfortunate–is often taught to Conventional Buddhists by their parents, but no more than in other families. Only the habit of "helping unfortunate people" might be slightly more frequently taught in Conventional Buddhist families (CB 47.8% vs. general 44.5%).

60 v16a: 79.5% (314/395) of the Conventional Buddhists think that their father is/was a Buddhist; v16b: 84.6% (334/395) of the Conventional Buddhists think that their mother is/was a Buddhist.

61 These percentages do not increase either even if one considers only the devout believers among the Conventional Buddhists.

v29		Conventional Buddhists
(16)	To follow the faith of my parents (跟父母信的)	67.1% (265)
(4)	To seek peace (尋求平安)	44.1% (174)
(1)	Self-cultivation (修身養性)	32.9% (130)
(11)	To seek spiritual sustenance (尋求精神寄託)	27.8% (110)
(10)	To seek consolation (尋求安慰)	22.5% (89)
(7)	To reduce worries (減少煩惱)	17.7% (70)
(9)	To bring good luck and avoid evil (趨吉避凶)	16.5% (65)
(6)	To seek wisdom (尋求智慧)	15.9% (63)
(5)	To understand the meaning of life (了解生命意義)	14.9% (59)
(3)	To seek the truth (尋求真理)	9.4% (37)
(14)	Due to the zealous introduction by relatives and friends (親友熱心引介)	8.1% (32)
(8)	To solve special problems (解決特殊困難)	7.8% (31)
(2)	To seek redemption or repentance (尋求救贖或懺悔)	6.3% (25)
(12)	To make friends (結識朋友)	6.1% (24)
(15)	The future fate of going up to heaven or encountering happiness after death (將來昇天或死後的福樂)	5.3% (21)
(17)	Other (please specify)	2.5% (10)
(13)	The attraction of the religious leader (宗教領袖的吸引力)	2.3% (9)

Table 6: Answers of the Conventional Buddhists in order of frequency to the question: "Why do you believe in your present religion?" (TSCS 2004.2, v29, percentage and frequency, more than one answer possible, n=395).

How does the belief of a Conventional Buddhist express itself in his/her daily life? Normally, Conventional Buddhists in general are not affiliated with any *Buddhist organisation* (v26). Recent Buddhist communities, like the Taiwan Zen Buddhist Association 台灣禪宗佛教會 of Miaotian 妙天 (0%, 0/395) or the Falun Gong 法輪功 movement (0.3%, 1/395), do not interest the Conventional Buddhists, nor do any of the well-known new arising monasteries, like Dharma Drum Mountain 法鼓山 (2.3%, 9/395), Foguang Shan 佛光山 (5.8%, 23/395) and Zhongtai Shan 中台山 (1.3%, 5/395), seem very attractive to them either. Only the Tzu Chi Relief Compassion Association 慈濟功德會, which concentrates mainly on charity work, and to which around 10% of all Taiwanese belong, is selected by around 15% of the Conventional Buddhists (15.2%, 60/395).

Far more frequently, the Conventional Buddhists visit *temples and shrines* (v31). A very few of them (3.3%, 13/395) never visit a temple, shrine or church. Around a third visit very seldom (30.4%), another third visit several times a year (31.4%) and the remaining 32.7% (129/395) of Conventional

Buddhists visit a temple, shrine or church at least once a month.[62] 60.5% of the Conventional Buddhists believe that they are protected by the gods or Buddha (v50: 139/395).

It is consistent that the Conventional Buddhists, in line with the general population, cherish dearly the *services* which are offered at the popular religious temples. In particular, the practices of *an Taisui* 安太歲 "Placating your zodiac year good" (v46.3) and *dian guangming deng* 點光明燈 "Lighting the brightness lantern" (v46.6) are widespread among the Conventional Buddhists (v46.3: 48.6%, 192/395; v46.6: 44.3%, 175/395). Also "putting on a peace talisman (on your body or car)–*peidai ping'an fu* 佩戴平安符 (*sui shen, che shang* 隨身,車上)" is practised by over a third of the Conventional Buddhists (v46.7: 38.7%, 153/395). None of these practices has any specific Buddhist meaning, but they are commonly followed at Taiwanese popular temples, regardless of whether they also have Buddhist altars or not, and the practice of lightening lanterns (*dian guangming deng* 點光明燈) is also common in the larger Buddhist monasteries, such as Foguang Shan.

The most spread general popular belief, although not obligatory, is the *veneration of ancestors and gods.* The Conventional Buddhists adopt this practice even more frequently than the average people in Taiwan: 93.9% (371/395) of the Conventional Buddhists venerate their ancestors and gods (v15a), while the rest of the population only follows this practice with a frequency of 82.4% (1224/1486).

Not only in their acceptance of popular religious belief, but also in their financial support (v55), the Conventional Buddhists are *not strictly exclusivistic*: while half of them (50.1%, 198/395) donate to Buddhist organisations, 11.9% (47/395) give donations to popular religious ones, and some donate to Daoist institutions (8.4%, 33/395). Even religious organisations without any obvious connection to their own belief, like Protestant and Catholic Christian, I Guan Dao or Islamic groups, sometimes receive single donations from the Conventional Buddhists (I Guan Dao 一貫道 0.8%, 3/395; Protestantism 1.3%, 3/395; Catholicism 0.5%, 2/395; and Islam 0.3, 1/395).

When asked "Why do you visit shrines?" (v32b), the Conventional Buddhists exhibit exactly the same interests as the rest of the population: the three main reasons for visiting a shrine are: 1) for health and peace (*shenti jiankang, ping'an* 身體健康, 平安), at 28.9% (114/395); 2) for smooth business (*shiye shunli* 事業順利), at 11.6% (46/395); and 3) to avoid disaster and

62 In this cross-comparison, we do not take into account the fact that the Conventional Buddhists who often visit might only visit their own organisation (v26). This may account for around a quarter of the Conventional Buddhists: assuming that nobody visits more than one organisation, 98 of the 395 people could even visit very often, making a maximum of 24.8%.

eliminate misfortune (*xiaozai jie'e* 消災解厄), at 9.6%; 38/395). A desire to earn a lot of money (5.6%), to pacify evil spirits that cause fear (*shoujing* 收驚; 5.3%), to foster social stability (4.8%), to solve family problems (4.6%), or successful studies (4.6%), as well as solving disciplinary problems with children (3.5%) or marriage (1.0%), are also mentioned.

The Conventional Buddhists feel more often than other people that their life is:

v68	Conventional Buddhists (n=395)	Rest (n=1486)
(1) More sorrowful than joyful (v68.2: 您會不會覺得人生真是苦多樂少?)	42.0% (166)	32.3% (480)
(2) Full of misfortune (v68.3: 您會不會覺得生命中有很多不幸?)	35.2% (139)	26.8% (398)
(3) Only vanity (v68.4: 您會不會相信人生到頭總是空虛一場?)	39.7% (157)	32.5% (483)

Table 7: Feelings of the Conventional Buddhists about life (TSCS 2004.2, v68, percentage and frequency).

These are three variations expressing a general dissatisfaction with life. It seems that, just as karmic retribution and rebirth were interpreted as an exhortation to endure family hardships, the first Buddhist truth–life is about suffering–is, apart from Buddhist orthodox doctrinal elaborations and separately from the context of the three other Buddhist truths, in the general perception of people, applied to confirm a negative view of life. Nearly a third of the Conventional Buddhists consciously recognise in accordance with the rest of the population the *uncertainty of life* (v68.1: 28.9%, 114/395; general: 28.3%, 532/1881).

Conventional Buddhism seems, after all, to be more a variant of popular religious belief than indicate a clear, distinct group of people. In fact, all cross-comparisons that we have undertaken so far reveal no significant differences between Conventional Buddhists and popular religious believers. The Conventional Buddhists' answering behaviour parallels that of the majority of the Taiwanese population.

The Socio-geographical Distribution of Buddhists in Taiwan

While the parallels seem to prevail, however, in the comparison between the Conventional Buddhists and the popular religion believers, a significant aberration in all of these parallels emerges when one considers the geographical locations where Conventional Buddhists live. In contrast to the popular religious believers and the rest of the population, the Conventional Buddhists are more likely to dwell in urban areas rather than in developing or even remote ones. While, in the remote areas, the percentage of Conventional Buddhists is only about 9.4%–popular religious believers constitute up to half the population here–it is higher in the developing areas (19.0%), and the highest of all in the urban areas (25.4%).

	Three Regions			Total
	Remote Areas	Developing Areas	Urban Areas	
Popular religious believers	51.1% (157)	28.4% (151)	25.7% (268)	30.6% (576)
Conventional Buddhists	9.4% (29)	19.0% (101)	25.4% (265)	21.0% (395)
Others	39.4% (121)	52.6% (280)	48.8% (509)	48.4% (910)
Total	100.0% (307)	100.0% (532)	100.0% (1042)	100.0% (1881)

Table 8: A cross-comparison of popular religious believers and Conventional Buddhists in the three socio-geographical regions of Taiwan (TSCS 2004.2, percentage and frequency).

This produces an insightful observation: *the more urban a region is, the more Buddhists seem to live there.* The applied classification into three regions–remote, developing, and urban–is based on the author's regrouping of the division of Taiwan into ten socio-geographical regions, as used by the TSCS and based on research by Luo Qihong.[63] For Buddhists as a whole, there is an increase from approximately 10% in the remote regions, to 20% in the developing regions, to 30% in the urban regions:

[63] For a more detailed explanation of the regional stratification, see chap. 10. Luo Qihong's 10 regions are: (1) newly emerged areas, (2) mountain areas, (3) industrial areas, (4) syndicated areas, (5) hilly areas, (6) remote areas, and (7) service areas; completed by (8) Taipeh, (9) Kaohsiung and (10) areas under the direct jurisdiction of Taiwan. These are regrouped by the author into three regions: Remote (including 2, 5 and 6), Developing (including 1, 3 and 4), and Urban (including 7, 8, 9 and 10).

Buddhists according to Regions of Taiwan

Absolute count and percentage

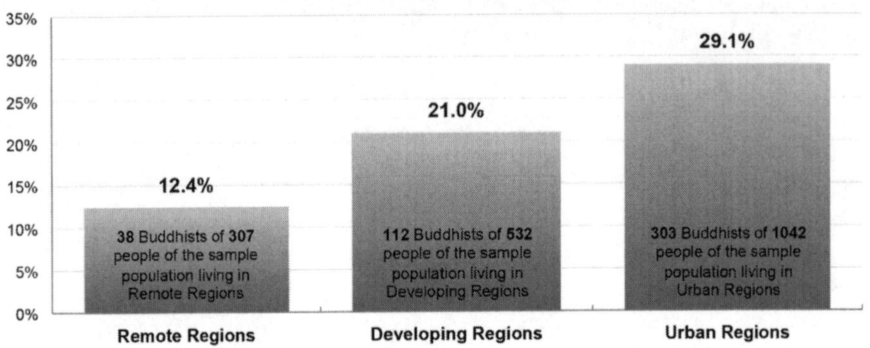

Buddhists are including Conventional Buddhists (CB = 395), Specifying Buddhists (SB = 45), and Buddhists who do not know what kind of Buddhists they are (NB = 13)
(total: 453 Buddhists, sample population total n = 1881)

Figure 4: Living places of Buddhists according to regions in Taiwan (TSCS 2004.2).

This increase is, compared with other religions, specific to Buddhist believers. *Buddhists in general are more likely to live in cities than the followers of any other religion, except for non-believers and Christians.* The latter two show the same pattern as the Buddhists: the numbers of non-believers, Buddhists and Christians all rise in frequency the more urban the region is. Among Buddhists, this increase is the most explicit of the three groups. While the numbers of Daoists and Buddho-Daoists are highest in developing areas, popular religion, in particular, is a phenomenon that becomes the more frequent the more remote the region is:[64]

64 The data provided here is taken from the TSCS 2004.2 as this was compiled closest to the time of the interviews analysed in Part I and II. The result for the TSCS 2014.2 however shows a similar increase for Buddhists living in urban areas in contrast to the countryside (tested variable of the TSCS 2014.2: stratum 2005).

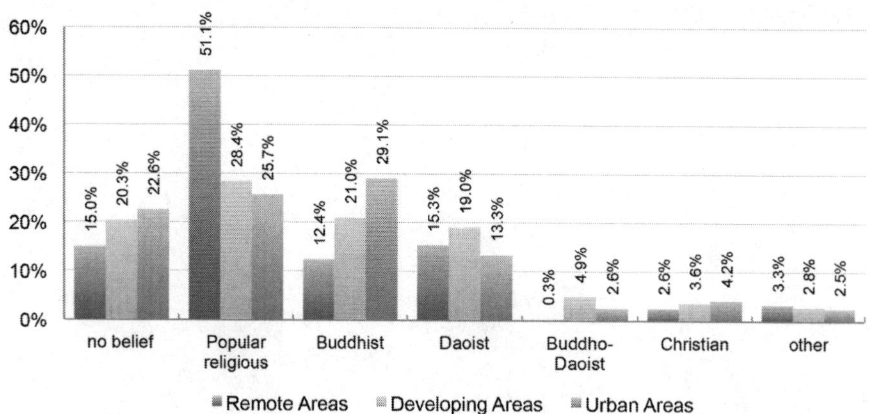

Figure 5: Religious belief according to regions of Taiwan (believers of each area add up to 100%; TSCS 2004.2).

v15b	Three Regions			Total
	Remote Areas	Developing Areas	Urban Areas	
No belief	15.0% (46)	20.3% (108)	22.6% (236)	20.7% (390)
Popular religious	51.1% (157)	28.4% (151)	25.7% (268)	30.6% (576)
Buddhist	12.4% (38)	21.0% (112)	29.1% (303)	24.1% (453)
Daoist	15.3% (47)	19.0% (101)	13.3% (139)	15.3% (287)
Buddho-Daoist	0.3% (1)	4.9% (26)	2.6% (26)	2.8% (53)
Christian	2.6% (8)	3.6% (19)	4.2% (44)	3.8% (71)
Others	3.3% (10)	2.8% (15)	2.5% (26)	2.7% (51)
Total	100.0% (307)	100.0% (532)	100.0% (1042)	100.0% (1881)

Table 9: The distribution of religious belief according to region (TSCS 2004.2, v15b, percentage and frequency).

Differentiating Buddhists into a) Conventional, b) Specifying and c) Buddhists who do not know what kind of Buddhists they are reveals that, in the countryside, the number of people who belong to the latter category is the highest (2.0%, 6/307). In contrast, there are 3% of those with a high probable knowledge about their belief, Specifying Buddhists, living in the urban areas, and these decrease in frequency–paralleling the decrease in the number Buddhists in general–in the countryside (with 2.1% in the developing areas and only 1% in the remote areas):

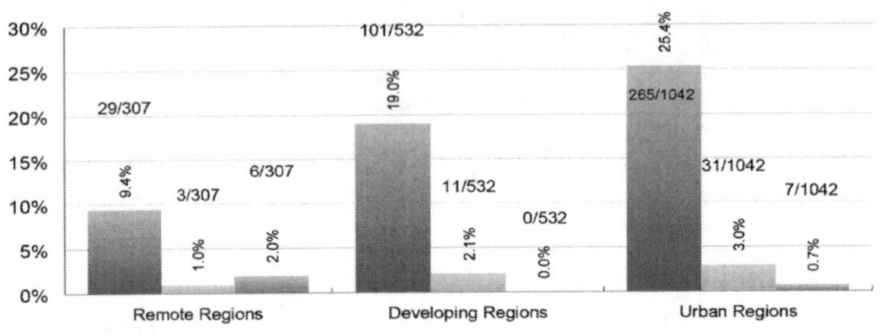

Figure 6: Living places of the different kinds of Buddhists according to regions of Taiwan (TSCS 2004.2).

With which silent expectations might one embark on an analysis of Conventional Buddhists, the main focus of this section? To the author, it seems that the Conventional Buddhists are extremely similar to the popular religious believers. Still, they denote themselves as Buddhists. Might it be that the Conventional Buddhists living in the cities are not so very different from the popular religious believers living in the countryside, but find it advantageous to consider themselves–perhaps it simply "sounds good"–"Buddhists"?

What could make Buddhism more attractive to urban people? To answer this question, the author turns now to concrete biographies of individuals on the basis of narrative interviews and investigates the role that Buddhism plays in the everyday life of Taiwanese people. Within this first part dealing with Conventional Believers, Lin Yongfu will be considered first–someone, who certainly would have ticked the option "*xinfo/baifo*" on the questionnaire.

7 Conventional Buddhists– Five Selected Cases under Consideration

7.1 Lin Yongfu–Naturally Protected by the Family and Temple Life

The following portrait of Lin Yongfu 林永福 (male, age about 66)[65] is somewhat unusual in comparison to the other interviews presented subsequently. It is located here at the beginning as it touches closely on the amalgamation between popular religion and Buddhism and reveals the structure that allows the integration of Buddhist elements into common religious practices. The interview is also exceptional due to its closeness to the usage of the Taiwanese dialect. It is based on an informal chat that the author had with Lin in December 2006 while stuck in his taxi for over an hour. It was raining and a public holiday, so it was difficult to hail a taxi. The author had to reach a different part of Taipeh urgently but, when she finally found a taxi, one traffic jam followed another, so the journey took far longer than expected and there was time to chat. Like many taxi drivers, Lin had several amulets hanging from his dashboard and rear-view mirror, which seemed to be of popular religious origin. Therefore, the interviewer was curious about his statement that he was a "Buddhist" (*fojiaotu* 佛教徒).

Lin Yongfu is, at the time of the interview, about 66 years old, married and proud of his grandchildren. By occupation, he is a full-time taxi-driver, driving during the week in Taipeh city and on holidays in Taipeh County. His family lives in the suburbs of Taipeh. Although he speaks Mandarin fluently with a Taiwanese accent, he occasionally drifts back into Taiwanese. He comes from a Taiwanese Chinese family, sees himself as a *bentu ren* 本土人. He appears at first sight to be a stable, positively-minded older man, who is satisfied with his life and his family. At the same time, he shows great curiosity and informedness about the researcher as a foreigner and foreign culture in general. He enjoys discussing how best to solve the conflict between Taiwan and mainland China and is interested in hearing the researcher's comparison of the situation regarding the unification of East and West Germany. Then, his attention shifts to the author's visit to Taiwan. As soon as he hears that she is conducting research in religion, he states that he is a Buddhist. A conversation unfolds about his belief, which forms the basis for the following analysis:

---

65 The names are altered and the locations rendered anonymous in the following portraits also; see methodology, chap. 4.

The first interaction, in which Lin discusses Buddhism, begins as follows:

(1) Lin: 佛教有好幾種 阿 有沒有 我們國語 那個講求 可以溝通	(1) Lin: There are so many kinds of Buddhism. A. Right? If we pay attention to our Chinese, to that, then we can understand each other.

Lin states that there are many different kinds of Buddhism, though what kinds of "Buddhism" are implied here remains unclear. This proposition might be intended to differentiate Lin's belief in Buddhism with the interviewer's occupation with Buddhism. Despite his desire to share his insights about the associations he experiences when hearing the term "Buddhism" (*fojiao*), Lin possibly assumes that his Buddhism and the researcher's occupation relate to the same subject. He might seek to avoid any possible conflict arising between different conceptions of Buddhism through his language behaviour. This interpretation is supported by the following "right?" (*you mei you*), as he intends to reassure himself that his conversation partner agrees. This harmonising performative language behaviour could imply that his following explications might not so much demonstrate his doctrinal knowledge as reveal an interest in social interaction. Lin might be relatively accustomed to requesting constant reassurance or feel uncertain about this specific subject. Up till now, his language style has been simple and casual. In the following sentence, Lin changes topic and states that mutual understanding is possible via concentrating on Mandarin as a means of communication. Is Lin simply surprised that the interviewer can speak Chinese? This is improbable as the conversation has been going on for some time. Perhaps, for Lin, it is not normal to speak in Mandarin–as supported by his Taiwanese accent–and he discovers, all of a sudden, that being able to speak Mandarin is useful as it gives him and his communication partner a basis for exchange. Lin is searching for a basis for communication–as the methods for believing in or studying Buddhism might differ, he points out that at least a shared language enables exchange. Still, one should consider whether Lin has sufficient vocabulary at his disposal and also whether he considers the religious topic especially challenging for his Chinese in the following. He continues:

(2) 有人拜了那個神像 有雕刻那個 有沒有 我們家裡是拜那個	(2) Some people venerate these statues of gods, the ones that have been carved–right? Our family worships these.

In the next sentence, Lin has returned to the topic of religion. One might expect him to enlarge on his first statement that there are many kinds of Buddhism. He continues: "Some people venerate these [carved] statues of gods". If Lin Yongfu is still talking about how he perceives "Buddhism", it is possible that he regards the group of people who venerate carved statues as constituting one kind of Buddhism or even equalling all Buddhists. What does the fact that the statues are "carved" contribute? Is the carving itself of significance to Lin as it is the process of bringing a god to life and to being efficacious especially with the final act of eye-opening, or does he simply assume that the interviewer as a foreigner might be more likely to have seen the carving of statues on the street than be familiar with religious life? He continues: "Our family worships (*bai* 拜) these".[66] It is clear that Lin sketches "Buddhism", at least for some, as an action, a "veneration", that is oriented towards (carved) statues of gods. His belief might be situated within the context of his family, as they are the actors performing the veneration.

(3) Interviewer: 是阿! 不錯	(3) Interviewer: Indeed! Fine.
(4) Lin: 甚麼觀音阿 觀音佛像阿 甚麼欸關聖帝君[tw] 阿 五府千歲[tw] 啦 這些阿 我們就是拜這個阿 還有太祖 阿 我才知道佛教有好幾種阿 有人沒有是拜這個像阿 有人是弄這個像來拜的. 是不是這樣 [b]	(4) Lin: Whatever Guanyin a. Whatever Buddhist figure Guanyin. Whatever ei Guangong a. Wufu Qiansui la. These a. We venerate that a. Also there is Taizu. A. Only then I knew that there are many kinds of Buddhism a. Some people don't worship these statues a. Some people take this figure and worship. Isn't it like that? [b]

The positive reaction of his conversation partner shows her interest in his explanation and could implicitly request an elaboration on it. Lin Yongfu continues with an enumeration, starting with the name of Bodhisattva Avalokiteśvara, Guanyin 觀音, a widely worshipped female bodhisattva and goddess of mercy in East Asia, which he describes not by using the Buddhist epithet "Bodhisattva" but as a "Buddhist statue" (*foxiang* 佛像).[67] It is unclear whether a "Buddhist statue" is also a "statue of a god" (*shenxiang* 神像), or forms a separate category of statues. Still, through marking Guanyin with "whatever" she gets enumerated in line with other "gods". None of the terms used up to now explicitly refer to Buddhism, despite marking Guanyin as a "Buddhist" statue. Might one hypothesise that he is simply describing these practices as being "kinds of Buddhism" and himself as a Buddhist because one of the statues he venerates is called a "Buddhist statue"? His enumeration proceeds to encompass the deified historical figure of the general Guan Yu 關羽–here called Guansheng Dijun and in Taiwan also often referred to as Lord Guan (Guangong 關公)–who is one of the most prominent examples of a historical figure being redefined and integrated also into Buddhist

66 The word "*bai* 拜" is translated in the following as both "to venerate" and "to worship", without any substantial differentiation between the two. For further reflection on this terminology, see chap. 8.1.

67 On the figure of Guanyin and its transformational history in the Chinese context see Yü 2001.

worship as a bodhisattva.[68] Guan Yu may, therefore, have a slight association with Buddhism. By Wufu Qiansui 五府千歲, Lin refers to a group of five "Wangye 王爺" gods. Their temple is, in this case, the Nankunshen Daitian Temple 南鯤鯓代天府 in Tainan. Founded in 1662, it is the most prominent of all of the Wangye 王爺 temples in Taiwan. Its founding legends revolve around a group of gods who appeared on the coast in a boat and were venerated from that point onwards in return for protecting the population and the success of its fishermen. Each year, especially during the annual celebrations, the temple attracts thousands of visitors from all over the island.[69] In the story of Wufu Qiansui, very few Buddhist elements appear although these may be integrated into contemporary veneration practice at temples

68 The general, who died in 219 AD, served under the warlord Liu Bei 劉備 at the end of the Eastern Han Dynasty and the Three Kingdoms era of China. This historical figure gained much of his popularity through the 14th century novel, "Romance of the Three Kingdoms", written by Luo Guanzhong 羅貫中. Starting from this literary work, Guan Yu was venerated and became deified probably during the Sui dynasty (581–618). Even today, he is commonly worshipped in Taiwan, as well as in southern China. He embodies the virtues of righteousness, bravery, justice and loyalty. His violent death is followed in the novel by an episode in which a Buddhist monk, Pujing 普净, features, and through whose help Guan's spirit learns not to roam around in search of his head (as he himself took the heads of many others). This is described as Guan's enlightenment. The temple of this monk, who counts also as a historical figure, might be where the worship of Guan Yu originated. Buddhist legends situated in the Tang dynasty report that Guan Yu appeared before the famous meditating Buddhist patriarch, Zhiyi 智顗 (538–597), formally converting to Buddhism by taking refuge and making a vow to become a guardian of the Buddhist dharma. Besides his Taoist or popular religious usages, even today, from the Buddhist side, he is integrated as a guardian under the name of Bodhisattva Saṃghārāma (Qielan Pusa 伽蘭菩薩). This figure is today also prominent in films and mangas, where he is mostly connected with the aforementioned novel and he can be presented having Buddhist aspects. There are several academic analyses of Guan Yu's story; more recently, by Liu (2004) or in German by Diesinger (1984).

69 The Nankunshen Daitian Fu is located in Beimen Township 北門鄉, Kunjiang Village 鯤江村. The temple is one of the most famous of all the Wangye temples in Taiwan as it is the oldest active Wangye temple in Taiwan and huge in size. It attracts large crowds of visitors each year. There seem to be several legends connected to the temple's establishment. The temple's website (http://www.nkstemple.org.tw, last accessed January 7, 2016) states that, during the Ming dynasty, a fisherman, while out at sea fishing, suddenly heard music. He saw a huge sailing boat approaching the coast. Next morning, the fisherman went to the coast and found a little old boat containing six statues (five gods and one general guarding them), bearing inscriptions. The fishermen venerated these figures and their fishing flourished. They wished to build a temple to them, but had no money for this, so they sent the figures back out to sea. The boat returned an hour later, so the fishermen decided to overcome their difficulties and build a temple for the five gods. There are different kinds of Wangye temple. The grouping together of five of the over 130 godly kings in one temple is common. In this case, their family names are Li 李, Chi 池, Wu 吳, Zhu 朱, and Fan 范. Also, the story that they came from the sea, sent from heaven to protect people, seems common.

(the veneration of "gods and Buddhas").[70] It becomes obvious how inseparably popular religious and Buddhist elements are combined, without distinction, probably also in the perception of Lin: Lin mentions both, Guan Yu and the Wufu Qiansui group, in Taiwanese and is obviously not used to conversing about them in Mandarin. His belief is situated in his Taiwanese cultural milieu. Adding Taizu 太祖, literally the "highest ancestor", to his enumeration, he refers to a god who is commonly included in Taiwanese ancestor worship, and might be adding to his definition Buddhism. Recognising that people venerate different selections of "statues" Lin explains that there are "different kinds" of Buddhism. The multiplicity of Buddhisms seems a consequence of the multitude of statues that one can venerate. The aforementioned figures become gradually less closely connected with Buddhism, but this might not be clear to Lin. From what he says, it is unclear whether he contrasts Guanyin with other figures or which inner differentiation he prefers. Having in mind a clear distinction between different religious traditions, Lin's enumeration might seem fuzzy, but in Lin's emic perspective he seems to perceive his enumeration as a consistent continuity, although–as he reassures himself frequently through rhetorical questions–he might feel that his own concepts might not fit the expectations of his conversation partner. Lin's answer finally exemplifies well what has been said previously about religious belonging as a non-exclusive behaviour and a historically young differential category (chap. 1).

(5) Interviewer: 還是如果是在家裡是 更好，對不對	(5) Interviewer: Still, if it is at home, it is even better, right?
(6) Lin: 阿 我們是我家 有沒有 我家裡拜的那個佛教有沒有 是觀音 還有關聖帝君[tw] 關聖帝君[tw]就是那個 有沒有松江路 的那個關聖帝君[tw] 有沒有 還有一個太祖 我家裡有	(6) Lin: A. I am/ My family–right? The Buddhism which my family is venerating–right? –is Guanyin, also Guangong. Guangong is just that/ right? The one of Songjiang Road. Guangong, right? There is also one Taizu. My family has [sc. him/them].

When Lin Yongfu stopped speaking, the interviewer tried to learn more from him, focusing on his practice within the family. Lin interprets this input as a request to specify his family's "kind of Buddhism": he repeats the names of three of the figures he mentioned before–Bodhisattva Guanyin

[70] The temple's website (see the previous footnote) describes practices including the veneration of "gods and Buddhas" (*shenfo* 神佛). This might be due to the fact that, at the Nankunshen Daitian Temple, actually two temples are combined, one dedicated to the Wufu Qiansui and the other to a god called Wanshan Ye 萬善爺: "Legend goes that Wanshan Ye was a shepherd boy of a Qing emperor. He practised Buddhist principles in Kanglang Mountain and became a Buddha here" (official tourism website of Taiwan, http://eng.taiwan.net.tw/m1.aspx?sNo=0002119&id=R105, latest access January 7, 2016).

and Guansheng Dijun, whom he locates geographically, and Taizu. These he links back to the keyword of family worship. Wufu Qiansui, who is obviously not worshipped at home, is omitted.

As he stops speaking, the interviewer tries to maintain communication by commenting on the traffic and referring to the fact that Lin Yongfu grew up in a Buddhist family environment:

(7) Interviewer: 不錯 [Because of traffic:] 好辛苦阿 那你長大在一個佛教的環境還不錯	(7) Interviewer: Fine. [Because of traffic:] How hard a. Na, you have grown up in a Buddhist environment. That is not bad.
(8) Lin: [laughs] 我們還有拜那個五府千歲 [tw] 阿 你看 我們這邊貼的 是五府千歲 [tw] 對不對	(8) Lin: [laughs] We still venerate this Wufu Qiansui. A. See. We stuck it here. It is Wufu Qiansui, right?

The author's statement strikes Lin as funny, as it seems that he would not assume that he had grown up in anything like a "Buddhist environment". While "Buddhism" to him might be loosely connected with the statues he venerates, a "Buddhist environment" is probably a secondary term which he is either unacquainted with or which at least he would never associate with his home. Still, he seems willing to continue the conversation and mentions the god he omitted when describing the veneration undertaken by his family: Wufu Qiansui. Lin Yongfu includes him in this second reference to the figures venerated by his family–a distinction that becomes plausible when one recalls that Wufu Qiansui is venerated as a figure only in his temple in southern Taiwan, while he is not present in the daily veneration behaviour of the family besides the protective amulets from the temple hanging in the taxi on which the god's name is written. Lin shows them to the interviewer, asking again for her consent, then continues with a new thought:

(9) 實際上講起來 有沒有 拜這個東西 有沒有 這個佛教 有沒有 不管基督教佛教也有 什麼教都好了 是拜一個 是拜 自己拜的是心安理得 那你真的是要做壞事的話 這個神也管不了你. 阿	(9) Practically speaking–right?–venerating these things–right?–this Buddhism–right?–regardless if [sc. it is] Christianity, Buddhism has it also. Whatever teaching is good. It is to venerate one/ It is venerating/ If you yourself venerate it is "to feel at ease and justified" [saying]. Na, if you really want to do bad, this god can do nothing about you. A.

Within this grammatically interrupted and colloquial statement, Lin transforms the conversation about "religious" belief into his own vocabulary and view that he denotes as "practical" or "realistic" (*shiji*): "Religions" as "teachings" (*jiao*)–a historically explainable equal semantic construction (see chap. 1)–stand interchangably besides each other united in the act of veneration. The veneration practice serves a double function: Firstly, one "feels at ease and justified". Applying a saying, the Chinese language itself provides an already well-established pattern for expressing the function of veneration and hints at the fact that *baibai,* veneration and worship are deeply-rooted in society. Central is the act of veneration itself; the object and venerated "figure" is simply a "thing" (*dongxi*). Placing Christianity and Buddhism side by side, for Lin, all "teachings"/"religions" (*jiao*) serve the principle of veneration and, in consequence, are recognised as being "good". The inherent logic of that positive estimation is explained as follows: all religions venerate gods (*shen*) who, in turn "pay attention to", or "care for" (*guan*), those who venerate, despite if this person plans to do "something bad" (*huaishi*). Here, the second function of veneration becomes visible: religions are "good" and valuable, because bad behaviour will not gain support through veneration. The one who venerates and has good intentions is allowed to expect care and attention (*guan*) and, at the same time, feels "justified" and freed from moral pressure. Speaking of human behaviour, Lin Yongfu concentrates on people's actions and shows a concept of moral concern about their actual behaviour when he recognises also a pressure-releasing, psychological function of veneration. His concept of religion might give him a sound basis in life, but so far it seems that it is normally neither questioned nor reflected upon, nor seen as a tool for a personal struggle about the meaning of life. Indeed, Lin's concept of "religion" and "veneration" is very "practical" and "realistic", as it serves the concrete function of personal justification and, in combination with moral intentions, leads to protection by the gods and the successful accomplishment of morally good actions.

In the following, Lin gives an example from his everyday life as a taxi driver to illustrate what it means to lack the protection of gods:

(10) 像我們台灣講的那個 喝酒不要開車 要開車/ 你喝酒開車那個神也保護不了你 對不對	(10) As we [sc. in] Taiwan talk about that "When you drink alcohol, don't drive". If you want to drive/ If you drink and then drive, this god'll also not protect you. Right?
(11) Interviewer: 對對	(11) Interviewer: Right.
(12) Lin: 你自己要有節制 說 阿 我要喝酒 我後來不開車. 不然的話我家裡小喝一點 後來睡覺 不開車 對不對 那 當然神明他會保佑你阿 對不對	(12) Lin: You have to restrict yourself saying: I want to drink, so afterwards I won't drive. Otherwise I drink a bit at home and sleep afterwards, don't drive. Right? Of course, the god'll protect you. A. Right?
(13) Interviewer: 對對 有道理阿	(13) Interviewer: Right. That makes sense.

"Not drinking and driving" is his example of a, morally-speaking, "good" behaviour. The example itself he takes as a commonplace for "good" behaviour in Taiwan: the morally "good" is provided by society, by "us", by "Taiwan"–not by the god. It is not questioned, but it is clearly apparent what is good and what is bad. The function of "this god" is to protect, and also know when to do so. It seems that the god knows, as well as "we [in] Taiwan", what is bad and does not deserve protection, and it is "natural" (*dangran*) that the god (*shenming*) protects one if one sleeps and does not drive after drinking, which means behaving according to the existing regulations for both humans and gods. In this sense, the insecurity of life is managed by the individual: the worship of gods ensures protection, while individuals, who naturally know about good and bad through society, are themselves responsible for engaging in morally good behaviour.

Structural Hypothesis

Lin Yongfu is a sociable, open-minded man with harmonising language behaviour, who is well-acquainted with Taiwanese culture. When questioned about religion and Buddhism, he defines, in an inclusive approach, religions through the act of worship. The consequence of worship, as he understands it, is the protection and justification of the worshipper's actions by the one being worshipped, which leads to inner peace. The *conditio sine qua non* for protection is the worshipper's morally responsible behaviour. The emphasis in his concept rests on action–the action of worship as well as the protection of actions. The code of "good" and "bad" is taken as given. Worship mainly takes place within the family. The distinctive characteristics of Lin's belief as a Buddhist remain unclear, as popular religious practice and the involvement of Buddhist statues are described as a continuum. Lin obviously calls himself a Buddhist as some of his venerated statues are associated with Buddhism. The term "religion" he constructs through a generalisation of his culturally average worshipping behaviour.

Further Elements

Lin Yongfu's becoming a Buddhist is obviously closely connected to the worship of a figure, probably that of Guanyin, in his home, which seems to have been freshly carved when he obtained it. Although Lin states that he has been a Buddhist since childhood, he sees the carving of his statue and the beginning of his actual worship as an apparently important stage in his definition of becoming a Buddhist. At least, the carving of his statue was so important that he remembers the date and mentions it during the conversation:

(S1) Interviewer: 所以你從小都信佛教嗎	(S1) Interviewer: So, you've believed in Buddhism since childhood?
Lin: 對 阿 我雕刻的那個佛像 是在民國 70 幾年的時候才雕刻起來拜拜的	Lin: Yes. A. That my carved Buddhist statue was carved and henceforth worshipped only in the 1980s.

Lin deems himself a "Buddhist" in a strict sense only after he had the chance to venerate his statue which, in contrast to his general belief from childhood onwards, occurred quite late in life. He continues:

(S2) 在家裡 有沒有 雕刻放在家裡 來拜拜 因為我們的祖先 有沒有 我們不能請出來 我們祖先 祖先牌位 阿 我們拜祖先的時候 過年 過節 會回去拜 平時都在家裡拜這個 神明 我們拜 全家都拜 小孩子都要拜啦 我的孫子 阿公我也要拜

(S2) At home–right?–it was carved and put at home. For worship. Because our ancestors–right?–we can't ask our ancestors to come out. The ancestor tablets a. When we venerate our ancestors, [sc. that is] at New Year, when we celebrate, we will return to venerate them. On normal days, we always worship these gods at home. We worship. The whole family worships. The children all want to worship la. My grandson: "Grandpa, I also want to worship!"

The worship of gods seems to be a standard practice within the family context, involving the participation of the younger generation. Lin Yongfu is proud that his grandson enjoys participating and that he can successfully pass on his tradition. The whole family is involved in the veneration and, through worship, the generations are bound together, including the deceased. Lin reasons: As the ancestors are represented through ancestor tablets at home and worshipped at New Year or during special festivals only, the worship on normal days addresses the gods. Still, ancestor worship is of major importance to him. This becomes clear, when he later states that, for this reason, he would not like his children to become Christians: "That would not be good for the family". In addition to protection, worship clearly helps to hold the family together and that is also why Lin enjoys handing it down to the next generation.

Lin gives a detailed description of the actions that he performs every morning and evening when worshipping through burning incense: he brushes his teeth while standing up, boils water for tea, burns incense, then goes out. In the evening, he returns home, has a shower, burns incense, and only then does the family eat. Worship is important not because of its content at that moment, but it gives everyday life a rhythmic structure and, through the order of the actions, respect is displayed for the gods and one's ancestors–the worship takes place before the communal meal.

The veneration undertaken on the 1st and 15th day of the lunar calendar month is especially beneficial. This is one of the few occasions during our conversation when Lin draws a distinction between the Buddhist figure Guanyin and other gods: the figure that he explicitly names "Buddhist" is distinguished by vegetarianism: "Guanyin is eating plain/meat-free" (*Guanyin shi chisu de* 觀音是吃素的); therefore, she does not accept meat offerings.[71]

Although Lin emphasises the importance of the action of worship throughout the interview, later, he tackles an ethical principal for social behaviour in a variant of the golden rule: "Only if you respect others will they respect you" (*Ni zunzhong bieren bieren cai hui zunzhong ni* 你尊重別人 別人才會尊重你), and mentions that he is behaving respectfully through his action of worshipping. For him, worshipping is connected to the quality of social interaction. It is also striking that this comes to Lin's mind as he is reflecting that, in terms of driving etiquette, the Taiwanese could learn something from the Japanese. His traditional *Lebenswelt* does not prevent him from being open to making international comparisons.

One might depict Lin Yongfu's perception of Buddhism in the following scheme:

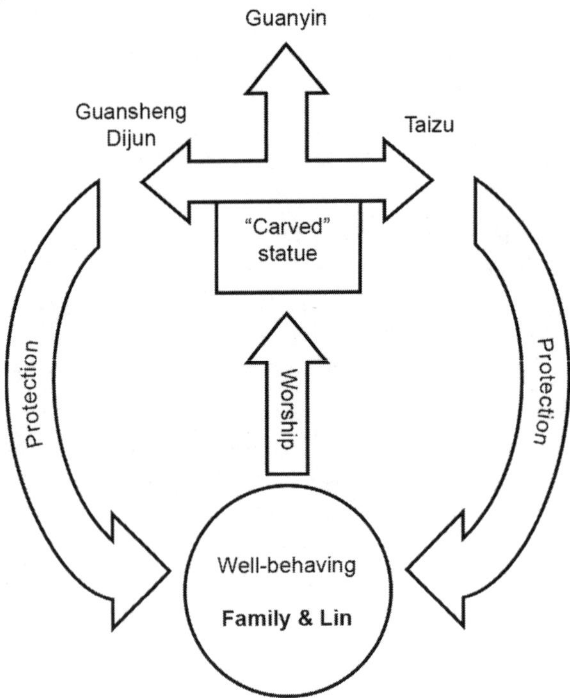

Figure 7: The function of "Buddhism" in Lin Yongfu's family.

71 It is interesting to note, on the linguistic level, that Chinese enhances in this case the thinking in action: while in English, one would normally make a statement about the intrinsic quality of Guanyin by applying an adjective like "vegetarian", the Chinese language naturally implies an action or behaviour of Guanyin, and makes no statement about the "nature" of Guanyin herself.

Besides the concentration on his family, the interview with Lin shows a second sphere in which his belief takes place–the temple. Interestingly, Lin is linked to a certain temple that is dedicated to the locally well-known Wufu Qiansui in Tainan. He visits this temple annually, and even actively supports it by being a commissioner (*weiyuan* 委員). In explaining his choice of temple, he states that this is unconnected with the god who is venerated there. Later, it becomes clear that the temple gods are all-protecting. The main differences between temples emerge from their leaders/managers' (*zhuchiren* 主持人) behaviour. The main danger would be that they are exploiting people's longing for the god's protection or the "change of luck" (*gaiyun* 改運) in order to make money. This, he claims, is "cheating" (*pianren* 騙人), and he thinks that supporting such a temple is *zaogao* 糟糕–terrible (*Zhe yang de miao gei ta zhanqi lai zhende zaogao* 這樣的廟給它站起來真的糟糕). Lin supports his temple because he believes that it is different. Firstly, it does not ask for money. "Our manager doesn't cheat you. You go and worship. Even if you don't give anything and come again, he'll still help you". Not only does the temple not cheat its visitors but it even helps people in need by acting as a social welfare

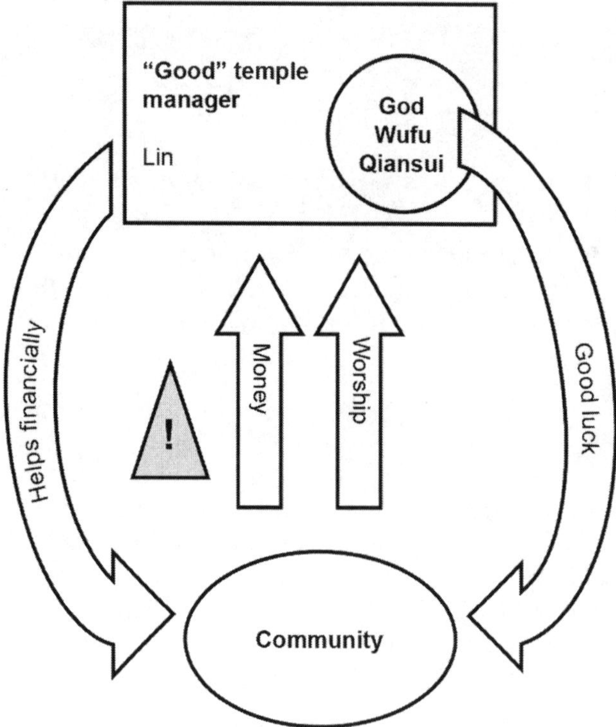

Figure 8: Reciprocal relationship with the gods as part of a functioning social community.

system. As health insurance is still a recent phenomenon in Taiwan, Lin will remember a time when ill people and their families were in great need. He is proud of the virtuous deed of his temple–about which he has only heard–when they gave money to such a family, without even informing the ill person. They offered help in this situation, without any desire to bind people closely to the temple or receive their gratitude. He also feels that it is important that, among the donor community, there is no mutual competition or comparison in terms of donations.

Searching for the role of Buddhism in this interview, we do not find that the term is applied very often. It is restricted to the existence of Guanyin and her vegetarianism. When explicitly asked by the interviewer about monks and nuns (*biqiu* 比丘 and *biqiuni* 比丘尼), Lin at first does not understand the vocabulary and, when the question is repeated using more common terminology (*chujia ren* 出家人), he remains with his topic of cheating and is unresponsive to the input. Also, Buddhist terminology is not within Lin's vocabulary. Even in a situation where a loose karmic argument would have been easy to apply, he speaks of a person's "opinion" and "thinking" like a conscious choice:

(R1) Lin: 那個不是好不好的問題. 那是個人的思想 個人的意念. 因為怎麼樣 我這個廟的 有沒有 怎麼樣 它的主持人 有沒有 對這一些事情 有沒有 他做得很理想 這個五府千歲[tw] 有沒有 怎麼樣說 我會信任他	(R1) Lin: This is not the question of good and not-good, this is the thinking of each person, the opinion of each person. Because how is it/my [sc. attitude towards] this temple–right?–its chairman–right?–for these things–right?–he does it very reasonably. This Wufu Qiansui [tw]–right? How to say? I trust in him.

His choice of temple is not a consequence of arbitrary circumstances, but the result of his personal attitude. It is noteworthy that the concept of "*yinyuan*", mentioned in the statistical introduction, is used here neither in combination with a personal opinion nor as an explanatory trope of fate.

Conclusion

Lin Yongfu's belief centres around two fields of action–the family and the temple–and is structured in both fields similarly: through worship and good behaviour, the family expects, as a reward for their veneration, the protection of the worshipped gods while implicitly upholding the boundaries between each other and the nexus between the generations. This reciprocal understanding is also the basis within the temple sphere. Remarkable is the fact that, although through worship the bettering of one's fate is expected from the gods, in a concrete material crisis, the temple cares about its worshippers. Therefore, in both fields, the community of those involved is central to the act of worship within the social system. Through veneration, it is strengthened and serves as a kind of buffer, providing social protection. One should be careful of considering Lin as a mechanistic practitioner who, according to the religio-historical well-tested principle "do-ut-des",[72] is expecting a claimable protection. Although his belief currently does not seem to be tested by negative incidences, one should take into account that his reciprocal relationship with the gods is accompanied by an intact social environment, a high sensibility towards monetary aspects and the possible misuse of the system through "cheating" as well as by his own obligation to display "good" behaviour. The moral code seems to be provided by his social environment, which one therefore must expect to be relatively homogenous in this aspect. His belief is also well-rooted in his daily experiences (not drinking while driving). Nevertheless, Lin does not create the impression of being a traditionalist, but is open-minded towards impressions from abroad, which he even uses as illustrations and integrates into the moral basis of his belief, defined in terms of a mutual respect.

Comparison with the Statistical Findings

Lin Yongfu's "belief" shows far-reaching parallels with the characteristics of "Conventional Buddhists", highlighted above. He calls himself a Buddhist but, as he constantly enlarges on his veneration practice and no Buddhist school is mentioned during our 40-minute conversation, we can suppose that he would–if deciding to define himself as a Buddhist in the questionnaire situation–choose the veneration option ("*xinfo, baifo*"). He explains his belief as a practice within his community, rather than a private spiritual one. As he marks the beginning of his being a Buddhist from the carving of his statue, an initiation ritual like taking refuge has no meaning for him. He might wear Buddhist beads by chance, but he would probably not connect with this any differentiated, intensified occupation with "religion" or "Buddhism". Nevertheless, he would claim to be "devout" and sincere in his beliefs, as this is essential for him. The nexus between the generations and ancestor veneration plays a major role, so we can assume that he sees himself in the tradition of his family and would not distance himself from his parents' beliefs. It is out of the question that Lin would never oppose the veneration of gods and ances-

[72] The phrases "Do ut des" or "Do ut possis dare", lit. "I do so that you do" or "I do so that you are enabled to do", respectively, refer to a veneration pattern that was widely-known in ancient Greek and Roman society. They hint at an imagined contractual balance here between the worshipper and worshipped. Examined within religious studies since the early 20th century (G. van der Leeuw), they are questioned (there is a risk of generalising inadequately the biblical concept of sacrifice) and challenged, but nevertheless established as a *terminus technicus* for a retributory veneration pattern. For details, see the Hoheisel (1990).

tors because of seeing himself as a Buddhist. He donates money to his temple, which in this case is not a Buddhist one. Lin does not visit "Buddhist temples" often–he explicitly states this also in the interview–but certainly visits temples and shrines, especially the temple to which he is dedicated. The purpose of these temple visits he describes by the term "*gaiyun*"–"to change one's luck". This practice is less common among Conventional Buddhists (see table 10 below), but the other practices also imply a more specific vocabulary and, finally, in a more general sense, all other practices can be summarised by the term "to change your luck". It might also be the case that the temple he visits in Tainan focuses on the practice of "*gaiyun*". Certainly, peace, self-cultivation and spiritual sustainability would also be a more natural consequence of his described belief than the search for truth and wisdom (v29).
Still, there remains the question of why Lin finally constructs himself as a Buddhist. He lives in the capital, Taipeh, although the socio-cultural expression of his belief is probably similar to that of a rurally situated popular religious practitioner. Herewith, he might be exactly one of those persons who are responsible for the fact that there are more Conventional Buddhists in the cities than in the rural areas. It seems that we are witnessing a terminological shift, which first takes place within the cities: while people keep up their religious practices and concepts, they are confronted with terms to which they have been exposed since the Japanese colonial period, like "religion" and "Buddhism". As Lin obviously perceives "Buddhism" in a positive light, which can even link him with the foreigner sitting in his taxi, he is very willing to label his practice of "worship of gods"–as he would normally call it–"Buddhism" and a "religion" without drawing personally any serious consequences from that. The

v46		Conventional Buddhists answering "I have done it myself" (自己有做)
(4)	Placated your constellation god (安斗[拜斗])	48.5% (192)
(7)	Put on a peace talisman (on body or car; 佩戴平安符[隨身, 車上])	44.3% (175)
(6)	Lit the brightness lantern (點光明燈)	18.7% (74)
(2)	Changed your luck (改運)	12.4% (49)
(5)	Called back your wandering soul and pacified evil spirits that cause fear (收驚)	8.9% (35)
(3)	Placated your zodiac year god (安太歲)	5.1% (20)
(1)	Sought help from a spiritual medium (找靈媒[找乩童, 牽亡魂, 觀落陰, 乩首, 找尪姨])	5.1% (20)

Table 10: Temple practices: "Have you or your family within the past year [from August last year to July this year] done the following, which is related to eliminating disasters and praying for blessings?" (最近一年內 [去年８月到今年７月] 您或您的家人有沒有做過下列與消災祈福有關的事情? (TSCS 2004.2, v46, percentage and frequency, n=395).

exposure to an urban multi-layered environment might induce, as one could trace in this case, a re-naming and, perhaps even in a second step, through chats like this interview, a process of re-thinking one's own tradition.

7.2 Luo Peirong–Coping with Bad Karma through Buddhist and Daoist Practices

Like Lin Yongfu, Luo Peirong 羅佩容 (female, age about 50) stands in a direct relationship of mutual benefit with gods and Buddhas (*shenfo* 神佛) but, in contrast to Lin, who makes a very harmonious impression throughout the interview, the basic tenor of Luo Peirong's whole interview is dominated by despair. She is the only interviewee who lost some of her composure during the session. Also, her narrations are far less coherent than those of the others. The chronological reconstruction of the major events of her belief's development demanded a most careful reading and rearrangement of the transcription.

Luo Peirong was, at the time of the interview, a housewife of about 50 years old, married, and probably with a grown-up son and daughter. Living in Taipeh County, she speaks with a strong Taiwanese accent and, at times, drifts into Taiwanese during the interview. Her friend, Kong Shuqing, is present for part of the interview, and intervenes when she feels that a translation into Mandarin might help. The antecedent of the fixed appointment dates back to the author's first visit to Kong a year earlier, in 2004. A friend for several years, the author had been visiting her at her home. Kong, by that time, was renting a room in a flat owned by Luo. During her visit, the researcher got the impression, that Luo was obviously following a strict Buddhist practice, which included vegetarianism and morning and evening recitations. A Buddhist altar dominated her flat. When the author returned to Taiwan in 2005, she asked her friend, Kong Shuqing, who had by that time moved elsewhere, if she would ask her former landlady to give an interview. Kong arranged for the interview to take place in her own new home. Especially at the beginning of the interview, Kong was mostly in the kitchen, preparing refreshments, as she knew that the researcher wished to be alone with the interviewee. The interview lasted about 75 minutes. In the end, the researcher's friend took over the communication and Luo made her excuses and left. She might have come mainly because she felt obliged to help her friend.

Introductory Sequence Analysis

The beginning of the interview is very unusual, as the first interactions do not lead quickly into the narration. Still, these initial interactions reveal a lot about Luo Peirong's perception of her current situation:

(1) Interviewer: 我以為她有跟你講	(1) Interviewer: I thought she'd have told you.
(2) Luo: 我忘記了. 因 因為我現在 我現在真的 阿 好像是問甚麼佛教未來的發展甚麼怎麼樣, 是不是?	(2) Luo: I've forgotten it. Be-/ Because I'm now/ I'm now really/ a/ I think, it was asking whatever Buddhist future development whatever, however, right?

Although informed in advance about the topic of the interview by my friend, Luo Peirong initially pretends to or has actually forgotten it, and she begins by stating this. She interrupts herself before mentioning the reason why she has forgotten–perhaps she finds her situation difficult to describe–but it becomes clear that she currently sees herself ("now") in a special situation. Once she has made this clear, she formulates from memory what her friend might have told her about this interview. Her formulation "the development of Buddhist future" omits her personal connection with the question. Perhaps she can, in fact, recall what Kong told her, or perhaps she is trying to avoid talking about herself. It could be that she would prefer to talk about the development of Buddhism in general rather than her own beliefs–due to her current situation at which she hinted or to the fact that she might feel awkward about a researcher showing interest in her personally. One certainly feels a certain restraint in Luo Peirong towards the interview.

(3) Interviewer: Yea. 也是你跟佛教的關係阿	(3) Interviewer: Yea. It was also about your relationship to Buddhism a.
(4) Luo: 我跟佛教的關係	(4) Luo: My relationship to Buddhism.
(5) Interviewer: 因為我還記得你是很認 真的佛教徒.	(5) Interviewer: Because I still remember that you are a very sincere Buddhist.
(6) Luo: [sighing]	(6) Luo: [sighing]
(7) Interviewer: 對不對. 很棒阿. 我那個時候來到你的房子那邊, 覺得很羨慕你, 一直在	(7) Interviewer: Right? Great a. I at that time came to your home there, and thought, I admire you very much, continuously/

The description of the topic as "her relationship to Buddhism" is carefully repeated by Luo. She might be trying to decide what to reveal, or wondering how to avoid this. The interviewer feels this and starts to modify her question–Luo answers this directly with a loud sigh. Does she feel a huge discrepancy between the description of her as a "sincere Buddhist" and her current situation? After further praise by the interviewer, she sums up her current situation with the statement:

(8) Luo: 現在都/ 都/ 都沒有一個信心哈 [laughs]	(8) Luo: Now I don't at all/ all/ all have trust ha [laughs]

Luo states that she has lost her trust; literally, her "trustful heart". Has she lost confidence in Buddhism and is no longer a sincere practitioner, as the interviewer constructs her? The statement could also be meant in a far broader sense to imply that Luo has somehow lost confidence in life and sees herself in a desperate situation. Certainly, this statement would explain her resistance to be interviewed. Does it seem ironic to her that, in her present situation, she is being asked about her strong Buddhist belief? Perhaps she feels that it is unreasonable to give an interview and wants to withdraw from it. This situation is unstable, and the laughter also helps to ease the tension and distance the communication partners from the topic, so that communication, despite Luo's tragic situation and the–in her view probably–useless meeting, remains possible.

(9) Interviewer: [laughs] 這樣子	(9) Interviewer: [laughs] Like that.
(10) Luo: 對阿 變化太大了	(10) Luo: Yes a. The change is too big.
(11) Interviewer: 什麼很大	(11) Interviewer: What is too big?
(12) Luo: ㄇ 這幾年變化很大了	(12) Luo: M. These years, the change is very big.
(13) Interviewer: 阿 [falling voice]	(13) Interviewer: A [falling voice].
(14) Luo: 這幾年變化很大 ㄇ	(14) Luo: These years the change is very big. M.
(15) Interviewer: 阿 [falling voice] 但是阿	(15) Interviewer: A [falling voice] But a/
(16) Luo: 我這幾年變化很大 ㄇ	(16) Luo: [sc. Concerning] me, these years the change is very big m.

The interviewer picks up her unsteady laughing. Perhaps she is surprised to compare Luo Peirong's current hopeless situation with that of the sincere Buddhist whom she remembers from the previous year. Luo explains this through a fourfold repetition of the "big changes" in her life, which is not explanatory but repeats the same formulation with little alteration. If Luo wanted to abandon the interview, she would probably have started to argue by now. In contrast, her fourfold repetition shows that she is caught up in her situation. The experiences seem to be painful and not yet fully processed. She might, therefore, be unable at this moment to arrange these separate experiences into a tide of events, to step back and describe the development of her belief. If the interview is to continue, it will probably centre around Luo's attempt to realise her current situation and integrate it into her life-concept.

(17) Interviewer: 還是一個佛教徒嗎	(17) Interviewer: You are still a Buddhist?
(18) Luo: 對 [laughing]. 佛教是我的目標我的宗旨	(18) Luo: Yes [laughing]. Buddhism is my aim and my mission.
(19) Interviewer: 哈?	(19) Interviewer: Ha?
(20) Luo: 哈	(20) Luo: Ha.

The interviewer intends to find a last base for an interview–even if Luo has lost confidence, does she still see herself as a Buddhist? Luo affirms this, without hesitation, and again laughs, recognising the tension between her lack of trust and her belief, explaining that Buddhism is "her aim and her mission". The formulation, contrasting with the previous choice of words, might recall vocabulary that is close to the proselytising attitude of the Young Buddhist Monasteries and could eventually be understandable in the context of Luo's latent longing to transform, as her "aim" and "mission", her environment, especially her family, into a Buddhist one. The interviewer reacts with surprise at the contrast between Luo's lost trust in Buddhism and her continuing adherence to it.

Finally, the talk ends up locating the beginning of Luo Peirong's belief about ten to 20 years previously when she came into contact with a Buddhist monastery. Again, it was her friend(s) who brought her there, she states (*ye shi pengyou dai wo jinqu* 也是朋友帶我近去). For Luo, it seems normal that one comes into contact with a Buddhist organisation via friends, who take the new member along with them. Luo escapes the personal narration one last time, enlarging repeatedly on the, at that time, unknown status of this monastery's abbot, whom she affectionately calls–as common in Taiwan–"our master" (*women shifu* 我們師父); literally "our teacher-father". She and her friends see themselves as sharing a close intimacy with the abbot, who at that time had been far more accessible. The accessibility of and personal contact with the master is central in Luo's memory.

The interviewer then asks Luo if she had been interested in Buddhism before that time, and Luo answers:

(22) Luo: 也不是沒興趣啦 因為 不是沒興趣 這是 因為我 是我自己個人的因素 因為 我還在療傷 [laughs, could also be weeping] 因為我這幾年 因為我這幾年運氣很不好 很不好 甚麼事情都有帶/ 你真的/ tsä/ 一剎那 接二連三 我都沒有辦法去承受的	(22) Luo: It is also not being not interested. Because/ It is not being not interested. This is because I/ This is because of myself. Because I'm still recovering [laughs, could also be weeping]. Because these years I came across/ Because these years luck is really not good. Really not good. Everything comes along with/ You really/ tsä/ In the nick of time [lit. *chana* 剎那 is skt. *kṣana*] one after another gets bad. I don't have a chance at all to accept [sc. it].
(23) Interviewer: 阿 這樣子	(23) Interviewer: A. Like this.
(24) Luo: 對	(24) Luo: Yes.

Luo Peirong here answers not the question asked, but enlarges on whether she is interested in Buddhism now. Perhaps she misunderstood the question, or perhaps is still, in her thoughts, trying to solve the discrepancy between being a Buddhist while having no trust/belief. From this perspective, it seems logical that she explains, in various stumbling sentences, the beginning of her relationship with Buddhism not as a matter of interest, but as a matter of her current personal situation. She presently would be "curing her harms" (*liaoshang* 療傷) and experiences her situation as severe. She continues with further reasoning: in the past few years, she has gone through a lot and has had very bad luck. Within a kṣaṇa,[73] everything would turn into misery and she would be unable to cope. We recognise that she naturally applies an Indian-Buddhist time concept, which does not necessarily have Buddhist associations, but could also just sound fashionable. Though normally speaking in a grammatically and semantically very simple way, Luo might be familiar with Buddhist terminology. The expression "*chengshou* 承受", here translated as "to accept" in the sense of "to bear", "to endure", is not necessarily a Buddhist term, but is likely to appear in Buddhist advice also. In the current context, it seems to imply a wish to endure and accept fate. As important matters in Luo's life have turned unexpectedly bad, she is trying to accept her situation. She might find her trust again and her interest in Buddhism, once she has recovered, as Buddhism remains "her aim" and "mission". Remarkable is the dialectic with which Luo constructs herself as a Buddhist. While she is currently not engaging in Buddhism, as she has lost her trust in it, she understands Buddhism to be her final goal and task and knows that she wants to handle her overall situation in the established Buddhist pattern as "acceptance". Is "Buddhism" assisting her to overcome a "non-Buddhist" phase in her life?

After Luo has finished explaining her general life condition, the interviewer asks why she once chose to belong to a Buddhist organisation. Luo simply states that this choice was by chance and starts to give details about how she came into contact with the monastery. The interaction runs as follows:

(25) Interviewer: 你那個時候為甚麼選 [..., monastery A] 那個時候還沒有很 有名 但是你還是常常去 還是/	(25) Interviewer: Why did you choose [..., monastery A] at that time? It wasn't very famous then, but you still went there often, or/
(26) Luo: 因為我之前那是偶爾 以前比較時常去	(26) Luo: Because I before that, that was by chance. Before I went there quite often.
(27) Interviewer: ㄇ	(27) Interviewer: M.
(28) Luo: 以前都時常去 時常去 時常 [...,monastery A] 都時常 有時常去 那我進入[..., monastery A] 的←因緣→ 這個緣分是從 這個一二十年 也是 怎麼講 也是因為我公公的問題啦 就是我們家族 的個人問題阿 我們家族 就是我公公 他平常都住在我這邊 公公你聽懂阿	(28) Luo: Before I went there always often/ went there often/ often/ to [..., monastery A] always often/ I went there often. Na, the ← karmic reason → why I entered [..., monastery A], this karmic connection came from these ten to 20 years. It was also/ How to say/ it was also because of the problem of my father-in-law. My family, this is just my father-in-law, he normally lived here at my place. Do you understand "father-in-law"?
(29) Interviewer: 國語懂 但是台語我不懂	(29) Interviewer: I understand Mandarin,

73 *Chana* 剎那 (skt. *kṣaṇa*) can be a noun in Sanskrit referring to a short moment or an instant in time. See FBD (2000), 3731 (entry "*chana* 剎那").

不好意思

but I don't understand Taiwanese, I'm sorry.

(30) Luo: 阿 沒關係 我不會講台語 我會講國語 這是我公公都住在我這邊嘛 那就是有一個家族 有是是非非 我也是沒辦法去承受 沒辦法去承受是說 我的大姑 就對了 大姑就是 說 我趕我公公走了 就是是非非一大堆 阿 沒有的事/ 強大就是是非非一大堆那一大堆 我真的 我那時候真的那是第一次的壓力 那時候 那後來 我們是住在 [..., name of part of Taipeh] [..., name of other part of Taipeh] 旁邊 我要去[..., name of a river] 河/ 跳河/ 後來一想不對因為這樣含冤歿死. 我就不甘 我有一點甘願 不對 那我就跟我朋友在講 那我朋友帶我進 就是我有一個朋友 她住在台北 從十七八歲交的朋友 那她現在 我講我的苦 從頭講給她聽 那她 就 我心情很不好 對不對 那他就帶我去師父那邊 到了師父那邊去見師父 因 那時候見師父很隨便 因為我門去那時候 因為要見不是像現在要見師父你見不到 對 因為他到處各國去他見不到 即使 即使就在台灣 我們這一些普通你見不到 像我們比較老一輩 我們就可以了 隨時說 師父阿 就可以了 阿那 那就帶我去師父那邊 而是師父講一些這個 這這 這個佛法 給我聽 阿 這樣我聽得 欸心理就滿舒服的 阿 那就是那個因緣進入 [..., monastery A].

(30) Luo: A. That doesn't matter. I won't talk in Taiwanese. I'll talk in Chinese. This is, my father-in-law always lived here at my place ma. There's a family, there's trouble, I also have no chance to accept that.
No chance to accept means: my sister-in law, that's right, sister-in-law said just: I drive out my father-in-law. [sc. That] just [caused] a big trouble. A. A small matter/ big and powerful just a big trouble/ I really/ I really at that time/ This was the first stress. At that time.
Then later/ We lived in [..., a name of part of Taipeh]. Near to [..., a name of another part of Taipeh]. I wanted to go to the [..., name of a river] river/ to jump into the river/ Then some thoughts [were there, that this is] not right. Because that way it is dying uncleared of a false charge [*hanyuan mosi*; saying]. So I didn't want it. I wanted it a bit–no [unclear]. So I told my friend. So my friend brought me in/ It is just, I have a friend/ She lives in Taipeh. A friend I made when I was 17 or 18 years old. Na she is now/ I told my sorrows. I got her to hear it from the beginning. Na she just/ I felt very bad [lit.: The sentiment/situation of my heart was really not good]. Right? Na, she took me to the master there. When we went there to see the master, because at that time it was very easy to see the master. Because when we went to see him/ Because when one wanted to see him, it was not like now going to see the master. You won't see him. Right. Because he's going to every country. One can't see him. Even if/ Even if just in Taiwan/ we these some normal [people], you won't see him. Like we from the older generation, we can. At any time saying "Master a!" then one can. A na, na she took me to the master there. And the master said some of these/ this/ this/ this Buddha's dharma for me to listen. A. Like this. I listened. Ei, my heart was very eased. A. This is that karmic reason I entered [..., monastery A] .

(31) Interviewer: ㄇ↓所以他講到的 是

(31) Interviewer: M↓ So what he talked

因果的	about was cause and effect?
(32) Luo: 對對對 阿這樣進入[…, monastery A] 那時候都時常 也唸 因為那時候也念佛嘛 誦經念佛 我都 對 我都時常會去 阿這是這個因緣 阿師父就跟我開始 終有一天我會水落石出 那真的 到後來 他們都 他們都 確實我 我那個大姑在造謠 不是 不是我的因素 這樣 阿就這個因緣進入	(32) Luo: Yes, yes, yes. A. Like this I entered […, monastery A]. That time I always often also recited, because at that time I also sang sūtras and recited the Buddha's name. I always for/ I always went there often. A. This is one karmic reason. A. The master explained to me, said: Finally there will be a day when the water subsides and the rocks emerge [*shuiluo shichu*; saying]. Na really until later, they all/ they all, truly my/ my sister-in-law started rumours. It was not/ It was not because of me. Like this. A. So this is the reason I entered.

At this point, Luo's formal narration comes to its first end. After a problematic start, she presents for the first time a coherent scenario: when she was under severe pressure from her spouse's family for the first time, she contacted a Buddhist monastery and met its abbot in person. In her family, her father-in-law passed away and, in the following weeks, her sister-in-law spread rumours, which led her to contemplate suicide. She shared her troubles with a old friend, who accompanied her to a monastery. Attending the monastery regularly, Luo asks its abbot for advice, listens to him and in the retrospective cherishes especially his personal accessibility. In addition, she engages in name recitation as a spiritual practice. The master's teaching she still recalls 20 years later as good metaphoric advice: one day, the situation will be clarified, the abbot told her, like rocks emerge when the tide goes out. This makes sense in the context of her contemplating suicide: while she feels that her family situation is unbearable and she wants to escape it by killing herself, at the same time she hesitates to commit suicide as this would make her look guilty or at least not help to clarify her situation. Participating in activities at the monastery serves therefore a double function: it eases her mind, reducing her stress and guilt and, through doing recitations–at deathbeds, as one learns later–she enters a new social field and can express herself in a new, unproblematic context.

At this turning point in her life, where she is helped in an existentially threatening situation by her friends' intervention and their introduction of her to a Buddhist abbot and Buddhist community life, she applies with emphasis–stretching out the words–the concept which, according to the statistical investigations above is commonly asserted in Taiwan–"*yinyuan*", a karmic connection.

Structural Hypothesis

Luo Peirong, with her fairly simple Taiwanese background, is actively familiar with a quite elaborate Buddhist vocabulary. Caught up in her current sense of personal despair, she only finds her way slowly into the interview situation. She describes herself as having lost her trust in Buddhism and as no longer practising it, but describes her situation in line with Buddhist argumentations as a task of "acceptance". Luo faces persistent problems in her life. The moment about 20 years ago, when she was feeling suicidal and a friend introduced her to a Buddhist community by putting her in personal contact with its abbot she describes in Buddhist terminology as happening due to *yinyuan*– "karmic connections". Through her personal exchanges with the master, she was able to take control of her life again and trust that the truth would one day reveal itself and clarify her situation. Besides her personal contact with the abbot, Luo also entered a new social field, the Buddhist community of the monastery, and started a spiritual practice of name recitation. The changes in her social field induced by Buddhism dominate Luo's narrations, while doctrinal explanations are not absent, but hardly enlarged upon. Buddhism is present in Luo's life as a practical method of fate management, opening up a new field of social interaction. At the time of the interview, she recognises herself as being in a process of recovery and momentarily disengaged from Buddhism. She describes her overall life-orientation as being dominated by Buddhism, which would be her "aim" and "mission". Buddhism, as Luo currently perceives it, stands for facing and accepting one's karmic situation–a formulation which might remind the reader of Kong Shuqing's description of the Buddhist essentials in the introduction.

Luo Peirong's current self-description conflicts starkly with her former life as a Buddhist. The question arises: through what circumstances has Luo's belief been challenged and how far might this have changed the function of Buddhism in her life?

Development of Personal Situation

Luo's later narrations are centred on tragic events within her family. Hospital scenarios, dreams, and miracles dominate her descriptions. There are several stories within the interview which, after a re-arrangement, can be reconstructed as the following course of events: Luo has been participating, with her female Buddhist friends, in the monastery activities for several years and been following Buddhist practice. Recently, her situation has totally changed. First, her son was involved in a car accident, then her daughter suffered an injury. Finally, her husband developed cancer. She had to sell the house to pay the medical costs. By the time of the interview, all three family members had recovered or were on the road to recovery. Around each of these three incidents Luo relates dreams and miracles, which serve the purpose of proving the "power" of gods and Buddhas, especially of Bodhisattva Guanyin and the Queen Mother of the West, Wangmu Niangniang 王母娘娘.

After the car accident, her son was in a coma for several weeks. She constantly engaged in name recitation, asking Guanyin for help. While reciting, the water on the altar changed colour. She gave it to her son to drink, and he regained consciousness a week later. Her son had two dreams, in both of which a lady appeared, whom Luo Peirong interprets as the goddess Guanyin. In the second dream, this lady drew her son away from some black doors–the doors to hell in her interpretation. Through the change in the water's colour as well as through her son's dreams, Luo believes that the goddess Guanyin rescued her son miraculously (*aomiao* 奥妙). Within the last year before the interview, first her daughter had an accident and severely injured her leg. After leaving hospital, the father took the family to a temple of Wangmu Niangniang. Upon their arrival, Luo recognised that she had seen the goddess before in a dream, in which Guanyin guided her towards the goddess. She took her daughter every week to the temple, and her leg healed quickly. Luo has, since then, been convinced of Wangmu Niangniang's miraculous power, and also that her husband is currently under this goddess' protection. The enormous strength of the "many gods and Buddhas", who rescued her husband, Luo emphasises by pointing out the time her husband faced a hopeless situation when he was diagnosed with advanced lymphoma. The fact that he is still alive and healthy demonstrates again the miraculous power of "gods and Buddhas". Her husband spent over two months in hospital, for which the costs were exorbitant. Finally, he seems to be cured and said that "all pain is over now". Luo interpreted this as a message from Guanyin, that all bad karma has been compensated for now. Some radiology treatment scared Luo and her husband. Luo took the shaman of the temple where her daughter was cured to the hospital, whom she believes possesses power granted by Wangmu Niangniang and, after falling into a trance, he rejected the conventional treatment. He agreed to accept responsibility for her husband's health in the future, but wanted to watch over him for five years. Since then, her husband has been in good health, and the shaman often visits Luo's family home.

At the time of the interview, Luo was not participating in the main monastic activities, nor following her private Buddhist practice. Still, her main conversation partner, especially with regard to critical issues, remains Guanyin. She discusses everything first with Guanyin. Also, name recitation seems to form part of her daily life. Throughout every stage of her narration, Buddhism as well as other religious practices serve the purpose of fate management.

Development of Belief

Luo Peirong came into contact with Buddhism after a family conflict, which was resolved when she built up a new social circle by entering a Buddhist organisation. It seems that she immersed herself in the field both practically and intellectually: she read all of the monastery's abbot books, performed morning and evening recitation daily at home, and visited the monastery regularly. She took refuge with the abbot, as she felt understood there: "Her heart opened" (*xin you kai le* 心有開了) when she visited the monastery. Although she did not receive the bodhisattva precepts, she can argue with common Buddhist topoi the reasons for that: it is better not to receive the precepts while knowing them than receive them and not be able to keep them. Breaking precepts would mean generating new bad karma and the method of continuous repentance would not be the right way. This echoes the widespread arguments of Buddhist leaders in Taiwan (such as that of Ven. Jingkong 淨空). As she copes with her family's various hardships, Luo cannot maintain her Buddhist practice and sees her belief as challenged, as other religious practices proved more successful in curing her family members. Luo adapts to her husband's religious practices which she calls Daoist, although her overall framework for interpreting her situation remains Buddhist in nature–the argument for extinguishing bad karma prevails. Although not engaged as a Buddhist pracitioner, Luo's Buddhist vocabulary remained active at the time of the interview. Describing her present situation, she admits that, to read the master's books, she now has to be in "good mood".[74] She regrets her loss of Buddhism and prefers the Buddhist monastery's environment, even though Daoist practices have proven very powerful at certain times of her life.

74 (S6) Luo: But my mood has to be good, only then will I read. Like when my mood is not good, I cannot stand reading [laughs] I really cannot stand it [laughs] Like, these last couple of years, I have not read his books at all. (Orig.: (S6) Luo: 但是要我心情好的話才有看 像我心情不好我都看不下去 [laughs] 我真的看不下去 […, tw] 像我這幾年我都沒有看他的書.)

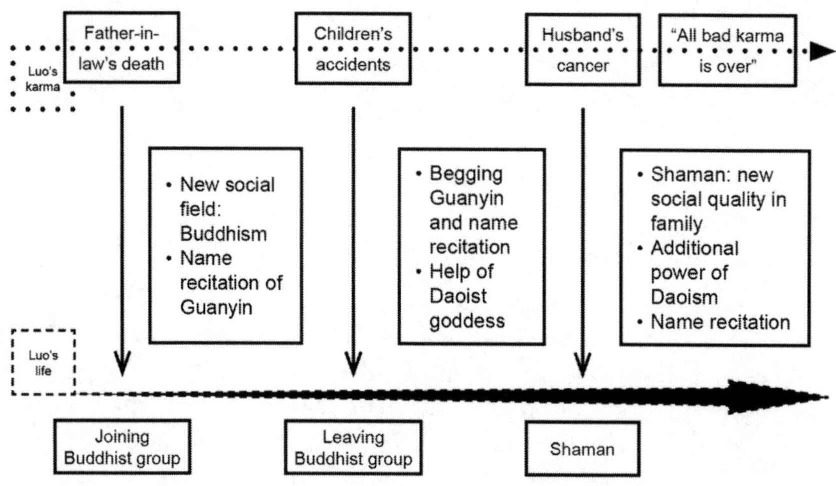

Figure 9: Development of Luo Peirong's belief in response to her family situation.

Role of Bodhisattva Guanyin

What remains constant in Luo's belief after the first phase of her engagement with Buddhism, and even intensifies it, is her close contact with Bodhisattva Guanyin. Luo recites the goddess' name constantly, especially during crises. She entreats her to help when her family members are injured or fall ill. She is engaged in dialogue with her both in everyday life and in dreams. These dialogues she imitates in a lively manner several times during the interview: she takes Guanyin to task, argues with her and questions her about the misery she is suffering. She tells Guanyin that she sees herself as an average woman who does not deserve such punishment, and she listens to Guanyin's answers. Guanyin not only answers her directly, but also through other people: a final explanation of her misfortune she perceives as coming from Guanyin through her husband in the hospital, which tells her that all bitterness is now over. Luo claims that Guanyin often appears in her dreams. Even when she first encountered the Daoist goddess, Guanyin led the way and they exchanged greetings. Luo interacted with Guanyin in her dreams, and in daily life she experiences her miraculous power. She consults Guanyin even before/instead of talking to her husband:

(S4) Interviewer: 我們繼續可以嗎 你有困難的時候 都會跟觀世音菩薩比較有關係對不對	(S4) Interviewer: Can we continue? When you are in difficulties, you will always be more in contact with Bodhisattva Guanyin, right?
Luo: 對 我都會跟觀世音菩薩講 我的內心實際內心話甚麼 甚至我先生我也都不會講	Luo: Right. I will always tell it to Bodhisattva Guanyin. My heart/ In fact what I

我都會問觀世音菩薩講

say in my heart/ Up to my husband I also will say nothing/ I will always ask Bodhisattva Guanyin.

Guanyin is, for Luo, a communication partner, on whom she can talk without restriction and with whom she can also argue. In this way, Luo might ponder on the events of daily life and these inner arguments may help to ease her stress, as we see her using Guanyin "to let off steam", which might have a harmonising effect upon her environment.

Luo's relationship with Guanyin is vividly depicted in her first, longer narration, in which she describes the days and weeks following her son's accident: after she heard the news, she instantly drove to the hospital. The next day, the physician told her the frightening news that he did not know whether her son would ever wake from his coma or whether he would be brain-damaged. She reacted to this news by reciting for days "the holy name of Bodhisattva Guanyin" (*Guanshiyin Pusa shenghao* 觀世音菩薩聖號). After spending a week at the hospital, she went home for a day and continued reciting at her home altar:

(S1) Luo: 一直求觀世音 但是我 那個 我的第六感很強 就是觀世音菩薩在 對 那我就跟觀世音菩薩 因為我一個禮拜回來 那時候我兒子還沒醒活來 那我就跟觀世音菩薩 就是講 就是我們講對 […] 我說 我進入佛教這麼久沒求過甚麼 那今天我兒子他醫生的宣佈 就是很不好的消息 但是我就跟觀世音菩薩講說 因為我那時候 第六感很很強的 我在講 觀世音菩薩都有在聽 我說 我 你既然 你是 我一個兒子 那我求觀世音菩薩你脫胎換骨的方式 在把我兒子帶回來 這樣那我就 我就一直唸觀世音菩薩 一直大悲咒那我就 我是這樣 就的說 因為 師父時常在開始 我以師父就開始這樣說 師父開始說佛法無邊 哈 醫學科學在怎麼發達 不如佛佛法無邊 那我現在就是觀世音菩薩 我要的甘露水 我要 *bagere* 水 [slurred] 那要你的 那求觀世音菩薩 你是 是 你給我這些東西 你賜我這些東西 我要大杯 要那個甘露水 要那個經典裡面有一些八功德水還有觀世音菩薩的甘露水 哈那觀世音菩薩賜給我

(S1) Luo: I continuously entreated Guanyin. But I/ That/ My sixth sense is very strong. That is, Bodhisattva Guanyin was there. Right. Na, so I with Bodhisattva Guanyin/ Because I came back after a week, at that time my son still had not woken up. Na, I spoke with Bodhisattva Guanyin, we just spoke with each other […] I said: I engaged in Buddhism for such a long time, and did not ask for anything. Na, today, my son, the announcement of his doctor. It was very bad news. But I said to Bodhisattva Guanyin/ Because at that time my sixth sense was very strong. I was talking, Bodhisattva Guanyin listened. I said. I/ You/ Since you are/ You are/ My only son/ Na, I entreated Bodhisattva Guanyin/ You [sc. use] the method of "taking out the embryo and exchanging the bones" [*tuotai huangu*, saying for "to cast off one's old self", "to be reborn", "to thoroughly remould oneself"]. Bring my son back! Like this. Na I just, I just continuously recited Bodhisattva Guanyin. Continuously the *Mantra of Great Compassion*. Na, I just/ I am like this, that means, the master often explained, I explained to the master in this way. The master said: The Buddha's dharma has no limits [BT]. Ha. However medicine

> and technology are developing. This is not like Buddha's dharma. Buddha's dharma has no limits. Na, I am now: Bodhisattva Guanyin, I want your Sweet Dew [BT; skt. *amṛta*] Water, I want *bagere* water [slurred], I want yours. So I entreated Bodhisattva Guanyin. You are/ are/ You give me these things, you grant me these things, I want a big cup, want that *Sweet Dew Water*, want this/ in the sūtras there is some *Eight Merits Water* [BT] and there is also Guanyin Sweet Dew Water. Ha. Na. Bodhisattva Guanyin granted it to me.

What follows is a narration about how a glass of water on the altar changed colour and how delighted Luo felt about that. She took the water to the hospital and gave it to her son to drink and, after three times drinking it, he regained consciousness.

The passage shows that Luo believes in Bodhisattva Guanyin as an existence whose presence can be experienced through a "sixth sense", a special ability of perception, which not everyone seems to possess. It also shows that Luo sees herself in a relationship of mutual benefit with Bodhisattva Guanyin. As she has never begged for anything before and has been interested in Buddhism for a long time, she supposes that she has a kind of huge deposit to which she can now resort by requesting a drastic change (reinforced by the saying "to take out the embryo and exchange the bones") in her son's physical condition. She describes in detail to Guanyin the situation, making clear to herself and Guanyin all of the available information about it, and accentuating the necessity to act. This mechanism of mutual benefit Luo shows in her relationship with Guanyin and, later, with any goddess, like Wangmu Niangniang. Characteristic is the fact that Luo sees the gods and Buddhas as having a duty to help her son, daughter and husband to recover, while she worries about the situation of others and quarrels with her personal bad fate. In this situation, again, karmic arguments come into play, helping her to accept her situation (see below).

Central to Luo's narration is a transformation miracle: the recitation of the *Mantra of Great Compassion* bestows on the water a healing quality. Luo knows several names for this water, such as "Sweet Dew Water" or "Eight Merits Water" (lit. for *ba gongde shui* 八功德水), the first of which she attributes to Guanyin and the second she has heard about through sūtras–possibly the *Amitābha Sūtra*, which is commonly recited in Taiwan and in which it is also mentioned.[75] Visiting Buddhist organisations all over Taiwan, one easily recognises the water bottles that are placed during recitations at the front of the recitation hall and taken home afterwards by the participants. The transformation of water through recitation is a widespread topos in Taiwanese Buddhist culture. In general, this water is not expected to change colour, but its positive powers are widely acknowledged. In Luo's case, the shaman interprets the change in the colour of the water as meaning that Bodhisattva Guanyin has put a fivefold medicine inside it, which would have initiated the healing.

Luo's abbot's Buddhist teaching, that Buddha's dharma is limitless and therefore she should not abandon hope of a recovery, she interprets as meaning that no miracle is impossible, while she waits for the power of Bodhisattva Guanyin to break the laws of nature or at least act against all medical probability. For Luo, it is important that the miracle is not only that a very improbable recovery occurred unexpectedly, but also that it took place because of the concrete, material interaction of Bodhisattva Guanyin.

Bodhisattva Guanyin remains Luo's only addressee during her son's illness. It seems that she de-socialises herself from her former Buddhist group and is alone with her belief in her tragic family situation. Later in life, when her husband falls ill, Luo also recites and entreats Bodhisattva Guanyin, but finds that she can no longer reach the goddess: "I continuously entreated Bodhisattva Guanyin without success" (*Wo yizhi qiu qiu Guanshiyin Pusa qiu bu dao* 我一直求求觀世音菩薩求不到). Finally, after Luo had also engaged the shaman and Wangmu Niangniang, her husband wrote on a tablet: "Everything is over now" (*yiqie dou guo qu le* 一切都過去了). She realises that this might be the answer of Bodhisattva Guanyin, meaning that every hardship is over and life from now on will be joyful, as there is no bad karma left.

With the shaman taking over responsibility for her husband's recovery, Luo gets back to a spiritual contact person.[76] At a time when the monastery's abbot has become famous and is increasingly inaccessible, and she can no longer attend her Buddhist group, the shaman comes to care about the situation, delivers a frame of interpretation and takes responsibility. He interprets the miracle and is directly accessible, even visiting Luo's home regularly, and creating an optimistic environment and stability which might also, from a medical perspective, be helpful for her husband's recovery. As is normal in popular belief, the shaman does not reject Luo's Buddhist belief, but includes

75 For a first explanation of *Bagongde* Water, see FBD (2000), 279 (entry "*bagongde shui* 八功德水").

76 For the role of a shaman, compare Shahar 1998, 171–219. The book exemplifies the medium cult dimension of the Jigong (Crazy Ji) figure and his appropriation by the monastic establishment, based on extensive fieldwork in Taiwan.

it even by interpreting it. Luo's understanding of Buddhism, centred on a mutual exchange, is clearly compatible with popular religious concepts. Even though she claims that she did not know anything about Wangmu Niangniang before she experienced her power, Luo naturally assumes that the new goddess is functioning in the same manner as Bodhisattva Guanyin.

How to Handle Bad Luck

Luo's concept of Buddhism is based on her understanding of karma. She states that, due to her knowledge about karma, she knows that she has to face her destiny and not flee it. Luo summarises this concisely as follows:

(S3) Luo: […] 因為如果沒有佛法 這幾年發生這麼事情 我真的/ 我就沒有辦法活下去 對 […] 這是我真的 我真的沒辦法再做下去 因為你就 因為你就會去了解說 阿可能我不到那一世 或是 或我該去還的 就是 所謂的甚麼 因緣果報 甚麼樣 我該去還 我還是去還它 逆境嘛 所謂的逆境 你知道嗎 對 所以你碰到逆境你不要去逃避它 你就是要去承受它 要去面對他 等逆境過的 人因為 來轉世 就是我帶業來的 那 這個業你要去消 你沒有消的話 你還還是就是一樣 帶業往生一樣	(S3) Luo: […] Because if I hadn't had the Buddha's dharma, these things that happened in recent years I really/ I just wouldn't have had a chance to continue living. Right. […] This is I really/ I really wouldn't have had a chance to go on again. Because you just/ Because you just will come to understand: "A, maybe I'm still not that far [or: maybe when I still was not in this world, sc. did something bad], or/ or I should repay it. That's what's called the result of karmic conditions [BT]. Like that. I alter it. I still go and pay it back. The adverse circumstances [partly BT] ma. The so-called adverse circumstances, you know? Right. So when you encounter adverse circumstances, you shouldn't flee them, you should accept them, should face them. When the adverse circumstances are over–because people turn to the next world, just I brought karma with me, na. This karma you should extinguish. If you don't extinguish it, you'll still/ still stay the same. It is like you take your karma with you when you die.

Understanding karma enables Luo to cope with her situation. On another occasion, she states that, due to Buddhism, she has "more energy" (*bijiao you liliang* 比較有力量). Accidents of fate can be controlled by the idea of karma: bad karma, in Luo's view, is bound to individuals and continues beyond death into their next life. Therefore, it is impossible to escape it. Accepting the concept itself and her current situation as a consequence of it, Luo can relinquish her sense of helplessness and perceives herself as an acting subject, managing her fate: she can make positive changes to it, and alter it by not fleeing but facing it. Coping with misery in everyday life becomes a question of salvation, providing a reason not only for the person to whom help is offered, but also for the helper, as he/she is "extinguishing (bad) karma" (*xiaoye*). Encountering "adverse circumstances", *nijing* 逆境–a term again possibly but not necessarily occurring in a Buddhist context–is therefore no reason to lose hope, but simply a sign of bad karma. Luo fails to question what encountering adverse circumstances actually means, but is, without deliberation, assumed when we examine her practice of entreating gods and Buddhas. Facing one's destiny means searching for a solution. For Luo, this does not mean, for example, using every medical means to cure her husband or learning about the medical details–the doctor's authority remains unquestioned. He is the only one whom she cites directly besides Guanyin during her narrations. To take matters into her own hands means, for Luo, involving the power of gods and Buddhas and handing her responsibility over to them and a shaman.

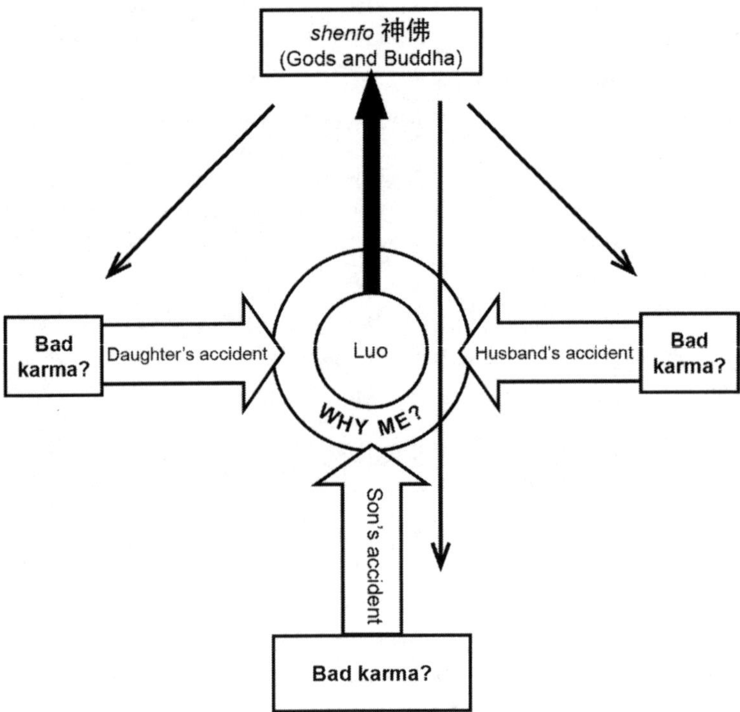

Figure 10: Luo Peirong praying for miraculous power–Entreating gods and Buddha to manage incidences.

Luo Peirong has vivid experience of the powers of "gods and Buddhas":

(S2) Luo: […; Her son regained consciousness.] 所以很奧妙 真的 這個佛法 你要/ 你要這個神佛/ 你要說沒有 他又有 他又有 他有一個/ tsä/ 你/你摸 摸不到 看看不到 但是他後面 有一個很強的力量 真的很奧妙 這個佛法真的很奧妙	(S2) Luo: […; Her son regained consciousness.] So very miraculous, really, this Buddha's dharma, you want/ you want these gods and Buddhas/ you want to say that they're not there, they are nevertheless there. They are nevertheless there. They have a/ tsä/ You/ You can't touch them, you can't see them, but behind they have a very strong power. Really very miraculous. This Buddha's dharma is really very miraculous

Luo repeats the sentence "You can't touch them, you can't see them, but behind they have a very strong power" four times during the interview, the content of which she never enlarges on further. She uses it after narrations and explanations to conclude and prove the miraculous powers of Bodhisattva Guanyin (three times) and finally of "gods and Buddhas" in general. Luo has acquired, through all three incidences within her family, vivid material-based experience of the power of gods and Buddhas.

*"One cannot reject Daoism"– Practising as a Buddho-Daoist (*Fodao shuangxiu *佛道雙修)*

Facing one's own karma means altering it. As Luo experiences the power of Guanyin and later of Wangmu Niangniang, she uses them to improve her situation. Within this encounter, she leaves the field of Buddhism and comes to venerate a Daoist goddess. This shift between two separate religions is a conscious one for her, although she emphasises that the division between Buddhism and Daoism is a recent phenomenon in Taiwan:

(S7) Luo: […] 對 甚麼拜拜 但是 不是 那時候沒有佛教 所以說 甚麼神 甚麼神 那時候沒有佛教 而是現在有佛教 才分佛教道教這樣子 […] 沒有那麼興旺 沒有那麼興旺 對 所以道教你也不能去忽略它 它確實 怎麼講 因為 我先進入佛教嗎 我是先進佛教 那後來這是這個因緣 這是我先生這個問題 才進入 這個道教 因為 我進入 那個 公廟 才去差不多一年多而已 剛開始我也不太習慣	(S7) Luo: […] right, whatever veneration. But it isn't/ At that time, there was no Buddhism, so one said this or that god. At that time, there was no Buddhism. And only now as there is Buddhism, do we separate between Buddhism and Daoism like that. […] It [i.e. Buddhism] was not so flourishing. It was not so flourishing. Right. So you also can't ignore Daoism. It in fact is/ How to say/ Because I first entered Buddhism ma. I first entered Buddhism. Na later this was this karmic connection. That's my husband, this problem. And only then I entered this

Daoism. Because since I entered that temple it is only about a little over a year ago. Right in the beginning, I was not really used to it.

Within this passage, Luo shows historical awareness. As she states that she came into contact with Daoism only recently, during her extreme difficulties, it seems that she has not been socialised via popular religious habits very intensively during her youth before she turned to Buddhism. She admits that she felt strange when she first came to learn about her husband's religious world, which is connected with Daoism. The passage sounds defensive, as if countering a fictive opponent–possibly the interviewer, whom she supposes to be only interested in her Buddhist belief, her friend, who knows her as a sincere Buddhist, or even her former Buddhist group members. She gives the impression that a Buddhist, in her understanding, would normally reject her veneration of a Daoist goddess, and she tries to convince her counterpart and maybe also herself by stating that she felt the same. Still, by now, she seems to be an expert in her new practice, and later presents herself clearly as also being into what she calls "Daoism":

(S8) Luo: 那我進去這一間廟 這個因緣也是從那裡起 你知道嗎 那時候 阿 我妹妹不是後來轉到[..., place in Taipeh county]嘛 哈在[..., place in Taipeh county] 哦 真的很奇怪 所以說 時間到了 因為在 我說真的 我剛才在說 佛教跟道教 真的息息相關 因為我在道教 進去道教 來這裡 真的我也了解蠻多的 我是覺得 某方面去學習 我也了解蠻多 因為 我接近道教 是從因緣來

(S8) Luo: Na, that I entered this one temple, this karmic connection is coming also from there, you know? At that time, a, my younger sister [i.e. her daughter] went afterwards to [..., place in Taipeh county] ma, right? Ha. In [..., place in Taipeh county] oh, really very strange. Therefore I say the time was ripe. Because when I tell the truth, I just said, Buddhism and Daoism are delicately interwoven. Because I in Daoism/ I entered Daoism up to here, really I also understand a lot. I think, one should learn some aspects, I also understand a lot, because I came into contact with Daoism for karmic reasons.

This sequence also provides Luo's main arguments for practising both Daoism and Buddhism: first, it is the Buddhist principle according to which she understands her life, karma, that led her from Buddhism to Daoism. It is actually Buddhism itself which justifies her contact with Daoism. Therefore, she changed her attitude slowly and, by the time of the interview, is convinced that one should learn broadly, as Buddhism and Daoism would be "delicately interwoven" (*xixi xiangguan*). What could this intimate connection imply? It has already been demonstrated that Luo applies equally the principle of mutual obligation and expects the same kind of miraculous help from a Daoist goddess as from Bodhisattva Guanyin.

The interconnectedness between Buddhism and Daoism Luo explains in detail in a further passage. Summing up her thoughts, one could interpret: Luo parallels the relationship between Buddhism and Daoism to that between Pure Land Buddhism (implying recitation), and Zen Buddhism (implying meditation). In her opinion, one must practise both together, because only if, in addition to one's personal meditation practice, one also recites sūtras, one can give something back to those to whom one is close in daily life [i.e. Bodhisattva Guanyin, for example]. If one does not recite and gives nothing back, one cannot extinguish any bad karma. Transferring the parallel to the relationship between Daoism to Buddhism, Daoism, to Luo, might parallel a kind of Pure Land, as it is closely involved in this mutual exchange process between humans and gods, and the reason for turning to Daoism in certain situations is that Buddhism is insufficiently strong. In Buddhism, one would not have a chance ("*zai fojiao nabian mei banfa* 在佛教那邊沒辦法") and the Daoist goddess is obviously seen as providing more power.[77]

Conclusion

Initially, we saw Luo Peirong struggling with a huge discrepancy. There was her former life, when she was a member of a Buddhist group, whose social field helped her to overcome her family problems and, in contrast, her recent situation: of her Buddhist belief and practice, only her attitude that one

77 Original passage: (S9) Luo: [...] If you want to practise, the broadest way is to practise both Chan and Pure Land. If you want/If you want to practise, you want to practise until everything is empty. If it is empty, then you practise until one/practise until one limitless world. A. If you want emptiness, you still have to recite. Only then will you have a chance to diminish. You have no chance like that. Only/ only sitting there, you have no chance to diminish. [...] You have to recite to give it back to God [/him/her]. We present it to God [/him/her]. In the Chan school, we just will not/ just will not disturb ourselves. Na, I feel, practising both Chan and Pure Land is just like practising both Buddhism and Daoism. My/ My thinking now is just both, Buddhism and Daoism. Because Daoism/ like we folks in general run into something, say/ We normally say/ Because I before/ Like I have some/ I have some movements, have some opinions, in Buddhism there is no chance. They have no chance. You understand. [She is getting very fast.] Friend: That is in the karma of that person. Luo: Right. A single person really has no chance [to change it, ?]. Therefore I say now: Practising both Buddhism and Daoism. Na, that is similar to practising both Chan and Pure Land. Therefore I say, it is delicately interwoven. [...] (Orig.: (S9) Luo: [...] 你要 修就是禪淨雙修最寬 你要 你要修的話 你要修到做下去整個都空 空的話 你就修到一個 修到一個無境界 阿 你要空的話 你還是要誦經才有辦法去消 你沒這樣辦法 只只有在那邊坐 你沒有辦法消 [...] 你就是要誦經回獻給祂[/他/她]嘛 我們獻給祂[/他/她] 我們在禪宗 才不會 才不會來打擾我們 那我是覺得 禪淨雙修 就像佛道雙修 我的我現在的想法 就是佛道雙 因為道教 像我們民間 一般碰到事情 說 我們平常是講 因為我之前 像我有些 有一些動作 有一些意義 在佛教那邊 沒辦法 他們沒辦法 你懂 [She is getting very fast.] Friend: 那是這個人的業裡 Luo: 對 個人真的沒辦法 *yu* 動[?] 所以我現在說 佛道雙修 那就是跟禪淨雙修 類似一樣 所我就是說 息息相關的 [...]).

has to face one's fate in order to extinguish bad karma remains, and she seems to be trying to recover and build new trust. The interview slowly reveals her family difficulties, which led her to abandon her Buddhist practice and involve into the "Daoist" practises her husband trusts in. While she does not mention any miracles when describing the first phase of her belief, Luo intensifies after the incidents in her family her relationship with Bodhisattva Guanyin, leaves her Buddhist community and develops a strong concept of mutual obligation to "gods and Buddhas". Although her situation appeared hopeless to her, miraculous healing occurs through experiencing the intervention of Guanyin and a Daoist goddess, which breaks the laws of nature. These miracles prove the power of these gods and Buddhas, as well as confirming Luo's belief in them. Luo compensates in her following phase for the loss of her social environment with an intense inner relationship with Bodhisattva Guanyin. This relieves her pressure as well as having a harmonising influence upon her environment. When her husband fell ill, a shaman became involved. His frequent presence at Luo's home alters the atmosphere within the family. Luo's search for meaning, her worries and fears are no longer answered within a separate community, but she finds a contact person within the family context itself. The situation appears to stabilise, as all family members are recovering and are psychologically accompanied by the shaman. Although Luo still prefers her former Buddhist environment, she takes pains to defend her transference to Daoism. She uses the Buddhist argument that karmic connection brought her into contact with Daoism and emphasises her expertise, focusing on the delicate interconnectedness between Buddhism and Daoism through her personally witnessed miraculous power of gods and Buddhas. Through Daoism even more strongly than through Buddhism, one is repaying the gods and Buddhas. Only through this does one extinguish bad karma–which seems to be similar to preventing future additional hardships.

A Comparison between Lin Yongfu and Luo Peirong

What does this analysis of Luo's belief reveal with regard to the different options for defining one's Buddhist belief in Taiwan? Are Luo's belief and practice ultimately fairly similar to those of Lin Yongfu? Both are from Taipeh County, from Taiwanese families and both consider themselves to be "Buddhist". Both see as central to their belief the veneration of "gods and Buddhas" (*shenfo*)–a term which insinuates that there is no categorical difference between the function of these two. This veneration or worship involves the concept of reciprocity, which assumes a relationship of mutual benefit between humans and gods or Buddhas/bodhisattvas. In both beliefs, concrete action stands central. Veneration and participation in the practitioners' community are important. They are not used to frequently reflect on their own belief and doctrinal considerations–maybe Luo is slightly more used to it, and both are hardly accessible for an interview. Doctrinal questions are the task of experts. Luo's attitudes are particularly clearly-oriented towards authority figures, such as the doctor, abbot, shaman, and, of course, especially Guanyin. For both Lin and Luo, the action of veneration is natural and unquestioned. Luo, when asked by the interviewer if she sees her Buddho-Daoist belief as something unique, replies that many of her friends at the monastery were also worshipping at common temples.[78] It appears to be very common in Taiwan to go to venerate/worship (*baibai*), as we already know from the statistics, and both Luo and Lin obviously see themselves as Buddhists while venerating gods (and ancestors). For Conventional Buddhists, we know, this is the norm, since 93.9% of them do so (TSCS 2004.2, v15a).

Still, Lin Yongfu and Luo Peirong are already outwardly in totally different situations. Of course, also, the challenge of the actual situation makes a difference: Lin's belief is not tested; his family situation is peaceful and harmonious. His only concern is the cheating behaviour of the temples–an issue which does not affect him directly. Luo is experiencing extreme hardship and fighting her bad fate. She visits the temple, like Lin, to entreat the gods for help and, like 5.1% of the Conventional Buddhists (see p. 88), Luo is searching for the help of a medium, in her case a shaman (*jitong*). These outer circumstances also have an influence on the actual role that Buddhist belief plays in their life: the action of *baibai* (veneration) functions within a different social frame. For Lin, it is an integral part of the family or temple's social field. The protection of the gods is, for him, natural and a consequence not only of worship but also of correct moral behaviour. The act of *baibai* is, for Luo, far more central to her belief, as she intends through it to oblige or even browbeat Guanyin and Wangmu Niangniang to break the laws of nature by performing miracles and healing her family members. The effectiveness of that veneration practice outside Buddhism is, for Luo, the main reason for her to leave her Buddhist practice, justifying it as a necessary consequence of her bad karma. Her relationship with gods and Buddhas makes a more mechanical, countable impression and it is an exclusive relationship in which her other family members are not necessarily involved.

In a crisis, initially, Lin Yongfu does not expect miracles and divine interaction, but the temple and its leaders to care materially for the community

78 (S10) Luo: Ei. That is all existing. At that time, I did not go to venerate this Daoism. But I heard it all: "I go there to venerate, [I] go there." It should all exist la. (Orig.: (S10) Luo: 欸 都有了 那時候我沒有去拜這個道教 但我都聽到 我去那邊拜拜 去那邊拜拜 去那邊 應該都有啦).

members, independently of any reward. Luo Peirong goes through several stages, the first of which is characterised, not by miracles, but by entering a new social circle and the abbot's personal care. Her transfer to Buddhism does not include her social environment. This has the advantage that the Buddhist field can serve as stress compensation and the disadvantage that the Buddhist community is inaccessible at times of extreme crisis, when Luo's family requires her whole attention. In the second phase, she therefore leaves the Buddhist community and enters an exclusive one to one relationship with Guanyin, expecting to experience the power of the bodhisattva through miracles rather than, for example, through a temple community. In the third phase, Luo establishes a relationship with a shaman, through which she again receives personal guidance, such as during the time when she joined the Buddhist organisation, but she can integrate this resource into her family environment. Still, her relationship with the shaman makes herself dependent, and might also run the risk of being cheated by the shaman. This parallels Lin's high sensibility towards the "cheating" temple managers: a defined payback, exploiting the one searching for help, is unacceptable. In contrast, he cherishes the fact that his community does not ask for anything from those in need, but helps them free of charge. In addition, Lin never built up two separate spheres: for him, his family not only joins in the home rituals, but even represents him at the temple if he cannot attend.

Abstracting the cases, Buddhism serves a different function for Luo Peirong and Lin Yongfu: Lin socialises via the religious field, which strengthens the links within his family as well as within the temple community, thus creating a mutual obligation among its members. The hardships of single people might be compensated for by this system of social safety. For Luo, Buddhism serves as a psychological aid. Literally, she states that, with her difficult destiny, she could see herself undergoing psychiatric treatment were it not for the help of Buddhism. Through Buddhism and Daoism, she attempts to manage her bad karma by asking for miracles using the popular system of worship and veneration, *baibai*. Her belief in Buddhism does not transform the widespread system of *baibai*, but is fastened and re-discovered even in her master's teachings: "Buddhism has no boundaries" in contrast to worldly science–this is the master's answer to her hardship. He adds that one can have hope even if medicine appears hopeless, as medicine can never provide an absolute description of the situation. Luo extends her interpretation: Bodhisattvas themselves can intervene in the situation and break the laws of nature in order to heal a patient. To enhance the intervention of bodhisattvas and gods, she exhaustively uses the system of *baibai* instead of developing a different view about the hardship itself.

While Lin Yongfu is concerned not only about himself but his thoughts are centred upon his family, Luo Peirong cares intensely about her family while also questioning her personal bad fate. Her behaviour seeks to extinguish and prevent further tragedy, and implicitly stresses her own suffering in the situation. Ancestors, whom we have noted are almost part of Lin's family, are of minor importance to Luo–she does not mention them. Probably, when asked on the TSCS questionnaire whether they follow a private spiritual practice, Lin would clearly say no, while Luo might agree. Luo's Buddhist practice separates her from rather than uniting her with her family: her husband is critical of it, while her children keep away from it. For Lin, his belief builds a nexus between all of his family members, especially between the different generations.

How far can Lin Yongfu and Luo Peirong be considered Buddhists, irrespective of the fact that they term themselves so? While Lin marks his beginning as a Buddhist with the carving of his statue, Luo sees herself as entering Buddhism via the initiation process that is commonly acknowledged by Buddhists, through taking refuge. Also, in terms of Buddhist vocabulary, Luo is highly informed. Although her language is grammatically and semantically simple, specialist Buddhist expressions emerge. As a consequence of the fact that he is relatively uniformed, Lin cannot recognise any conflict between Buddhism and Daoism. Luo, in contrast, repeats throughout the interview–initiated by the interviewer who wants to know how she found her way to "Buddhism"–why, as a Buddhist, she is following Daoist practices at present. Luo feels uncomfortable about Daoism, but fears to reject the veneration of Wangmu Niangniang as she sees herself in such a hopeless situation that she is deeply dependent on the "power" of the most powerful, who is Daoist in this case. In both cases, it is striking that the monastic community itself and the relationship to it play virtually no role. Lin does not even understand the question, and monastics simply do not exist in his social life. Luo is so deeply involved in her family's situation that she does not mention monastics despite the abbot featuring in her interview.

Summing up, Lin is integrated into a closed traditionally established functioning system of religious practice with highly social functions. He did not choose his belief freely, but grew up within it, and is deeply rooted in his tradition. His first step in re-naming his own culture as Buddhism has made no real impact upon his self-definition, and his international openness does not lead to a visible transformation of his mental concepts or practical behaviour. The complex system seems stable. Luo is living between competing systems, whose benefits she therefore can only partly enjoy. To rectify a combined practice of Buddhism and Daoism, she makes high intellectual efforts to construct a Buddhist metanarrative in order to harmonise the two. We can see that Luo is influenced by a process of differentiation, where new experiences with young Buddhist institutions lead her to an awareness that Buddhism can go beyond the veneration of Guanyin in a popular religious context. Luo recognises the differences between Daoism and Buddhism and would perhaps even redefine herself as a Buddho-Daoist on the questionnaire (53/1881: 2.8 % of the population, TSCS 2004.2, v15b). The beliefs and practices of people in Taiwan are in transition. Luo created, by joining a Young Buddhist Organisation, new social spaces for herself, but these were less stable than a well-established Daoist or popular religious system might be. Her transition to Buddhism excluded her family. In consequence, she falls back upon a–reduced–traditional system, re-interpreting veneration as an act of getting gods under her control, leaving out the moral implications and the full social immersion, but concentrating in her pain on miracles. Later, she fully re-integrates herself into a Daoist or popular religious shamanistic practice, which is culturally well-established and fully-fledged, providing ideological stability and social coherence in times of hardship. A Buddhist organisation in Taiwan created a new choice for Luo, meeting the needs of her family for stress compensation. Socially, this organisation could not integrate Luo's family, and, ideologically, the organisation did not transform Luo's concept of veneration and worship, *baibai*. In contrast, within her Buddhist group, she finds that many of her colleagues worship various gods simultaneously. Although she enjoys her new environment and the knowledge she gains there, her new way of life does not prove in a crisis: the abbot, who is responsible for her guidance, becomes unavailable and, once the crisis starts, she does not have time to meet her group. As her social circle dies away and her personal guidance disappears, Luo's way back to popular religion starts, with painful legitimisation efforts. She admits that she would now have to be in a "good mood" to read the master's books and, recently, would be unable to read them. Quarrelling with her fate, the master's books, which contain Buddhist philosophical explanations for understanding human life, might feel like mockery and be like adding insult to injury. Luo remains, throughout the interview, caught within her pain.

Buddhist organisations develop their networks in urban areas. Their density is highest in the metropolitan area of Taipeh. In this environment, it is more likely that Luo would come into contact with Buddhist groups, attend regular activities and develop a specialised belief. More intense involvement has consequences: what for Lin remains a carefree re-naming of his own tradition becomes for Luo a painful re-interpretation process of her traditional culture.

7.3 Cai Chenhao– Member of a Long-established Lay Buddhist Community

While Lin Yongfu was well socialised in a pseudo-Buddhist environment and Luo Peirong was unable to socialise herself successfully in a new Buddhist movement but drifted into the retributionary veneration behaviour of solitary fate management, we see in Cai Chenhao 蔡宸豪 (male, age about 30) someone who is well-integrated into a traditional Buddhist lay community–one with a locally fixed centre that creates even more intense social cohesion than Lin's temple. The kind of "Lotus Society" (*lianshe* 蓮社) in which Cai participates does not seem to be becoming increasingly attractive to the masses over the last few decades, but Cai, as a young single man, integrates fully into his community. His whole life he defines according to his conscious "choice" (*xuanze* 選擇) to be a Buddhist lay person. What self-concept underlies this young man's choice to identify so closely with his community? What are his motivation, beliefs and practice in the light of the two previous cases? Does, finally, his option of living a lay Buddhist life make him structurally different from them?

Cai Chenhao is a single who after his studies in Taipeh has recently moved into a dormitory in his community. He comes from a Taiwanese family from a city in central Taiwan. The community in which he now lives is located in a different city, but still in central Taiwan. After leaving high school, where he first came into contact with the Buddhist lay association to which he now belongs, he attended university in Taipeh and obtained a B.A. and then an M.A. in religious studies. While doing his M.A., he also participated in classes held by his community. After finishing his M.A., he started working formally in the community, helping with the community magazine. Founded in the 1950s by a mainland Buddhist intellectual refugee, the interviewer undertook a day trip to the well known traditional lay Buddhist community. Cai felt, since a friend had introduced them, obliged to act as her guide. When she finally requested an interview with him, he agreed, after enquiring about its purpose. Although he did not appear very enthusiastic about it, he felt that researching lay Buddhism in Taiwan was worthwhile and wished to support it. For the interview, he chose the community's exhibition hall. The sound of films and music could be heard in the background. A woman was overseeing the exhibition hall, preparing tea for the guests. She came over from time to time to refill our cups. The interview took place out of earshot of anybody else, but the atmosphere remains the community's public hall. While this might lead the interviewee to talk less personally and more as a representative of his community, it also provides him with a safe frame in which he does not have to expose himself and in which he may feel more comfortable about talking to a foreign female of about his own age. Before the formal interview began, Cai Chenhao appeared restrained, fearing that he would be asked too many questions. He seemed unsure about the conceptual freestyle of the interview, as it seemed very unusual to him.

The interview took place on a weekday afternoon in March 2005. It lasted about a hour and was interrupted once by the interviewee's friend, who had heard that the interviewer was coming. As this person was short of time and left after a brief conversation, the interview continued.

Introductory Sequence Analysis

The introductory stimulus of the interview posed a question about how Cai Chenhao first became involved with Buddhism and what he would say about its development. Cai began:

(1) Cai: 應該就是我們高中的時候有/ 我們學校有一個社團 它就是在介紹佛教 就是一個佛學社團 那, 我就是有參加這個社團 所以說/ 就是開始接觸佛教 那就是老師有上一些課 然後就開始接觸佛法觀念. 那, 開始是這樣子 [b]	(1) Cai: It should just be, when we were in high school, there was/ our school had a club. It was just introducing Buddhism. It just was a "Learning-Buddhism-Club". Na, I just joined this club. So/ I just came into contact with Buddhism. Na, the teacher just gave some lessons, then I just started to come into contact with Buddhist thinking. Na, the beginning was like that [b].

Within this first sequence, Cai Chenhao gives an extremely rough, brief summary of his introduction to Buddhism. He starts with "It should just be"–and seems to speculate about his own past. Perhaps because his introduction to Buddhism was such a long time ago and being a Buddhist is so natural to him that he has almost forgotten how it began. At least, he does not seem to talk about it very often. Beginning with an assumption also leaves him the freedom to change his story later. It could be that Cai is primarily interested in satisfying the interviewer with his response and less interested in telling his story. Also, the particle "*jiushi*" (often not required to be translated, here always as "just") supports his desire to tell a normal, unproblematic story. The formulation "just" (*jiushi*) is inflationary, being repeated in nearly every semantic unit–a total of six times here. The following sentences describe a situation which is free from any personal involvement. The first content-wise information we receive from Cai is his reference to the time when "we" were going to high school. Recalling his school days, Cai sees himself as part of a group. Buddhism is here a way of socialising in a peer group. His family–who also could be the main transmitter of cultural and religious socialisation–is not mentioned at this point. The implicit group orientation remains central in the following: his school ran a Buddhist club–something which the two previous interviewees, being a generation older, did not mention–which he joined. A teacher taught "some lessons" and he learnt about Buddhist doctrine. His introduction to Buddhism is constructed as an intellectual event. Buddhist "thinking" can be taught and is accepted by the student without any apparent problem. Cai depicts his initial contact as a constellation of facts and the events that took place, without mentioning his own involvement or any inner process with regard to Buddhism. His introduction to Buddhism appears to have taken place during his late adolescence and is described as a happy accidental event, in which Cai does not play any active role. As his personal motivation to join the group remains–perhaps purposefully–completely hidden, the interviewer tries to probe more deeply:

(2) Interviewer: 其實, 為甚麼對佛教有興趣?	(2) Interviewer: Why in fact were you interested in Buddhism?
(3) Cai: 為甚麼對佛教有興趣呢. 阿. 應該就是小時候 有看一些/ 自己順便想看一些佛教的東西 對阿 就是覺得蠻有趣的. 所以說高中的時候參加那個社團/ [b]	(3) Cai: Why was I interested in Buddhism? A. It should be when I was small, that I saw some/ I myself liked to see casually some Buddhist stuff. Right a. So I just thought it's very interesting. So I participated during high school that club/ [b]
(4) Interviewer: 有怎麼樣有趣的?	(4) Interviewer: In how far were you interested?
(5) Cai: 不曉得. 就是/ 就是/ 看到一些佛教經典, 就拿了 看一看. 阿.	(5) Cai: I don't know. It's just/ it's just/ I saw some Buddhist sūtras, and took them to read. A.
(6) Interviewer: ㄇ.	(6) Interviewer: M.
(7) Cai: 或是聽到某一些佛教的想法或觀點. 就是會注意一下那個. A.	(7) Cai: Or if I heard any Buddhist thoughts or attitudes. I just paid attention to them. A.

Cai Chenhao continues his dry narration which might constitute a compromise between complying with the interview but not exposing himself too much either. First, he repeats the question to himself as if considering how to answer it. Certainly, the question about why he became interested in Buddhism does not lead to enthusiastic story-telling on his side. He takes a step backwards in his life into his childhood–again introducing through the tentative prephase "*yinggai jiushi* 應該就是" (It should just be)–and talks about himself as before: he passively came across some undefined Buddhist "*dongxi* 東西" (stuff, things) and became interested in it. The concrete situation is suppressed. He does not describe any details, which could have led to his particular interest in Buddhist books. Still, he exhibits no frustration when asked a second time about how interested he was. He simply admits that he does not know and tries to explain his interest again by replacing Buddhist "stuff" with Buddhist "*jingdian* 經典" (canonical scriptures, sūtras). As the interviewer still appears dissatisfied, he adds that he heard about some Buddhist "*xiangfa huo guandian* 想法或觀點" (thoughts or attitudes). The fact that neither the reading nor the hearing is content-specific, and might even be exchangeable ("or"), leaves the auditor with the impression that he simply "*zhuyi* 注意" (paid attention) to anything Buddhist he came across, besides the frame of the group to which he belonged. This attention appears as if naturally arising–reading Buddhist sūtras and hearing Buddhist thoughts are in general two well-established narrative patterns for people's introduction to Buddhism. It remains unclear whether this is due to the interviewee, who is by his nature interested in Buddhism, or Buddhism, to which, in his view, anyone would feel attracted on reading or hearing about it.

Structural Hypothesis

It is difficult to draw a preliminary conclusion from this early interaction. Cai Chenhao demonstrates his situational managerial skills, confronting the interviewer with a minimal solution. He neither refuses the interview nor responds to the questions openly, taking instead the path of least resistance. His narration is based on facts and actions, and fails to deliver inner insights. The habitus of a strong group orientation can be seen in his youth as well as through his will to present the community in a positive light without becoming involved himself or mentioning his personal engagement or commitment. Cai is "paying attention" to what he encounters and one might even get the impression that his present life in his Buddhist community is a result of his habit of integrating himself into a group rather than due to his personal development. The non-informative linguistic style may be attributed to several reasons: perhaps Cai does not know how to add content to his answers because being a Buddhist is so self-evident to him that he cannot remember how it started, or because his Buddhist engagement is based on pragmatic and social reasons. On the other hand, the motivation underlying his engagement could also be more severe so that Cai feels unable to discuss it during the interview.

Final Sequence in Comparison

With the interviewee following his minimalistic style, the interview quickly proceeds to a discussion of his past and then present life as a Buddhist, describing the community and then tackling more abstract questions like the relationship between lay people and monastics. After his friend's interruption, the interview proceeds, ending with a variation of the author's initial question about why Cai finally would define himself as a Buddhist. Here, Cai again mentions his youth and, although the whole scenario remains highly abstract, he provides a far more detailed description about his relationship with Buddhism:

(S12) Cai: 阿 阿 阿 這應該說 阿 就是自己個人的重點.因為我小時後聽過這種 就是自己關於這種生死的問題. 然後我覺得在我	(S12) Cai: A. A. A. One should say. A. This's just my own personal focus. Because when I was small, I heard this kind

接觸過這麼多宗教的想法之後 我覺得 佛法它是我比較接受的. 佛教的講法是比較可以說服我阿.	of/ I just myself paid attention to these kinds of life-and-death questions. Then, I think, after I came into contact with the thinking of so many religions, I think, Buddha's dharma is, what I can pretty well accept. The statements of Buddha's dharma can pretty well convince me a.

The whole interview was meant to be about Cai's "*ziji geren de zhongdian* 自己個人的重點" (personal focus) but, even at the end of it, he finds it necessary to highlight that he is making a personal statement. As he works during the day as a representative of his community, he feels uneasy about changing to a personal narration within the interview, and bears the positive representation of his community in mind. Again, he starts talking about his childhood, using the same formulation as at the beginning–this time without inserting the formulation "it should just be". The memory seems to be less constructed by now, as he does not say in general that he liked to see "some Buddhist stuff" or "sūtras" or "heard some Buddhist thinking", but corrects himself: he "*tingguo* 聽過" (heard) something but, before naming it, he starts downplaying it like before: "*jiushi ziji guanyü zhezhong shengsi de wenti* 就是自己關於這種生死的問題"–he was "just by himself paying attention to these kinds of life-and-death questions". The scenario of a child pondering questions of life and death is a description of a grown-up in retrospective. The child's language itself at that point of encountering "questions of life and death" might be far more experience-centred and concrete. One would expect less an abstract occupation with a philosophical question than we would expect children to ask concrete questions while experiencing angst directly, like someone close to them dying or falling ill. Cai's formulation might be a hint that he is highly abstracting what happened in his youth. Still, whatever events occurred, it seems that they initiated his search for life orientation, which led to him focusing on religious studies and undertaking a comparative reflection of religions. The result was that Cai "*jieshou* 接受" (accepted) Buddha's dharma", as it "*shuofu* 說服" (convinced) him. This "convincing" he explains as follows:

(S13) Interviewer: 怎麼樣的說服?	(S13) Interviewer: Convinces you in what way?
Cai: 就是佛教講這一套輪迴的觀念阿就是可以透過修行然後跳出這個輪迴 我覺得這是佛法這樣子的觀念我覺得蠻受用的.	Cai: Buddhism just talks about this idea of rebirth a. That just is, one can practise thoroughly and then jump out of this rebirth. I think this Buddha's dharma, this kind of idea, I think, is full of benefit.
Interviewer: 是幫你理解世界	Interviewer: It helps you to understand the world?
Cai: 對對對對. 它有幫助我理解有關生死的問題.	Cai: Yes, yes, yes, yes. It helped me to understand questions of life and death.

Cai summarises the basic concepts of Buddhism–the idea of rebirth and how to escape it through practice. He again notes that these ideas helped him with "life-and-death questions". Cai might have some clear event in his mind which he fails to explain further. Still, Buddhism in this context and probably also later in his life is "*shouyong* 受用", full of benefit and practicably applicable. He goes on to explain how far his understanding actually helps:

(S15) Cai: 理解有甚麼樣的幫助. 因為. 就是我理解佛法這樣的觀念之後 我知道應該怎麼做. 對阿, 因為就是我們修行到佛法這樣的觀念之後它是我說可以怎麼做怎麼做 而我自己有去做之後 覺得真的有改變這樣子.	(S15) Cai: In how far this understanding helps. Because. Just after I understood these kinds of ideas, this Buddha's dharma, I knew, how I had to do it. Right a. Because just after we practised until this kind of idea, Buddha's dharma, it told me how to do it, how to do it. And after I'd done it myself, I think it really has changed, like this.
Interviewer: 有怎麼樣改變?	Interviewer: How has it changed?
Cai: 比如說想 就是透過一些 比如像我唸佛 我們家唸佛, 會幫我們的心情比較平穩.	Cai: For example, like, just thoroughly going through some/ For example, like, I do name recitation, my family does name recitation, this'll help our heart to be peaceful and stable.
Interviewer: 平穩	Interviewer: Peaceful and stable
Cai: [...] 或者一方面就是說 阿 讓他就唸佛幫助自己就是解決人際關係啦. 因為就是我們在講說 透過唸佛 如果說你可以把這個唸佛的好處然後回向給別人的話 阿 你跟別人的關係就會好一點. [b]	Cai: [...] Or one aspect is just, let him/her do name recitation, that will help him-/herself and this just solves interpersonal relations la. Because we say: Thoroughly reciting Buddha's name/ If you can take advantage of this name recitation and then give it back to other people, then your relationships with other people'll be slightly better. [b]

The emphasis of the first passage clearly lies on action–Buddha's dharma enables Cai to act. What exactly can be done is unclear, but it changes something. In the second passage, he explains this change, using his family as an example: they perform name recitation, like him, and that makes their heart "*pingwen* 平穩"–peaceful, stable, or balanced. Interpersonal relationships improve, so it is possible that this experience, of name recitation solving family problems, possibly even those connected to life and death, forms the basis of Cai's firm belief and consequent engagement. It is reasonable that he finds Buddhism especially convincing, because of the successful role it has played over the years in his daily life, especially in his close relationships, like that with his family. Therefore, his final statement in the interview is highly consequent:

(S16) Interviewer: 你覺得我們還有甚麼我們沒有提到的你還想說的?

Cai: 想說的其實就是 就一個居士而言阿. 阿. 一個居士選擇作一個居士 阿. 來作他就是 就是 一個居士要作成為一個居士有他的想法跟理由. 那是說 像我 因為覺得 這樣的方式蠻適合我的. 對阿. 因為 阿 我可以這樣子一方面就是 學習佛法觀念. 然後一方面也可以 就是很盡責的在我世俗方面的東西阿. 阿. 因為就是像我們 我如果選擇在家的生活我可以繼續 可以繼續孝順父母然後跟 跟一些就是 應該怎麼講 阿 跟出家生活比起來 就是會更/ 比較多的時間可以在自己世俗方面一些人際關係或者工作方面可以可以多盡心盡力這樣子.

(S16) Interviewer: Do you think there's anything which we haven't covered now that you'd like to say?
Cai: What I'd like to say, in fact, is just, just concerning a Buddhist lay person a. A. A lay chooses to become a lay a. Becoming he just/ just/ When a lay wants to become a lay, he has his ideas and reasons. That means like me/ because I think, this kind of method suits me very well. Right a. Because a, I can this, on the one hand, just learn the ideas of Buddha's dharma. Then, on the other hand, I can also just with full responsibility be with the things in my daily situations a. A. Because just like us, if I choose a life at home, I can continue, can continue to be filial to my parents, then with/ with some/ just/ How should I say that? A. In comparison, with a life leaving home, it's just more/ pretty much time I can spend on my own daily situations, on some interpersonal relationships or work situations. I can/ I can more [sc. engage] with my whole heart and energy, like that.

Interviewer: 很好.
Cai: 大概的意思是這樣.

Interviewer: Very good.
Cai: My view is approximately like this.

Being a lay is a conscious choice for Cai, because Buddhism is a means for him to change his daily life, and engage fully with and change his family, his other relationships and his work environment positively. Cai is pragmatic in the basic sense of the word–his interest is to master his daily life, to be able to take action (gr. "*pragma*") within it.

In the sense of pragmatic life-mastery also, the initial interview sequence becomes less ambiguous: as his belief is situated in his experience, how it changes his environment, his narrations are focused on action. Also, Cai probably regards the interview itself as an action in which his Buddhist practice proves, through a stable and peaceful relationship, that he is loyal to his Buddhist community and in principle accessible to an external interviewer. What also could be described as the path of least resistance seems also to be a sensitive and wise balancing of the events unfolding in his own life, the stabilising and important function of his community within this life, and of a direct interviewer of curious innocence. Cai surely recalls the conflicts of his youth, but abstracts them to a level where he feels that they might be sufficient to illustrate his convictions–but not that open that they could endanger his successful integration into his community.

Additional Markers of his Religiosity

Through a comparison of the first and last sequence, Cai's pragmatic life mastery through the means of Buddhism becomes clearer and his life orientation unfolds in three dimensions–his high doctrinal informedness and obligation, his commitment to his group and the concrete interview, through his presentation of stylised, exemplary answers.

Cai's informedness and obligation to Buddhism constantly underlie the interview: he is the only member of his family to have become a Buddhist, and is aware of his formal belonging by having taken refuge: "I have taken refuge, so I count as a Buddhist" (*Wo guiyi guo le, suozi suan shi fojiao tu* 我皈依過了 所以算是佛教徒), he states explicitly. He tries his best to adhere to the five precepts as well as the bodhisattva precepts, and so has been a vegetarian since university. He also tries to protect life within his daily life; for example, by not killing mosquitoes. Never having taken refuge with any other master than that of his community, he participates in the morning and evening chanting and deeply embraces name recitation. Whenever he has time, he participates in the community's activities and ceremonies. While studying for his M.A., he also participated in courses there. Through this, he not only explored its belief in detail intellectually but also seems to have experienced its quality and power at a deep level. He expresses this through describing miracles that occurred during deathbed recitations of which he has heard, believing in which he feels increases his "trust" (*xinxin* 信心). Through his constant and integrated engagement, he became an esteemed member of his community and, as a consequence, after completing his studies, began working as an editor of his community's magazine.

His pragmatic life-orientation is illustrated by his commitment to his community. He identifies with it, holding an inside-outside perspective, when stating that his belief is not the same as that of normal people outside ("*Wo zai xuexi zhe ge fofa zhi hou, jiu shi/ jiu shi you hen duo guannian jiu hui gen/ gen waimian yiban ren bu tai yiyang* 我在學習這個佛法之後就是/ 就是有很多觀念就會跟/ 跟外面一般人不太一樣"). He does not ignore other communities and their beliefs but likes to be informed about them, provided that he does not start to engage in any spiritual practice which is unrelated to his community. His longing to integrate with it as much as possible is clear from his efforts to participate in every activity of his community. Still, he seems to maintain a very sensitive balance throughout the interview, which can be exemplified by two formulations that he uses regularly and which mark his linguistic style: "*jinliang* 儘量" and "*ou'er* 偶爾". He "tries as far as possible" (*jinliang*) to follow the lay precepts, adhere to bodhisattva precepts, and participate in his community's activities, but "occasionally" (*ou'er*) the community holds releasing life activities, and he "often occasionally just tries as far as possible to participate them" (*Na jiu shi fangsheng pingchang ou'er jiushi hui jinliang qu* 那就是放生平常偶爾就是會儘量去). "Occasionally", he participates in monthly, seven day recitations ("*foqi* 佛七") and has "occasionally" heard during his studies in the community of other followers' spiritual experiences. He visits other communities "occasionally" and, during the evening recitation, they "occasionally" also recite a sūtra.

Cai exhibits conservative behaviour (what he calls "*baozhi* 保值"), while being at the same time highly flexible and integrating smoothly into his community. His harmonious relationship with everyone–his family, friends and especially community–seems to guide his actions and act as his *Handlungsmaxime*. Although he seldomly applies karmic argumentations, Cai mentions at one point that he sees himself as part of the community and as having taken refuge with his master merely due to a "karmic chance" rather than because of a conscious decision or choice:

(S1) Interviewer: 為甚麼選那個 [..., abbot F] 法師皈依?
Cai: 因為我開始接觸佛教就在這邊. 然後那個時候剛好就是[..., master F] 法師就在這邊有/有/ 有開那個 要皈依的那個法會. 這樣子. 所以剛好有那個機緣, 就像說來這邊皈依那位師父這樣子.

(S1) Interviewer: Why did you choose to take refuge with the Master [..., master F]?
Cai: Because I made my first contact with Buddhism there. Then, just at that time, it was only the Master [..., master F], just in that place having/ having/ having opened that/ that dharma assembly, if one wants to take refuge. Like this. So there was right at that time that lucky[/karmic] chance, meaning just that one can go there and take refuge with this master, like this.

Cai takes part in group-establishing processes, while playing down his personal doctrinal convictions. His Buddhist conviction seems to be best expressed in his final statement: Buddhism enables people to act better and improves their relationships. This is central to Cai's belief as he presents it–which includes a pragmatic orientation, a sincere obligation towards practice and a strong group orientation.

All of his other statements throughout the interview are in some way ideal, exemplary answers that one might expect from a traditional Buddhist lay practitioner who is representing his community. The lay-monastic-relationship he defines, for example, as monastics being the real practitioners who are responsible for their supporters. Lay people he describes as secondary and respectful of monastics, from whom they receive spiritual guidance. When questioned about his hopes for his own future as a Buddhist, Cai answers:

(S10) Cai: 對自己的未來方面, 希望能夠終期一生 都護持佛法可以在這方面多學一點, 多學一點. 因為佛教的經典很多道理很深.	(S10) Cai: In respect of my own future, I hope I can throughout my whole life always protect Buddha's dharma and learn a little more in this respect, because Buddhist sūtras make lots of sense and are very deep.

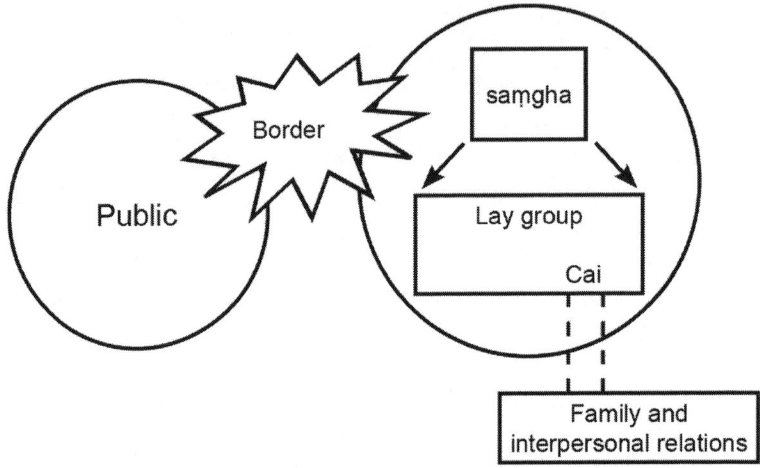

Figure 11: Cai Chenhao's view of society–Being a lay Buddhist through a conscious choice.

Conclusion

Cai Chenhao has made a conscious choice to live as a Buddhist lay person. This implies, for him, being part of the lay Buddhist community with which he identifies. His personal reasons for this close engagement remain concealed, while it is clear that his Buddhist practice as well as his integration into the group successfully solve this problem, not only replacing his primary socialisation but also improving his original relationships. Cai regards Buddhism as enabling him to lead a satisfying social life. Insofar as Buddhism serves this function, his choice to be a lay Buddhist appears reasonable, displaying his general pragmatic orientation. He is seriously devoted to Buddhist doctrine and his narration reveals a deep experiential dimension of personal and private religiosity within Pure Land Buddhism and the framework of name recitation. His close identification with his community leads Cai to embrace society but also to build up an exclusivistic self-definition.

Comparisons

Linking Cai Chenhao's case to the previous statistical investigations, a couple of observations can be made: Cai uses the term "karma" once during the interview. Karmic retribution is a widespread topos of belief in Taiwan, acknowledged by about three quarters of the population. Cai uses this term only in the context of his choice of community. Besides its direct usage as an argument, it also enables Cai to avoid making a qualitative comparison and disqualify other Buddhist organisations. Still, in his self-concept as a lay person, Cai speaks of his conscious "choice" not to join the monastic community. He is knowledgeable about Buddhist doctrine and aware of his formal belonging by having taken refuge (only 14.7% of Conventional Buddhists have done so). He would certainly regard himself as a highly-dedicated, devout believer. Like most people (93.9% of Conventional Buddhists), he venerates his ancestors. Although he does not state so explicitly, one can assume that the practice of name recitation also forms part of his personal spiritual practice in addition to the group recitations he attends. He would certainly consider himself to be a convert, as he clearly recognises himself as distinct from his popular religion-oriented family. Cai has started, through his Buddhist engagement, to transform his family environment: he mentions how his family relations have improved due to his practice and that his family now also engages in name recitation. Can one still regard Cai as a Conventional Buddhist? Unlike the majority, he neither visits temples or shrines, nor makes any reference to "*baibai*" (veneration). The differential criterion for Conventional Buddhists was an attachment to a Buddhist school. What response would Cai have selected here? Perhaps he would even have taken his community's central practice as his school affiliation and called himself a "Pure Land Buddhist" but, for him, this certainly would be a secondary category. His primary identification is with his local community.

As noted briefly above, Cai's community is a good example of the first wave of Buddhist revival in Taiwan after the Second World War. Together with the refugees from the mainland, there also arrived Buddhist intellectuals, including the founder of Cai's community. The community started in the 1950s and still had less than 1000 members by 2005. It owns several houses on a street in a large town in central Taiwan. In addition to their recitation hall, they also, for example, run an orphanage, hospital, old people's home, and library. Although the community is influential all over the island, they mainly function locally. The intention was to provide a local community for Buddhist and also traditional Chinese education and, at the same time, build up a social network and functioning social community.[79] Cai joined the group from outside, which might indicate the organisation's changing orientation

79 On the role of Buddhism in Taiwan after World War II, see Günzel (1998), 27 ff. On the historical development of this kind of community, see ter Haar (1992), who also describes in detail the engagement of the Lotus Societies in society. While beyond the scope of this book, the phenomenon of the Lotus Societies in East Asia would be an interesting topic for further research.

over the past few decades as, due to its declining membership, it is seeking to delocalise and attract followers from outside. Still, in Cai, we witness a successful socialisation into a traditional Buddhist community. This immersion into the community and integration into the social network that it provides make it possible to liken Cai Chenhao's situation with that of Lin Yongfu, since the former's Buddhist lay community appears to be "conventional" in providing a social-functional parallel to the temple community. Both communities are "traditional" in the sense that they are locally bound and provide a socially complex net, which will buffer their members' hardships. Cai's Buddhist community makes, in that respect, an even more differentiated and reliable impression than the temple community and could be seen as a successful local substitute for the popular religious system. Communities like that of Cai are usually endangered by the processes of urbanisation and modernisation, as local, closed communities tend to dissolve once people's mobility increases and their interests become more specialised. As soon as individuals start to choose their own lifestyle, it is plausible that highly differentiated offers will attract more attention than inclusivistic communities. The new Buddhist monastic organisations attempt to cater for these newly arising niches and succeed in attracting many followers, although we can see in Luo Peirong's case that they do not provide a reliable social network for all, and that famous abbots and female group activities that are suddenly withdrawn and have little connection with their adherents' daily life do not always provide a sound basis for a stable belief. Lin and Cai's communities create boundaries and strengthen the nexus between the family members. The involvement of every generation of the family is even stronger in the case of the temple community, but even Cai states how his family relations improved due to his new practice of name recitation, in which his family seems to participate. Cai might face a problem regarding his family bonds in future, as his community is designed for families that live together within it but, during the interview, he tries to avoid discussing issues connected to his family.

The replacement of popular religion through Buddhism seems complete: Cai Chenhao neither speaks of veneration (*baibai*) nor refers to any popular religious, mechanistic bargaining with gods and Buddhas. There is no mention of a do-ut-des-type formulation during the interview. Cai is accustomed to reflection, but concrete actions and spiritual practices are central for him. Like Luo Peirong, Cai discusses mysterious experiences but, in contrast to her, he sees them as strengthening his belief in general and does not embed them functionally within the context of fate management. They are not proving the power of gods and Buddhas nor competing with the laws of nature, but they incidentally illustrate the positive effects of deathbed recitations. Also, Cai does not imply the concept of "extinguishing bad karma", as does Luo Peirong, but emphasises the positive social effect of behaving in harmony with the situation. The idea of karma is here less connected to a system of punishment through various hardships, but seen positively as the range of opportunities that people encounter. The main parallel between Cai and Luo seems to be their shared emphasis on name recitation. While Luo establishes an exclusivistic and solitary relationship with Bodhisattva Guanyin through name recitation, Cai improves his social relationships through recitation. He usually recites with his community and probably also in private. Through this, he combines the psychological benefit of the practice with its social factors within a consistent system. To conclude, Cai's case indicates that a traditional lay Buddhist community with strong local boundaries and an intense educational programme has successfully replaced a popular religious community. Its member is able to express his belief in Buddhist terms without intermingling it with popular religious concepts. This successful replacement cannot be seen on the level of the religious self-definition of the individual alone but also in the reliable, dense social network that this community provides to its members.

7.4 Li Zhiqiang– Patron and Promotor of a Young Buddhist Monastery

So far, we have considered a conventional popular religious temple adherent, a person struggling between popular religious thinking and the possibility of participating in a new Buddhist movement, and someone who is conventional, in the sense not of sharing popular religious attitudes but of totally integrating himself into a conventional–especially locally bound–Buddhist lay community. Is a conventionally oriented Chinese-Buddhist self-construction only possible within the context of a group, which is sustained through closed borders, and the set of beliefs and practices of the group?

During her field-research, the author conducted a couple of interviews with followers of one of the Young Buddhist Monasteries in Taiwan, having informed the monastery in advance of her intention to contact their followers of all kinds. She was granted an opportunity to interview one of their patrons who supported them financially. An appointment was arranged at short notice on a weekday afternoon in March 2005, and the researcher visited an international trading company director in his office. He was a serene man of about 60, probably married, with children, but unwilling to discuss this. He seemed to be a routine conversationalist, open to being interviewed about his life. Like Cai Chenhao, he avoided discussing personal issues, preferring to enlarge on his views about the Buddhist monastery, its abbot and institutions. Later in the interview, his understanding of Buddhism became clearer. His partly conventional Chinese Buddhist views, combined with his role as a supporter and patron of a new Buddhist monastery, enabled him to reflect on options for Conventional Buddhists' self-definitions.

Li Zhiqiang 李志強 (male, age about 60) comes from a Taiwanese family from Southern Taiwan. He speaks fluent Mandarin, but with a strong Taiwanese accent, and sometimes had difficulties understanding the interviewer. He has travelled widely and visited South America on business. Currently, he is back in Taiwan and has recently become more engaged with the Buddhist monastery, which led to meeting the author. The researcher was guided to a high building situated on one of Taipeh's large arterial roads. Finally, she found an open-plan room and was shown into the director's private office. The door remained open, but nobody could overhear the interview. After a short introduction and exchange of business cards, the interviewer began to explain the purpose of the interview. She asked how Li Zhiqiang first encountered the monastery and how his relationship with it developed. The questions were not about Li's general relationship with Buddhism. As this was the first meeting, and also because the monastery implicitly hoped that the researcher would not trouble Li, one of their main supporters, it seemed appropriate to narrow down the question, which may have made the interview less personal in nature. In addition, Li was in his office, giving instructions to his secretaries and claiming natural authority also over the interviewer by first asking her questions and checking the situation. The anonymity of the interview surprised him–probably because he is well-known. In granting the author an interview, he seemed well aware that he was in control of the image he wishes to convey, and so was in control of how much of his private life he was willing to share.

Introductory Sequence Analysis

While the interviewer was explaining her method of allowing interviewees to talk freely, Li interrupted her, starting his narration:

(1) Li: 在一九九八年吧 (2) Interviewer: 欸	(1) Li: In the year 1998 ba. (2) Interviewer: Ei.
(3) Li: 一九九八到現在 九九 應該在一九九七年 九七 九八 九九 二千年. [b] 兩千 欸應該是一九九七年 [breathing in]	(3) Li: From 1998 till now. 99, it should be in the year 1997, 97, 98, 99, 2000 [b] 2000, ei, it should be in the year 1997 [breathing in].

Li Zhiqiang interrupts the interviewer and starts his narration. He has decided what he wants to reveal, and further methodological explanations will not influence his choice about what he is going to narrate and how. Perhaps even the statement that he can talk freely without answering too many questions gave him the impression that he could structure the situation himself. Having been given this choice, he does not hesitate. His narration starts by mentioning a year and, after an asserting interjection by the interviewer, he mentions a duration: "from 1998 till now". One may assume that this might be the period–about seven years–for which Li has been in contact with the monastery. Since he is 60 years old, his involvement with the monastery is still comparatively new while, depending on its intensity, Li also has had enough time to become acquainted with it.

In the following, he attempts to reconstruct the exact year when he first made contact, counting to himself and finally ending up with a year earlier, 1997. He seems to take the task seriously and is not satisfied by stating the wrong year. He also takes his time deliberating. Even if one were unaware that he is a company director, his use of language shows that he is accustomed to structuring situations and taking the initiative, and that he naturally claims authority, while giving an impression of engaging in sincere deliberation.

His fixation on the numeric fact, the exact year, occupies him. Starting his narration with a date gives it a clearly identifiable beginning, frames the whole story, and creates the impression that he is revealing reliable "hard facts" in the manner of a manager used to controlling his economic success through numbers and years, as well as making the story less spontaneous. Like the year when a temple or company were founded, Li's relationship with his monastery also has a standardised beginning. In such a narration, a personal search might be less central than his desire to construct a tellable, representative story, which fits into the social frames of both a company and a monastery, being a well-recognised director of the former and a cherished supporter of the latter.

After determining the exact year, one would expect Li to proceed to enlarge on the event which formed the basis of the relationship. As if starting a longer narration, Li takes a deep breath:

(4) Li: 在一九九七 九九八年的時候 我有一位很好的朋友 介紹我跟[…, abbot B]認識哈 那 因為我從小也都是在佛教 這個佛教跟寺廟 台灣有很多寺廟 哈 道教是廟嘛 佛教叫寺嘛 哈	(4) Li: At the time, 1997, 1998, I had a very good friend, who introduced me to […, abbot B]. Ha. Na. Because, from childhood onwards, I also was always in touch with Buddhism. This Buddhism with temples [*simiao*]. Taiwan has a lot of temples [*simiao*]. Ha. Daoism is *miao* ma, Buddhism names *si* ma. Ha.
(5) Interviewer: ㄇ.	(5) Interviewer: M.

The precise, reliable impression that Li creates persists when he begins his narration, not choosing just one of the mentioned years but taking both into consideration. Around that time, he made contact with the monastery, via one of his close friends. "*Guanxi*", connections, led to his introduction not only to the monastery, but also to its abbot. The formulation "me with [abbot B]" (*wo gen* [abbot] B) insinuates an equal relationship between two leaders. He does not go there to venerate or visit (*canfang* 參訪) the Master, but is "introduced" there to "get to know" him (*jieshao...renshi* 介紹...認識). He was enlarging his network of friends at that time and there was no special religious connotation yet. Li is answering the question precisely about how he became involved with the monastery. Still, in the next sentence, he seems to feel the need to justify his contact with a Buddhist monastery by going back to his childhood: he sees a continuity between the Buddhism he experienced in his youth and that at the monastery now. He immediately explains, almost correcting himself: not Buddhism alone, but Buddhism and "*simiao* 寺廟" (a common term for popular religious temples), made up–we might amend–the religious experience of his youth. Considering that the interviewer is a foreigner, he dares to give a graphic, simple explanation about how he understands the term "*simiao*"; namely, by allocating the two parts of the expression to the two traditions of Buddhism and Daoism. This is a definition which reflects his daily experience that most popular temples in Taiwan that have a Buddhist flavour are named "*si*". In fact, temple locations not involving the term "*si*" are likely to place no emphasis on Buddhism-connotated worship. Still, of course, this is by no means a generally valid categorisation from a historical perspective for Chinese Buddhism.[80] Li appears capable and comfortable about explaining his religious world in simple or simplified terminology to a foreigner. He might hesitate to reveal his hypothesis to those whom he considers experts, such as a group of monastics. In the frame of the present narration, his explanation reveals that he grew up within a popular religious context that combined Buddhism and Daoism:

(6) Li: 就是在這個寺跟這個廟裡面 從小就在那邊活動 那我以前在南部 有在[..., name of a mountain location in South Taiwan] 有一個[..., name of an 18th century Buddhist temple in South Taiwan] 那裡住了幾個月 那 後來我就在[..., city in Southern Taiwan]的[..., monastery C] 時

(6) Li: This is in this *si* and this *miao*, since my childhood I was active there. Na, I was in the South before. In the [..., name of a mountain location in South Taiwan] there is a [..., name of an 18th century Buddhist temple in South Taiwan]. There I lived for some months. Na. Later, I often

80 In general, a "*miao* 廟" is associated with an ancestral shrine or hall, but in Buddhism it can hint towards a *stūpa*. A "*Si* 寺" can be an official building and, in the Buddhist context, a Buddhist temple (DDB, accessed September 30, 2015). The Buddho-Daoist distinction of Li therefore simply reflects the association that something characterised as "*miao*" is hardly ever Buddhist in Taiwan, while major and recognised popular religious temples that also enshrine Buddhist statues like Longshan Si in Taipeh or Buddhist temples, like Fagu Shan's Nongchan Si 農禪寺 or Chengtian Si 承天寺 (Founding abbot: Guangqin 廣欽), regularly are characterised as *si*.

常去那邊拜拜阿 去那邊玩	went to [..., monastery C] of [..., city in Southern Taiwan] to venerate [*baibai*] a, went there to play.

His narration reveals that his life consists of three stages: first, as a child, he recalls being "active" in Buddhist and Daoist temples, and subsequently lived in a traditional Buddhist temple for a short time, before returning to secular life in the third stage, in which he visits a newly founded Buddhist monastery for the purpose of worship and recreational pleasure. One would like to learn more about the motives behind his decisions. His rough summary of his belief development in childhood helps to legitimise his engagement with the concrete monastery. Through all three stages, his natural involvement in religious affairs is apparent. Being active in a temple awakens the child's imagination as he plays near the village temple–the centre of social life–from time to time following the veneration instructions of his relatives or other grown-ups. It means a natural socialisation within a sociocultural environment, in which the distinction between "religion-culture" and "Buddhism-Daoism" are irrelevant. Still, this natural involvement led Li to a stage in his life where he lived in a Buddhist temple for two months. One can only guess about his motives at that time–economic difficulties, an adolescent interest to reflect on a tradition which one perceived naturally as a child, introduction by "a friend", or a mixture of these. One may consider, when listening to the rest of the interview, how far his current belief and practice may have been influenced by that period, and how far they may be consequent, conscious, or reflected. Still, the third stage, venerating and relaxing in a Young Buddhist Monastery, is in accordance with the behaviour of most Taiwanese people when in a Buddhist temple. At least Li's stay at a temple did not lead him to engage in distinct religious behaviour subsequently. "*Baibai*" also seems to be, for him, the central religious activity, and mirroring what has been said in the introduction concerning "Buddhism and travelling", veneration or belief for Li is not only a parallel category to organising one's leisure time, but these can be combined with ease. Li Zhiqiang continues his summary of the religious stages of his life:

(7) 那後來我到台北來的時候 就跟道教比較接近 好 佛教也有 到[..., name of suburb of Taipeh]那邊也有一個佛教 我也有去過了 哈 那我有一個同學是[..., name of a monk] 是 在那個[..., name of a central road in Taipeh]. 跟[..., name of another central road in Taipeh] 那邊有一個[..., name of a recitation hall, *jingshe* 精社] 那個[..., monk's name]也是[..., name of a university in Taipeh] [..., name of this university]的碩士畢業的 出家當法師 那我	(7) Then, afterwards, when I came to Taipeh, I was closer to Daoism. OK, there also was Buddhism. In [..., name of suburb of Taipeh], there also was Buddhism. I also went there. Ha. Na, I've a colleague, [..., name of a monk], he's where that [..., name of a central road in Taipeh] with [..., name of another central road in Taipeh]. There's one [..., name of a recitation hall, *jingshe* 精社]. That [..., monk's name] is also from [..., name of a univer-

在七十四年跟他同學 有一個訓練班同班的同學 以後我就時常去那邊拜拜 所以到 一/ 等 一九八五年的那個時候 哈 我就時常去那個寺廟 那個[…, name of recitation hall]拜拜

sity in Taipeh]. Graduating with an M.A. from […, name of the university], he left home and became a monk [lit. Buddhist master, *fashi*]. Na, I was studying with him in year 74 [i.e. 1985]. There was on the training course a classmate of mine. Later, I just often went there to *baibai.* So, until the time of one/ wait the year 1985. Ha. I just often went to this temple [*simiao*], that […, name of recitation hall] to *baibai.*

Li Zhiqiang grew up in the South and obviously migrated to the Northern Region, to Taipeh, where he became engaged with Daoism. Still, he admits, that there "was also Buddhism" and that he went to a suburb of Taipeh for this. As time passed, Li describes his involvement with religion according to the religious sites that he visited rather than according to his inner recognition of a religious truth, nor his dedication to a particular religion. He compares his involvement with Daoism and Buddhism, without mentioning an inner change occurring to mark his transfer between the two. Thereafter, he enlarges on a fellow student, who became a monk. We see Li again engaging in a religious activity due to his personal connection with a religious group. Through a friend, he becomes involved with the monastery in question, and because of a fellow student at his university, he joins his Buddhist group. As if to enable the interviewer to find it herself, Li describes this group's geographical location in detail. He fails to mention any content related information that would convince him of his friend's activities, but goes to perform the same activities as before in the new Buddhist monastery in the South–he goes to "*baibai*", to venerate. Again, he tries at this point in his narration to fix his story by adding external facts. Here, not the location, but again the year is mentioned. As at the beginning of the interview, he does not remember the date clearly and therefore summarises that, from the time when they studied together in 1985 onwards, he often visited his friend to "*baibai*". This activity remains the same, independent of the location, and therefore it is unsurprising that a typical Buddhist recitation hall (*jingshe* 精社) he first calls a temple (*simiao*). It seems that all of his religious activities are connected to the same action as well as his attitude.

(8)那到一九八七年八八年的時候 ←阿→ 一九八五 到一九九七 九八 剛才講 一九九九六 九七年的事 人家認識 我 介紹認識[…, abbot B] 好 我就加入 這個[…, monastery B]的 的那個行列 那 我從那個時候開始 認識[…, abbot B] 那我發覺到[…, abbot B]跟其他的法師的 這是一 年紀比較大的法師 他很隨和 而且很活潑 而且很樂觀 阿 他跟人家開示的話/ 講講話的時候 他

(8) Na, until the year 1987, 88 ←A→ 1985 until 1997, 98. I just said, the things of the year 199, 996, 97, someone let me know, introduced […, abbot B] to me, OK, so I entered the procession [i. e. followers] of this […, monastery B]. Na, since then I began to know […, abbot B]. Na, I discovered that […, abbot B], in comparison to other masters, this is relatively old mas-

就很平常話 阿 大家這很 這個很容易親近一樣	ters, he is very amiable, and very active, and also very optimistic, a. When he talks to people/ When he talks, he is talking very casually, a, everybody [can] this very/ this like very easily be close.

He attended his friend's group for over a decade, then changed to that very monastery once he got to know its abbot. He struggles with numbers and it seems like a casual slip of the tongue when he replaces the year of the beginning–1997/98–with a date a decade earlier. The constant search for dates also suggests that Li's primary experiences are not linked to certain years, but his habitus shows a strong desire to undertake a secondary reconstruction according to a timeline that might be linked to his idea of telling a representative story.

He later repeats that he was introduced to the abbot, adding that the natural consequence of this was that he entered the "procession" (*hanglie* 行列) of the monastery as a follower. The term "*hanglie*" is normally used to indicate an actual row of people, vehicles, etc. Using it here to denote someone entering a community of followers is slightly surprising and creates a secular, practically-oriented impression. Li describes in the following the qualities of the abbot, making it plausible that he remained a follower of the monastery and became engaged with it. What impresses him about the abbot is not his spiritual, intellectual or religious qualities, but the fact that he is "*suihe* 隨和"–"accommodating", "amiable", "smoothly flexible", "*huopo* 活潑"–"active", or "lively", and "*leguan* 樂觀"–"optimistic", and "positive-minded". Li expects from the abbot less religious guidance and Buddhist expertise–which he might take for granted–than the qualities that one seeks in a good friend or business partner. He states that people can understand the abbot easily and feel close to him because of his use of casual language. The abbot's accessibility and lack of conceit are received positively by Li and suit his more practical approach to religion, following wherever his personal connections lead him while maintaining his practice of veneration and combining it with his leisure time.

(9) 那到 一九九八年開始 他 要我幫他組織這個護法會 阿	(9) Na, from 1998 onwards, he wanted me to help him to organise this Dharma Protection Society [in the following, DPS]. A.
(10) Interviewer: Hm.	(10) Interviewer: Hm.
(11) Li: [..., monastery B]佛教教團護法總會 的工作 那個時候 我就開始投入幫忙他 把整個護法會 的一些組織 重新作一個規劃 規劃一個組織 那我規劃這個護法會 護法總會的組織 把它設立的三個層級	(11) Li: The work of the Buddhism-Teaching-Group DPS of [..., monastery B]. At that time, I joined and helped him to plan some organisation of the whole DPS. Making a plan once again from the start. Planning an organisation. Na, I planned this DPS, the organisation of the DPS, and set it up in three layers.

Shortly after meeting the abbot, he was asked to help to build up the organisation which seems to oversee the monastery's external relations and contact with its lay followers. Li's expertise is requested by the abbot, and Li portrays himself as a cherished, vital partner in the organisational, secular desiderati of the abbot's institution. In the 1990s, many monasteries established this kind of society due to a change in Taiwanese law in 1989, which guaranteed freedom of association to religious groups. Li proudly states how he took responsibility for planning the organisational structure "*zhongxin* 重新" (once again from the start), portraying himself as one of the main organisers of the whole process. He stresses how he implemented a structured concept–the organisation had three layers, as will be discussed in more detail below. Li's general habitus is clear up to here and therefore a first structural hypothesis can be formulated:

Structural Hypothesis

Li Zhiqiang is following, in his introductory sequences, a strong narrative concept behind which his will can be seen to construct a representative, unproblematic story that fits the frame of legitimising his engagement and role in the Buddhist monastery that he supports. Li is well aware of the interview situation as such and is handling his task with ease as he is accustomed to presenting himself and structuring situations. His situational competence is accompanied by a self-confident self-representation as a vital, responsible partner of the monastery and the abbot's personal friend. His narration emphasises the reconstruction of the exact dates, numbers and locations, while his personal development connecting the different events of his life remains more or less hidden. The main selective criteria for Li's engagement in a religious community seem to be his personal connections (*guanxi*) and pragmatic considerations. He joins a Buddhist group because its leader is a former fellow student and he is introduced to the monastery by another friend. Li relies on social networking, using his network to become actively involved. He supports the monastery through his organisational skills and–according to the monastery–also financially. His positive emphasis on pragmatic engagement can be seen in the direct layer of action (*Handlungsebene*) of being one of the monastery's patrons, but it consistently recurs throughout his approach to the interview: he is willing to be interviewed, attempting to adapt to the foreigner's needs and showing during his narration a serious concern about stating accurate dates. He describes a religious authority, the abbot, without a primary religious notion, as an accessible, sympathetic friend. This does not necessarily include any kind of secularism, as he also demonstrates a strong commitment to religious behaviour, staying in a temple, actually engaging, and having a natural acquaintance with basic Buddhist ideas.

Concerning his religious belonging, Li was socialised in his youth in a popular religious context, which he divides during the interview into a dual construction between "Buddhism" and "Daoism". Still, the concepts are naturally applied and function as an adequate representation of his belief. Li prefers simple, applicable concepts. He praises the abbot's easy, accessible habitus but also adopts the same concept himself, feeling capable and comfortable about explaining his religious world in simple terminology to a foreigner (*simiao, hanglie*). While much of his personal belief goes unmentioned, the central religious action that Li performs from childhood throughout the various stages of his life is "*baibai*", veneration. Though important to him and frequently mentioned, it does not seem to include the construction of a separate religious sphere, and Li easily incorporates it into his leisure time.

As Li's prevailing pragmatic habitus becomes evident, attention will be paid in the following to challenging and complementing this with further elements and specifying his notion of "Buddhism" or "religion". Is there an ethical concept underlying the ostensible dichotomy between (secular) pragmatism and religious commitment? What role is Buddhism playing here? Is there a more differentiated belief, in which Li's practical behaviour is rooted?

A Buddhist Organisation Determined for Growth

During the interview, Li Zhiqiang elaborates in detail about the organisation he is supporting, its threefold structure and its respective functions, as well as about two major events: the Water and Land Ceremony (*shuilu fahui* 水陸法會, S5), a one week recitation in the seventh month of the lunar calendar, and some emergency assistance organised for the victims of a huge earthquake a couple of years ago.

Li summarises the three functions of the Dharma Protection Society (DPS): first, as an organisation, one must interact with society. People from outside should be able to learn about the monastery through participating in activities, either through the regular programme or through events in society. The second function of the DPS would be to serve the organisation's followers by offering education and courses on various aspects of Buddhism, such as sūtras, meditation, "Buddhist knowledge" or even planning pilgrimages. Thirdly, it is important to help members who are in difficulty, especially in relation to childbirth, illness and death (*linzhong guanhuai* 臨終關懷). In introducing the organisation, Li illustrates his narration with many details, naming a multitude of possible classes and events.[81] He describes his aim as follows:

81 (S1) This is the DPS, just the whole society of followers. That society again in each county or city established a regional branch. A. Each village established a sub-branch. Like that, the whole organisation was established in three layers. A. That is the whole society, the regional branches and sub-branches. These three layers. A. In this system of organisation, there were established three functions. The first function is the function of the growth of the followers and service. This means the function of the service for followers who have not entered [..., monastery B]. How was this service to be provided? One just goes inside the recitation hall to organise lots of classes, which establish ties (*jieyuan*) with the mass of society, like flower arrangement classes, language classes, calligraphy classes, children's painting classes. A. Family classes a. Or choir sessions. A. Including establishing Chan practice classes. Letting lots of people from society come to participate in that activity. Within this process of participating in activities knowing [..., monastery B] Na, if he/she is interested entering Buddhism. This is the first system. The system of this organisation, na, the leading people in this system participate again/ participate also in activities out in society. A. Introduces [to] communities from the outside, letting them know [..., monastery B] Na, the second system is the system of the development of the whole organisational work [within the DPS]. This development of the organisational work is just the organisation of [our] own followers. Our own followers, we want to give him [/it, meant "them"] training in sūtra education. Also, give them classes in Chan practice. Also, [we] want [to give] them classes in Buddhist knowledge education. Also, there is this pilgrimage to holy places. To go to India and Nepal for a pilgrimage. Organise dharma recitation activities. And also the activities of all the members. To care about this work of service. Helping the followers [..., monastery B] to be able to/ First is the work [with] people from outside. Second is the work [with] followers inside. Third is caring about people near to death including childbirth and also if someone in the family falls ill. And also death. This care for people near to death, from birth to old age, na, this care is coming out of the organisation of our followers. Has/ has that/ When someone is dying, he has something like going to him and reciting for him the Buddha name, and also after someone in his family has passed away, helping him to organise a funeral/ that dharma assembly a. Dharma assembly of reciting sūtras. Ha. Na, this is like helping his family to make funeral arrangements. Like this, a system of caring about people near to death. (Orig.: (S1) 這個是護法總會 就信徒的一個總會 那總會 再來每一個縣市 成立一個區會 阿 每一個鄉鎮成立一個分會 這樣把它整個組織三級化 阿 就是總會區會分會 這個三級化 阿 在這個組織的系統裡面建立了三個功能 第一個功能就是信徒的擴展跟服務的功能 這是說沒有加入[..., monastery B] 的信徒服務的功能 這個服務的功能的工作要怎麼做 就是要在講堂裡面 辦很多跟社會大眾結緣的班 像插花班 語言班 書法班 兒童畫畫班 阿 親子 班阿 或者合唱班 阿 合辦禪修的班 讓很多社會大眾來參加這個活動 參加這個活動的過程裡面去認識[..., monastery B] 那他[/她]有興趣加入佛教 這是第一個系統 這個組織的系統 那 這個系統的幹部 再去參加 也參加外面社團的活動 阿 來介紹讓外面的社團 來認識[..., monastery B] 那 第二個系統 是整個會務發展系統 這個會務發展就是自己信徒的組織 自己信徒 我們要給他一個經典教育的訓練 還有給他禪修的課程 還要佛學知識教育的課程 還有這個朝山朝聖 到印度尼泊爾去朝山 辦法會活動 還有整個會員的活動 關懷這個服務的工作 協助[..., monastery B] 的信徒 能夠 第一個是外面人的工作 第二個是信徒內部的工作 第三個是臨終關懷包括嬰兒出生還有家人有人生病 還有死亡 這個臨終關懷 從出生到老 那這個關懷是我們信徒裡面組織出來的 有 有那個 人家死亡的時候 他有這個等於去把他唸佛 還有他家人死亡以後 幫他辦喪 那個法會 阿 誦經法會 哈 那這個等於是協助他的家人辦喪事 這樣一個臨終關懷的系統).

(S2) 所以這個組織設立三個層級 建立三個任務功能的系統 把它建立起來 那建立起來把這個推動 推動這些組織的功能 還有組織的任務 那 讓這個會員就一直成長 這是這一邊 那麼從一九九八年開始 整個 [..., monastery B] 的會員成長 就一直壯大 一直壯大 一直成長 那慢慢把這一些人把它組織起來 你那個信徒越多的話整個動力就越大 就是這方面 那是從 一九九八年 一九九九 把它推動過來	(S2) So, this organisation was established in three layers, setting up a system of three functions of duties. Establishing it. Na, through establishing it pushing forward/ pushing forward this/ the functions of this organisation. There are also the tasks of the organisation. Na. Letting the members just constantly grow. This is on this side. Na, since the year 1998 the number of members of the whole [..., monastery B] grew. Just continuously growing in strength. Continuously growing in strength. Continuously growing. Na, slowly bringing up these people and its organisation. If you [sc. make] these followers more, the whole power grows. This is just this aspect. That is since the year 1998, 1999, promoting it.

Once Li's threefold structure was established and proposed, its efforts became clear as it began to grow. Repeating the growth time and again, Li creates the impression that the quality of his advice about this structure bore fruit in terms of the organisation's growth. The three layers–going out into society, offering entertainment to its members and building up a social network for them–could also make up a flourishing concept for a secular company. Li is confident of his ability to enable a company to develop through having a well-organised structure. He is convinced of the abbot's personal qualities–amiable, active, optimistic–and supportive of his friends. How far does Li assign the task of defining the organisation's Buddhist content to the abbot? Li explains that the organisation, since 1998, had been continuously growing, and continues:

(S3) 目前當然一直在修正 這個組織 哈 因為我 我對整個佛教不是認識非常深 所以這個組織從開始到現在修改了十次 哈 我們要迎合 這個信眾的需求 佛教的規定 還有社會上的狀況 去修正這個護法會的組織組織的條文 能夠迎合 各方面的規定可以應用的內容 所以我就這樣子推動	(S3) Currently, of course, [sc. we] are continually improving this organisation. Ha. Because I/ I don't understand deeply this whole Buddhism, so this organisation has been altered ten times from its origin till now. Ha. We want to play up to these believers' needs and the rules of Buddhism, and also the situation in society, and make up the structure of this DPS. The organisation's regulations can play up to the rules of every aspect. [sc. So] one can apply the content. So I promoted it just like that.

Li describes the frequent adaptations of the organisation since its foundation as flexibility and stresses without hesitation that he is not deeply interested in Buddhism. Avoiding a collision of interests, this might also facilitate his cooperation with the monastery by restricting himself to the organisational task while the monastery or its abbot provides the content. Li describes the content itself as "Buddhism" (*fojiao*) without further specification.

A Short-term Monastic Stay and its Consequences

a) Buddhist Ethics for Managers

Does Li assume that the Buddhism of different monasteries or temples is similar and that only the personal qualities of individuals make a location more attractive to him? What life experience is connected with Buddhism? Halfway through the interview, the interviewer questions Li again about his Buddhist past, and this time he provides a more detailed report of his youth:

(S9) 那[...]我從小都是會去廟裡去拜拜 那麼到二十歲以後 我就會比較跑去寺廟拜拜 那我在二十三歲的時候曾經在[location]的[traditional Buddhist temple name] [explanation of the name] 一個風清很特別的聖地[...] 我在那邊住了幾個月 所以開始讀那個佛教的事情. 讀那個佛教的事情. 開始對佛教比較有認識跟興趣.

(S9) Na [...] From childhood on, I always visited temples [*miao*] to worship. Na, after I was 20 years old, I would visit temples [*simiao*] more often to worship. Na, when I was 23 years old, I had the experience of the [Buddhist temple name] of [location]. [...; explanation of the name] A holy place, where the scenery was very special. [...] I lived there for a couple of months. So I began to read these Buddhist things/ to read these Buddhist things. And I began to know more and to become more interested in Buddhism.

Li mentions again his sojourn at a long established Buddhist temple, and although one does not learn exactly what led him to join the life of this temple–throughout the interview, Li never discusses any personal developments or crises –, still this seems to be the time when his commitment to Buddhism took root. Without any direct reference to his temple stay, later in the interview, he is asked about the value of being a monastic, to which he presents a double argument, starting with the value of being a monastic for a short time:

(S11) [Sc. 當一個出家人]也有他的理想 阿 日本早期 的 那個企業集團的負責人 都要短期出家 哈 那短期出家的用意 有幾個 他們到佛教 裡面去出家 可以讀到很多佛教的經典 去領悟人生 還有社會的事情 那佛教的經典是有哲學的/ 其實裡面也有領導 同意管理 內容都很豐富 阿你如果有這樣佛教的精神 跟佛教的智慧 跟知識的話 你出來經營企業 你就 不會走偏了 你就不會去作違法 犯

(S11) [Sc. Getting a monastic] also has its own reasons. A. Those in charge of the business groups in early Japan all had to leave home for a short period. Ha. This short-term "leaving home" [BV] produced several benefits. They embraced Buddhism, leaving home, and could read many Buddhist sūtras and understand human life. Also, matters of society. Na, Buddhist sū-

紀的生意 不會去騙人家 你會很遵守你的信用 那遵守你的信用 你才會長年下去 哈 阿你如果都沒有佛教 知識 沒有宗教知識 你就自己怎麼做就對 你慢慢的可能會了為了賺錢 為了私利 你會偏了 違反社會道德阿 沒有道義啦 就是說 阿 產品有危險性了 食品有毒啦 他都不管 那都沒有道義 那品質也不管 只有賺錢就好 那會慢慢走偏了 那會/ 到最後人家都不喜歡你 你公司就垮掉 但是你企業負責人參加了很多佛教經典 很多活動你會慢慢領悟到 信用是很重要 那不正當的獲利是不應該 賺你應該賺的錢 那你這樣企業才會有經營的長久.

tras have philosophical/ Inside, there're also leaders, which is like management. The content is all very abundant. A. If you have such a Buddhist mind[/spirit] with Buddhist wisdom, with knowledge, [concerning] your later business management, you just will not become biased, you just will not engage in illegal business. You won't cheat everybody. You'll observe your credibility. Na, only when observing your credibility, you will stay on for a long time. Ha. A. If you don't have Buddhism at all, knowledge, if you don't have religious knowledge, you just think it's right however you are doing, you slowly perhaps will be/for making money/out of selfishness/you'll be biased, violating the morals of society a. It doesn't have morality and justice la. [sc. This] means, a. The goods are of a dangerous character, the food is poisonous, he doesn't pay any attention to it at all. Na, doesn't have morality and justice at all. Na, also doesn't care about the quality. It is only OK, if one makes money. Na, he'll slowly become biased. Na, will/until finally nobody likes you. Then, your company collapses. But if your people, who are responsible for the business, participate in lots of Buddhist sūtras, lots of activities, you'll slowly become aware that credibility's very important. Na, the not regular making of profits should not be. You should earn the money you deserve to earn. Na, if only such a business of yours'll last for a long time.

A short monastic stay has a direct positive influence on one's business behaviour, Li concludes, by drawing an international historical comparison with Japan. Reading Buddhist sūtras makes businesspeople more aware of society's morality, and prevents them from recklessly pursuing financial success. The philosophy of Buddhist sūtras guides people's life, giving insight into "*shehui de shiqing* 社會的事情" (matters of society). Guided by Buddhist sūtras, one can learn about management and, within this splendid "*jingshen* 精神" (spirit), "*zhihui* 智慧" (wisdom), "*zhishi* 知識" (knowledge) of Buddhism, one will not cheat anyone nor engage in illegal business, but "preserve" one's "credibility" (*zunshou ni de xinyong* 遵守你的信用). A long list follows of what goes wrong through the failure to observe Buddhist or religious knowledge in general. For Li, religions obviously serve the function of delivering moral knowledge and standards which are compatible with society's moral standards (*shehui daode* 社會道德). Buddhism is cherished as it helps to uphold social morals, and obeying the social moral leads to long-term business success. Morality is not cherished as such, but operationalised, functioning to serve business persons' mind maps. Finally, Li's arguments promote sustainable success and, as the audience, one can also imagine a group of businesspeople aiming at economic well-being by adopting Buddhist values.

b) Buddhism and Family Life

Still, Buddhism is not only serving the enterprises' interests, but also has a positive effect upon family life:

(S13) 如果你全家都信仰佛教 你的小孩子可能因為結緣 善緣的關係 就比較不容易變壞 哈 他的思想就會跟佛教的 就是與人為善 凡事以善為出發 這小孩子就不會變壞 不會吸毒 殺人 當流氓 哈 個性就比較溫和 不要很暴力行為 哈 你全家人就會比較融洽 阿 全家人比較融洽 中國講了一句話 家和萬事興 和氣生財 對不對阿 阿 家庭都很和氣 都沒有人出問題 這個家庭就很興旺 那容易賺到很多錢 阿吉祥的事情都會出來	(S13) If your whole family believes in Buddhism, your children possibly are less likely to become bad, because of karmic connections and good karma. Ha. Their thinking will just with Buddhist/ Just having good intentions, encountering people [saying], beginning everything with goodness. These small children will just not become bad. Will not take drugs, kill people, become gangsters, ha. The character will just be more stable. [Sc. It] should not [sc. be that they engage in] violent acts. Ha. Your whole family'll just be more harmonious. A. China has a saying: if a family is in harmony, ten thousand things arise. Harmonious energy leads to wealth. Right? A. A. The whole family is very harmonious. There is no one who is coming up with a problem. A. Auspicious things will all come up.

A family which adopts Buddhism intends to make humans better (*yuren weishan* 與人為善) and creates good karma, so there are fewer family problems. As the children are "gentle" (*wenhe* 溫和) and avoid engaging in "violent behaviour" (*baoli xingwei* 暴力行為), the family is "harmonious" (*rongqia* 融洽). Buddhism seems, according to Li, to have a positive influence upon children: they do not "take drugs", "kill people", or "start leading a vagabond life" (*xidu* 吸毒, *sharen* 殺人, *dang liumang* 當流氓). These problems are obviously, for him, the worst imaginable activities in which children can engage and may place them beyond their parents' control. In these situations, Buddhism is given the role of positively influencing whatever is happening beyond the parents' direct influence. The awareness of the power of "Buddhism" has, in this concept, a stabilising effect on families and removes pressure from the parents. Li finally links back the Buddhist family to economic success: a consequence of inner-family harmony is that it is easy to make "lots of money". Li seems to be closely-linked with the business field, and money-making and company growth are unquestioned values to him. As in the DPS, whose good guidance one can see through the growth of its followers, like a businessperson, whose company flourishes in the long-term because of Buddhist ethics, a Buddhist family can be recognised by the fact that a high income is possible–in the structure of a family business, as is common in Taiwan, or possibly through the father, as Li sees himself.

Li not only fails to really question the social standards but also the family standards in terms of Buddhism. Buddhism is seen as stabilising the traditionally established roles–like that of a businessperson or a family, both long-existing social functions in Chinese society.[82] Li's perception of Buddhism seems traditional in that sense and, in this traditional view might even be more necessary in Taiwan, as a rapidly-changing country, in which the social boundaries and social support are endangered and the frightening image of children following "the wrong path" might strongly affect parents who are experiencing a time of social change.

Monasticism as Determined through Fortune-telling

When questioned about the difference between lay people and monastics, Li sees Buddhism not only as a task for monastics, but also assigns them their own role in society. Because of society's boundaries, lay followers cannot explore Buddhism as deeply as monastics can. They remain "*shehui ren* 社會人", members of society, with their restrictions. Li clearly recognises the advantage of being a monastic, but the tension between these two ways of life and the possible accusation of not following Buddhism fully as a lay person he answers through recourse to Chinese prognostic traditions:

(S12) 那最出家的時候 當然我/ 我們中國人比較相信那個八字的命運 一個人生下來我們/ 年月時 哈 欸 你是幾年 幾月 幾時 幾分 生的 阿 所以我們中國一個人的命運裡面有算命的/ 有 *tianzi* 哈 八字 阿 *tianzi* 阿 天干地支 八字 八字 哈 那這個八字是怎麼來得 啦 年 月 日 時 這個 這個 這個 八 這個 四字[meant 柱?] 人家 就是說 你的/ 你	(S12) Na, when [sc. it is] basically [about] becoming a monastic, of course I/ we Chinese people believe rather in the fate [i.e. *mingyun*] of that Eight Characters [i.e. *bazi*]. The passing of a human life. We/ year, month, daytime ha. Ei. Which year, which month, which daytime, which minute you're born. A. So, in the fate [i.e.

82 It is a well-known topos that Confucius saw the family as lying at the heart of society's well-being and focused his ethics also on filial piety. Also, Confucianism's impact on family life from a sociological perspective in East Asia has been well-studied, see Slote and de Vos (1998).

的命運裡面有 細條 台灣話講 四字四字 年月日時 那中個這個八字/ 四字裡面有分成八字 八字就是像了/ 我那一年生了就變成戊子 兩個字 對不對 阿 阿 欸 這樣兩個字這樣排起來 這樣八個字 這個八個字構成裡面 可以從這個八個字裡面 算出你的命運 哈 阿 所以如果你的佛緣很深厚的人 在這個八字 裡面 可以算出來/ 算出你有沒有這個佛緣/ 佛教的緣分 以前我在[..., name of a Buddhist temple]住了幾個月在那裡看了一本書 就是大達摩祖師 有一本算命算時命理師 早期在台灣二三十年以前如果你要出家 他開始算你的八字 你是不是適合出家 你如果不適合出家 他就不收你 阿所以這個八字很重要 哈 在中國的命理學上面哈 那裡面有算出來 是你出家的命 才讓你出家 因為你才知道你不會還俗 阿你跟佛教才有緣 阿你才會終生當出家人

mingyun] of us people from China, there is fortune-telling [i.e. *suanming*]/ there is *tianzi* [i.e. probably the *jiazi* 甲子-cycle] ha, *bazi* a, *tianzi* a, the *tian'gan dizhi* [i.e. Ten Heavenly Stems and Twelve Earthly Branches, which is the *jiazi* 甲子-cycle to designate the time]. *Bazi bazi* ha. Na, these *bazi*, how are they coming, la? Year, month, day, daytime. This/ This/ These *bazi*, these *sizi* [pronounced: Four Characters, probably meaning: Four Pillars?], everyone says, your/ in your destiny there are "little lines" [i.e. *xitiao*]. In Taiwanese, one says: Four Characters, in the Four Characters we divide the year, month, day, and daytime. Na, these Eight Characters/ Four Characters one divides into Eight Characters. Eight Characters are just like/ In the year when I was born, I got *wuzi* [i.e. one possible combination of the *jiazi*-cyclus], two characters, right? A. A. Ei. Like this, two characters. Like this rowing [them] up. Like this, eight characters. In the composition of these Eight Characters, one can count from these Eight Characters your fate. Ha. A. So if your Buddhist karma is very deep/ you are [sc. such a] person, in these Eight Characters one can count/ one can count, if you have this Buddhist karma/ Buddhist karmic connection. When I once lived in [..., name of a Buddhist temple] for a couple of months, I read a book, this is just the big Patriarch Bodhidharma. There was a book about counting fortune, counting time, a fortune-telling teacher. In early times in Taiwan, 20, 30 years ago, if you wished to become a monastic, he started to count your Eight Characters. If you suit becoming a monastic or not. If you didn't suit becoming a monastic, he didn't accept you. A. So these Eight Characters are very important. Ha. In the Chinese teaching[/art] of fortune-telling, ha, na if in that one counted that you've the predestination to become a monastic, only then one lets you become a monastic. Because only then, you know, you won't resume normal life. A. Only then will you have a karmic connection with Buddhism. A. Only then will you become a monastic for the rest of your life.

Becoming a monastic is not a personal decision, but is already determined by one's exact time of birth. The evaluation of the date is performed by a master from the monastery, who decides who is accepted for monastic life. The counting itself is complicated and Li recalls the outcome: born in the year *wuzi* 戊子, he was not predestined to become a monk. The system of "Four Pillars" or "Eight Characters" on which the fortune-telling is based is a method that attributes to the exact time of birth (year, month, day, time) a set of characters, the interpretation of which explains one's whole life course. The years are counted according to the *jiazi* 甲子, a sexagenary cycle that combines the ten heavenly stems (*tiangan* 天干) with 12 earthly branches (*dizhi* 地支). The 60 potential combinations add up to 60 years, after which the cycle restarts. The year mentioned by Li is–assuming that he was around 60 at the time of the interview–1948 (lying between Feb 25th, 1948, and Jan 28th, 1949). While Li may be unfamiliar with the history of fate-calculation,[83] he appears familiar with the Four Pillars system. "We Chinese" believe "naturally" in predestination by that method, so he begins his excuse for not becoming a monk. He recognises the prognostic technique as his cultural heritage, in which he naturally believes. Its cultural bounds do not hinder his belief in its reliability. He implicitly awakens the expectation that the modern practice might be different, but also does not distance himself from it.

Although the interpreter may influence the outcome of the counting, Li narrates the reason for the decision as a fact–the time of his birth–that makes no judgement about the potential novice's personal ability. The decision against him might have been a fact that requested his reorientation in life, but it remains an entertaining story and is at the same time also a means for the monastery to restrict entrance without passing judgement on the aspirants' personal qualities. More than 30 years later, Li appears content with the life he has led as a consequence of the monastery fortune-teller's decision. In general, for Li, upholding a traditional system of Buddhist practices and attitudes justifies his being a businessperson, positively values his busi-

83 The Four Pillar system, which developed in various forms in China, Japan and Korea, dates back to the Ziping method of fate-calculation. The method's name refers to a man about whom little is known. According to Ho Peng Yoke, Xu Ziping 徐子平 was probably a fate-calculation expert in the second half of the tenth century, who already used the four categories (year, month, date and time) to calculate people's fortune. The *Sanming Tonghui* 三命通會, written in the 16th century, is the most authoritative commentary on it. For an introduction, see the paragraph on "The eight characters (*bazi* 八字)" in Ho (2003), 156–160, within the overview about the Ziping method (Ho 2003, 153–164) and his book on the Ziping method, He (1988).

ness success, acts as a moral guide in his business behaviour, and gives him the strength to engage with his family under the positive influence of good karma. Buddhism plays therefore a stabilising, supportive role in important aspects of Li's life. In his own life and behaviour, Li witnesses these positive influences of Buddhism, as he feels more "*tashi* 踏實", "firm and reliable". Life is "calmer" (*wenzhong* 穩重).

Buddhism in Society: Education

Not only in his own life, but also with respect to society, Li Zhiqiang is explicitly aware of the function of religious groups and Buddhism: society, Li states, is described in China via two traditions, and he explains, quoting the beginning of the Three-Character-Classic (*Sanzi Jing* 三字經), commonly recited by Taiwanese primary school children, that Mencius and Confucius claim human nature to be good while–and here her replaces the classical Chinese philosopher Xunzi 荀子 (3rd century BC) by the founding figures of Daoism–Laozi and Zhuangzi and therefore also Daoism would start from the general assumption that human nature is bad.[84] Religious groups, as a result of this situation,

84 (S8) In China, there are very big books. Confucius and Mencius' position is: the character is/ the character is basically good. Ha. A. But in Laozi the character is bad. Therefore, in the development of Daoism, the character is bad. Na, only if it is bad, one has to make it better. A. Na the teaching of Confucius and Mencius/ the teaching of Confucianism thinks that, when a human is born, his/her character is good. Because there are lots of bad things in society, it leads this human to become bad. A. To become bad. Therefore, basically, humans have a good character. In society, there are also lots of not good/ influencing him to do bad things. We religious groups should just influence the bad things happening in society to become good. Na, every group agrees about doing good things in society. But Laozi, the thinking of Laozi, they think, when a human is born, [sc. he/she] is bad. Basically [sc. he/she] is just bad. Just, therefore, he says, the things that are done in society are first done badly. Therefore, our original character/ Make this bad character/ through education to change it into a good character. [sc. In] one [sc. case], goodness emerges. In a second, bad emerges. Two different teachings. These two teachings are not the same in China. Na, Buddhism is rather partial to this side of this goodness of Confucianism. Ha. This means, because it is too bad [sc. if it's not the case] Na, humans are good. Just they are under society/ the big stream of society's influence and become bad. Therefore, Buddhism says: We hope, before he turns bad, first to educate him not to become bad. A. Let perish all things of society. It is like this. (Orig.: (S8) 中國裡面有很大的書籍 孔子孟子他[sc. 們]主張 性是 性本善 哈 阿可是在老子裡面 性是惡的 所以道教的發展性是惡的 那惡的才要把它變成好的 阿 那 孔子孟子的學說/ 儒教的學說 是認為人生出來性是好的 因為社會上很多不好的事情 讓這個人變壞 阿 變壞 所以基本人是善性的, 社會上還有很多不好的/ 把他引導去作壞事. 我們宗教團體就應該把社會上的事情的壞事把引導為好的. 那每個團體都訂的社會上好的事情來作 可是老子 老子思想他們認為 人以生出來是惡的 本來就惡了 就所以他說社會上作的事情先作惡的事情所我們性本/ 把那個惡的性 把它教育為好的性 是一個是善的出來 二個是惡的出來 兩個是學說不一樣 在中國兩派學說是不一樣 那佛教是比較偏向儒教的這個善的這一面來講 來作 哈 就是說因為太不好了 那人是善的 就被社會 社會的這個大洪流的這個影

react and must work hard to improve society: “Our religious groups just shall guide the bad things of the things in society towards the good” (*Women zongjiao tuanti jiu yinggai ba shehui shang de shiqing de huaishi ba yindao wei hao de* 我們宗教團體就應該把社會上的事情的壞事把引導為好的). Buddhism especially would be nearer to the “Confucian” view that human nature is good. As humans are good, Li argues, they come under society’s bad influence so, in Buddhism, one would try to educate them, before they turn bad. Buddhism provides “education” (*jiaoyu* 教育). This is why Li also suggested renaming the DPS as a group for “Buddhist education”. Buddhism has an educative mission in society, preventing people from turning “bad” just as, in the family, the children, with the help of Buddhism, also set off on the right path.

Buddhism educates people. Li elaborates on aspects of the content of this education while discussing the success of the Water and Land Ceremony: its first effort would be to release the participants’ ancestors from purgatory; the second, to release those who die suddenly in tragic circumstances; and the third concerns educational efforts:

(S6) Li: 第三個讓參加的人了解到 人是會有死亡的 可是在死亡以前 他怎麼去修行好 這個世 裡面的 行為 語言行為 還有整個社會上的事情 把它修得很好的時候 讓他往生的時候 會不會找到更好的幸福 輪迴回來 能夠在輪迴回來 當人的時候 會不會比以前更好 各方面更滿意 更好 更幸福 大家都在追求這個 所以那個水陸大法會 變成真的非常大 而且是水陸空大法會 哈 那這樣連續十一年連續十一年 來 譬如說 從這個法會的超渡過程裡面 去教化現在現有的人 在你的人生過程裡面去作善事 作好事 哈 一些佈施 種福田 讓你得到更好的基因 還有好的因果 讓你往生以後 得到更大的福報 或者說 你把你的祖先都超渡 好了然你這一輩子最好的基因 最好的福田 能夠給遺留給下一代去承續 那中國人 都是希望把自己最好的留給後面的下一代 所以希望把這樣的作 所以水陸大法會作得非常成功

(S6) Li: The third is letting the participants understand that people are dying. But, before they die, how is one practising well? The behaviour in this world, the language behaviour and also the things of the whole society. If one practises them very well, if he[/she] faces death then, will he[/she] fare better? If he returns through rebirth, if he can return through rebirth and become a human, will it be better than before? Better in every aspect? Luckier? Everyone pursues this. So this Big Water and Land Ceremony became really very big and it’s the Big Water and Land and Air Ceremony. Na, like this continuously eleven years/ Continuously eleven years. For example: from the process of liberation of this dharma assembly to go and educate the people of now who are there. Do in your life-process good things, do good things. Ha. Some alms-giving. Plant the acre of merit. Let you reach better genes. And also good karma. Let you after your death attain a bigger, good reward. Or, say, you’ve liberated all your ancestors already, then you can give the best genes of this life, the best acre of

響 變惡的 所以在佛教裡面是說 希望他要變惡 以前 先教育他 不要變惡 阿把所有社會上的事情 消滅掉 是這樣)

merit to the next generation to continue. Na, Chinese people all hope to give their best to the next generation. So they hope to act like this, so the Big Water and Land Ceremony can be very successful.

The most basic teaching that Buddhism has to offer is the doctrine of rebirth. Li Zhiqiang turns this doctrine into a means of improving people's behaviour: if one knows about rebirth, one tries to obtain a better one. To do so, one does "good things", give alms, plants the field of merits, etc. Giving alms in this concept helps to improve one's destiny. Lin Yongfu's and Luo Peirong's system of mutual retribution from the gods is here given an inner-worldly turn: the gods do not receive offerings–which do not directly contribute to society–in exchange for protection, but people undertake charity work to obtain better rebirths. The system of reincarnation depersonalises the retributional exchange. Still, the Mahāyāna ideal of compassion towards all living beings as a motive does not feature in Li's reasoning. He is also offering a variant, which he declares to be typically Chinese: if one does not seek better circumstances in the next life, one can at least try to pass on one's merits to the next generation. This also looks like a good motive for encouraging people to adopt determined behaviour, emphasising their efforts and social morality.

Karmic Connections

Li, at a focal point in his life, credits prognostication with his failure to become a monastic. In the same manner, he uses the–as we have already seen, widespread–argument of karmic connection to legitimise his engagement or non-engagement in religious organisations:

(S10) 實際上我在高中的時候也參加 基督教的青年團體阿 天主教的活動 我也是有參加 可是一個人是一個機緣嘛 這是你剛好到甚麼時候 阿剛好有朋友有參加甚麼活動 阿請你去參加 阿這是一種機會跟緣分的行程嘛 像我在高中的時候 同學有甚麼基督教團體請我去參加 我會去參加 對不對 天主教甚麼辦活動 我們也會去參加 我們並沒有排斥 我們都是一樣參加 哈 [...] 那後來 二十歲到寺廟 現時 我就開始到寺廟去拜拜 如果到那個地方有寺廟 或是廟 我都拜拜 阿進去拜拜啦 哈 那 以前在南部 跑到 [name of temple] 後來到北部 我也幫忙 [name of monastery] 一段時間 阿就是到一九九七 左右人家介紹說 有 [name of monastery] 這個佛教團體 阿我加入以後 我才虔心了來幫忙他 對

(S10) In fact, when I was at high school, I also participated in the Protestant church's youth club a. Catholic activities I also participated in. But a person's an opportunity ma. This means, right at which time you're just a, right at which time there's a friend participating in which activity a, asks you to participate a, this's a kind of process of opportunities and karmic connections na. Like when I was in high school, my classmates asked me to participate in whatever Protestant group and I would participate, right? Whatever activities the Catholics planned, we'd also go and participate. We certainly didn't refuse. We participated in them all in the same manner. Ha. […] Na,

> afterwards, when I was 20 and went to the temple, I began to visit temples [i.e. *simiao*] to worship [i.e. *baibai*]. If at a place there was a temple or a *miao*, I'd always worship a, go inside and worship la, ha, na, before, in the South, I went to the [name of a Buddhist organisation], afterwards in the North I also helped [name of a monastery] for a while, a, until around 1997, when everybody told me of [name of monastery], this Buddhist group. A. Only after I entered it, I started with devotion to help him. Right.

In his youth, Li participated in everything he came across, and argues that this was dictated by whatever opportunities happened to present themselves. It seems that he floats between suggestions made by his colleagues, without any personal dedication. After his brief temple-stay, this changed: he has felt the necessity since then to worship at every temple he passes. We learn nothing further about his worshipping behaviour. *Baibai* in Taiwan is normally perceived as a practice, which is taken as given, clearly distinguished and long established, so that normally–except to children–one does not explain it or give it a personal meaning. In the following, he becomes increasingly engaged with helping Buddhist organisations, but his selection of organisation he also attributes to karmic connections rather than a conscious choice. Still, he is clear about his function, helping the organisation as such and not participating in any activities, as he would not have the "karmic connections" with that, and he is still following the same principle as in his youth, not to "force" things ("*Wo bu hui zai renhe tuanti limian zuo shiqing. Yinwei you xian de shiqing ye xuyao you jiyuan. Wo bu hui qu qiangqiu, zhe shi zui zhongyao de.* 我不會在任何團體裡面作事情. 因為有限的事情也需要有機緣. 我不會去強求, 這是最重要的".).

Buddhist Practice?

While his outer engagement might therefore have a moment of arbitrariness, one could ask how far Li is dedicated to specific Buddhist practices and regulations. Firstly, he would see himself as following an orthodox religious belief (*zhengjiao* 正教), which includes Christianity and Islam and which he generally finds acceptable in contrast to being superstitious, a word which he associates with the New Buddhist/Religious Movements, whose leaders would claim to possess mysterious powers. Secondly, Li states that he follows a personal recitation practice as, if something happens, he says that he recites the *Heart Sūtra* or the *Great Compassion Mantra*. In general, he recites the *Diamond Sūtra* when he has time. Sometimes, he also recites the *Lotus Sūtra* in full. Li follows a personal spiritual practice, but does not mention meditation or name recitation specifically. He is reading sūtras. This seems consistent, as we know that he is convinced that knowing the sūtras means possessing Buddhist knowledge, which leads to the improvement of oneself, one's family and society.

When asked about formal initiation, Li answers directly that he has taken refuge on two occasions, once during his temple-stay and once with the abbot of the monastery that he currently supports. He seems aware of the meaning of formal belonging and the initiation into Buddhism. Still, although he took refuge, he does not follow the five lay precepts and points out that he would not have participated in a ceremony about holding these. The question of whether he is vegetarian he finds at first funny then irrelevant. For him, it is natural to eat meat. Still, he respects vegetarianism and states that he does not eat meat for breakfast as a first step towards it, including it within his whole theory of the different grades of intensity of vegetarianism.

Conclusion

In summary, one can say that Li regards himself as a supporter of Buddhism by offering to an abbot his organisational skills to build up a foundation in which Li himself does not participate. Being a company director, Li feels close to and easily makes direct contact with the abbot, who is in charge of the monastery. Their combined efforts, uniting organisational skills with Buddhist knowledge, enables the flourishing and adaptation of the Dharma-Protection-Society (DPS), which spreads "Buddhism"–i.e. the doctrine of the monastery–in society, among its members and through spiritual charity work. Although Buddhism can be lived in a more intense way within the monastic order, Li describes its moralising and stabilising effect on himself, families, business, and society in general. As he believes in karmic retribution, his support of Buddhism is consistent with this.

Li Zhiqiang demonstrated his pragmatic approach to Buddhism throughout the interview while his concept of Buddhism underlying his engagement became differentiated through the further analysis. In his 20s, Li got interested in Buddhism and spent a couple of months living in a traditional Buddhist temple, but was subsequently denied the chance to become a monk. Li accepted this refusal, that was based on prognostication, and adapted what he had learnt about Buddhism in his later life as a successful lay Buddhist. By the time of the interview, Li has recovered from the possible personal crisis of his youth, and is able to construct a strong narrative, within which his temple-stay provides the legitimation and foundation for his actual life as well as

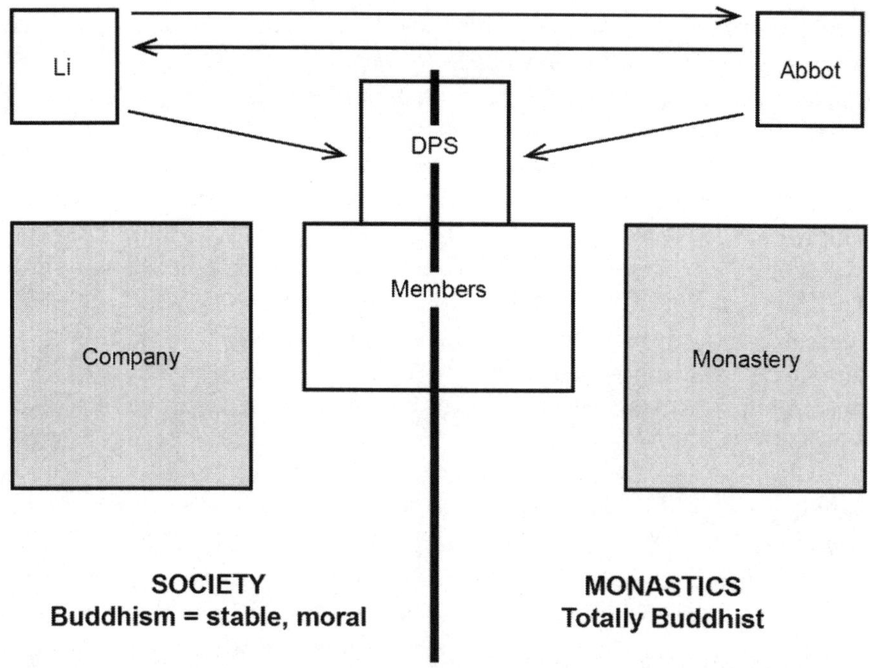

Figure 12: Li Zhiqiang positioning himself as the organisational supporter of a Buddhist organisation.

of his views about the role of Buddhism in society. He strongly supports a Buddhist organisation, as he is of the opinion that this improves his karma, leading to a better rebirth as well as the merits that will also be passed on to the next generation. Li does not mention the idea of compassion and, therefore, it might not form part of his primary motivation.

The role of Buddhism in secular, i.e. non-monastic, life Li sees in a broad variety of social levels: in general, the task of Buddhism would assume, together with the culturally dominating role of Confucianism, the "good nature" of people. The social task of Buddhism would therefore be to educate society to follow the "good" and protect people from turning "bad". In the business world, Buddhism helps to recognise, what is, in general, assumed by society to be good in the sense of traditional, socially-recognised morality. He enumerates here the awareness of the worth of life or even managerial qualities. Within families, Buddhism helps children to stay on the "right path"– also according to the traditional moral standards. He himself feels that he is firmer and more reliable due to Buddhism. In all aspects of social life, we see that Li constructs Buddhism in the role of preserving society's traditional moral values, but the social reality includes, for Li, also the realms of the deceased, especially ancestors and those who die tragically. Their care and the release of their souls is central for him and so he especially values dharma meetings, which serve this purpose. Buddhism here plays a unique role, which has been established in Chinese society for centuries.[85]

Therefore, we cannot regard Li as someone who is blindly donating or supporting a Buddhist institution, although he clearly supports the view that monastics can serve Buddhism to a far higher degree than lay people. Li never assigns the task of interpretation to the monastics or the abbot, and simply expects good karmic retribution in exchange. Still, in direct cooperation with the monastery, he uses his understatement "of not understanding Buddhism" as a rhetorical means, which has a harmonising effect upon the cooperation. Arguments about karmic connections can serve the same purpose for him. Li follows an elaborated Buddhist practice, although it is influenced by popular religion. He has taken refuge and seems to regard this as a formal initiation. His high self-esteem shows that he does not see himself participating in any of the activities offered to lay people, but as following a double practice of reciting privately Buddhist sūtras and visiting temples to worship (*baibai*). Through the first practice, he is consistent in his conviction that Buddhist knowledge, as it is transmitted through the sūtras, helps one to adopt the appropriate moral behaviour in society. Through the second practice, he is paying respect to his ancestors, the souls of the deceased, and probably also the "Buddhas and gods" we already know from Luo Peirong–although he does not mention them specifically. This embeds him within the traditional social context of Taiwanese popular religious society. Li is not, through his Buddhist practice, excluding Daoist practices, nor does he oppose the combining of Buddhism with Daoism throughout the interview, which means that he continues to see himself as acting in harmony with his traditional environment.

Li structures his biography in a linear way: he attains his self-concept through a temple-stay after a non-selective popular religious socialisation during his youth. The Buddhist knowledge he perceived there differentiates his position, but does not pervert it. Veneration (*baibai*) remains central for him. His attained knowledge he employs in his later career. He sees his role as that of helping, through secular skills and resources, Buddhism and society to interact. It is striking that Li's traditional, linear conception seems to be in harmony with Taiwanese contemporary society. One should note this as a characteristic of Taiwanese modernity: Li might present an option of living a conscious life as a lay Buddhist in contemporary Taiwan, which is aimed at an active, pragmatic orientation and is consistent, in accordance with the traditional values of his society, centred around moral values related to business, the family and active social engagement. Therefore, a dichotomy between a secular and a religious realm cannot be seen in the habitus of Li.

---

85 For the development of the *Shuilu Fahui* see, for example, Stevenson (2001).

How far does Li Zhiqiang fit into the picture of the Conventional Buddhists that we developed earlier? Firstly, Li must be recognised as a Conventional Buddhist believer according to the formal criterion that he would select the option of "to believe in, venerate Buddha". He also does not distance himself from popular religion. Unlike a popular religious believer, he is used to talking about and rectifying his beliefs, convictions and practices. His commitment, although highly conventional, can be by no means characterised as slight. Li is a consciously average Buddhist. Like an average Taiwanese, he believes in, and is also able to formulate, the idea of karmic retribution, which he connects with the need to pursue moral behaviour. He is popular religious in the sense of visiting and worshipping at temples. Conventional Buddhists tend to see themselves as devout. Li Zhiqiang would certainly count himself as such. Still, unlike the majority, he has taken refuge (14.7% only of Conventional Buddhists) and follows a personal spiritual practice (27.3% of Conventional Buddhists). His personal commitment never conflicts with traditional values: he is following, like the Conventional Buddhists in general, his parents' belief, would certainly regard himself as filial and naturally venerates his ancestors. The aims that inspire his temple visits are probably in line with his expectations of the positive effects of Buddhism: peace in the sense of social harmony is certainly an important *Handlungsmaxime* for him. Also, self-cultivation and spiritual sustenance will be in accordance with his intentions. Throughout the interview, Li never mentions the search for truth. During his temple-stay, he learnt about Buddhist "spirit", "wisdom", and "knowledge" (*jingshen* 精神, *zhihui* 智慧, *zhishi* 知識), but never describes a time in his life when he questioned the traditional cultural-religious practices or doctrines. The rule of his youth was never to reject any chance to participate and even now he believes that one should never "force" anything. His direct requests at temples might be about business (as 11.6% of the Conventional Buddhists) and money-making (5.6% of the Conventional Buddhists), but he certainly would never avoid requesting health and peace. One can only speculate whether Li would see life in general as sorrowful. He tends to worship whenever he passes a temple. As a successful businessperson, he appears confident. Still, one can assume that he is aware of the Buddhist view that all life is suffering.

Can we see any hints in Li Zhiqiang's narration why Buddhists live more frequently in urban areas? Li, after his temple-stay, moved into the world of business. The earning of money is seen positively in the Buddhism he experiences and he considers himself a successful businessperson. Buddhism even provides an essential means for him to remain a successful entrepreneur in the long term. In addition, Li sees a chance to intensify his Buddhist belief by engaging in supportive action and, in the urban region, he is able to maintain personal contact with the Young Buddhist Monastery, which fully appreciates his engagement. One could say that the traditional concept of Buddhism to which Li is exposed is easily intensified when one enters the virulent, urbanised business-world of the fast-developing Northern Region of Taiwan.

In comparison with the cases analysed previously, Li's case is certainly closest to that of Lin Yongfu. Both are socially active via their "Buddhist" communities–Li Zhiqiang via a Buddhist monastery and Lin Yongfu via a popular religious temple. Both support their respective organisations actively as well as donating money to them. Still, Lin Yongfu clearly donates to the temple community and expects social retribution as a result, while Li, in contrast, experienced the social buffer of a temple in his childhood and later in his youth, where he lived there for a couple of months. One could regard his engagement as a kind of retribution within Buddhism, but to another institution. The question arises of whether this kind of retribution would cause the Young Buddhist Monastery that Li supports to offer the same kind of social help to Li as Lin Yongfu can expect from his temple. Both cases originate from a popular religious context. Buddhism in both cases does not oppose popular religion and as a result gains donors. Even a transfer from the popular religious field is not visible, apart from the fact that Li adopts the formal vocabulary of "religions", dividing "Buddhism" and "Daoism". The social reality does not picture this shift, but Buddhism and popular religion are not clearly separated from each other.

As a successful businessperson, Li is striving for more social recognition via his engagement than Lin Yongfu, who seems to follow a less elite and more egalitarian-social self-concept. Li does not mention engaging in any private spiritual practice. All of his religious practices are rooted within the context of either his family or his temple community. While, for Lin Yongfu, Buddhism in his family has a mainly social dimension, Li lays greater stress in his narration on the moral influence of Buddhism upon a family. The social reality is not really present to him and he might be less engaged in the processes of Buddhist family life as a businessperson who is spending his leisure time helping a Buddhist organisation.

Li and Lin both recognise the stabilising function of Buddhism in society and Lin Yongfu especially regards it as connecting the generations. They are both familiar with the traditional, socially-stabilising religious context and open to international influences, both being curious about the foreign interviewer and both having travelled abroad.

Still, the main difference is that Lin Yongfu stays in his popular religious environment, simply renaming it as a Buddhist one, while Li Zhiqiang actually changes his affiliation, making contact with a Young Buddhist Monastery. By contrasting these two cases, one can witness how young Buddhist organisations can successfully absorb popular religious practitioners and support them with doctrinal concepts which do not oppose their original cultural-religious socialisation but embrace and even support it, so that some of them can become highly socially and economically successful. From this success, the monasteries can also profit. The background of retributionary thinking enhances the relationship with potential donors. Turning to the level of the individual, there is the option as a popular religious believer to redefine oneself–following the urban fashion–as a Buddhist without changing the field, or to follow the traditional Buddhist concepts, achieving success through one's own ability and the offers of society and starting to support Buddhist organisations. From the very beginning of Buddhism onwards, lay people have been active in society in the well-established role of donors (see also McNair 2007).

A comparison with Luo Peirong is also telling. The difference between retelling one's life story through the topos of a crisis in contrast to a linear development is obvious. Also, miracles occupy a different position: Li Zhiqiang involves in his Buddhist missionary visions all layers of existence, but miracles do not feature. He is, in his narration, constantly describing his external acts like, for example, worship and he does not speak of any inner relationship to Guanyin. He also does not engage in name recitation. In addition, he found in his monastery one that meets his expectations, being Buddhist without rejecting popular religion and having an abbot to whom he can feel personally connected, while Luo had to fall back upon popular religion and Daoism as the Buddhist monastery failed to help her with her situation.

While Lin Yongfu and Li Zhiqiang show similar patterns of socialisation via "Buddhism", Cai Chenhao and Li share the traditional Chinese perception of Buddhism in common: care in the context of death rituals is part of Li's Buddhist organisational concept, and deathbed recitations are included in the daily practices of Cai's community. In explaining causalities, Cai, who is at least 20 years younger and better educated than Li, does not employ the pattern of karmic connections to explain his own choices. Li does not describe any real choices, but formulates his life in terms of karmic connections. Cai can at least, when faced with a foreign interviewer, describe his life as following his interests and making his own choices: he pursued religious studies, because he was unsure about the meaning of religion in his own life, and later chose his community. He does not completely avoid using the terminology of karmic retribution, but is able to replace it. The reliability and social support of the chosen community is strongest in Cai's local lay Buddhist group, looser in Lin Yongfu's temple and questionable with regard to its mutual character in Li's Buddhist monastery. But the obligations of the members are reciprocal: Cai has to live in his community, which is locally fixed, while Lin Yongfu visits his local temple regularly, and Li's organisation can move or open branches, while he can determine himself, when he wishes to contribute to it. A social network, it seems, requests the actual presence of the person, and the more locally a community is bound, the more it provides social security for its members.

7.5 Gu Puzhong–Intellectual Buddhist Publisher

The following interviewee represents the outer range of Conventional Believers as believers without any Buddhist school affiliation. Gu Puzhong 谷甫仲 (male, age about 65–70) holds a world view, dominated by a sharp East-West dichotomy. Traditional Buddhist resources are being reshaped according to "Western"- and "modernity"-compatible criteria and serve the function of a positive self-reconstruction of the "East". Still, Gu's developed views do not lead to his affiliation with a certain school, which induces reflection including the whole of the results from Part I centring on: a) a differentiated description of the tentative field of more conventionally oriented Buddhists; and b) the question of how Taiwanese modernity, with its specific historical dimension, on the one hand, and its massive urbanisation process on the other, impacts on Conventional Buddhists' beliefs and concepts.

Gu Puzhong is happily looking back upon a successful life. Born on the mainland during the Second World War as the only child of rich parents, he was taken to visit Taiwan at the age of eight. His father returned to the mainland–he never saw him again–and the rest of the family were impoverished and so stuck in Taiwan. He was brought up by his grandmother, later studied Chinese, became a journalist, had a family, earnt a good living and, at the age of 40, began studying Buddhism for five years. He opened a small publishing house specialising in Buddhist books. After a serious illness, he retired at the age of 50, but even today remains engaged in various activities in his neighbourhood, teaching on a lifelong learning course, and advising his former publishing house. He has published guidelines for laypeople and is currently compiling a dictionary of Buddhist terminology in casual Chinese. His Mandarin is fluent, without any Taiwanese interjections, but his narration is vivid and, at times, surpasses any clear pronunciation or grammatical word order. While the interviewee creates a lively impression, his friend is concerned about his health.

Gu Puzhong's friend suggested him to the interviewee. He also listened to and recorded the interview, as he is interested in this story of a "highly interesting Buddhist"–Gu's friend would surely not spontaneously call him a "Conventional Buddhist". The interview took place in the publisher's office in a suburb of Taipeh in January 2007. It lasted nearly two hours and has an unusual structure, as the interviewee first dominates the informal chat and the interviewer asks questions, which normally would occur at the end of the interview. In the second phase, the interviewer has an opportunity to pose the original introductory stimulus. Its answer will be subject to the following introductory sequence analysis.

Introductory Sequence Analysis

After Gu Puzhong had described his understanding of Buddhism, the role that Buddhism should play in everyday life and in a systematic world view, and the meaning of being a monastic, the interviewer tried to lead into the originally intended interview:

(1) Interviewer: 你這麼深入佛法/	(1) Interviewer: As you are deeply immersed into Buddhism /
(2) Gu: [very fast, loud, excited] 我沒有深入佛法. 我只是需要去做啦.	(2) Gu: [very fast, loud, excited] No, I am not deeply immersed in Buddhism. I only have to do it.

The interviewer starts concluding Gu's explication of Buddhism by admiring his in-depth study of it. Instead of accepting the compliment, Gu interrupts the interviewer, denying the proposition vehemently. He appears impatient, and speaks loudly and quickly. Has the interviewer totally misunderstood his main point about his Buddhist belief? One expects the explanation to follow. "I only have to do it". Is Gu associating the idea of "being immersed in Buddhism deeply" (*shenru fofa* 深入佛法) as simply engaging in Buddhism intellectually without putting it into practice? Is this perhaps even a strong response due to the potential accusation or an inner conflict with himself, as he is intellectually trained? Or is it a common misunderstanding that Buddhism would involve learning rather than practice? Is therefore Gu's reaction not only a protest against the interviewer's implicit assumption but also revealing his dissatisfaction with an intellectual Buddhism that is inconsistent with life conduct? As Gu dominated the conversation up to this point, he gives the impression that he feels he has something to say about Buddhism. Being an elderly man, he might be aware that his action in spreading Buddhist teaching is a pleasant intellectual involvement, not necessarily connected to his own efforts to put it into practice. His protest might even imply that, to put Buddhism into practice, one does not have to intellectually "be immersed in Buddhism deeply", but can practise it even without it–one "simply/just" (*zhi* 只) has "to do" (*zuo* 做) it. The emphasis on Gu's interpretation of Buddhism lies, in any case, on actual practice.

It follows a sequence, whereby Gu Puzhong and the interviewer are talking nearly simultaneously:

(3) Interviewer: 然後	(3) Interviewer: Then/
(4) Gu: 我以前穿衣服隨便穿/	(4) Gu: Before I wore clothes without paying attention to them/
(5) Interviewer: 你還	(5) Interviewer: you still/
(6) Gu: 我現在/	(6) Gu: I'm now/
(7) Interviewer: 是想起來 你是怎麼跟佛法	(7) Interviewer: remember how you came /
(8) Gu: 很快樂	(8) Gu: very happy
(9) Interviewer: 接觸的	(9) Interviewer: into contact with Buddhism?
(10) Friend: 她是問 你怎麼接觸/ 開始接觸佛法/	(10) Friend: She's asking how you came into contact/ you began to come into contact with Buddhism/

Gu Puzhong's excitement continues, while the interviewer tries persistently to pose her question. Finally, Gu's friend repeats the interviewer's question to him. The interviewer is determined to have the introductory stimulus posed as a whole, probably considering the need to follow the formal criteria. The relationship between the author and the interviewee has already been established and the interaction shows that Gu is far from narrating his story, but trying to transfer a mission of Buddhism to the interviewer. He is not paying attention to the interviewer, which one might ascribe to several reasons: perhaps because the interviewer is a foreigner and so he might not understand her motivation clearly. Is it because she is a far younger, female foreigner that he feels a need to explain the whole of Buddhism in plain words? Also, his friend could have informed him in advance about the presumed topic of the interview. Within this situation, his friend feels obliged to help the interviewer and repeats her question clearly.

Meanwhile, Gu Puzhong makes a statement which might be interpreted as a very concrete exemplification of his understanding of "doing Buddhism": without irritation, he brings his sentence to an end and states that he changed his habit of dressing casually and became "happy" (*kuaile* 快樂). Does "doing Buddhism" imply for him dressing in a specific way? There is no connection offered between the two statements. Perhaps the concept of "doing Buddhism" can be reconstructed from the preceding phase of the interview? If not, Gu probably would like to enlarge now on exactly this link and one will see from the following answer to his friend whether he is open to engaging in this new topic.

(11) Gu: [very fast] →那是我祖母.←	(11) Gu: [very fast] →This's my grandmother←
(12) Interviewer: 對. 祖母. ㄇ.	(12) Interviewer: Yes. Grandmother. M.
(13) Gu: 她不識字. 她很簡單. 她就喜歡做/	(13) Gu: She was illiterate. She was very

做/ 做好事	simple. She just liked to do/ do/ do good things.
(14) Interviewer: 口	(14) Interviewer: M.

Gu changes topic abruptly and answers concisely without hesitation. This is probably not the first time he has thought about how he came into contact with Buddhism or his grandmother's influence. His grandmother may have played an important role in his life. The fast change of topic and hasty answer also show that Gu is willing to comply with the interview and that it is probably his long life experience and strong personality which make him enthusiastically impatient and prevent him from listening. His Buddhist belief is directly connected to a person–his grandmother–whom we would expect to command respect and who, belonging to the previous generation, may have passed on the tradition to her grandchild. Gu sketches her in three short phrases: for him, it is important that his grandmother was "illiterate" (lit. "did not know characters", *bu shi zi* 不識字), "simple" (*jiandan* 簡單) and "(just) liked to do good things" (*jiu xihuan zuo haoshi* 就喜歡做好事). He regards it as worth mentioning that she laid emphasis on acting while not being formally educated. Gu seems to appreciate his grandmother's simplicity without making an intellectual issue out of it. There is a certain parallel in Gu's emphasis on "doing Buddhism" and his grandmother's attitude, to do "good things": Gu cherishes concrete action and pays respect to someone who is illiterate but acting, while he is upset about "being immersed in Buddhism deeply". Has Gu adopted his grandmother's habitus and is trying to live according to her ideals, despite being highly educated? What role does Buddhism play here? Has "to do Buddhism" to be understood as "to do good things"? At least for his grandmother, one would expect her belief to be connected to being engaged in "good" matters. But how far? Gu continues:

(15) Gu: 那是我小時候我家很有錢. 她也把錢/ 錢阿 去拿去 第一個是要幫人家蓋廟 幫助廟裡面 第二個她幫助窮人 她常常住在廟裡 我的祖母阿	(15) Gu: That's when I was young and my family had lots of money. She also took the money/ money/ took it. First, she helped everyone to build temples. She helped in the temple. Second, she helped the poor. She often lived in the temple. My grandmother a
(16) Interviewer: 你的祖母/	(16) Interviewer: Your grandmother/
(17) Gu: 住在廟裡 因為我祖父做生意	(17) Gu: lived in temples. Because my grandfather was doing business.

Gu Puzhong returns to the experiences of his youth and points out the wealth of his family. Is he proud of this wealth? He does not hide the fact as such, but wealth is also just the necessary basis for his grandmother's charity work. Gu portrays the event by concentrating on material matters and his narration builds up in a realistic, pragmatic way. His grandmother was spending his family's money, which suggests that she was probably part of a family wherein, traditionally, the earning of money was not her task, but she was allowed to spend it. Gu's narration is clearly structured when he divides his grandmother's activities into two fields: building temples and helping the poor. Her help with temple building was not dedicated to a specific project, but a general attitude, and this help was not only a financial matter but a general engagement "within" the temple (matters; *bangzhu miao limian* 幫助廟裡面). The second statement about "helping the poor" (*bangzhu qiongren* 幫助窮人) receives no further clarification, but Gu is specifying the background to his grandmother's engagement: the assumption that she does not have to earn money proves correct. She even seems to be on her own, as her husband is away on business. Gu reasons that his grandmother lived in temples because of this. Living in temples was perhaps uncommon, as he sees the need to justify it. The reason for living a temple life itself–a husband doing business–is not unusual. The scenario makes sense in the context of a rich family, whose grandmother has a kind of elite self-understanding.

Gu Puzhong was obviously, in his early youth, socialised in the context of a rich mercantile family and witnessed his grandmother engaging in–as the "good things" are specified–two traditional, long established fields of lay support: temple construction and charity work. She lives in a temple. Is this temple explicitly Buddhist? Or she simply a more religiously-oriented person, whose engagement is not bound to a certain doctrine? How does Gu's own connection to Buddhism unfold in this context?

After a short interlude of trying to concretise this engagement in temple-building activities, Gu enlarges on his grandmother's charity work, who collected money without asking much about the spiritual or actual merits she would gain from that, but being innocent about any differentiation, just wishing to do something good. Any selfish acquisition of advantages was far from his grandmother's thoughts, as she was very austere (*jianpu* 儉樸). This Gu illustrates by portraying her eating habits:

(26) 像吃飯 我都看在眼裡阿 家裡很多錢 但是她吃飯 她吃素 她的飯很簡單 那時我們沒有米阿 都只是有那個麥 做成粉 這樣和在一起 就像這個咖啡一樣 她就吃一點 吃饅頭 吃完了以後 杯底用開水 沖一沖 因為還有一些粘的東西阿 洗乾淨 再喝下去 哈 就在那裡 三拜 感謝一些眾生阿 從佛始 法界一切眾生 通通在那裡感謝

(26) Like when eating. I saw it all with my own eyes. The family was very rich, but she ate her meals/ She was vegetarian. Her meals were very simple. At that time, we had no rice a. All we had was that wheat for making flour. Like that, we mixed it together. Just like this coffee. She just ate a bit. Ate steamed bread. When she was ready, she used boiled water for the bottom of the cup, poured it, because there was still some sticky stuff left [in it]. Washed it clean. Swallowed it. Ha. Then there–three bows. Thanking all sentient

beings. From Buddha starting through the *dharmadhātu* and all sentient beings she thanked there.

As when talking about clothing before, Gu enlarges on a very concrete everyday matter. Rich in detail, he describes how his grandmother ate. One can easily visualise him watching his grandmother intensely as a child, observing her actions precisely and storing up a long-lasting impression of them. More than 50 years later, he still recalls the family's lack of food and his grandmother not taking advantage of their wealth but eating a very simple vegetarian diet, fastidiously cleansing her bowl and not wasting any food. Finally, her eagerness is rounded off with a thankful dedication to the whole world, starting with Buddha. His grandmother's behaviour appears considered. She is not simply following a mere traditional Buddhist habit of vegetarianism and Buddhist meal prayers, but each of her actions seems to be leavened by a clear will which might be founded in what Gu would call "Buddhism".

(27) 從小我們就看這個 她管我們很嚴 那我們被她管了 她常常把我們帶到廟裡去 她帶到廟裡去 就開我們智慧 這個很笨 就開智慧 常常在那個城裡廟裡去 因為我們城裡面很有錢 那 後來到台灣沒有錢 但是她學佛不斷

(27) Since childhood, we watched that. She watched us very strictly. Na, we were watched by her. She often took us to the temple. To open up our wisdom. "This [sc. child] is very stupid". So to open up our wisdom. We often went to the temple in this city. Because we were very rich in this city. Na. Later, we came to Taiwan and had no money, but she studied Buddhism without interruption.

His grandmother's influence was already strong, even before he came to Taiwan. Together with other children he was "*guan* 管" (watched/cared) for by her "*henyan* 很嚴" (very strictly). Again, the link between belief and money emerges: they often visit a temple because they are rich. Wealth means social recognition. Visiting a temple is probably an important action in terms of being seen or taking an active part in community life. Wealth also makes it possible to donate to the temple, which–as we saw in the interview with the taxi driver, Lin Yongfu–takes over the welfare function in society. Still, the grandmother's obligation to Buddhism continued, even when she was poor in Taiwan. She did not stop "*xuefo* 學佛" (studying Buddhism). "*Xue*" (Studying) has to be seen in a wide sense, as a kind of "coping"/"keeping busy" with Buddhism, and actions such as visiting the temple and helping the poor might even be subsumed under it.

The children are taken to the temple with the intention of "increasing their wisdom" (lit. "opening wisdom", *kai zhihui* 開智慧), Gu recalls. Taking children to a temple first includes familiarising them with the religious or Buddhist temple life and making them receptive to its atmosphere. Children will unconsciously become acquainted with the social dimension of temple life. "Increasing their wisdom" might also imply calling some religious power upon them. One does not learn here whether Gu appreciated his grandmother's strict education, but her statement about him being a "stupid" child in front of others shows that he either accepts his grandmother's authority or will oppose her with great difficulty. It seems that her influence was inescapable and Gu may have sought later to find a way to match his own concepts and experiences with his dominating grandmother's clear instructions. What exactly was the Buddhist heritage that his grandmother handed down to him?

In the following, he continues his story: how he visited her every weekend in the temple where she lived, enjoyed the advantage of having fruit to eat there and, although he does not fully appreciate its master, he acknowledges his respect for him, a respect one could even have towards a Napoleon or a Hitler. On the other hand, he also used the opportunity to pray for success in exams. When his grandmother passed away, he finally realised her power (*Wo zumu guoshi nage shihou wo hen gandong cai zhi nage liliang hao da* 我祖母過世 那個時候我很感動 才知那個力量好大). In her testimony, she had determined a sea burial of her ashes baked in steamed bread, symbolising the 48 vows of Bodhisattva Amitābha. This touched him and initiated his interest in Buddhism. His answer to the introductory stimulus ends with the following sequence:

(34) 這我感動 我非常非常感動 以前還有時候還有很討厭她 因 因為她要求很嚴 拜不能 papapa [sound of beating] 你要規規矩矩 要拜 阿 […, slurred] 都按規矩 拜 那個時候去亂拜 譬如說一百拜 我珍惜 罵了 打我得 她就 對 那後來我發現到的 那個時候她對佛教是交心交義 當然也聽了一些很不可思議的事情 阿 真的 還不是假的呢 有時候也會被我碰到不是我上 是看到別人製作 病好了 很多事情就這樣 不可思議 那後來她一死 這個人這個那麼厲害阿 我們中國人是在講屍體保存的很好 很好的棺材 她不要 那個 丟海 還在叫我去丟 那好 我丟丟丟了和平島 租支船就去 哦 我覺得 她太厲害吧 她不識字 識字 可她會背金剛經 金剛經阿五千多字 五千八百多字 都不要念的 就是背的 不看經本 keoioioi [throaty sound] 一直念 一分得到第三十二 哦 這麼厲害 我都背就背得很爛 都背不起來所她這麼厲害 這是第一個 所她死的時候 我就很感動 真的很了不起 這樣/ 這樣能夠大死 那我就開始需要對佛 開始要

(34) This [i.e. her death] moved me, I was very, very moved. Before, still, sometimes I also hated her a lot. Be/ because she was strict. Worship. You can't *papapa* [sound of beating]. You have to behave, you have to worship a […, slurred]. All according to rules. Worship. That time I worshipped improperly, for example, 100 times, I was severely scolded, she beat me, she just, right/ Na, later I discovered, that time she was with her whole heart and mind [idiomatic; *jiaoxin jiaoyi*] into Buddhism. Of course, I also heard some unimaginable things. A. Really, not fake ne. Sometimes, I also witnessed them. Not by myself, [sc. but] seeing others making it, illness being cured, lots of things were like that, unimaginable. Na when she later died, this person was so great a. We Chinese say: Preserve the body well, a very good coffin. She didn't want it. Throw that into the sea. And even ordered me to throw it away. Na, good. I threw/ threw/ threw it.

看看佛經阿 看不懂阿 嗯 比較深阿 那後來慢慢體會自己去想找書 找書 找書 後來看 後來 我是看 那個祭壇 很大 結果我祖母 哦 台灣所有的大和尚都到那邊去做那個氣 好可怕 所有的大和尚都到了我跟這個人 這個力量怎麼那麼大 所以我覺得 在這個裡面有東西可以學習阿要去探秘 解開秘密 所以我這樣慢慢讀

At Peace Island, rented a boat and went. O. I think she's really great na. She was illiterate, illiterate. But she had memorised the *Diamond Sūtra. Diamond Sūtra*, more than 5000 characters. More than 5800 characters. She didn't need to read it. Just memorised it. Didn't look at the textbook. Keoioioi [throaty sound] read continuously. Once up to Chapter 32. That's great. I was very poor at memorising. I can't remember it. So she was that great. That is the first. So when she died, I was really moved. Really unimaginable. Like that/ being able to die a great death like this. Na, I just started to have to for Buddhism/ wanted to read Buddhist sūtras a. I didn't understand them. A. En. Was a bit deep a. Na, later I slowly realised things and went myself to consult books. Consult books. Consult books. Later, I saw/ Later, I saw that huge burial. Finally my grandmother. O. All the eminent monks of Taiwan came there and did it. That atmosphere was so scary. All the eminent monks were there. I with that person/ This power was so great. So I think in this there are things one can learn. A. One has to investigate the mystery, open up the secret by understanding it. So like that I slowly studied.

His grandmother's Buddhist heritage is of a heroic character: austerity means, for her, denying herself even in death, and serving herself up to the fish. The highly symbolic act itself she asks her grandson to perform. Deeper than any intellectual explanation, this might lead him to internalise and be obliged to follow his grandmother's message. Indeed, although he admits his hatred for her due to her ill-treatment of him, he feels deeply touched by her death, and it is this death which initiates his interest in studying Buddhism–he wants intellectually to understand and "open up" his grandmother's "mystery" (*jiekai mimi* 解開秘密) to reach the source of her "power"/"strength" (*liliang* 力量) and "unimaginable" character (*liaobuji* 了不起), as he stresses repeatedly during the interview. Gu Puzhong might try to understand her dedication by putting it into practice in his own life and continuing through his life his grandmother's heritage. Her performative adhortation is as strong as an imperative and successful: in retelling the story and in spreading his Buddhist mission, Gu brings into action in his life and in the interview itself the strength and the will of his grandmother.

In addition, Gu seems an accomplished, talented speaker. His narration about his grandmother is so far clearly floating and logically structured, finding its biggest intensity in the final lines and ending in a dramatic bow in his obligation to study Buddhism. The narration itself he enforces through tropes which he assumes to be well-recognised patterns, ensuring his grandmother's authority and integrity: always first outlining her missing education and illiteracy, he transforms his listeners' doubts into admiration, contrasting his grandmother's simplicity with her dedication and bright memory. Her authority receives support from the fact that he witnessed healings as well as the fact that "all of the eminent monks of Taiwan" (*Taiwan suoyou de da heshang* 台灣所有的大和尚) attended her burial. Simplicity and austerity are an intense combination, which Gu underlines by frequently exclaiming, how "*lihai* 利害", how fierce and great his grandmother seems to him.

Structural Hypothesis

Gu Puzhong is used to dominating a discourse while being open to the interview as such. Well-meaning in intention, he finally opens up to the introductory stimulus and shows a high degree of reflection about his biographical encounter with Buddhism. An intense description of scenes from his youth prove him a talented narrator who is precisely sketching situations and vividly evoking the past. The most formative figure during his early years was his grandmother, a person whom he describes through a discrepancy between a minimal education and a high austerity and obligation towards Buddhism. Buddhism, as he experiences it through his grandmother's impact, means being self-less until death, engaging in temple matters and helping the poor while living an ascetic life. His grandmother passes on her mental heritage to her grandson, requesting that he feed her ashes to the fish. The theatrical strength of this act initiates Gu's decision to study Buddhism and try to understand the "mysterious" depth of her belief. The event has far-reaching consequences since, at the time of the interview, Gu is *de facto* enacting his grandmother, emphasising already in his initial phrase the importance and necessity of action ("I only have to do it") over intellectual deliberation. Still, his fixation on action is verbally expressible, while his grandmother was performing it through her own deeds. This is the basis for Gu's missionary enthusiasm, which nearly makes him unable to listen to the question of the interviewer.

One might expect, in the rest of the interview, that not only will Gu's life-story become clearer, but also his current concept of Buddhism. In the sequence analysed so far, only his disinterest from his selfish praying and pragmatic interest in food during his youth becomes evident. By mentioning wealth repeatedly, one can also deduce that Gu probably has a realistic, fact-based primary orientation.

Practice

Gu holds a basically materialistic opinion, which he sees as a precondition for any occupation with Buddhism: "eating" comes "first" to him:

(S12) 吃飯還是第一啦 你沒有飯吃 你天天拜佛 我看也不行 還是要一個經濟好一點 可以吃飯 可以吃得飽 不要給別人煩惱 吃飯吃不飽有兩個煩惱 一個自己煩惱 一個你爸爸媽媽煩惱 那是我沒有 我爸爸 我沒有錢 我爸媽開始吃不飽 太難過 所以你必須要這個家安置好 要把一匹豬養好 我們自己也是豬的 剛剛講的 這個豬養的肥肥有吃有睡有休息 阿 就很好了 那這樣去學佛 就比較好一點 因為我們就是凡人嘛 本來沒有錢找你學佛嘛. [..., name of monk of his grandmother]也沒有很多學佛嘛 就是出家 那我們不是那一種人 沒有那個福報 也沒有那個根基啦 必須一點一點慢慢去 所以後來我就變這樣

(S12) Eating is still the first la. If you've nothing to eat, but daily venerate Buddha, it doesn't work in my view. Still, there has to be a slightly better economy. One can eat, can eat until one's full. One should not give others worries. Not eating until one is full has two concerns: one is worrying oneself, the other is worrying your father and mother. Na, I have not done [that]. My father, I don't have money. [Then] my parents don't eat up, [that would be] too sad. Therefore, you have to arrange for this family well, you have to nourish well one pig. We ourselves are also like pigs, as I just said. Nourish this pig to be fat. Can eat, can sleep, can have a break. A. Just very good. Na, like this to go and learn Buddhism is just a bit better. Because we are just common people ma. If one originally has no money, and asks you to learn Buddhism ma. [..., name of monk of his grandmother] also did not study a lot Buddhism. Just left home. Na, we're not that kind of people. We don't have this luck, also don't have this basis la. We have to go bit by bit slowly. So afterwards I got like this.

His opinion is based on his concept of responsibility for those around him, i.e. his family, and his–normally emphasised in traditional Chinese culture–respect for his parents. Bodily satisfaction–eating, sleeping, having a break–are the basic requirements, which he describes through the metaphor of the needs of a pig. Pigs are here supposed to be passive farm animals, depending on the care of humans. They are not engaged in any kind of productive work besides finally being determined to become food for humans, but just consuming and relaxing. Gu acknowledges the worth of having these basic needs fulfilled: "Just very good" this is. Also, in this respect, he shows a realistic, pragmatic orientation, being in line with his own and his grandmother's obligation to take action and appreciate the actual effects of Buddhism in his life. Gu is taking over his grandmother's pragmatic habitus and does not consider himself as superior to her because of his education. Counting himself as one of the "common people", he admits that he was neither rich nor the kind of a person with the (karmic) "luck" to become a monastic. "Common people", among whom the average lay Buddhist has to be counted, are restricted in their ability to study Buddhism, they have to go "bit by bit", slowly.

Gu takes the path that his traditional environment expects of him, taking the role one expects of a man in a patriarchal culture, nourishing his family and caring for the finances, while concentrating in his mind primarily on the role of men: when talking about "we", the "common people", how they "run the family" and nourish it, one thinks more of the role of the family's father than the mother, who traditionally does not earn. Gu is managing his task successfully and, having established a firm basis, he studies Buddhism. Again, following his grandmother's heritage in this second step, at the age of 40, he is working through Buddhist doctrine, seeking to understand her "mystery".

Gu attempts many times to explain this "mystery", which in the interview is a synonym for the essence of Buddhism. Practice–*xiuxing*–remains the central term for him throughout his whole narration. Even at the beginning, he states:

(S2) 我覺得修行蠻重要. 這個佛教我們 怎麼活 怎麼死 活得很快樂 死得也很快樂 所以我學佛的用意在這裡	(S2) I think practice is most important. This Buddha teaches us how to live, how to die, to live very happy, to die also very happy. So my use of learning Buddhism is there.

Buddhism is not just constructed as truth about life which, happy or unhappy, one has to accept, but Buddhism, according to Gu, is a teaching that enables one to lead a life of profound happiness, one that even includes a joyful death. If Buddhism teaches people how to live and die, one asks about the content of this doctrine. What makes one happy and what shall one finally practise?

His longing to put things into practice has been shown to be mainly inspired by his grandmother, so one would expect him to define practice through being austere and free from selfishness. To what extent does this include any concrete instructions? Gu states later in the interview:

(S9) 修行在人間阿 佛法在時間 不離時間法 啦 不一定說 用這個東西 這個不直啦 佛說 *bawansiqian* [slurred] 三千煩惱絲剪掉就沒有煩惱了 原來是如此 佛也是割髮嘛	(S9) Practice is among people a. The Buddhadharma is within time. It doesn't leave the law of time la. It's not certainly saying: use this thing, this's not right la. Buddha says: *bawansiqian* [slurred]. If one cuts off the 3000 fine hairs of sorrow, one is without sorrow. Originally, it's like that. Buddha is also cutting his hair ma.

Practice is done in the field of social life and, through that, Buddhism is concretely bound to the realm of time. Buddhism and Buddha himself Gu Puzhong relativises as being part of the world. The historical Buddha himself has, in Gu's view, to practise so that he is without sorrow–metaphorically enacted through cutting his hair. How far is concrete hair-cutting obligatory? Which performative qualities does Gu see in concrete Buddhist practice? The concrete example stands in contrast to his statement, that Buddhism would not "certainly say" what to "use" (*fofa [...] bu yiding shuo yong zhe ge dongxi* 佛法[...]不一定說用這個東西), and therefore might be meant figuratively. Is finally the meaning of Buddhism dissolving Buddhism as a distinct entity itself? At least, Buddhism seems not to give any concrete instructions; it is "not certainly saying" what one has "to use" or what is not "right" (*zhi* 直).

It is therefore no wonder that Gu exemplifies the perfect practice of Buddhism through relating a life-experience that does not include the conscious notion of Buddhism at all:[86] it seems that he lived for some time in Canada.

86 The story Gu summed up as follows: "(S4) Gu: So Buddhism has lots of things which I think are very good. These things are reconstructing my soul [sc. and are] finally saying: one has to practise by oneself. You in your daily life. Ei. Inside. Then it is good. When I came to Canada, when I went to Canada the first time, I was really touched. This/ I think this is just practice. Na, my English is not very good. I studied Chinese. A. Still OK. When I was at high school, it was still OK. Later, when I studied in the Chinese department, it didn't work. Later, I myself went to work [in the field of] journalism to work. This English I just encountered rarely. Basically it's still OK. O. One day, I came into a very big/ that/ [..., name of department store] In Canada it's very big/ now it's also very big/ one floor very big, very big. Just overly big. Everything in Taiwan I saw, there is none like this. Several streets all in that underground. O a! We in Taiwan have an advantage. It says this "restroom" [in English] or "lavatory" [in English]. Interviewer: Right. Gu: wash room [in English]. It says it all very clearly. Restroom [now in Chinese]. Made very big. In the foreign, it is not. Small. Written: Restroom. You search half a day and don't find it. So I searched for a foreigner. I just asked: Where's the toilet? He said: Follow me [in English]. He took me with him. After he took me there a, he said: I'll wait for you at the entrance. When you've had a pee, a a, you come out. OK, OK. So I went in. When I had washed my hands a, I also ran into a thing: there was a foreigner. [I] was touched. Just East and West are not quite the same. I think. Na, Canadians are fine. Their folk is educated. He just used that paper and wiped that clean. I just watched from the side. Ei. How can there be this kind of/ this kind of a person [laughs]. He did not make it wet. It is other people who made that wash basin wet. He did like that there. Wiped once, twice. I was very touched. I watched it to the end and went out myself. Ei. That fellow [lit. "older brother"], who took me to the toilet, was still there, waiting to take me back to the original place again. Hai a. Too touched la. Too touched. I just/ I this think is practice la. Interviewer: This is real practice despite they are not necessarily Buddhists." (Orig.: (S4) Gu: 所以佛教有很多東西我覺得很好 這東西是重建我的靈魂到底說 自己要修行 你在日常生活 欸 裡面 就好好的 我到加拿大 第一次去加拿大 很感動 這/ 我覺得這個就是修行 那我英文不是很好 我是讀中文的 阿 還可以了 高中的時候還可以了 後來我念中文系 就不行 後來自己從事新聞工作 這英文就很少接觸 基本還可以了 哦 有一天到了很大的一個 那個[..., name of department store] 在加拿大很大 現在也很大 一層 很大 很大 就超大 台灣我所看的 沒有一家 幾條街都在那個地

Soon after he arrived, his English was poor and, while shopping in a department store, he found himself unable to find the toilet. He felt the need to rectify both issues: excusing his poor English, he states that, as a journalist who had graduated in Chinese, he did not have much contact with English. Still, in other passages, he partly applies English expressions as being more precise than the Chinese ones–one has to live in the "Here and Now", Chinese "*dangxia* 當下" (R4)–which shows that he estimates English as such. Being unable to find the toilet, he complains that toilets abroad are unclearly marked. He prefers his homeland in this respect, but clearly points out that he valued the Westerners' behaviour that he experienced in the department store. The incident he does not see in the light of a cultural difference alone, but also as a positive attitude in everyday life: in search of a toilet, he asked a native person. He led him to the toilet personally and waited to escort him back again afterwards. In addition, when washing his hands, Gu saw someone wiping dry the wash basin, which had been wet by someone else. The combination of these two events overwhelmed Gu. Both actions showed him the selfless attitude he had seen in his grandmother. Still, his grandmother led a life which had clear Buddhist markers of prayer and engagement in the Buddhist community, Gu's enthusiastic exclamation, that what he had seen there in Canada would be the real practice, is answered by the interviewer by pointing out that these people were not necessarily Buddhists. Gu counters this:

(S5) Gu: 他不是佛教徒 就是你不管是哪一個徒來 全世界的人好 有紅人白人 看你白的 我們兩個黃的 也有黑人 有紅人 可是血是紅的 可見人是平等的嘛 所以佛說 阿耨多羅三藐三菩提 真正正覺 這是要修呢 修就是作嘛 簡單嘛 就是 你平常時時刻刻 你心在改變自己 不斷修正自己的錯誤 修行我覺得要從這方面 去作

(S5) Gu: [They are; lit. he/she/it] not Buddhist. You just don't care what follower comes. The people of the whole world are good. There are red people, white people. See, you are white, we two are yellow. There are also black people. There are red people. But the blood is red. [So] one can see that people are equal ma. So Buddha says: *anuttara-samyak-saṃbodhi* [BT, i.e. unexcelled complete enlightenment]. Real true awakening. This is what one should practise ne. Practice is doing

下 哦阿 我們台灣有一個好處 它寫這個 restroom 或者 lavatory. Interviewer: 對 Gu: wash room 它都寫得很清楚 化妝室 作很大 外國不是 小小的 寫的 化妝室. 找半天找不到 我就找一個老外 我就問 這個洗手間在哪裡 他說 follow me 他把我帶去 帶去以後阿 他說 我在門口等你 你撒尿完了以後 阿 阿 你就出來 好 好 我就進去 我洗完手 阿也碰了一件事情 有一位外國人 很感動 就是東西方不太一樣 我覺得 那加拿大人不錯他國民教育 他就用那個紙 把那個擦乾淨 我就在旁邊看 欸 怎麼有這種/ 這種人 [laughs] 不是他弄濕的 是別人弄濕那個洗手檯 他就是在那邊弄這樣子 擦一次 兩次 我很感動 我看一看完了 我自己出去 欸 那個老兄 帶我到廁所去 還在那邊 等我帶我回到原處去 咳阿 太感動 啦 太感動 我就是 我這覺得修行啦 Interviewer: 這是真正的修行雖然他們不一定是佛教徒.)

ma. Simple ma. Is just: You in normal moments, your heart changes itself, correcting without interruption your own faults. Practice, I think, has to start from this aspect.

The question of real practice, in a Buddhist sense, seems to be connected to being a human as such. In Gu Puzhong's view, people are equal and he supports that by referring to the bodily knowledge that, although outwardly different, people are equal. The idea that blood through all ethnicities is red seems to guarantee this truth of human equality. Bodily knowledge, in accordance with the common basics of the natural sciences, guarantees the truth of this equality. *Anuttara-samyak-saṃbodhi*, "Unexcelled complete enlightenment", is the key term for Gu's Buddhist description of the situation in general, which later becomes for him the decisive criterion about other traditions (see below for his comment on Islam). Reformulating the Sanskrit key term in semantically meaningful Chinese, Gu Puzhong emphasises that this would be the aim of all practice, but what does "real true awakening" imply? That it is connected with "doing" and "simplicity" has already been repeated frequently, but Gu's explanations mostly ended there; this time he enlarges on them, taking the essence of his story to aid his understanding of the nature of correct Buddhist practice: Buddhist practice means that, usually, "your heart changes itself, incessantly practising your own faults". The practice of Buddhism is connected with observing one's own behaviour and correcting oneself constantly. This means awakening in a very pragmatic sense as being aware of one's own actions and constantly reminding oneself to make the effort to engage oneself, "being able to lift up yourself" (*nenggou tisheng ziji* 能夠提升自己; S8), as Gu later in the interview refers back to the message of this story.

While criticising Taiwanese believers who go to temples simply to pray for their own advantage and therefore being very selfish,[87] Gu actually holds a view of Buddhism which, put into practice, would have as a consequence the reform of the Buddhist world or at least would marginalise the common

87 "(S6) Gu: But, today, Taiwanese Buddhism, I see, Buddhism, [on] the mainland [it] is also the same, all took off the Buddhist character, the human character came out. How scary! Humanity has a bad character. A. [...] Taiwanese are very selfish ma. They go to worship. That is just very selfish ma. Right? You don't have this kind of feeling? They are, ei, asking Buddhas and bodhisattvas: let me win. They are asking Buddhas and bodhisattvas: I'm going to take an exam, let me pass. A. I donate a bit, right, a lot of money. This is talking about business ma. Only making this/" (Orig.: (S6) Gu: 但是今天 台灣的佛教 我看 佛教 大陸也是一樣 都把佛性拿掉了 人性出來了 好可怕 人有劣根性 阿 [...] 台灣人很自私嘛 他去拜佛 就是很自私的嘛 對不對 你沒有這種感覺 他是 欸 求佛菩薩 讓我中獎 求佛菩薩 我去考試讓我考取 阿 我投資一點 對不對 很多錢 這談生意嘛 只有把這個/).

boundaries within it. Gu denies the importance of the dharma meetings, that were so essential to the donor, Li Zhiqiang, and seems to dislike all markers of difference, like signs or even temples. Referring back to Buddha himself as the final authority, he claims that he would not have established any of these institutions, but simply been enlightened sitting under a tree. Jokingly, he adds that one cannot simply put up a sign to which death one goes to or which afterlife:

(S7) 就佛教也沒有了 他搞 以前了也沒有搞搞甚麼法會 搞這個這些牌子[?] 以前 我覺得 佛當初沒有搞這個東西 阿 佛是/ 佛是搞這個阿 沒有阿 樹下 他是在樹下悟道.	(S7) Buddha just didn't teach that. He established/ Before he also didn't establish/ establish whatever dharma assembly, established this/ these signs [?]. Before I think, Buddha in the beginning did not establish these things. A. Buddha is/ Buddha established this a/ No a. Under a tree. He was enlightened under a tree.
Interviewer: 對	Interviewer: Right.
Gu: 他不是在這個大廟裡面 沒有這樣搞 阿 也沒有說蓋大廟甚麼 貼牌子 貼長生 貼消災延壽 貼到死到往生 沒有用啦 我覺得 公修公收 收到功德, 婆修婆收, 不收不修不收, 自修自收 在修行 佛教不是很難的東西啦 我/ 我覺得啦.	Gu: He didn't in this big temple inside build like that a. He also didn't say "build a big temple" or something like that, hang up signs, hang up "long life", hang up "extinguish disasters and prolong life". Hang up "to death", "to rebirth". This has no use la. I think, a man practises, a man receives, receive merits and virtues, an old woman practises, an old woman receives, not achieving, not practising, not achieving. Self practising, self achieving. In practise, Buddhism isn't a very difficult thing la. I think la.
Interviewer: 所以修行也是在生活裡面的對不對	Interviewer: So practice is also in life, right?
Gu: 對對對 非常重要 它不是 一種宗教你去拜	Gu: Right, right, right. Very important. It's not a religion you go to venerate.

Buddhism in this concept is returning to its historically initial phase and overcomes what was so important for his grandmother and for most of the other believers discussed so far–veneration. In that sense, Buddhism, for Gu Puzhong, is not a "religion". Gu follows, nevertheless, religious practices in his own life, as will be seen later.

Returning to its roots means, to Gu, putting into question all later established developments of Buddhism and trying to concentrate on the inner attitude of the person only. Gu even enlarges upon the well-established institutions as one of monastics, herewith reinterpreting the role of lay people and monasticism. As a good Buddhist, he explains, one has to practise, which means watching oneself carefully. A monastic, for Gu, is supposed to be an ideal Buddhist, and therefore he thinks, that the essential question would be whether one is a monastic in one's heart rather than in one's body:

(S8) 我功力夠的話 我今天做總統, 我今天看你的法典, 我一樣是一個大出家人. 這個心出家 身不出家吧.	(S8) If my power is great enough, I'll become president today. If I look at your Buddhist scripture today, I am the same as a big monastic. This heart leaves home, the body doesn't leave home, ba.

Contrariwise, returning to the roots and referring to the practice of Buddha himself does not mean that Gu would follow a Theravāda Buddhist oriented path of belief, as he clearly cherishes the Mahāyāna bodhisattva ideal of opening up the possibilities of enlightenment to everyone. The vow of the bodhisattva to "bring everyone through" (*du zhongsheng* 渡眾生), to liberate everyone, makes no distinction between people, assuring their equality as science does:

(S13) 真正正覺人就是平等的嘛 你不分這個嘛 不過他有緣無緣 我都要渡他 對不對 我沒有甚麼公益甚麼 不可以說有對價條件 或者 你信 那我給你永生 你不信 給不給永生不知道了 這是基督教的論調了 可是佛教不是 他都要渡了 不管你有緣無緣 我都渡到只要你是要渡的 我覺得這個那個佛教的心[hic!]的量非常大 就是佛教的文字 因為離我們太久遠 就反過來從白馬寺以前到現在 太久了 對阿 兩千年阿 我們那裡現在不懂阿對不對 我們把它現代化 大家懂阿 對不對那 才有用 對人有沒有幫助啦	(S13) Really right, people are just equal ma. You don't separate this ma. Regardless of if they have karmic connections or not, I want to bring them all through, right? I don't have any use for that. I can't say, that I have countervalue conditions or: if you believe this, I'll give you eternal life. If you don't believe, I don't know, if I give you eternal life. That is the point of discussion in Christianity. But Buddhism is not. It wants to bring them all through. Regardless of if you have karma or not. I bring them all through. Only, you have to want to be brought through. I think this is the capacity of the heart of this/ that Buddhism. Very big. It's just Buddhist written language, because it's too far away from us. On the contrary, just before the time of the *Baima* Temple until now is too long. Right a. 2000 years a. There we don't understand it now a. right? We modernise it, everyone understands, right? 2000 years a. We there now do not understand a. Right? We modernise it. Everyone understands a. Right? Na, only then it has a use. For the people, it is no help la.

Gu Puzhong is convinced of Buddhism, because he thinks that its goodness is its universal promise of salvation. Buddhism has been a great help to people over the centuries and, because of this long period, Gu argues that it has become incomprehensible. He sees his task as making the old Buddhist texts understandable again through modernising them and, later in the interview, even states this to be the task of his life: "This is a kind of thing that I hoped throughout my life, helping the not comprehended" (*Zhi shi wo yisheng xiwang de yi zhong shiqing bangzhu bu dong de* 這是我一生希望的一種事情 幫助不懂的; R13). The aim of making Buddhist texts understandable is based on a cognitive concept, assuming that the value of the texts lies clearly in their content which, according to him, can be separated from the form of the language. Also, the transmitted texts are not appreciated in any other aspect, despite their content. Most Buddhists treat Buddhist sūtras, for example, with great respect. Would Gu oppose something like that? In his intellectual reflection, at least, it looks as if he holds a rationalistic and pragmatic basic concept of Buddhism.

East-West Dichotomy

As mentioned in advance, Gu is critical of Taiwanese who egoistically venerate in temples to gain advantages. Elsewhere, he states that Taiwanese Buddhism consists only of business interests (R9). This criticism of his own culture is part of a strong East-West-dichotomy, which dominates especially the beginning of his talk. During the interview, he wears a cap from Canada and immediately shows an interest in the researcher's home country while starting to chat about his experiences in Canada. Talking about research centres in Taiwan, he states:

(S1) 有時候是要用西方的方法來研究東方的東西 東方的方法不太好 這是沒有方法 這是個人個做個的 對不對	(S1) Sometimes, one has to use Western methods to research Eastern matters. The Eastern methods are not that good. This is: they don't have a method. This is, each does his/her own, right?

How are "Western methods" to be understood? Later in the interview, Gu states that painting and music are good ways of making Buddhism understandable and provides numerous examples of this (R10). He adds elsewhere that science should now provide the best research about Buddhism (R5). Art and science are therefore examples of "Western methods" for Gu, while "Eastern things" parallel Buddhism. So, for example, it would be good to compose Buddhist music using Western composition techniques. It would also be perfect to draw paintings with Buddhist topics in the Western style. Both attempts have been made and Gu names two artists, one from Malaysia and one from Hong Kong, as examples (R1; R10). While Western music has more "system" and Western paintings and architecture have more "spirit", Gu states:

(S10) Gu: 所以說可以從任何 文字 音樂 繪畫 對不對 我們看 米開朗基羅的東西 就很	(S10) Gu: Everything can be said in written language, music, paintings, right? We see

感動阿 你跑到那個山洞裡面去 看敦煌的東西 你就很感動 你不是搞得金光閃閃的 金光也可以了 但是你要有真正藝術的修養 那是工匠作的 他就表達不出來 那個 這個形象以外的東西 精神不出來 必須要精神出來.	Michelangelo's things are just very touching a. China always stayed the same. You go to this cave and look at the things of Dunhuang, you're just very touched. You didn't build it very shiny [fixed expression]. Shining is still OK, but if you want to have real art mastery, that was done by an artificer. Performing he could not express it. That. These things apart from the figure. The spirit doesn't come out. The spirit has to come out.

Gu Puzhong denies any development in Chinese art history, while a "Western" picture like that of Michelangelo would be "touching" (*gandong* 感動). The role of the Dunhuang caves in this example is certainly clear to the speaker, but less clear in the actual passage. Is Dunhuang here an example of the non-developing China? The visitor seems touched by it. Is Dunhuang not an example for China, but of how Chinese art can be influenced, mixed with art from other cultures and therefore become very touching? However one decides upon the example, Gu's point is clear: he values art of which he has the impression that "the spirit comes out" (*jingshen chulai* 精神出來).

Gu has received a comparatively traditional Eastern education, studying Chinese, and can speak very little English, as noted above. Still, the interview is dominated by the East-West-distinction. On the one hand, this might be a reaction to the interviewer and some of Gu's polite praise of the West he might emphasise less in other contexts but, on the other hand, this reaction is also understandable, given his biography. His grandmother's heritage emerged from a strongly traditional way of life. Gu had to face the challenge of how to combine his grandmother's heritage with the rapidly-developing 20th century Taiwanese society. Modernity in Taiwan is undergoing a multitude of foreign influences, especially the cultural-political influence of America (see chap. 10). Therefore, social change is challenged by extreme tension.

Gu formulates his East-West dichotomy by separating categories similar in form and content, the first being Western and the second Eastern. While he reduces the essence of Buddhism to practise in everyday life, to "lifting yourself up" (*tisheng ziji* 提升自己; as cited above), the concept of belief is unconnected to Buddhism. As the above citation already shows, in contrast to Christianity, Gu sees the role of Buddhism as not in asking for belief. The role of receiving belief he applies to science:

(S3) 這一些是我自己也要/ 對佛教堅信不已的 的原動力. 他說佛教是現代科學所必須. 現在就是 問題不能解決 只有這個 佛所講 都出現了 我們必須好好去研究這個 那好好去修行 很重要 要解決現在的問題	(S3) These I want also/ [sc. to have] for Buddhism the/ the original moving power [i.e. motive power] of absolute faith. He says that Buddhism is, what contemporary science needs. Now, it is just: one cannot

現在科學要研究佛教 我覺得說得很好 所以我原來是不懂科學的人, 我這個人不科學, 非常不科學, 但是我相信科學.

solve the problem. Only all that the Buddha said has appeared, so we have to research this well. That we have to practise well. It's very important, to want to resolve the present problems. The present science is to research Buddhism. I think that this is well said. So, despite the fact that I'm originally someone who doesn't understand science, this person is not scientific, really not scientific. But I believe in science.

Gu holds a positive, enthusiastic view of science – an attitude that emerged in the Buddhist reformatory period already (see p. 209ff.). This can be seen from the implicit argument that science guarantees the equality of people (S4). With pleasure, he once listened to a "scientific" explanation of the *Diamond Sūtra.* He thinks that scientific education is the most required for monastics, and is convinced of the alliance of science with Buddhism: Buddhism is what science needs, as scientific knowledge is becoming complemented by the practice, which is provided by Buddhism. Therefore, he believes in science and, for all illnesses, which cannot be cured by science, he practises, as practice heals unknown diseases (R6). The high compatibility of Buddhism with science he explicates also elsewhere, mentioning that the Buddhist time unit of a *kṣaṇa* would be even shorter than a scientific Western second. This simple example shows Gu's pride in Buddhism, which far surpasses Confucianism in terms of exactness (R10). Gu is deeply convinced of the ultimate measure one can get from the Buddhist principle of *anuttara-samyak-saṃbodhi.* This leads him even to make a negative judgement of Islam:

(S15) Gu: 不是 我是都好 我天主教基督教都好 除了這個不太好 我覺得回教不太好 因為你看很基本沒有道理 太離譜了 怎麼可以討十一個太太 是合法的 還可以不合法 但是 五十五 這甚麼多不阿耨多羅三藐三菩提 沒有平等阿 對不對 哈 這個回教不要 我是讀可蘭經 因為那個時候誰在教這個比較宗教 [name of teacher] 我這個師父很多錢阿 因為他是基督徒 他說 我本來不要作基督徒 我覺得佛教太好了 可是我爸媽讓我受洗 我不能換教 我自己沒有受洗過 我就隨緣

(S15) Gu: No. For me, everything's fine. For me, Catholic, Protestant, everything's fine. Besides, this isn't very good. I think Islam is not too good. Because you see, very basically it doesn't make sense. Too far from normal. How can one take 11 wives. It's legal. Still, it can't be legal. But 55. So many is not *anuttara-samyak-saṃbodhi*; it has no equality a, right. Ha. This Islam I don't want. I have read the Koran. Because, at that time, who taught this comparative religion? [name of teacher]. My, this master has a lot of money a. Because he's a Protestant. He says: I originally didn't want to be a Protestant. I think Buddhism is too good. But my parents had me baptised. I can't convert. I myself wasn't baptised. I followed my karma.

Gu Puzhong sees his principle of "unexcelled complete enlightenment" (*anuttara-samyak-saṃbodhi*) being violated when, in Islam, the equality between the sexes is violated by polygamy. This adds to his understanding of his doctrinally unbound principle of the dimension of the constant practice of one's own faults the dimension of "equality" (*pingdeng* 平等). The concrete interpretation of "equality" he supports through the remark that polygamy is too far removed from "normal" (*lipu* 離譜). Gu, besides his abstract principle, holds in addition also unconsciously reflected assumptions about normal acceptable social behaviour. Although intellectually holding a very abstract principle, in his actual judgements and everyday behaviour, Gu has a clear opinion of which behaviour he can cherish and which not. The argumentation leads him here to an interreligious comparison. While, for the religion of Islam, he mentions a content related example, for the case of Christianity, he takes the statement of a confessing, wealthy Christian, who recognises Buddhism as superior to Christianity, but uses the Buddhist argument of "following his karma" to decide not to be a Buddhist. The question arises of how far the construction of Buddhist doctrine is, for Gu, bound to a concrete, religious specific doctrine. This might shed light on Gu's perception of "normality" by asking how far he, in his everyday life, is practically rooted in the Buddhist tradition.

Ritual Practice

When asked about the Buddhist practices he actually follows, Gu names a variety of habits. Firstly, he tried meditation, but was unconvinced:

(S16) 本來我是打坐 打坐也不要去參 canchan 很難阿 我父母會生我 我是誰 想不出來啦 [laughing] 我從那裡來 猜不出來 不知道 但是有好處 打坐學靜心 我/我自己覺得 我唸到 我其實我打坐 這是我必須要作的 我還要作香功 阿 因為運氣 打坐有一個好處 這是自己會靜下來 在你要光想一個光想很偉大的事情 阿 都不要來 光想不出來了 越來越煩 [laughs]

(S16) Originally, I meditated. I also didn't want to participate in meditation. Really difficult. My parents gave birth to me. Who am I? I couldn't find an answer. [laughing] Where am I from? I didn't guess it; I didn't know it, but it has an advantage: through meditating, one learns to calm one's heart. I/ I think by myself/ I recite until/ I, in fact, I'm meditating, this's what I have to do. I still have to put up incense [?, *xianggong*] a. Because, luckily, meditation has an advantage that is that one becomes calm. If you want to consider [constantly]/ consider a very big thing, a, it all doesn't come up. Considering it doesn't come out; it's more and more concerning. [laughs]

While meditation calms his mind, he finds it difficult to meditate on the basic questions of life. He feels unable to solve major questions through meditating about them. While his meditation practice, therefore, did not last long, between the lines, when enlarging on his grandmother's life, Gu relates how she obliged him to go to a popular religious temple once a month after her death:

(S17) 那我觀念跟那個不太一樣 因為我祖母命令 我每個月去 [..., name of a popular religious temple]一次 因為祖母說 她死後 你每個月去 阿 不是很好的地方阿 因為那是雜教 前面中間是一個觀世音 後面甚麼文昌帝君, 玉皇大帝, 媽祖, 關公, 駐生娘娘, 甚麼一大堆亂放 世界大同 沒有耶穌 [laughing, slurred]. 那這是她遺命我 我要孝 中文講 我就去 有時候多去一次 不一定 因為那個觀世音菩薩 我覺得還不錯 [..., slurred], 不是很好了 藝術性不是很高 可是他的臉 不能那個/ 我覺得還不錯 所以我做的時候 因為要加強自己能夠靜下來 就光想他 看了反光 祈禱不是要祈禱自己. [...]

(S17) Na, my view's different from that. Because my grandmother ordered me to go once a month to [..., name of a popular religious temple]. Because grandmother said: when I'm dead, you go every month. A. It's not a very good place a. Because, there's a mixed religion. In the front, there is a Guanyin, in the back there's whatever Wenchang Dijun, the Yellow Emperor, Mazu, Guangong, the Queen Mother of the West. Whatever a big pile put there in a mess. The Great Harmony of the world. No Jesus [laughing, slurred]. Na, this's her wish. I have to be pious, one says in Chinese. So I go. Sometimes, I go once more. Not necessarily. Because this Bodhisattva Guanyin, I think, is quite good. [..., slurred], it's not very good. The artistic character isn't very high, but her face can't that/ I think it's not that bad. So when I do it, because I want to increase my ability to calm down, just, she. One sees the light's reflection. When one prays, one shouldn't pray for oneself. [...]

By altering the habit of praying for one's own fortune to praying for the welfare of all sentient beings–which is in line with his conviction about selfless practice –, Gu goes along with a highly abstract Buddhist belief in a very traditional context, which is not even exclusively Buddhist. He is not even necessarily cherishing the belief of the temple that he attends, when he states elsewhere that he hopes that religion in China will decrease (S8), but pious behaviour is more important to him than any other doctrinal considerations. It is remarkable that, at the age of nearly 70, he still follows his grandmother's testimony and goes to worship at a temple. Although intellectual about his own belief and highly eloquent in general, Gu cannot describe the exact value he gains from worshipping the Guanyin statue at this temple. It seems that something in her facial expression touches him beyond words. Gu's intellectual approach to religion does not hinder him from following this heartfelt veneration monthly. He combines his highly reflective position on Buddhism, which actually is void of the necessity of a religious practice like veneration, with a ritual practice that is totally integrated into normal Taiwanese veneration behaviour. The intellectually-centred concept enables him to access his traditional resources anew by not changing them but reinterpreting them.

Gu Puzhong mentions, besides his temple visits, a regular recitation practice which seems to be his main practice in everyday life:

(S18) Gu: 第二個我會持咒 一百零四遍 藥師咒 這是因為我懷念 因為我那個時候不太把我媽弄好 我現在在還債 早起的時候我唸佛最多 因為譬如說我坐捷運 因為在 *fa* 那個 *wanjie* 的 [..., slurred] [laughing] 我不要了 我就 阿彌陀佛 阿彌陀佛 看沒有人就唸出聲音 有人我就默唸 或者唸那個心經 我想到甚麼就唸甚麼 [...]你這樣不會浪費時間阿 但是你覺得說 那個車怎麼還沒來 沒到 那你走路也是要小心一點 [...] 這我就是在作 我做甚麼 我都在唸 我沒事我去念佛 也沒有意義 也沒有所求 只是說不要太無聊 亂想 空想 這/這/這沒有意思 你現在就把它擺著 我心不亂 沒有阿 我沒那麼功夫阿 就是說我要作無益的事 那你要回想 回想全世界法界一切的眾生 那除了佛菩薩觀音 那鬼呀人呀 我都會想給他 *chusheng* [i.e. 出生?] 我也有一個好處 我是全世界的一份子 那 [...] 就這樣去作

(S18) Gu: The second is, I'm reciting mantras. 104 times the *Medicine Teacher Mantra.* That's because of my bad thoughts. Because I didn't care very much about my mother at the time. I'm now repaying [my debt] from earlier. In the morning, I recite mostly Buddha's name. I mostly recite the name of Buddha, because for example when I sit in the subway, because I'm [..., slurred] [laughing] I don't want it. I just: Amitābha. Amitābha. If there're no people, I recite with sound. If there're people, I recite silently. Or I recite that *Heart Sūtra.* Whatever I think of, I recite. [...] That way, you don't waste time a. But you think: how come this car didn't come, didn't arrive. Na, if you walk, you don't have to be careful at all. [...] That's what I'm doing. Whatever I do, I always recite. If I've nothing to do, I recite. It has no meaning. It's also not longing for anything. It's just that I don't want to be too bored, weird thinking, empty thinking. This/ this/ this's no meaning. You now say it. My heart isn't confused. No a. I'm not so skilful a. It's just, I want to do something that isn't useful. Na, I want to remind, remind the whole world, the *dharmadhātu* and all living beings. Na, besides Buddha and Bodhisattva Guanyin, na, these ghosts and these humans I'll think of them all [to give birth to them?]. I also have an advantage. I'm part of the whole world. Na [...] That way, I just do it.

Gu follows an extensive recitation practice which includes, for example, the *Medicine Buddha Mantra*, the *Heart Sūtra* and especially the recitation of the name of Bodhisattva Amitābha. Again, Gu acts in a very traditional way, but does not claim to experience any special effect as a result, performing it in a selfless way and thinking of the world in all six of its paramitas, to feel part of it, and reciting to combat the uncontrolled thoughts in his own mind. Again, it is interesting to see how Gu combines the two strata. Claiming to believe in science, he obviously sees the six realms of living beings as compatible with the scientific world view.

Recitation practice also plays a central role in Gu's preparation for his own death: at the very beginning of the interview (R2/R3), he states that, as an old man, with grown-up children, who has nourished his family and contributed to society through his Buddhist publications, he feels: "I'm ready to die". Sometimes, he relates, he feels unhealthy and, when everybody around him gets excited, he starts reciting. Death one should face and not start creating chaos is his opinion. Gu is trying to live and die as honourably as his grandmother, whose "big death" (*dasi* 大死, Interact (34)) impressed him that much as a young man, leading to his recitation practice through which he is fighting against all sorts of fears, even the fear of death itself.

The choice of the actual mantra or name is unimportant to Gu, and he does not see himself as having a school affiliation:

(S19) Interviewer: 你會覺得你會靠近一個宗派嗎?
Gu: 我沒有阿 我來我都喜歡

Interviewer: 因為你是唸阿彌陀佛, 淨土? 也不一定/
Gu: 我不一定 我也唸 omeme [starts singing] om meme beme hong om me 你自己快樂就好阿 本來法喜 就在這裡阿 不是你自己一定要 我覺得 不能僵化 欸 佛告訴我們隨緣吧 對不對 你不是隨緣嗎 隨緣不變 那基本中你不能變 你那個追求智慧 要發那個慈悲心的東西 不能變阿 因為佛教主要追究一個般若嘛 就是智慧 大智慧 我有智慧 我們必須這樣 我們智慧不夠嘛 所以這個這個到那邊不行

(S19) Interviewer: Do you think that you are close to a Buddhist school?
Gu: I don't a. What I come up with, I like it all.

Interviewer: Because you're reciting Amitābha, Pure Land? Also not necessarily/
Gu: I, not necessarily. I also recite omeme [starts singing] om meme beme hung om me/ If you're happy yourself, it's fine a. Originally rejoicing in the dharma is just here a. It's not that you yourself really want, I think, that's talking, ei. Buddha told us to follow our karma ba. Right? You don't follow your karma? Following one's karma doesn't change. Na, originally you can't change. You pursue that wisdom. Have to develop that things of a compassionate heart. That can't change a. Because Buddhism mainly wants to pursue one *prajñā* ma. That's just wisdom. Big wisdom. I've wisdom. We have to do this. Our wisdom's insufficient. So this/ this until there doesn't work.

"*Ni ziji kuaile jiu hao a* 你自己快樂就好阿" (If you're happy yourself, it's fine) is Gu's decision criterion and, demonstrating how happy he can be flexibly shifting between the traditions, he starts empathetically singing the well-known invocation of Avalokiteśvara "*oṃ maṇi padme hūṃ*", here probably imitating the Tibetan sounds.

The argumentation about the possibility either of shifting or not between the traditions has already occurred a couple of times in the other interviews as well as here: *suiyuan* 隨緣–"following one's karma" is the guiding principle for deciding whether to become a monastic or not (S12), for legitimising the simplification of the classical Buddhist texts to make them understandable to everyone, to prevent saying to someone else that they do not have the karma to understand (S10) and for giving a reason not to convert, even though one sees one's own religion as inferior (S11). The first usage functions as a convenient excuse for choosing a more comfortable lay life and prevents any further private investigations of the conversation partner. The third usage has a similar function: it harmonises the talk, explaining and legitimising why there are religious differences between conversation partners. The second usage draws attention: the flexibility of the *suiyuan*-argument seems endless and easy to misuse, as happens, for example, in the second case for justifying the barriers to understanding as classical texts are. At exactly this point, Gu denies the right application of the argument. While not reasoning heretofore by what criterion he makes a judgement, whether the *suiyuan*-principle should be applied or not, within this sequence (S19), Gu adds to the *suiyuan*-criterion a principle of its application: the principle of *suiyuan* he parallels with the statement that one cannot basically (*jiben zhong* 基本中) change. What this basis consists of he explains as "pursuing wisdom" (*zhuijiu zhihui* 追究智慧) and "developing a compassionate heart" (*fa cibei xin* 發慈悲心). For the interpretation, this also helps to solve the question of the applicability of the *suiyuan*-principle in different situations: while becoming a monastic and converting to another religion might be seen as "pursuing wisdom" and might not be immediately connected to the argument of "developing a compassionate heart", hindering the understanding of Buddhist texts opposes certainly the argument about compassion, if not also that about pursuing wisdom. Gu transfers the idea of wisdom and compassion into the Buddhist terminology of *prajñā*, which he interprets as being without boundaries and surpassing human wisdom. One can conclude that, with human wisdom as a means at hand, one should not set up boundaries regarding which traditions to employ. With the argument that compassion and wisdom are the leading criteria for the application of the *suiyuan*-principle, Gu certainly gains from it an impression of pure arbitrariness and convenience, while the applicability of compassion and wisdom in other cases would be speculative.

Inconsistencies

Up to now, one could say that Gu has, through his long-standing studies, found a principle of selfless practice and karmic criteria in combination with wisdom and compassion for actual decision-making. His basic insights are in accordance with his grandmother's lifestyle. Having decoded his grandmother's "mystery", Gu feels like spreading it throughout Taiwan via his publications. He has even written a handbook for laypeople, in which he sums up his insights and adds some of the expectations regarding lay people. His grandmother's heritage has inspired him to make a huge effort regarding constructional and reflective work, which pervades the interview.

Mapping out Gu's whole world view as he presents it in the interview here is impossible and also not intended. Still, it must be admitted that the reconstruction work of analysing the interview emphasises the coherence rather than the inconsistency, which surely also can be found, e.g.: on the one hand, Gu aligns Christianity with Buddhism, as if he considers it the same. On the other hand, he disqualifies Christianity as a "belief" and proudly cites a scholar and Christian who claims that Buddhism would be far more profound than Christianity; he just unfortunately had been baptised and could not convert. Also, the concept of the "East" and its equivalence with "Buddhism" is not precisely formulated as Gu, on the one hand, holds up Eastern phenomena to be researched, but on the other ranks Buddhism far higher than Confucianism. The estimation of the East is only partly a self-estimation, as Buddhism did not originate in China. Still, this does not hinder Gu from regarding Buddhism as the means for a positive self-reconstruction of the East. For him, science needs Buddhism, and Western methods are highly applicable to Eastern topics. Also, the estimation of Buddhism or the East, with its focus on practice, easily attains, through the illustration of social behaviour in Canada, on the one hand, its general meaning; on the other hand, it becomes clear that Gu's missionary enthusiasm is mainly oriented towards Taiwan or the "East". His publishing house specialised in publishing foreign books in Taiwan and making them accessible to the Taiwanese. The vision Gu holds is bound to the cultural context of Taiwan and the question of how to combine Taiwanese science and modernity with one's own traditions and values. The reflection on the "original meaning" of religious practice, like the practice of selflessness, is therefore intended to constitute a positive re-evaluation of Taiwan's own culture. Turning this round, it is unclear, from the "Westerners'" point of view, who have "science" and obviously already naturally behave correctly, even in toilets, why they should embrace Buddhism. Consequently, one might conclude that one should not do so. Following one's karma, a Westerner would naturally avoid engaging in Buddhism. Perhaps this is also what Gu would emphasise. On the other hand, during the interview, he is enthusiastic about foreigners who are interested in Buddhism, so perhaps he simply feels appreciated and honoured as an "Eastern" person. His view of Buddhism is certainly not formulated as a "mission" to bring a more profound wisdom "to the West" (compare Xu Wenhua below in chap. 12.2). Gu Puzhong is used to the Taiwanese audience. One can conclude from this that, for him and his audience, Buddhism might serve the function of a positive self-reconstruction.

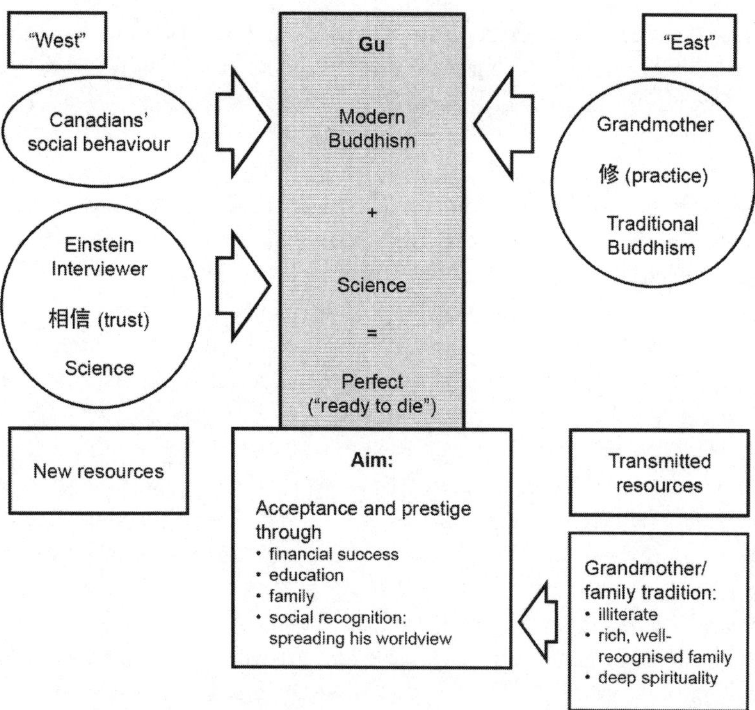

Figure 13: Gu Puzhong–Positive self-reconstruction through the transformation of transmitted resources and acceptance of new resources.

Conclusion

Gu Puzhong is a very reflective narrator of his own biography and enlarges on his Buddhist world view in detail. Born on the mainland, he grew up in Taiwan under his grandmother's supervision, a Buddhist woman, whose mysterious selfless austerity became Gu's intellectual life-task.

Gu shows first a strong sense of responsibility towards his family and a deep respect for the older generation. His realistic, pragmatic life-orientation is situated in a traditional and patriarchal social environment. Practice–*xiuxing*–is strongly emphasised throughout the interview as leading to profound happiness and is defined as the basic message and function of Buddhism. In addition, Buddhism stands for a selfless attitude of constant self-observation leading to the correction of one's own faults concentrated in the Buddhist term "*anuttara-samyak-saṃbodhi*"–unexcelled complete enlightenment. It is important to Gu that the practice of unselfishness is not bound to the notion of Buddhism through the practitioner. In contrast, Gu refers back to the Buddha's lifetime, before Buddhism had been established as a formal religion. Gu marginalises the importance of any concrete markers of religious boundaries as veneration activities, dharma meetings, formal school establishments, or monastic-lay differences for true Buddhist practice. Holding up the Mahāyāna ideal of universal liberation, he sees it as his life's work to make understandable the Buddhist message of the importance of sincere practice as "being able to lift up yourself" (*nenggou tisheng ziji* 能夠提升自己) for the average person in Taiwan. Intellectualising and enacting, *de facto*, his grandmother's attitude, he pragmatically has a family, studies Buddhism and opens a publishing house to spread his understanding of Buddhism throughout Taiwan.

His grandmother's heritage has led him to make a huge effort to engage in constructional and reflective work. Growing up under the influence of her traditional Buddhist belief, he must reshape and re-ascertain his world view as he encounters the 20th century Taiwan's rapidly-developing society and modernity. He does this by applying a strong East-West-dichotomy in a for hundred years well-established pattern (see below), which combines Western science and art with Eastern Buddhism. Science as a "belief" needs Buddhism as a "practice". Enthusiastically embracing the concept of science, Gu ascribes to it the quality of guaranteeing the equality of humans ("all human blood is red"), while Buddhist practice in the sense of *anuttara-samyak-saṃbodhi* also supports the argument about equality and delivers a criterion for judging other religious traditions. Within the later argumentation, it becomes clear that Gu enacts his highly abstract Buddhist belief in a very concrete traditional context, which partly still forms his normative opinion.

Gu's ritual practice is dominated by name recitation in combination with regular visits to a popular religious temple. He has abandoned meditation. His regular temple visits result from a combination of filial piety towards his grandmother and a non-intellectually grounded piety towards the venerated statue. Piety and devotion go beyond his intellectual claims. An extensive recitation practice, involving resorting to a variety of sources, accompanies his everyday life and proves of great assistance in overcoming his anxiety and fear of death. Gu's intellectual reconstruction of his grandmother's testimonial enables him to access his traditional resources anew, reinterpreting them and striving for a non-egoistical performance.

As Gu Puzhong's concept of unselfish, sincere practice is quite open in terms of its actual content, he adds which tradition one should practise in everyday life, he explains the common, socially-acknowledged views and the widespread idea of "following one's karma"–*suiyuan*. Preventing a misuse of the karmic idea for legitimising inequalities, Gu mentions as the leading criterion for the application of the *suiyuan*-principle the argument that compassion and wisdom lead to the Buddhist idea of perfect wisdom, *prajñā*. They serve the function of taking from the karmic principle the impression of pure arbitrariness and convenience.

While Gu's intellectual concept contains several inconsistencies, such as the varying position of Christianity, or a not entirely coherent concept of the East-West-dichotomy, the overall impression is that Gu is, in his own words, "*ready for death*", looking back at a successful life, having managed its practical needs, found an intellectual concept to face it and successfully generalised his personal challenge of his grandmother's heritage into an enthusiastic message for the average Taiwanese, promoting a positive image of an Eastern self-reconstruction that is characterised by selfless practice and karmic criteria in combination with wisdom and compassion for actual decision-making.

Comparisons

Outwardly Gu Puzhong appears similar to the majority of Conventional Buddhists. He is not affiliated to any particular school and would count himself within the category of believing in or venerating Buddha. He also regards himself as following his grandmother's tradition and therefore would not see himself as opposing his parents' beliefs nor as a convert. He certainly believes in karmic retribution, although he does not seem to use it in a mechanistic manner to control his fate. Also, he fits perfectly the model of a frequent temple visitor, who performs veneration, *baibai*, there. The reinterpretation of the intention of prayer as not entreating Buddhas and bodhisattvas for oneself can scarcely be analysed through the questionnaire. His frequent temple visits and veneration-behaviour match his devotion within the frame of the average Conventional Buddhist. Still, his individual profile is reflected in the fact that he follows a private practice and has taken refuge twice. Also, in his ideals, he might give a different answer than the average Buddhist, as he may see himself as seeking for truth or at least the path to it, where he is consciously questioning and reasoning about the essence of his practice. He is not simply a passive participant but actively builds up his own opinion about a tradition which leads him back, in consequence, to his original traditional behaviour but with a different inner attitude. As a child, he begged Buddha for good exam results and now he prays for all sentient beings.

How more likely is it for someone to be this kind of a Buddhist in an urban area? Gu profits greatly in his belief development from his education, his Buddhist studies, internationalisation and a flourishing book market. The urban environment enables Gu to fall back upon new resources and bring them into fruitful contact with his own tradition. Urbanisation, therefore, is a basis for the development of his belief. Reflection on Buddhist belief, re-interpreting one's own tradition in the light of science and modernity, seems therefore a phenomenon that needs, for its differentiation, a vivid intellectual environment which is more likely to be found in the cities, especially in the metropolitan area of Taipeh.

In comparison with the other believers discussed so far, Gu stands out because of his explicitly Buddhist grandmother and considerable engagement in re-thinking the essence of Buddhism. This independence and intellectual efforts are not found in the other four interviews. Still, some major similarities and contrasts are found, which might help to differentiate between the believers discussed so far.

Lin Yongfu comes from the same popular religious environment as Gu, and the action of veneration is an essential element of religious practice for both. While Lin is as aware as Gu that one has to be careful about retributionary thinking, Lin seeks a solution through a practical approach, acknowledging that the temple leaders do not cheat those in need, but support them. Gu solves this problem by adopting an intellectual approach, reinterpreting the meaning of action itself and depriving it of its personal, retributionary sense. One detects a similar difference because of their educational background in their handling of the term "religion". While Lin unconsciously picks it up and re-names his own tradition Buddhism, Gu, throughout his life, seeks consciously to re-interpret Buddhism, making it compatible with the values and developments he experiences in everyday society. Still, both are, despite their very different educational backgrounds, very open-minded about the new developments in Taiwanese society and the new resources which are now available to them due to democratisation and internationalisation.

Luo Peirong's venerating behaviour of entreating Bodhisattva Guanyin and the Daoist gods to solve her family's various health problems involves practising an egoistical understanding of veneration, which Gu opposes. Luo is entering a spiral of fate management, which causes her to focus on the worshipping rituals. Like Gu, Luo believes in miracles but, while Gu talks of miracles to demonstrate the depth of his grandmother's belief and point out the betterment of health in general and cures for unsolved scientific illness through Buddhist music or recitation, Luo attempts to rescue her family members by her will and veneration miracles. Her miracles are not expected to cure unsolved illnesses, but those for which science sees no hope. Luo belonged, for some time, to a Young Buddhist Monastery. This link to recently established Buddhist organisations Gu never discusses. He studies with various monks and visits his grandmother's monastery but never joins a recently established group and would never consider himself a group-member. Finally, for Gu, Buddhism seems to be his natural heritage in which he grew up and which he wants to make fruitful by reflecting on his present and future. His contact with Buddhism does not, as in the case of Luo, arise out of a crisis, but is a result of his admiration for his grandmother and his curiosity about the austerity of her belief.

Like Cai Chenhao, Gu is very consciously a lay Buddhist, a choice which has had direct consequences for his life. Both are deeply engaged in name recitation, which Luo also favours. Like Cai, Gu has a similar understanding of karma, as they both oppose any bargaining through veneration. Gu talks only of following his karma (*suiyuan*), which means, to him, being open to the options available to him. He explains differences in belief through this, using it as a means of harmonising people's different decisions. Cai would fully agree with this concept of karma, as he sees it as his field of possibilities. Miracles are part of Gu's demonstration of the power of belief. Gu applies miracles with the same functions in his arguments, discussing the deep effect of deathbed recitation. Again, as with Luo, Gu differs from Cai, due to his independence from any Buddhist organisation or closed group.

Li Zhiqiang follows a twofold practice of Buddhism through veneration, which he sees, in contrast to Gu, under the clear aspect of personal retribution, and intellectually-oriented sūtra readings, which ensure his morality in everyday life. Buddhism, for Li, is functionalised as communicating moral standards. Gu does not speak about morality or any concrete values that emerge from Buddhism but reduces everything to the practice of selflessness. The necessity of defining values besides non-egoistical behaviour he denies. Still, both Li and Gu possess a strong pragmatism which puts any occupation with Buddhism second and the satisfaction of one's bodily needs first, following the successful earning of money by a father who is responsible for his family.

8 Reflections– Mental Concepts, Historical Traces, and Urbanites' Attraction

Having portrayed Conventional Buddhist believers, who are chosen on the criterion of not linking their belief to a Buddhist school, it seems reasonable to ask, if this is a mere statistical, arbitrary definition. Does making school awareness a decisive criterion impose an artificial view of modernity as a process of functional differentiation upon the religious field? Or do underlying common strata of mental and practical orientation exist, which make it reasonable to discuss the statistical definitions of a field of conventional orientation within lay Buddhist belief in contemporary Taiwan?

Like all models and secondary reflections, of course, any field or so-called typology must be a structured simplification that intends to develop our understanding of reality. The five cases analysed so far vary greatly in terms of defining their Buddhist belief: Lin Yongfu presented himself as a traditional popular religious temple believer, while Luo Peirong was attempting to manage her personal bad luck with the help of a young Buddhist organisation. Cai integrated himself totally into a long-established Buddhist community, but Li Zhiqiang, as a successful businessman, saw himself in the role of his good friend's donor and supporter, the Buddhist abbot. Gu Puzhong, in contrast, has been on a mission throughout his life to bring the essence of his grandmother's traditional Buddhist austere belief into the "modern" Taiwanese world. In these five cases, habitus-options intermingle that show varying degrees of intensity to define oneself a Buddhist in contemporary Taiwan: 1) one can stay within the popular religious field, 2) take elements of a Buddhist cognitive concept like "karma" to manage life decisions, 3) separate from society by entering a closed traditional Buddhist setting, 4) enhance one's economic and social success by making generous financial and practical donations to the Buddhist field, or 5) try to bring a Buddhist mission to society and re-evaluate tradition for modern life.

However, it would certainly be misleading and inadequate for the complex field of reality to be reduced to a static picture of five options. Reviewing the cases presented, one can regroup and re-differentiate the five concrete choices that the interviewees have taken according to the results of the qualitative analysis. Within the following, the author therefore will try to trace the mental concepts which appeared dominant in the analyses, seeking which historical frame the cases reveal and which current process of social development they reflect.

8.1 *Underlying* Mental Concepts

Screening through the conclusions and comparisons of all of the cases, several concepts recur or have a huge impact on single cases. The interviewees frequently refer to concepts of causal interconnectedness when describing interactions within their environment, while they partly follow a veneration behaviour, which is based upon mutual benefit. They show a strong orientation towards social harmony, respecting authority and avoiding conflicts and discussion.

"Karmic" Thinking?–Yinyuan *因緣 and the Like*[88]

Causal interconnectedness was frequently used as an explanatory means in four of the five interviews. While the taxi driver, Lin Yongfu, was the only one to refer explicitly to a personal, individual reason for choosing his temple,[89] the rest of the interviewees employ explicitly the concept of karmic causalities as well as casual terms for causal interconnectedness and the concept of rebirth.

Through anthropological investigations about karmic thinking in South and South East Asia, a twofold usage of the karmic concept has been analysed, which can also be found in our interviews: in the introduction to the single anthropological study "Karma. An Anthropological Inquiry", Keyes notes an "explanatory" and "predictive" aspect (Keyes 1983, 5) of applying the karmic concept. The first is mostly used in retrospect to explain predestined fate, especially misfortune, while the second predicts the future, enabling people to act by observing moral responsibility.

Both aspects can be clearly observed in the interviews: Luo Peirong's main reason for sticking to her Buddhist belief (see Luo S3) is that it makes her acceptance of her bad luck and current suffering reasonable and explicable as a diminishment of her bad karma (*xiaoye* 消業). The "psychological

---

88 Although originally a direct translation of the Sanskrit *hetu-pratyāya* ("causes and conditions"), the term *yinyuan* 因緣 soon came to possess a broader meaning of causal connectedness or co-dependent origination (see also Sharf 2002, 129–131, here 129). The *Digital Dictionary of Buddhism* (DDB 2016) collects for the term *yinyuan* a number of explanations: "In the most basic sense, the character [*yin*] 因 refers to a main cause (Skt. *hetu* […]), which directly incurs a result, while [*yuan*] 緣 refers to an indirect cause (Skt. *praty[ā]ya*) which helps or participates in producing the result. In terms of the description of the causal factors involved in a mental event in Buddhist philosophy, this term denotes conditions that are direct causes (Skt. *hetu-praty[ā]ya* […]) […] [Charles Muller;…]." Besides concrete applications in Buddhist philosophical schools and a large number of specific usages, *yinyuan* can also refer to a causal situation (skt. *nidāna*), a logical cause or reason (skt. *kāraṇa*), and dependent origination (skt. *pratītya-samutpāda*).

89 See Lin (22): "this is the thinking (*sixiang* 思想) of each person, the opinion (*yinian* 意念) of each person."

uncertainty" of asking when the stream of bad karma is going to finish, as already stated by Obeyesekere (Obeyesekere 1968, 21), finds its expression in Luo's karmic reinterpretation of her husband's words, that "all suffering is over". Karma, in Luo's eyes, is reduced to bad karma and its extinction is the main aim, leading her to a peaceful life and a good rebirth. The nirvāṇic idea does not come into play here. Her friend, Kong Shuqing, in the same interview, also mentions the explanatory function of karma, even going a step further than Luo: karma not only enables her to endure misfortune, but even equips her with an optimistic view of life, as she follows the motto: "[I]t's over, just forget it. It just diminished one karma". (*Guo le jiu suan le, jiu shaole yi ge ye* 過了就算了 就少了一個業, see ann.2). The predictive field of usage of karmic thinking we encounter with Li Zhiqiang, who stresses the consequences of following a Buddhist belief in family life: the good karma created would result in the children's moral behaviour (Li S13).

The passages mentioned so far all explicitly imply the idea of causal interconnectedness. Luo and her friend even apply the correct Buddhist term equal to Sanskrit "karma"–which basically means "action" and is commonly used to refer to a universal law of cause and effect[90]–"*ye* 業" (Luo S5) resp. "*yinguo* 因果 /*yinyuan guobao* 因緣果報" (Li S6, Luo S3). Still, the majority of the instances during the interviews where karmic thinking features do not really make it the topic of the conversation, as it is applied with ease between the lines: Particularly the lexemes "*yinyuan* 因緣", "*yuanfen* 緣分/份", "*jiyuan* 機緣" and "*suiyuan* 隨緣"[91] tend to be used in situations where people argue about why something has happened as it did or why they are currently not choosing something else–because they follow their karma. As in Gu Puzhong's case, the karmic connection in itself does not provide a principle for its correct application, but in most conversations is referred to without further reflection. Gu Puzhong and Li Zhiqiang make an exception here by providing a guideline about the application of karma. Gu Puzhong does so by enlarging on "*bore* 般若" (*prajñā*, "wisdom") being the leading principle for deciding what it means to follow one's karma (Gu S19), while Li connects in the process of deciding whether to join a monastery the karmic argument with a guideline for its application, the Eight Characters (*Bazi* 八字), a traditional method of fortune-telling based on one's birth dates (Li S12). It ap-

90 For an analysis of the principle of karma in Classical Indian literature, see the outcome of a conference and the precedent to Keyes' anthropological approach, O'Flaherty (1980).

91 Various combinations of *yuan* are hard to imitate appropriately in the translation. While the last–*suiyuan*–can be clearly translated as "to follow one's karma", *yinyuan*, *yuanfen* and *jiyuan* are mostly combined with *you* 有 (to have). They all refer to something, like having a karmic connection or relation with something/-one else. For *jiyuan*, see below.

pears easy to combine karmic thinking with various backgrounds. Besides straightforward Buddhist principles and Chinese astrology, references to other sources could also probably be discovered in further field research.

While the terms "*ye*" and "*yinguo*" are more technical Buddhist terms located at the core of the Buddhist translations of the Indian concept of karma, the Buddhist usage of "*yuan* 緣" is continuing and re-focussing a term that was already used before the introduction of Buddhism to express causal relations. In pictographical terms, referring originally to a hem as the border of a garment, it can express a desire "to ascend"[92] and something "being in conformity/accordance with", a cause or plausible reason[93] and, in combination with a question particle like "*he* 何", it can serve as an interrogative pronoun.[94] At first glance–as this is not the place to go into etymological details–one therefore can locate the word *yuan* as a Buddhist enlargement that may channel an existing causal concept. The Buddhist reinterpretation raises the word field of "*yuan*" to a cognitive map of understanding the course of human life. The qualitative deepening of an existing concept may have led to the success of the casual utilisation of the *yuan*-related terms today.

It is unsurprising, therefore, that, in contemporary Taiwan, one finds the reasoning in the word-field of *yuan* widely-applied, when people intend to say that things happen as they do because particular circumstances came together: Cai Chenhao (Cai S1) took refuge, because there "just was that opportunity" (*ganghao you nage jiyuan* 剛好有那個機緣). Luo went to a young Buddhist organisation, because of her *yinyuan* and *yuanfen* (Luo (28)). Also, it was her *yinyuan*, when she went there often to practise, finally receiving the master's explanation (Luo (32)). Because of her *yinyuan*, Luo entered Daoism (Luo S7) as it was her *yinyuan* that helped her sister to recover with the help of a Daoist temple (Luo S8). Even Gu Puzhong does not constantly fill the karmic argument with content when he states that he was not baptised because he "follows his karma" (*suiyuan*, S15).

92 As in the well-known saying "climbing a tree to search for a fish" (*yuan mu qiu yu* 緣木求魚), which goes back to a passage in Mencius in which he explains to King Xuan of Qi (齊宣王, reigned 342–324 BC) about governance by warfare and imperilling the people: "Seeking the fulfilment of such an ambition by such means as you employ is like looking for fish by climbing a tree." (以若所為，求若所欲，猶緣木而求魚也; *Mengzi* I.A.7, trsl. Lau 1970, 57).

93 As in *Hanfei Zi* 20 (*Jielao* 解老).7: "*wu yuan er wang yi du ye* 無緣而妄/忘意度也" refers to an arbitrary way of assessing without being grounded in good reason (Mögling 1994, 161, translates: "sich unbegründeten Spekulationen hin[geben]").

94 This preliminary overview was obtained via the help of the TLS-database (accessed April 1, 2009). Further verification, involving accessing also later texts, such as the writings of the pilgrim Faxian 法顯 or an analysis of the usage in the *Shishuo Xinyu* 世說新語, may shed light on the semantic development of the word.

In all of these situations, implying the karmic argument means, firstly, providing an explanation of the situation. In the actual interview, people probably are convinced that referring to their karma means referring to the entirety of the situation and providing a proper explanation for an action as the result of circumstances. An analysis of the actual conversational situation, keeping in mind Austin's speech act theory,[95] reveals in addition that the application of karmic arguments can also have perlocutionary effects. As in the case of baptism, Gu Puzhong, for example, stated that he was not baptised, because he was not convinced of it. This would create a possibility of starting an argument with the conversation partner. Implicitly, the listener would wonder whether the interviewer agrees with the choices on which the narrator enlarges. Especially as the listener is a foreigner, whom the interviewee might assume to be Christian or at least to hold a different belief from himself, the narrator seems culturally used to or even interested in maintaining situational harmony. Implying karmic arguments has the side effect of avoiding insults: it does not challenge the listener with arguments with which she might disagree. Beyond the primary content, the karmic tropes fit, therefore, also into harmonising language behaviour. The popularity of the karmic argument might not only result from the general conviction and attention paid to the causal interrelatedness of matters, but resorting to karmic tropes also prevents confrontation and further investigation into overly sensitive or personal questions.

A closer look at the argumentations provided reveals a second layer beyond the depicted establishment of situational harmony: besides the implicit excuse of "I did something different from you, because the circumstances in which I was were just different", using karmic tropes can also help the interviewees to escape any evaluative questions, which implies a ranking or qualification of others: Cai (S1) and Luo (28.32) do not disqualify any other Buddhist organisation, and Gu (S15) does not talk negatively about baptism, but all three made their own choice: Cai likes his community, while Luo still appreciates her young Buddhist organisation and Gu, despite having lived for over a decade in Canada, does not identify himself as a Christian. In addition, Luo, when granted the privilege of talking with her master, does not stress her personal qualities in comparison with others (Luo (32)). Analysing the usage of karmic tropes in the interviews, one can see that they have a tendency to avoid competitive evaluation. The more formal

95 Austin (1962). Simplified, Austin divides between locutionary, illocutionary, and perlocutionary acts of speech. A speech act can be analysed on all three levels. Locutionary is the act's utterance with phonetic, syntactic and semantic features. Illocutionary is its intended meaning. Perlocutionary is the actual effect, which is not necessarily intended. The psychological consequences of a speech act belong, therefore, to the perlocutionary level of speech.

the interview setting, the greater the possible reluctance to be critical of other concrete people or organisations and the greater the likelihood of activating, especially because of centring on Buddhism, well-trained harmonising language use.

A third usage of the karmic argument in these interviews is as a leading principle for making choices about personal engagement: Later in the interview, Li Zhiqiang states that he does not donate to any Buddhist community, but seeks one that is suitable, with which he has "*jiyuan* 機緣".[96] He explains: "I'm not forcing things, this's the most important". (*Wo bu hui qu qiangqiu, zhe shi zui zhongyao de* 我不會去強求 這是最重要的). One can see that the application of karmic formulations assists, among other means, the finding of appropriate roles in group processes. Karmic arguments are used in the context of smooth group integration and show the deep respect of the interviewees for the situation and their subordinate role within it.

The *yuan*-tropes seem, besides their direct explanatory purpose, to be a convenient, inflationary applied means of conversation for avoiding confrontation. They support conversational behaviour, which–while not necessarily conscious in the speaker–in effect has a tendency to create situational harmony, avoiding disagreement with the listener, maintaining privacy without directly rejecting questions and preventing negative judgements about third parties. They serve as a means of group integration. The harmonising and convenient conversational effect of karmic tropes could explain why they enjoy great popularity and are statistically widespread in Taiwan.

The only sequence in which a karmic argument is rejected within the interviews is its usage as a means of exclusion. Gu Puzhong rejects the idea of denying people access to Buddhist literature because of their lack of education, countering the argument "you just don't have *yuan*", i.e. a karmic connection, with it. Gu argues that the incorrect application of the principle through Buddhist doctrine is not in accordance with the ideal of a bodhisattva, who would intend to rescue all beings equally (S13). While Gu is the only interviewee who explicitly refers karmic arguments back to the deeper Buddhist doctrine, it is still remarkable that even this reference to Buddhism is in line with an avoidance of attitudes that could endanger integrative thinking.

In Taiwan a wide range of karmic argumentation seems common. The interview material was not collected with the intention of elucidating the different usages of karmic thinking in Taiwan, so naturally the analyses cannot map out the range of possible applications. One would have to elicit in this respect not only ideas about fate and destiny management, but also go fur-

---

96 *Jiyuan* might be considered a combination of either *shiji* 時機 (right moment, opportunity) or *jihui* 機會 (opportunity, chance) with *yinyuan* and can be used in Buddhist as well as non-Buddhist texts and formulations.

ther into ideas of rebirth and merit-making. With such a widely-acknowledged trope as causal interconnectedness, one should expect a complex field of usages, just as one would try to analyse the multiplicity of usages of English native speakers when exclaiming "Oh, my God!", which is–needless to say–not necessarily linked to Christianity. Still, the preliminary results allow to add at least one type of specific Taiwanese usage of the karma idea, which has not been outlined in the anthropological inquiry of Keyes about the use of karma in South and South East Asia.

Keyes summarises in his introduction the main ways in which different cultures apply the idea of karma: Hindus, as analysed by Babb, see in karma a "theory of causation that supplies reasons for human fortune, good or bad, and that at least in theory it can provide convincing explanations for human misfortune" (Keyes 1983, 3), while Theravāda Buddhists "see in karma an explanation of conditions that have emerged in one's lifetimes only on rare occasion, conditions that must be accepted because there is nothing one can do about them" (ibid.). Among Tibetans, Lichter and Epstein point out that karma is used as an "ironic contemplation of life's unhappiness based upon the realisation that 'ultimately there is no happiness in the realm of karma'" (Keyes 1983, 206). For Tibetans and Theravādins, the focus would be more on prospective speculation than retrospective explanation.

This emphasis on action and prospection might be underrepresented in narrative biographical interviews in general, as the interviewees attempt to shed light on their past. The "Hindu" view as providing convincing explanations about human misfortune can also be seen in our interviews. Once again, this shows that the karmic idea might be more Indian than Buddhist in origin, although it could have been implemented into Taiwanese-Chinese thinking by Buddhists.[97] Still, the "Hindu" usage of explaining misfortune seems, in Taiwan, to be only one aspect of a broad variety of possible applications–which might lead to a second look at the broader Hindu culture. The "Theravādins'" usage of explaining "rare occasions" through karmic tropes contrasts with the inflationary implementation in colloquial Taiwanese language. The ironic aspect of "Tibetan" expression modes is an interesting addition that one could explore by interviewing further Taiwanese Buddhists. Besides all of these single observations, one could add to the South and South East Asian investigations an East Asian perspective, which adds to the content-oriented explanatory and predictive usages of the karmic idea via various combinations of the term "*yuan*" a performative usage: Karmic tropes can be used in Taiwan to create situational harmony during conversations. In communication, it can serve as a means of protecting one's privacy, avoiding dis-

97 R. Gombrich argues that Buddhism can even be constructed in isolation from the idea of karma and rebirth; see Gombrich (1975), here 215.

agreements, preventing questions about specification and pejorative declassification, and fostering smooth group integration–karmic tropes are a highly flexible integrative means of communication.[98] In contrast, karmic argumentation was not applied where it could lead to people's exclusion. Chinese, as it is used in daily life in Taiwan, contains a variety of sayings around karmic expressions (especially the application of the term *yuan*), which have a Buddhist–or Indian–flavour. The karmic idea becomes a trigger, emphasising causal relations within Chinese culture. While it would be interesting to explore further the classification of doctrinal explications of the karmic idea in Taiwan, one can state that the doctrinally-logical approach occurs as an elaborate idea in the Taiwanese Buddhists' explications, but the occasional harmonising usage is far more prevalent in everyday language.

Social Relations: Family, Authorities, and Monastics

Detecting the perlocutionary effects of karmic tropes in daily language, the question arises of whether, within everyday relationships, an integrative tendency through Buddhist tropes is also to be found.

Lin Yongfu, the taxi driver, showed a strong family orientation and his belief strengthened his family's social cohesion. Luo Peirong's problems all relate to her family. She uses religious resources to improve the situation of her relatives, but the Buddhist act itself is separated socially from family affairs. While the community integration in Luo's behaviour is less visible, she shows a strong commitment to authorities. She is highly respectful of the Buddhist master of the monastery and regards his advice as beyond challenge. The shaman who visits her home grants her husband's health. While Lin autonomously explains the functions of gods and temples, and no further authorities feature in his narrations except for gods who are predictably protective, the unpredictive power of gods and Buddhas leads Luo to subordinate herself in a spiritual hierarchy and see her wisdom in the correct choice and application of religious resources and authorities. Subordination to the authorities as well as his community dominates Cai Chenhao's narrative style. Without any rejection, he is integrated into his community and recognises its masters. He emphasises that his family relations were improved by his practice and he uses this fact to demonstrate its positive effects, such as name recitation. Improved relations are, in his case, a strong argument for following a practice. The donor, Li Zhiqiang, did not question the monks' decision not to accept him into the monastic community. He respects Chinese astrology and Buddhist monastics. In his position as a donor,

98 In the author's personal experience, the karmic idea is also frequently used to strengthen friendships ("We seem to have *yuan*.").

he also accepts the Buddhist abbot's religious authority. This self-restriction facilitates cooperation within the organisation for him. Gu Puzhong rarely refers to the monastic authorities as persons to whom he is subordinated. The abbot in his youth he puts in context with the narrations about his grandmother. Another monastic he describes as his fellow student at university. His family seems to Gu to be a task that has to be successfully faced in its economic aspects. He shows, through the concentration on his grandmother within his narration as well as through his veneration behaviour, a strong filial piety towards her.

Do the interviewees see themselves as following their parents' belief, as most Conventional Buddhists are supposed to do? Lin Yongfu certainly sees himself within a family tradition. Luo finally admits the strength of the Daoist tradition into which her husband is socialised, and follows the tradition of the previous generation though not necessarily that of her parents. Gu observes his grandmother's heritage. Only Cai has broken away from his family, while pointing out that his new belief alone improved his family relationships. The donor Li does not mention his family at all, but nor does he oppose the general Taiwanese belief through which he has been socialised since his youth.

The interviewees are, in general, respectful towards the authorities, whenever they mention them. Only Gu criticises the abbot whom his grandmother followed, and Lin criticises corrupt temple managers in general. The authorities in the narrations can either be human or spiritual in nature; for example, Luo's intimate relationship with Bodhisattva Guanyin. A focus on the relationship with monastics reveals that, for Lin, who is socialised in popular religion, they do not form part of his social world. The question about becoming a monastic does not arise for him. Luo, in contrast, had a challenging encounter with a Young Buddhist Monastery led by monastics. On joining the organisation, Luo already had a family and therefore it was difficult for her to become a monastic. Through karmic argumentation, she accepts her situation, while her friend assured the author during the interview that Luo, in the past, had seriously contemplated leaving home. Still, Luo shows great respect for the abbot's advice and affectionately calls him—as is common in Taiwan—"*shifu*", literally "teacher-father", which implies a personal closeness and respect. Meanwhile, Cai's practice helps to improve his relationships. Leaving home seems counterproductive in his eyes. He adopts the respectful habitus which unites his community in its reverence for its founder and the authorities. The donor Li is well aware of the monastic-lay distinction, but has personally left behind the phase of life-decisions. He recognises the authority of the monastics, but sees his business world as a relationship of mutual benefit with monastics. Gu is the only one who intellectually challenges the *saṃgha* and develops a differentiated understanding of Buddhism, which makes sense of being a Buddhist as a lay and does not necessarily see lay people as religiously subordinate to the *saṃgha*. Still, in his critique of the abbot, whom his grandmother cherished, he remains moderate.

Summing up, it is safe to say that the interviewees' belief is closely connected with their social relations. The desire to make family matters central and integrate into a social network might be specific to neither Buddhists nor Taiwanese. Still, one can see that Buddhism influences their social relations. The presented cases value harmony in their social life, in their family, and in their relationship with the previous generation and in general regard monastics with respect and affection, insofar as they are aware of them. Any criticism of monastics is uttered discretely. None of the "Conventional Buddhists" sees themselves as part of a revolutionary generation, opposing their parents or their (Buddhist) belief.

*Veneration–*Baibai *拜拜-Religiosity?*

The respectful recognition of authorities and elders is in line with one of the most central acts of general veneration behaviour in Taiwan, commonly referred to as "*baibai* 拜拜". "*Bai*" generally means "to pay respect to", "do obeisance", and is not necessarily bound to a primarily "religious" context, but can also be about respecting others. It is used in combination as a verb to request someone to do something, inquire after or visit someone, or even express gratitude or congratulations (*baituo* 拜託, *baifang* 拜訪, *baixie* 拜謝, *baihe* 拜賀). In its repeated usage, *baibai*, it clearly refers to worshipping at a temple. The act of *baibai* was frequently mentioned by the interviewees and seems to be deeply-rooted in their everyday experience. This certainly relates to the central act of religious behaviour during Lin Yongfu's interview, who, in nearly every statement, mentions this term. To him, the characteristic of a religion seems to be the act of veneration (*bai*) which, in his eyes, is the central way to realise his belief in practice. The quality of a religion is to be seen through the quality of the protection that its respective god offers. The effect of veneration as protection is accredited by 60% of the Conventional Buddhists (see chap. 6, p. 69). Veneration for Lin includes material donations, and he shows a high sensitivity against misusage.

Also, for Luo Peirong, the act of veneration is, in her personal historical memory, the "original" form of religion, while the separation between Buddhism and Taoism is secondary, only emerging in her later historical awareness. When severe problems arise, Luo does not maintain the distinction between Buddhism and Daoism, but simply venerates the gods or Buddhas, which she experiences as having more effect and being more helpful. Donations, for her, naturally form part of veneration–she is surprised when, at the Daoist temple, the owner does not want any money. The veneration of gods, therefore, becomes enlarged by "Buddha/-s", which are literally added to the expression itself: "venerating gods" (*baishen* 拜神) is extended to "venerating gods and Buddhas" (*bai shenfo* 拜神佛). The act itself remains the same. As Luo is distressed by her situation, she tests the system of veneration for its effects and becomes convinced that the Daoist gods are more powerful in her concrete case. The usage of the system of veneration develops, in her context, an extremely mechanistic connotation. Through the linkage with karmic thinking, discussed above, Luo tries to put "gods and Buddhas" as Bodhisattva Guanyin under pressure to help her to resolve her situation. Li Zhiqiang is softly switching over to Buddhism, when he recalls that, after a certain age, he went more frequently to Buddhist temples to venerate than to Daoist ones. He changed the location, but the action itself remained the same. Even when he describes how he is going to a colleague and monk's Buddhist centre, he says that he goes there for veneration (*baibai*). *Baibai* is a collective term, which requires no further explanation for the interviewees. It is often used, but never explained. They take it as well-known and suppose it to be easily communicable. Li mentions it in the same breath as "playing" (*wan* 玩): In his youth, he went to temples for "veneration" and "playing". The natural combination of these two actions was implanted in Li since his early childhood and he also later places the performance of "*baibai*" in the realm of an everyday behaviour. "Veneration" appears to be common and conventionally recognised as enjoying oneself, playing like a child.

In the case of Lin Yongfu, Luo Peirong, and Li Zhiqiang, Buddhism is smoothly integrated into the concept of veneration without alteration. For Lin Yongfu, at home, the Buddhist statue is simply an addition to his pantheon, which he venerates also. While he does not really recognise any essential difference between the different kinds of "gods and Buddhas", Luo far less easily shifts back from Buddhism to Daoism and marks this shift consciously as she tries to justify it repeatedly during the interview. Still, to her, the act of *baibai* seems to be a natural consequence when encountering problems, and she also experiences it as normality in her Buddhist environment: "I heard [from colleagues also participating in Buddhist activities]: 'I go there to venerate, I go there to venerate'. That should be common. Because like when you encounter something, you want to ask, you want to find out this answer" (Luo S9). Even though she feels slightly uncomfortable about visiting a Daoist temple for veneration, she tells herself, that it would not be a bad thing ("Na, going to venerate is also not a bad thing. Na, [so] I went to venerate. *Na qu baibai ye bu shi huaishi. Na qu baibai* 那去拜拜也不是壞事. 那去拜拜"). This discomfort about the idea of veneration, while unable to imagine it as something bad, demonstrates Luo's situation precisely: on the one hand, she seems to be aware that venerating Daoist gods might not fall within the sphere of being a Buddhist, which she would prefer, but, on the other hand it is unimaginable for her to regard such a common social experience as unacceptable. Although uncomfortable, she does not abandon the concept and, as a consequence, integrates Buddhism into her veneration behaviour. Content-wise, she accomplishes this through karmic argumentation, which assures her that her Buddhist world view would lead her into Daoism. Li Zhiqiang is not only continuing his veneration practice, shifting to Buddhist temples, but also stresses the importance of Dharma assemblies. To him, they form a parallel to the veneration practice, as they serve one's ancestors and the deceased. A significant difference to veneration behaviour at a temple is that it is less possible to start bargaining with the addressees, but one intends to care for them, and one is also personally interested in preventing negative events, wanting to assure oneself of protection, and even seeing it as a chance to earn merit. Buddhism presents itself as transforming the act of veneration into an organisational form. Li clearly thinks that, by respecting people's desire for veneration, a Dharma assembly like the Water-and-Land Recitation is of great importance and also convinces himself of the quality of the Buddhist monastery.

For Lin Yongfu, Luo Peirong and Li Zhiqiang, veneration (*baibai*) is central to their religious experience. They integrate their definition of Buddhism within its frame. In this frame, they are assured that their Buddhist religious behaviour will protect them and improve their fate.

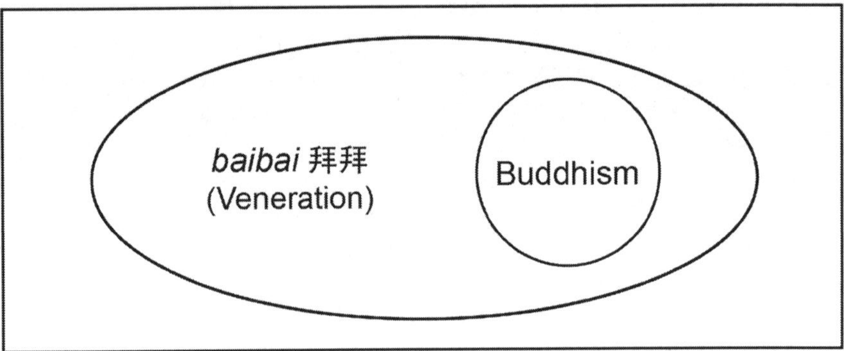

Figure 14: Lin Yongfu, Luo Peirong, and Li Zhiqiang see Buddhism as harmoniously fitting into popular veneration behaviour.

Although there are slight differences between the role that veneration plays in each of the three cases, they can be grouped together when contrasting them with the relationship that Gu Puzhong and Cai Chenhao have towards the act of *baibai.*

Cai never once, during the interview, implies veneration or even uses the term *bai.* He emphasises his practice of name recitation, which improves his family relationships. Cai does not even recognise this most common field of religious activity. Interestingly, this accompanies the building of strong boundaries against "others"–i.e. the rest of society, which does not belong to his group–and living in social isolation.

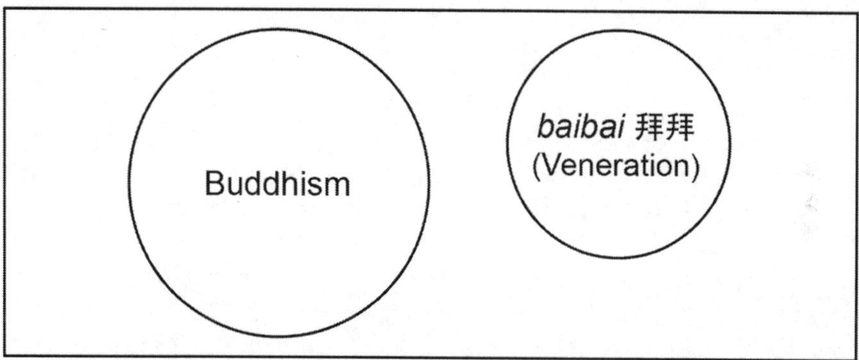

Figure 15: Cai Chenhao does not talk of veneration. He constructs his understanding of Buddhism independently of common veneration behaviour.

Gu Puzhong does not cut himself off from society, but sees himself as having a mission within it. Buddhism, in his eyes, should be lived in everyday life and therefore "Buddhism is not a religion you go and venerate". Still, Gu himself maintains a practice of veneration, which is outwardly no different from the first three cases. This becomes understandable through the deep respect and personal devotion that he pays to his grandmother, who obliged him to follow this practice frequently in his youth. Still, Gu displays a different attitude within his veneration behaviour. While he recognises that, in his youth, he had selfish motives for engaging in veneration, like wanting to pass exams, he inherited from his grandmother a desire to engage in veneration for the sake of all sentient beings. He opposes any mechanical bargaining character, personal purpose or answer-searching through veneration, reinterpreting it rather as a selfless act that extends to the whole world.

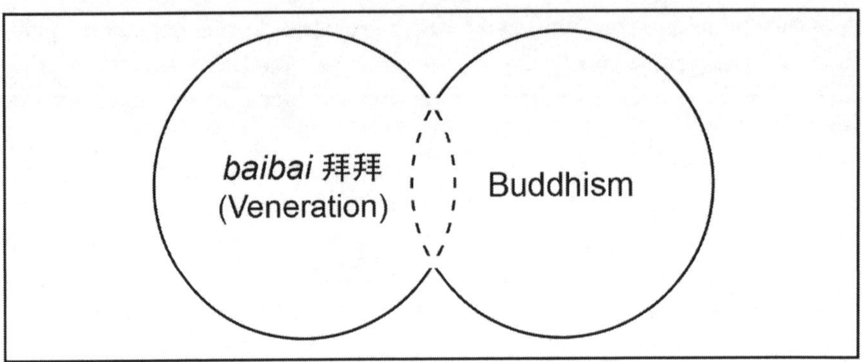

Figure 16: Gu Puzhong gives the action of veneration a new meaning with the help of Buddhism.

Within Buddhism, there seem to be tendencies for a doctrinal reinterpretation, negligence, or even denial of the popular act of veneration, which is so common that the act of "venerating Buddha" is, even for those who designed the TSCS-survey, the exact equivalent of "believing in Buddha" (TSCS 2004.2, v15, is asking about venerating *or* believing in Buddha). Still, the field of Conventional Believers seems to require differentiation, as those who regard Buddhism simply as part of their general veneration behaviour have considerably different notions of Buddhism than those who construct their belief separately from the common veneration practices or opt for a profound re-conceptualisation of the act of veneration itself. The second part of this book will test the borders and see which life-concepts are expressed by the lay Buddhist believers in Taiwan who do not form part of normal veneration behaviour.

*Effects upon Daily Life: Moral (*lunli *倫理), Practice (*xiuxing *修行), and Miraculous (*aomiao *奧妙) Happenings*

The karmic argumentation is closely connected to the idea of rebirth, which is generally seen as being determined by karma. This suggests that the concept of cause and effect motivates people to engage in good behaviour. The tendency towards an egoistical motivation in bettering one's karma by engaging in good conduct and good deeds to attain a better rebirth is formulated by Li Zhiqiang explicitly. For him, Buddhism fosters moral behaviour, and he is the only interviewee to mention this. How far are morality and belief for Conventional Buddhists connected to each other?

As explained in chapter 4, the *Taiwan Social Change Survey* asks about the influence of religion in life as well as ethical and moral values in relation to parental guidance. The majority of the interviewees affirmed that they were taught the basic rules of social behaviour by their parents during their childhood and youth. These include respecting others and pursuing the ideals of uprightness and fairness. Also, the need to help disadvantaged people is seen as being transmitted by parents. On closer examination, the questionnaire does not ask whether these ideals are connected to religious institutions. At least, the questionnaire designers see it as parents' responsibility to teach their children values, and this is supported by all of the responses: in all cases, the majority of people (65–87%) recall that their parents taught them not to bully others, lie or push into queues, but to help the unfortunate:

v83	(1) Not to bully others (不欺負別人)		(2) Not to lie (不可以撒謊)		(3) Not to push into queues (不可以插隊)		(4) To help the unfortunate (幫助不幸的人)	
	Frequ	%	Frequ	%	Frequ	%	Frequ	%
Often	1065|222	56.6|56.2	1200|253	63.8|64.1	740|157	39.3|39.7	851|189	45.2|47.8
Sometimes	465|96	24.7|24.3	444|90	23.6|22.8	496|93	26.4|23.5	619|116	32.9|29.4
Seldom	200/37	10.6|9.4	127|22	6.8|5.6	352|72	18.7|18.2	243|50	12.9|12.7
Never	124/35	6.6|8.9	86|25	4.6|6.3	267|68	14.2|17.2	140|34	7.4|8.6
Don't know/ forgotten	11/2	0.6|0.5	8|2	0.4|0.5	10|2	0.5|0.5	12|3	0.6|0.8
Don't want to answer	3/0	0.2|0.0	3|0	0.2|0.0	3|0	0.2|0.0	3|0	0.2|0.0
Parents already passed away	13/3	0.7|0.8	13|3	0.7|0.8	13|3	0.7|0.8	13|3	0.7|0.8
Total	1881|395	100.0|100.0	1881|395	100.0|100.0	1881|395	100.0|100.0	1881|395	100.0|100.0

Table 11: When you were growing up (at junior high school), did your parents often teach you to behave in the following ways? (TSCS 2004.2, v83). Frequency and percentages provide the data for Conventional Buddhists and for the whole sample side by side (whole population|Conventional Buddhists).

Still, people in general seem to recognise that their thoughts and daily behaviour is influenced by religion (TSCS 2004.2, v30.4, agreement 60%) and the majority assumes that religion gives them a direction in life (TSCS 2004.2, v30.5, agreement 55%). Buddhists are even more convinced that religion affects people's thoughts and behaviour in daily life and can give life a direction:

v30		v30.4: Religion influences the thinking and behaviour of people's daily life (宗教能帶給人日常生活的想法和行為)	v30.5: Religion can bring people a direction in life (宗教能帶給人人生的方向)
Agreement among the whole Population	Very much	25.6% (482)	20.4% (384)
	Somewhat	34.4% (647)	34.6% (651)
	Subtotal	60.0% (1129)	55.0% (1035)
Population	Total	100.0% (1881)	100.0% (1881)
Agreement among Buddhists	Very much	36.0% (163)	29.4% (133)
	Somewhat	40.2% (182)	42.6% (193)
	Subtotal	76.2% (345)	72.0% (326)
Buddhists	Total	100.0% (453)	100.0% (453)
Agreement among Conventional Buddhists	Very much	33.4% (132)	25.3% (100)
	Somewhat	42.3% (167)	44.8% (177)
	Subtotal	75.7% (299)	70.1% (277)
Conventional Buddhists	Total	100.0% (395)	100.0% (395)

Table 12: Agreement with the statements about the relationship between the interviewees and religion (TSCS 2004.2, v30.4 and v30.5, percentage and frequency).

When exploring the reasons for visiting a temple, moral issues were not considered by the questionnaire designers. Practical matters, like health, peace and careers, scored highest among the Conventional Buddhists who visit temples,[99] and who followed their religion mainly because of their parents' belief (TSCS 2004.2, v29.16: 67.1%). Still, 9.4–15.9% of the Buddhists stated that they adopt a Buddhist belief in order to "seek wisdom", "truth" or "un-

[99] Details of TSCS 2004.2, v32.1: For what main reason do you visit the shrine?: Of the 162 Conventional Buddhists who visit temples (out of the 395 Conventional Buddhists, i.e. 41%), the following proportions responded in the affirmative, when asked about the respective purposes (from highest to lowest): (01) Health and peace (*shenti jiang-kang, ping'an* 身體健康、平安): 114 people; (02) A smooth career (*shiye shunli* 事業順利): 46 people; (10) Avoiding disasters and eliminating misfortune (*xiaozai jie'e* 消災解厄): 38 people; (03) Earning serious money (*zhuan daqian* 賺大錢): 22 people; (12) Other (*qi ta* 其它): 22 people; (11) Pacifying evil spirits that cause fear (*shou jing* 收驚): 21; (08) Social stability, national prosperity and peace (*shehui anding, guotai min'an* 社會安定、國泰民安): 19 people; (04) To have good exam results (*dushu, kaoshi shunli* 讀書、考試順利): 18 people; (07) Family problems (*jiating wenti* 家庭問題 18 people; (05) Problems with children's discipline (*zinü guan jiao wenti* 子女管教問題): 14 people; (06) Problems concerning relationships and marriage (*ganqing hunyin wenti* 感情婚姻問題): 4 people; (09) Changing feng-shui (*gai fengshui* 改風水): 0 people.

derstand the meaning of life" (v29, see chap. 6). The answers do not explain the impact of belief on guidance in life and the role of morality in connection with belief: three quarters of the Conventional Buddhists think that their belief influences their daily life and gives them direction, but this deep influence is not necessarily connected with the search for truth, wisdom, and the meaning of life as a reason for resorting to a religious belief. So how does religion influence daily life? Can the results of the qualitative analysis shed light upon this connection? How do the interviewees describe the influence of Buddhism upon their life?

The taxi driver, Lin Yongfu, did not learn moral behaviour through Buddhism, but it did lead him to adopt morally-acceptable social conduct. Buddhist veneration is continuously needed in order to ensure divine protection. In the case of misconduct, the gods and Buddhas do not protect the venerating person. For him, the question of how to define good behaviour does not arise, but is supposed to be general social knowledge. His example of not drinking and driving demonstrates a morality which is sustaining a stable, undisturbed family situation. Personal pleasure, like drinking alcohol, is acceptable provided that it does not lead to short-sighted behaviour that endangers the safety of the individual and causes concern for the family. The self-evidence with which Lin is assuming a given social morality hints that he experiences morality in his social life as being not up for discussion. Also, the other interviews suggest that morality is seen as an assured knowledge: none of the interviewees struggled to define values as good and bad or judgements as right or wrong. For Luo Peirong, morals are not a question. She makes efforts to improve her situation by engaging in ritual behaviour, leading to a healthier, more harmonious environment. Statements such as "*baibai* is not a bad thing, so I go" (see above) reflect how natural veneration is for Luo. In her social life, the value of *baibai* itself is self-evident. The effect of veneration is the standard by which it is judged. Cai Chenhao, like Luo Peirong, fails to address the topic of morality, but is fascinated by the effects of name recitation upon his social life. Buddhism, in his view, delivers an understanding of life and death whereby his life improves. Cai does not reflect upon what such an improvement brings. He assumes, naturally, that a stable social environment and better relationship with his parents constitute an improvement. For Cai and Luo, there are clear moral values, which are not under discussion, revealed in their natural judgement of issues, especially their social life. Health and a conflict-free relationship with their social environment are, without doubt, considered positive values.

For the taxi driver, Lin Yongfu, Buddhism secures moral behaviour through ritual acts and personal good behaviour. In contrast, for the donor, Li Zhiqiang, Buddhist morality is not located in the ritual dimension, but constructed as a cognitive issue. He learnt about moral values by living and studying in a Buddhist monastery for a couple of months and, in his subsequent personal actions, tries to apply this knowledge. Buddhism delivers, for Li Zhiqiang, the rational motivation for behaving morally, as it provides direct guidance and insights into the consequences of good or bad behaviour with regard to family and business issues. Li Zhiqiang links Buddhism to morality so strongly that not only does he elaborate on it, but it becomes the dominant topic of the interview. Socially fair behaviour includes legal, upright conduct leading to a sustainable business development. Within his family life, a positive effect can be seen in his children, who behave well. The effect of his knowledge, the actual behaviour, is what Li Zhiqiang described as convincing him of Buddhism. Buddhism gives Li Zhiqiang insights into the consequences of his behaviour, which guarantees moral teaching about right and wrong, while the emphasis lies on convincing people of the advantage of socially fair behaviour, not on the construction of what is to be defined as good. For Li Zhiqiang, it is not a question of *what* is right or wrong, good or bad, but he is enthusiastic about the positive effect of its *application*. This is also the reason why, when asked about his choice of religion, Li Zhiqiang might not answer that it gives him moral values, but that it enables him to engage in sustainable business development and have well-behaved children. Buddhism, in his eyes, prevents people from falling into laxness, i.e. from thinking "it's right, however you're doing" (Li S11).

Summing up, in Taiwan, as represented by the interviewees' general assumptions about "good" and "bad" at least, Buddhists' experience is constructed as a homogenous moral code which is rooted in the social discourse, the values of which are not based upon primarily religious orientations. This code seems to centre around social well-being, health, business success, and a smooth and unproblematic family life. Still, Buddhists can experience the upholding of the moral code as ensured through Buddhism, either in its ritual function connected with the protection of gods or in its cognitive function as a knowledge and insight into the karmic advantages of paying attention to the moral code. "Buddhism", therefore, has an impact on life not by delivering the moral code itself, but by sustaining it. In an increasingly changing environment, Buddhism might even gain greater attractiveness by ensuring the binding character of moral values.

The author exempted the case of Gu Puzhong from the discussion of morality. Gu does not emphasise Buddhism in combination with the generally-acknowledged social values very often, but stresses frequently the value of acting according to his grandmother's maxim–selflessness. No other values seem to be needed, not even the notion of Buddhism. Only selflessness counts in his verbal reflection while, in his biography, practical necessities like securing the family's financial well-being are unquestioned, and he also integrates himself into the common Taiwanese standard biography of a family's father. Still, selflessness is not a theoretical principle for Gu, since he explicitly emphasises action and practice, as discussed at length in the analysis of his case: Buddhism is about practice (*xiu jiu shi zuo* 修就是作, Gu S5), about putting selflessness into practice. One shall practise on one's own faults (S5) and shall practise instead of building temples and uttering wishes there (S7). This *principle of practice* has the potential to initiate reformatory agendas within the Buddhist tradition. Gu is eloquent in pointing out the importance of *xiu* 修 as enacting Buddha's teaching. Buddhism is perceived as a form of self-cultivation which does not concentrate on moral theoretical constructions. Also, in the other interviews, practice, *xiu,* comes into play: similar to Gu, Li Zhiqiang speaks of applying practice in behaviour, language behaviour and "the things of society" (*xingwei* 行為, *yuyan xingwei* 語言行為, *zheng ge she hui shang de shiqing* 整個社會上的事情, S6). Luo Peirong describes her own belief through the expression "to practise both Buddhism and Daoism" (*fodao shuangxiu* 佛道雙修, Luo S9) just as one has to practise Zen and Pure Land together to improve one's karma. Cai wants to practise (*xiuxing* 修行, S13) to escape the cycle of rebirth and aims to practise "until Buddhism" (*xiuxing dao fofa* 修行到佛法, S15). Practice seems to be important to Buddhism, but not restricted to it. "Practice" is often discussed during the interviews, and is mentioned very naturally without special emphasis by the interviewees, while analysing their concept of morality required far more reconstructional efforts. Why is this so? What is the role of practice and cultivation within Buddhism or even Chinese history?

Screening through the standard dictionaries and encyclopedias of Buddhism in search of a reference to "practice", few entries can be found.[100] To the author's knowledge, there is, to date, no comparative anthropological fieldwork on the multiple concepts of "practice" in Buddhist cultures. A first study collects a broad array of Buddhist practices across cultures (Harding

[100] There is no entry either for "practice", "(self-)cultivation", the Sanskrit term "*caryā*" or the Chinese term "*xiu*" in the Encyclopedia of Buddhism (2004), The Shambala Dictionary of Buddhism and Zen (Fisher-Schreiber, Eberhard, and Diener 1991) and the Oxford Dictionary of Buddhism (Keown 2003). While "meditation" is discussed at length in the Encyclopedia, it is critically recognised as a Western construction by the Oxford Dictionary of Buddhism ("English word often used to translate a range of more specific indigenous terms denoting techniques and practices designed to concentrate and focus the mind." Keown 2003, 176, entry "meditation"). Still, this does not lead to a differentiated description of social reality, but, fleeing old patterns and generalisations about "meditation" and a "practically" oriented "Buddhism", the topic seems to have been avoided. It is the Princeton Dictionary of Buddhism that discusses "practice" shortly under the entry "bhāvanā" (Buswell and Lopez 2014, 112). The social sciences might reveal a helpful tool for scholars of Chinese Buddhism, to overcome blind spots, understand the historical investigations into the "beyond" of texts and also provide a systematic approach to contemporary culture as helpful for a "dense description" of reality.

2012). Consistently, the term "practice" is listed as an entry in a joint study on "Critical Terms for the Study of Buddhism" (Bielefeldt 2005) and reveals a well-known reason for this *desideratum*: while Western interest in Buddhism since the late 19th century was centred on doctrinal issues and meditation practices, the historical reality and social practices have often been neglected by academics. Recent trends in Buddhist studies attempt to reveal the historical social reality behind the transmitted texts. The article indicates this shift within Buddhist studies. Picturing the social reality of Buddhist life through interdisciplinary cooperation and methods of social research remains a Buddhological task also in the future.[101]

While lacking a profound study of the concept of "*xiu*" in Chinese culture, a preliminary overview of the Classical Chinese usage might offer an initial, tentative conceptualisation of it: the term itself is already common in early Chinese sources.[102] Also written as "*xiu* 脩", the expression is often used as a transitive verb referring to cultivating or refining something or oneself (esp. *xiuyi* 修己, *zixiu* 自修). It can also mean to "train" or "exercise" in military contexts or refer to an act of building or producing, as in to "maintain" or "repair". It can be used in the passive voice in the sense of "to be well cultivated". Nominalised, it refers to a cultivated person or personal cultivation. In combination with "*shen* 身", basically the "body", "*xiu*" refers to a standard principle in Confucian thought: "*xiushen*", to cultivate one's own personality, is the prerequisite for any outer action. The classic reference for this idea is to be found in *The Great Learning* (*Daxue* 大學) that, with Zhu Xi (朱熹, 1130–1200), became a standard part of general *literati* education: "*xiu shen zai zheng qi xin* 脩身在正其心" "The cultivation/practice of the body/person consists in rectifying one's mind".[103] The passage shows how the concept of the "body"

---

101 The open concept of "critical terms" leaves space for historical discoveries and the article's bibliography confirms that there seems to be no study analysing the concepts of "practice", be it "caryā", "bhāvanā", "*xiu*" or any other indigenous term.

102 In the following, the TLS-database (accessed Jan 21, 2016) was used to gain a preliminary overview of Classical Chinese usage.

103 *The Great Learning* is counted together with *The Doctrine of the Mean*, the *Analects*, and the *Mencius* among the "Four Books", the essentials of basic *literati* education. Legge translates the seventh chapter of *The Great Learning*: "所謂脩身，在正其心者，身有所忿懥，則不得其正，有所恐懼，則不得其正，有所好樂，則不得其正，有所憂患，則不得其正。心不在焉，視而不見，聽而不聞，食而不知其味。此謂修身在正其心。
1. What is meant by, 'The cultivation of the person depends on rectifying the mind', may be thus illustrated: —If a man be under the influence of passion, he will be incorrect in his conduct. He will be the same, if he is under the influence of terror, or under the influence of fond regard, or under that of sorrow and distress. When the mind is not present, we look and do not see; we hear and do not understand; we eat and do not know the taste of what we eat. 3. This is what is meant by saying that the cultivation of the person depends on the rectifying of the mind" (Legge 1861, 232). See also Unger 2000, 99, who in his entry "siu^1 shen^1 修身" translates this term lite-

encompasses the whole personality–a "bodily practice" is in this context meant to be a cultivation of an individual's whole personality. Moreover, the "bodily/personal practice/cultivation" of someone brings peace to his family and to those beneath him.[104] Bodily practices in the sense of the cultivation of one's own character, as Legge translates it, serve as the fundamental principles of successful ruling as setting up the "way" (*dao* 道) by virtue and proper conduct.[105] A detailed analysis of the concepts of bodily practices within Classical Chinese literature lies beyond the scope of this book. Still, it is already clear from this preliminary excursus into Classical Chinese texts that the Buddhist tradition coming to China mingles–similar to the karmic reinterpretation of *yuan*, see above–in Chinese culture with an already existing discourse on self-cultivation. The concepts linked to "*xiu*" receive a Buddhist re-interpretation and the availability and importance of the *xiu*-concept in China eases the spread of Buddhist ideas about human conduct and self-cultivation (Skt. *caryā*, *bhāvanā*, *yoga* etc.).

Within the sociological framework followed here, the results from the Conventional Buddhists, explaining their belief on the folio of Taiwanese society today, can be captured: the Conventional Buddhists easily resort to expressions that describe the importance of Buddhism as a religion through the effects it has upon their lives—it changes their spiritual and practical conduct. *Xiu* also seems difficult to categorise in the interviews. "Practice" can refer to everyday life as well as to religious traditions, as in the inter-

---

rally as "die eigene Person pflegen", and interprets it as "sich selbst zur sittlich gefestigten Persönlichkeit heranbilden".

104 This also reflects in the *Lunyu* 論語, the *Analects* of Confucius, through self-cultivation (*xiuyi* 修己) as bringing peace to society (to people and to the Hundred Families, *Lunyu* 14.42).

105 In *The Doctrine of the Mean* (*Zhongyong* 中庸) it is stated that the cultivation of oneself (*xiushen*) is the prerequisite of establishing the Way (*dao*). Knowing about self-cultivation one would know how to govern people. Self-cultivation would consist of three aspects: knowing about the importance of learning resulting in knowledge, determination resulting in humaneness, and the knowledge when to be ashamed resulting in courage. It also reaches out to outer appearance and proper conduct (see Legge 1861, 271–275, i.e. *The Doctrine of the Mean*, Chap. XX, 10–15: 子曰：「好學近乎知，力行近乎仁，知恥近乎勇。知斯三者，則知所以修身；知所以修身，則知所以治人；[…] 修身則道立 […] 齊明盛服，非禮不動，所以修身也；[…]」; The Master said, 'To be fond of learning is to be near to knowledge. To practice with vigour is to be near to magnanimity. To possess the feeling of shame is to be near to energy. He who knows these three things, knows how to cultivate his own character. Knowing how to cultivate his own character, he knows how to govern other men. […] By the ruler's cultivation of his own character, the duties of universal obligation are set forth. […] Self-adjustment and purification, with careful regulation of his dress, and the not making a movement contrary to the rules of propriety:—this is the way for a ruler to cultivate his person. […]').

views, but is certainly also connected to the broad field of bodily practices, including meditation.

A harmonious, generally acknowledged social knowledge about morality, in combination with an emphasis on practice, leads to the fact that the interviewees can, almost univocally, describe their practice of Buddhism in terms of its *psychological function*. Lin Yongfu describes this through a saying–*xin'an lide* 心安理得, feeling at ease and justified (Lin (9))–which emphasises the connection between feeling personally calmer and knowing that things in general are ordered appropriately. Cai Chenhao describes the effect of meditation practice as making his heart "peaceful and stable", which in consequence would lead to improvements in his social relations (Cai S15). Li Zhiqiang thinks that, through his knowledge about Buddhist values, he is more reliable/firm (*tashi* 踏實). Life is calmer (*wenzhong* 穩重) and when he needs to calm down, he also recites, but sūtras (the *Heart Sūtra* or *Great Compassion Mantra*). While Cai is engaged in name recitation mainly of the name of Bodhisattva Amitābha, Luo Peirong is invoking the name of Bodhisattva Avalokiteśvara. The invocation intensifies into a fictive communication. Luo states that, without her Buddhist belief and intimate relationship with Bodhisattva Avalokiteśvara, she would be unable to cope with the hardships of life, and be in hospital. Gu Puzhong recites whatever Buddhist invocation or mantra comes to his mind to avoid confusion and unnecessary concern. Recitation is a tool of mental control for him. Although the believers adopt different approaches to Buddhism, they value their belief and the practices connected to it, especially as these have a releasing and appeasing psychological effect upon their daily life.

Searching for the function of Buddhism in daily life, about which, according to the statistics, three quarters of all Conventional Buddhists are convinced, one can therefore say that it serves to secure a socially-acknowledged morality ritually or cognitively, but is mainly experienced as a practice with dimensions in daily life and especially in the form of a recitation practice, whose psychologically tranquillising effects are clear to the practitioners.

When it comes to rectifying their choice of Buddhism, some of the interviewees within their biographical narrations talk about *miraculous happenings*: Lin Yongfu and Li Zhiqiang have the most unproblematic life stories, and their belief is constructed without miraculous happenings. Still, the world of existing beings is–in line with traditional Buddhism–filled for Li Zhiqiang with ghosts and ancestors. Luo Peirong narrates a conflict, where Bodhisattva Guanyin wins over medicine and makes a medically highly improbable cure possible through miracles, by changing the colour of the recitation water. This story supports the power of the bodhisattva and makes reasonable Luo's commitment to Buddhism as well as her shift to Daoism, when

Buddhism is no longer strong enough to win over medical probabilities. For Cai, miracles illustrate the power of deathbed recitation. Like Luo, these miraculous incidents support his strong commitment to his Buddhist group. Even Gu Puzhong finally, after a long interview that fails to refer to any incidences standing in contrast to the laws of nature, finally points out his deep appreciation of his grandmother, which he supports by adding that not only did all of the important monks in Taiwan attend her funeral, but also that he witnessed her enormous spirituality when, through her sincere practice, others were cured of illness (Gu (34)). Of course, all of these miracles have a direct impact on the daily life of the practitioners. When asked about the influence of their belief upon their life, they still do not mention miracles. It might be that miracles are too extraordinary to be considered as having an impact on *daily* life. Still, it should also be considered that the miracles in all of the narrations so far served the clear purpose of justifying the practitioner's commitment to his/her belief.

The influences of Buddhism upon daily life are therefore certainly manifold. At its periphery might stand the perception of miraculous happenings that were evoked by highly-committed practitioners in extreme situations. The field of influence upon daily life centres, according to the interviewees, upon a psychologically tranquillising function of Buddhist practice, which has a positive impact upon their social life. In addition, Buddhism is perceived as a tool which secures, ritually or cognitively, the common social morality, centring around social well-being, health, business success, and a harmonious family life.

8.2 *Five Cases–Three* Historical Layers

Lin Yongfu–Popular Religion and Early Buddhism in Taiwan

All of the five cases connect in some way to the historical continuity of the Taiwanese Buddhism surrounding them. Lin Yongfu shows how vividly popular religious veneration behaviour, influenced by Buddhism, can structure a person's daily life. Summing up the case of Lin, he describes religious behaviour as an act of veneration, which he himself practises intensively. His belief is well-integrated into his daily family life and also expressed in his engagement with a temple committee. He recognises himself as a Buddhist, as he counts his home-statue Bodhisattva Guanyin as belonging to Buddhism, being served a vegetarian veneration diet. Lin lives in a relatively homogenous social and moral environment, in which he feels comfortable and on which basis he is curious and open-minded towards his environment. His veneration practice has supported the social bonds of the family through the generations and with the temple community. Psychologically, it ensures the feeling of being protected while behaving in accordance with the standard social norms. The role of Buddhism is, in Lin's religious practice, scarcely separated from his concept of veneration, which is here refered to by the general term "popular religion" (see ann. 6 in chap. 1). But what role did Buddhism play, historically, in Taiwan and how does the veneration of Bodhisattva Guanyin integrate into this?

The veneration of Bodhisattva Guanyin is common in Taiwan today. There are numerous temples dedicated to her: in 1959, 441 temples in Taiwan were found to be officially dedicated to Guanyin.[106] She is also often placed among other gods and goddesses. There are two female figures who are widely worshipped in Taiwan, of whom Bodhisattva Guanyin is one. The other is the goddess Mazu, whose female aspects stand central, while Guanyin would serve more in her motherly aspect as a deity (Lin 2007). Mazu is not usually associated with Buddhism, but the case of Guanyin is different. Although, in fact, she is often not even addressed as a bodhisattva, but as a *Fozu* 佛祖, i.e. "Buddhist ancestor", or "mother" (Guanyin Ma 觀音媽) and worshipped among other deities, the temples dedicated to her were, after 1945, generally registered with the Buddhist Association of the Republic of China (Zhongguo Fojiao Hui 中國佛教會). Meanwhile, other temples were registered with the Daoist Association (Zhonghua Minguo Daojiao Zonghui 中華民國道教總會). This, at least in the view of those who are closely connected to the temple, gave them the impression that they were Buddhists. The temples dedicated to Guanyin are, according to the research conducted by Lin Meirong, sometimes several centuries old and can date back to the 17th century.

Buddhism is assumed to have come to Taiwan with immigrants from the Chinese mainland. The early history of Buddhism in Taiwan is hardly traceable. Only in the 1980s, after the start of the democratisation process, did research on the history of Taiwan become possible. In particular, documents about religious life before the Japanese colonial period (1895–1945) were often destroyed due to the Japanese prosecution of religious movements. Still, even before the Dutch colonial period (1624–1661), the Chinese settled in Taiwan.[107] The Dutch were expelled by Koxinga (Zheng Chenggong 鄭成功) in

106 Cited according to Jones (1999), 5; Lin Meirong 林美容 (2007) discusses in detail the question whether to talk of Buddhism or popular religion in the case of the belief in Guanyin. She especially enlists the temples dedicated to Guanyin. In the following, the information about Guanyin is drawn mostly from her publication.

107 On colonial rule and the interplay between Dutch and Chinese colonists in Taiwan, see Andrade (2008), who worked on what he coined "co-colonisation" in 17th century Taiwan, referring to the interplay between the Dutch and the Han colonial forces on the island. On the general history of Taiwan, see Manthorpe (2005) and on the context of the history of Buddhism, also in the following, see Jones (1999).

1661, who was loyal to the Ming dynasty (1368–1644) and fled with his troops from the South East coast of China to Taiwan. Koxinga died shortly afterwards, in 1662, and the Qing dynasty (1644–1911) took over Taiwan in 1683. Also, after Konxinga's death, people continued to migrate to Taiwan. After 1661, Taiwan therefore witnessed its first big wave of Chinese immigrants from Fujian and Guangdong provinces, bringing with them their dialects. The dialect of the Fujianese people, the *Minnan Hua* 閩南話, is today commonly referred to as Taiwanese and is widespread throughout Taiwan. Still, a smaller group of people speaks Hakka (*Kejia Hua* 客家話) or Kantonese at home. The immigrants brought with them their beliefs. According to Charles B. Jones, already "during the early Qing period, the Bodhisattva Guanyin was the most worshipped Buddhist figure in Fujian province among the common people" (quoted in Jones 1999, 5). The immigrants often had connections with their homeland temples, brought images from there or named temples after them. As the exchange across the Taiwanese Strait remained dangerous, the knowledge about statues, their appropriate handling, and the belief associated with them could easily be lost. Buddhist offerings are usually vegetarian, as were the offerings made to Guanyin. Still, in Taiwan in 1943, a Japanese government report notes that 304 temples were dedicated to Guanyin Ma, while she was worshipped as a Daoist deity with meat offerings (see Jones 1999, 7). Lin Yongfu is naturally acquainted with the figure of Guanyin and seems able to fall back upon this historically-traceable knowledge, when he states proudly that his Guanyin is a bodhisattva, who follows a vegetarian diet.

Buddhism as a developed distinct religion did not exist in the early Qing period in Taiwan, but there are traces of single monks living on the island. As early as 1675, the first known fully-ordained monk, Canche 參徹, arrived in Taiwan and was highly revered for his Buddhist monastic practice. Still, for a long time, full ordination as a monk–which requires among other things ten witnessing monks–was impossible in Taiwan and novices had to travel to the mainland for proper ordination. Properly-ordained monks remained rare in Taiwan. There seem to have been very few nuns at this early stage while, at the end of the Qing period, women's ordination ceased. Only recently during the last few decades has the number of nuns increased and, today, more than three quarters of Taiwan's monastics are female, which gives them an extraordinarily strong voice compared to nuns in other East Asian countries.[108] The majority of monks and nuns today do not live in long-established temples, but rather in one of the five Young Buddhist Monasteries. Long-established temples usually

[108] Günzel (1998), 52–53 provides what is still the most reliable estimate of the number of monastics in Taiwan–by that time, about 14.000 people (the common estimate is 30.00–40.000 people). Looking at the gender ratio in the ordination rituals, Günzel analyses that there tended to be more than 75% females among the ordained.

consist of smaller communities in Taiwan, though they exist, as in the case of Li Zhiqiang, who spent several months during his youth on retreat in one of these older temples. He recalls that he learnt sūtras and acquired a basic Buddhist knowledge during this time. His ordination was refused because of his inauspicious birth date, calculated according to the Eight Characters. The narration reflects some characteristics of the older monasteries: they do not, in general, seek to attract monastics to fulfil a specific mission in society. The criterion for accepting somebody as a novice is, first of all, connected to the question of whether he is suited to monastic life and celibacy. Although the author has no historically verified information about fortune-telling as a criterion for choosing candidates,[109] this seems very much in line with the general expectations. The temple focuses on passing on the Buddhist doctrine, and letting novices recite and study Buddhist texts. Li Zhiqiang showed an interest in entering the monastery because he practised Buddhism there, without stating that he would like to be engaged in society, like the propagated aims of Engaged Buddhism in Taiwan often suggest (see chap. 12.6). The old monasteries were mostly inhabited by, not necessarily well-educated, males, who lead a simple, tranquil life. Until the Japanese colonial period, temples gained their income from land taxes, and later they could preserve at least the ritual services. The latter are frequently sought out by the population following a death. Monastics commonly oversee death rituals to ensure that the dead experience a smooth passage within the 49 days after death. These rituals provide an important source of income for the monastery or temple itself.

The general population therefore came into contact with Buddhism either: a) through the veneration of single statues like that of Bodhisattva Guanyin or Buddha Śākyamuni; or b) on the occasion of a death. Still, Taiwan has another specialty of Buddhist lay belief, called Zhaijiao 齋教, which was and partly remains a religious practice of lay believers, many of whom are female. Following a vegetarian diet, they avoid the consumption of meat (including fish), alcohol and the five kinds of bulbous plants. Adherents observe the Buddhist lay precepts, but their belief also includes elements of Daoism and Confucianism mixed together. A general overview of Zhaijiao in Taiwan is now available in the form of Nikolas Broy's study (2014).[110] The history of Zhaijiao combines three schools, the Longhua 龍華, Jinchuang 金幢 and Xiantian 先天 school (*pai* 派), and even sub-branches of these, which differ from each other significantly. The schools emerged on the mainland, and all of them have branches that are to be found in Taiwan in

109 There is, to the author's knowledge, for example, no hint at this practice in the case of mainland Buddhism in the groundbreaking ethnological study by Welch (1967).

110 For an initial overview of Zhaijiao, see Jones (1999), 14–30. See also: Wang Jianchuan (1996); Zhang Kunzhen (2003); Wang Jianchuan and Li Shiwei (2004).

the form of vegetarian halls named Zhaitang 齋堂. The followers take the Three Refuges, the Buddha, the dharma and the *saṃgha*, but take refuge in the *saṃgha* by redefining the monastic community as the followers' community. They also follow the Five Lay Precepts, try to keep the Ten Virtues and recite scriptures. People are married despite belonging to the Xiantian sect, which gave the schools the impression of a lay movement. The contemporary disappearance of Zhaijiao surely marks the biggest change in the popular religious-Buddhist field–followers of Zhaijiao are rarely found in urban Taiwan today. The Zhaijiao option as a believers' option ceased for political reasons mainly. Already during the Japanese colonial period, Zhaijiao was oppressed harshly after a revolt that started from a Zhaitang.

Becoming a practitioner in Zhaijiao is highly improbable–though not impossible–for Buddhist lay believers today. New Buddhist lay movements and especially the Young Buddhist Monasteries seem to overtake the mainstream of practitioners in responding to the psychological and social needs of average people–as we have seen in the case of Luo Peirong. Still, the general field of popular religion with its Buddhist elements did not disappear and people like Lin Yongfu–and also Li Zhiqiang in his early youth, playing in the temples–experience Buddhism mainly as part of their veneration behaviour. Buddhism is integrated, for these lay Buddhists, into their religious temple and family experience. Popular religion as the veneration of gods and goddesses in temples, often situated at the heart of the social life of villages, was the main religious practice of the early Chinese immigrants and can be seen as the historically oldest layer of Buddhism present in lay Buddhist believers even today. Buddhist lay believers in urban Taiwan reflect the fact that popular religion, as one of the oldest and most stable resources, is also, in the urban sphere, still present and is not necessarily vanishing. The question of whether popular religion in the urban areas is even growing lies beyond the scope of this book. Still, popular religion comprises elements of Buddhist practice. How far–figuratively speaking–the re-naming of Li Zhiqiang as a lay Buddhist will remain stable will depend especially on the development of the public notion of Buddhism. This notion is influenced by the Buddhist movements which are inspired by the reformist ideas that originated in mainland China during the Japanese colonial period and especially through the stream of refugees who arrived in Taiwan after the Second World War.

Cai Chenhao and Gu Puzhong–Mainland's Buddhist Modernism

In contrast to Lin Yongfu, Gu Puzhong and Cai Chenhao are both affected by a movement that began among Buddhists in China in the second half of the nineteenth century and was first called a "Buddhist revival" by Holmes Welch

(Welch 1968, 1). The Taiping movement in the 1850s and 60s led to the destruction of the Buddhist heritage in the Lower Yangzi region and the depreciation of monastic property. At a time when the European mercantile and missionary interest opened up the Chinese harbours for trade suiting their condition, the Chinese intellectuals saw the urgent necessity for a positive self-reconstruction of their "Eastern" or Chinese heritage. Within a most vivid discourse, Buddhist resources were also rediscovered and reinterpreted. Even throughout the Republican Period (1912–1949), a reorientation within Buddhism took place, the implications of which have been initially researched within the last decade and have contributed especially to the understanding of the major players within the Buddhist field, including lay Buddhists such as Yang Wenhui 楊文會 (1837–1911), Ouyang Jingwu 歐陽竟無 (1871–1943) and the internationally highly active monk Taixu 太虛 (1890–1947).[111]

For the Buddhist renewal, which is referred to under the heading of "Buddhist Modernism", several terms have been suggested (see Tarocco 2007, 9ff.). Reformers like Yang Wenhui, an intellectual lay Buddhist reformer and editor, referred to it as the "New" Buddhism, but the expression "modern" was used as well at an early stage. From a later perspective, scholars such as Donald Lopez see "Modern Buddhism" already as one sect within the multitude of Buddhist traditions. The movement is paralleled by another movement at the end of the nineteenth century, which had its roots in Sri Lanka under the leadership of people like Anagarika Dharmapala (1864–1933) and Henry Steel Olcott (1832–1907), emerging as a positive reformulation of an indigenous Asian tradition countering the work of the Christian missionaries. As the movement within Theravāda Buddhism oriented itself by taking over the main features of the Christian missionaries while at the same time trying to lead to a positive self-reconstruction, Heinz Bechert spoke of a "Protestant Buddhism" in the Theravāda context. The development within China did not occur in ignorance of the Theravāda movement, as particularly the monk Taixu was internationally highly active, but was clearly situated within the Chinese context, trying among other things to discover Buddhism as a source of Chinese nationalism. The development and discourse within Buddhism and among the Chinese intelligentsia is, in terms of its intensity, inseparable from the Buddhist publishing explosion that followed the 1911 Revolution.[112] According to Francesca Tarocco, "religious

---

111 Selected publications: Müller, Gotelind (1993); Pittman (2001); Goldfuß (2001); Bechert (1966ff.); Bechert (1995); Tarocco (2007); Lai (2013). Günzel (1998) analyses in detail the critiques of the monastic community during the Japanese colonial period. On Taixu see: Goodell (2012); Ritzinger (2010).

112 This enormous number of Buddhist periodicals has recently been edited to form part of a huge collection (MFQWJ 2006, MFQWJB 2007), enabling scholars, for the first

periodicals served as a central means through which new forms of representation, including new approaches to history and religious identity were being tested across religious lines" (Tarocco 2007, 75).

Magazines like Nanying Fojiao, published by the South Seas Buddhist Association (Nanying Fojiaohui 南瀛佛教會), reveal a lot about the ongoing process of self-reflection, which in its impact upon the development of the monastic community was analysed as being based upon a fourfold criticism of the *saṃgha* (Günzel 1998, 22–25): firstly, the journalists point out that a low moral and intellectual level dominates the monastic community, and is linked to a popular religious orientation which does not centre on the Buddhist doctrine itself, but tries to hide away from the world. Secondly, the *saṃgha* would be neither educated properly nor up-to-date. Not only should the rituals be known to the monks, but also monastic rules and secular knowledge. Thirdly, solidarity within the *saṃgha* would be lacking, so that problems could not be treated as a whole. Fourthly, the *saṃgha* would not engage sufficiently with society. The Chinese Buddhist monastic community feels the necessity to react to the Christian and Japanese Buddhist charity engagement.

The flood of publications consists not only of the directive reflections of intellectuals but the new, easy accessibility and spread of the print media also led to the emergence of new genres of literature, as the level of the language becomes closer to daily usage. Vernacular Chinese is used within the publications and small Buddhist groups print their own magazines, within which the process not only of the reformation of the monastic community is visible, but especially the dynamics through which lay Buddhists attempt to find their own voice. While these newly arising voices certainly would need their own investigation, the general threads of discourse during the Republican Era seem to resemble Gu Puzhong's concept of Buddhism as a resource for a positive Eastern self-reconstruction.

Summing up the case of Gu Puzhong, he has taken it as his life-task to adopt his grandmother's mental heritage. After having understood intellectually, through enrolling in Buddhist studies, what his grandmother expressed through her deeds in an extremely dense way, he started spreading his new understanding of Buddhism to people in Taiwan by opening a publishing house to bring the fruits of his own life-process as a message to all, especially the Taiwanese. The essence of his insights and the intellectually adequate expression of his grandmother's behaviour is that Buddhism is about practice, which means being aware of oneself and behaving selflessly in everyday life, following one's karma, and paying attention to wisdom and compassion. Through the reflection of the transmitted resources, he is able to

time, to trace the threads of the discussion and start to overview the press development of that time.

reformulate them in a way that makes them a means for a positive self-reconstruction. The identifying community, "we", being Buddhist, is redefined as representing the "East". In naming the "new" resources, Gu Puzhong concentrates on the term "science", in which he claims to believe. This highly authoritative science he sees as being in need of Buddhism. Through that combination, he constructs a re-estimation of the East via Buddhism and a mode of compatibility of traditional and new resources in Taiwan. His new definition of Buddhism allows him, on the one hand, to make the essence of Buddhism independent of any concrete ritual practice, veneration and even the category of a religion, but allows him on the other hand to practise these traditional religious rituals without making any outer change but in the spirit of selfless prayer for all sentient beings.

In his biographical narration, Gu never refers to the Buddhist reformers, but constructs his motivation solely on his personal experience with his grandmother. Although she came from the mainland, she does not show any influence of Buddhist reformism, but in contrast is portrayed as being immersed in the traditional Buddhist temple life. Only through Gu's background in having enrolled in Buddhist studies and run a Buddhist publishing house does one assume that the era of Buddhist reformism must have come to his attention. This is even more the case given the fact that, in Taiwan, the heritage of one of the most active figures in Buddhist reformist activities, the monk Taixu, is well-known among Buddhists. His disciple, the monk Yinshun 印順 (1905–2005), lived in Taiwan in later life and continued his heritage, editing his collected works, but also propagating his mission of a socially Engaged Buddhism, *renjian fojiao* 人間佛教, taking the reformation of Buddhism seriously as a new approach to the early Buddhist sources.[113]

For Gu, the reformist programme became his own as he makes it his life-task to combine the traditional Buddhist practice of his grandmother with his urban life-style as a highly-educated journalist and publisher. Buddhism is reinterpreted in this context and no longer seen as a "religion of veneration", but as a practice based on the principle of perfect enlightenment, which comprises the Mahāyāna bodhisattva ideals of compassion and love towards all sentient beings. The equality of humans is, for Gu, a basic consequence of his understanding of this wisdom, *prajñā.*

Bearing this in mind, a statement of Liang Qichao (梁啟超, 1873–1929), one of the prominent public intellectuals and journalists of Buddhist Modernism, claims: "Buddhism is a rational belief (zhexin) and not superstition (mixin). It trusts in one's own strength and not in the strength of others. On account of the bodhisattva vows, Buddhism believes in universal goodness and not in individual goodness. It also teaches equality and not differentia-

113 For details on Yinshun's Buddhist philosophical orientation see Travagnin (2009).

tion because all living things possess the nature of Buddhas" (translated in Tarocco 2007, 83). Gu would probably agree with this, even though he himself might have chosen slightly different words. Buddhism for him also is more than the propitiation of Buddhas or bodhisattvas, asking them to fulfill one's wishes. Buddhism is seen as a practice, which can be rationally defended as reasonable and as relying upon oneself. The emphasis on a universal dimension including all living beings and especially equality are central for Gu. Equality for him even offers the decisive criterion of judging the quality of other religions, especially Islam.

The monk Taixu discussed vividly the options of Buddhism with regard to contributing to politics and nationalism, but also to prove itself socially relevant and a scientifically unquestionable answer to the challenge of the West. As for Gu, science is for Taixu a huge challenge to the religious world: "Scientific discoveries have brought about a certain doubt as to religious evidence. The old gods and religions seem to have been shaken in the wind of science, and religious doctrines have no longer any defense, and the world at large seems to be handed over to the tyranny of the machine and all those monstrous powers to which science has given birth" (translated by Pittman 2001, 162–163). Buddhism, as Taixu conceives it, is the only religion which is compatible with science, while Buddhist wisdom even surpasses scientific knowledge, as enlightenment brings more profound insights than any instrumental investigations can ever achieve (see Pittman 2001, 166. 165–168).

Like Gu also, Taixu attempts to correlate his experiences about science and religion with geographical cultural regions:

> You may take the cultures of the world and divide them into three kinds. The first is a culture that cultivates a holy and pure inner mind; the second, one that improves human relations; and the third, one that manages material capabilities. Developing respectively from these three types are Indian culture, Chinese culture, and Western culture. In the past, China and India have made enormous contributions to the world. However, now both are being influenced by the West. On the unfortunate path taken by Western culture, human beings and material things are considered to be of equal worth. Therefore the world's crises deepen every day. I hope that in the future we will not lean to any one extreme. Material resources must be developed while at the same time our spirits are cultivated and ethics emphasised (translation of Pittman 2001, 163).

Gu used the same frame concept for attributing major geographical spaces to mental and behavioural concepts. While Taixu is following a threefold partition of his world map into Indian, Chinese and "Western" culture, Gu's map is bipolar, moving more in the direction of the non-Buddhist specific discussion within the modernisation debate which employed phrases like "*Zhongxue wei ti, xixue wei yong* 中學為體, 西學為用." Best translated as "Chinese learning for essential values, Western learning for practical values", this is a saying that dates back to Zhang Zhidong 張之洞, an important reformer of the Qing dynasty, who became politically relevant at the end of the 19th century. In terms of content, it coheres with the insight to accept "Western" knowledge as a tool, while the Chinese or Buddhist side delivers "essential values", as it shows for Gu the way, how to live life.[114]

Gu's commonality of interest with the Buddhist reformers around and shortly after 1900 centered on the search for solutions in the confrontation with the "West" and "science" through a positive self-reconstruction falling back upon Buddhist sources. In addition, Gu shares with his predecessors the fact that, as a Buddhist publisher, he uses the medium that the Buddhist reformers discovered as a basis for discursively developing their vision, the Buddhist press. Even the re-discovery of other traditional communicational means, such as music, Gu shares with the Buddhist reformers in Modern China who discovered the change in traditional Buddhist music and its adaptation as essential for spreading a socially relevant doctrine.[115] Gu's enthusiasm for Buddhist music is demonstrated particularly at the beginning of the interview, when he wants to share new Buddhist records from Malaysia with the interviewer, to make clear to her the appealing beauty of Buddhist modern music.

Luo Peirong and Li Zhiqiang–Young Buddhist Monasteries and Engaged Buddhism

While Lin Yongfu was affiliated with a long-established popular religious temple and Cai Chenhao and Gu Puzhong were more influenced by the effects of the mainland's reformist movement, two of the five cases presented showed the influence of the so-called Young Buddhist Monasteries that were established in the second half of the 20th century. These organisations, at whose core always lies a Buddhist monastery, are accompanied by a multitude of small and sometimes less orthodox-oriented lay movements. The whole development can be seen in its relation to the movement of "Engaged Buddhism"–within Taiwan and internationally–and is therefore presented in the second part of this book in the context of contemporary Buddhist development (chap. 12.6). In propagating an "Engaged Buddhism", these organisations are clearly following in the footsteps of Buddhist Modernism, but develop their own profile by answering the needs of urban citizens. In their organisational structure and aims, they pick up the visions of their mainland's predecessors, but also react to the

114 The arguments presented here, as related to Taixu, of course form part of a much larger and important discourse on the relation between Buddhism and science in the early 20th century–Erik Hammerstrom (2015) made it the topic of his analysis and identified discussion threads and recurring topoi. The idea that Buddhist knowledge precedes, in its structure, scientific discoveries was, for example, one of the popular ideas in the 1920s and 30s. For any further comparison, the reader is therefore referred to Hammerstrom's study.

115 Tarocco 2007, Part 2, p. 97–145.

urban climate of Taiwan. This can be seen in Luo Peirong and Li Zhiqiang's biographical narratives, who have both transferred from a long-established popular religious or even Buddhist environment to a recently-established organisation. While the latter estimates his flexibility in contributing to it, the former suffers from the uncertainty and unreliability of the connection, when her organisation grows and the abbot can no longer help her to cope with her family problems. The Young Buddhist Monasteries are attracting followers, who are not necessarily grounded in Buddhism, but Luo and Li both originate from materially and intellectually simply-structured social backgrounds. Exposed to the urban climate, they are more likely than Gu Puzhong, Cai Chenhao or even Lin Yongfu to open themselves up to the well-organised, urban-centred Young Buddhist Monasteries, whose existence is therefore closely intertwined with the urban development.

8.3 What Makes Buddhism an Attractive Choice in Urban Spaces?

In the introduction to this first part, the statistical investigation led to the hypothesis that Buddhist believers tend to live in urban areas. In concluding this first part, one therefore should ask if, through the analysed cases, one can reveal the plausibility which makes Buddhism an attractive choice in urban spaces.

The Impact of Urbanisation upon the Cases Analysed

Looking back at the cases, we recognised with Lin Yongfu that the rising mobility gave him the chance to maintain a relationship with a temple in the south of the island. Living in an urban environment meant that he was more exposed to social discourse: his notion of Buddhism does not imply any deeper doctrinal understanding, but he experiences "Buddhism" as a positive label, enabling him to communicate successfully with the foreigner sitting in his car. He plays in a relaxed manner with the new religious and international sources. Being Buddhist is, for him, a re-labelling of his veneration behaviour, which leads him to participation. Luo Peirong used the same but enforced retributionary patterns as Lin Yongfu to explain her belief, but enters a separated social field through her religious practice. She gets to know "Buddhism" through a Young Buddhist Monastery, which tries to solve her family problems. For Luo, it is more likely to dip into Buddhist funds crossing the urban space in comparison to living in rural areas. The increased proximity and accessibility of Buddhist organisations and the short time slot enable her to participate in a same sex peer group, develop a differentiated Buddhist vocabulary, and sets her on a journey towards a painful re-interpetation of her own belief. Cai Chenhao is about a generation younger than the previous interviewees and has in his own education profited from the rising standards in the densely-populated areas. In his case, "Buddhism" presents itself as attractive as it–in contrast to Lin Yongfu–leads him again out of urban society and provides him with a niche which promises social stability. His withdrawal is conscious to him and he exhibits a high degree of reflexion as well as a differentiated Buddhist terminology. "Buddhism" is, for Cai, in the form of a closed community re-placing the challenging city. Facing the multitude of choices associated with urban society, his decision to seclude himself within a small society is more a conscious withdrawal than a resignation. The multifaceted contemporary urban space in Taiwan offers also the choice to limit oneself to a socially-closed subgroup. Li Zhiqiang, a successful entrepreneur, has gained in his youth an understanding of Buddhism which is based on uprightness because of karmic retribution. His belief easily intensified once he entered the urban business world. He experiences "Buddhism" not only as cherishing his wealth, but for him it is important that the dense urban network of Young Buddhist Monasteries not only led him to bump into a sympathetic abbot, but also granted him huge flexibility in his financial and organisational contribution to the development of the monastery's institutions. As in Luo's case, the monastery probably would not bring him social security, but nor does it bind him too closely. Li is experiencing Buddhism firstly as re-stabilising his traditional values in a rapidly-changing environment and secondly discovers it as a new resource for gaining social recognition. Gu Puzhong's biography is unthinkable without the resources of the urban areas. He is highly internationally-oriented, and received a long secular as well as Buddhist education. His later professional career depends on a flourishing book-market, which equips him with a resource for unfolding his Buddhist mission. Gu's mission grows within the confrontation between the Buddhist "tradition"–personalised in the heritage of his grandmother–and an international, "scientific modernity" experienced through his life environment, the area of Taipeh, as the field to which he wishes to transmit his Buddhist message. Buddhism serves Gu as a stabilising resource that enables him to go through a long lasting re-definition process. It can prove itself in the urban environment through its capacity to complement the "scientific, western world" with the "eastern wisdom for a happy life conduct".

Buddhism proves itself to the interviewees to be a positive source of well-being in urban spaces through mere re-labelling, participation in the offers of the Young Buddhist Monasteries and seclusion within a small-scale society, as a means of re-stabilising one's traditional values, gaining social recognition, and even functioning as a positive eastern self-reconstruction.

In the urban field of options for lay Buddhist self-construction, historically distinct movements remain available and fill niches. Buddhist donors and supporters from the monastic community are well-anchored in the urban spaces. Long-established forms within Chinese Buddhism, like Lotus Societies, continue to attract members. The movement of Buddhist Modernism and the Young Buddhist Monasteries as forms of a Taiwanese adjusted "Engaged Buddhism" are able to find an audience. Besides the historically-recognised movements, lay followers search for new ways to express their belief. The huge diversification in consumption patterns, which allows the interviewees to search for their own way into Buddhism, is based on the fact that the interpretation and social manifestations of "Buddhism" in Taiwan are not bound to a hierarchically organised structure. The major players in the discourse, like the Young Buddhist Monasteries, shape the general perception of Buddhism and form a monastic stronghold for the revival of Buddhism in Taiwan, but do not exclude doctrinal and social diversity. Prior to democratisation in Taiwan, since about 1989, the Buddhist Association of the Republic of China (BAROC) held a monopoly over admittance to monastic ordination, although the field of lay believers was never controlled. Even ritual initiation cannot form a clear identity marker for a lay Buddhist believer, as there are not only recently established lay Buddhist organisations, who question this initiation, but also people in Taiwan do not necessarily recognise the act of taking refuge as an act which establishes a strong bond with Buddhism. Some people take refuge a couple of times in their life, not always counting themselves as Buddhists, while others declare themselves Buddhists without ever taking refuge. The field of Buddhist discourse has loose boundaries, but organisational and discursive threads. Through these, "Buddhism" can serve as an integrative, dynamic movement that builds up its means to serve the needs of urban citizens through the inductive mutual feedback of the participating forces.

The large grey area between believers and non-believers is supported by the fact that the field of Buddhism has low entry barriers: the Young Buddhist Monasteries rarely argue in an exclusive manner against the followers of popular religion. In contrast, they integrate ancestor worship, accepting common *baibai*-religiosity and the wish of followers to stay in harmony with previous generations and their family. They tend to provide doctrinally-easy formulations, and rarely create a distance from the reduction of karmic thinking as a direct explanatory pattern for misfortune. The idea of karmic retribution remains easily applicable from various backgrounds. Bearing in mind the particularised and enlarged network of people in the densely-populated areas, the possible general impression that happenings are linked to each other in a complex way might connect well with the idea of karmic retribution. Also, the emphasis on Buddhism as a field of "practice" and a "way of life" does not add an intellectual challenge to the planned life of a businessman like Li, but delivers a simple, user-friendly concept. This can serve as a guideline for behaviour and also reduce bodily stress, as a low entry barrier can also be counted the general positive notion of successful business behaviour which easily embeds successful businessmen like Li in the Buddhist field as supporters of the Buddhist community. This possibility of a smooth transition into the Buddhist field seems especially important for the attractiveness of Buddhism in urban Taiwan, which development is based on industry and trade. Summing up, one can conclude that the Buddhist field has low entry barriers as: 1) in general, common religio-social behaviour is not opposed; 2) Buddhist doctrine is formulated in a simple, applicable manner being reduced to a minimal doctrinal set of discourse threads oscillating between karma, practice, and veneration; and 3) its positive attitudes towards business enable potential supporters to perform a "soft switch" and make a smooth transition into the Buddhist field. Low-entry barriers imply, therefore, not only a missing obligatory formal initiation and set of knowledge but also reveal that a concrete mental or social change is not necessarily a prerequisite for entering the Buddhist field. Besides a mere re-labelling, the gradual participation in concrete offers in search of daily life mastery up to a full engagement in Buddhist matters are all counted under the term of being a "Buddhist".

The loosely-organised, dynamic field with its low-entry barriers gains attractiveness through the positive notion of "Buddhism" in society. All five interviewees are proud of being a Buddhist and Luo struggles throughout the interview to rectify her re-orientation to Daoism. The well-respected status of Buddhism in Taiwanese society is in accordance with the role of Buddhism in Chinese history. For centuries, the elite in society have kept themselves busy with Buddhist literature and, therefore, Buddhism in Taiwan today is still linked with the educated literati (Zhang and Lin 1992). In addition, Buddhism, at least in the construction of Gu Puzhong but also in line with Buddhist Modernism, presents itself as up to date with science and "modern" life. It holds as an intensified belief the option of transforming one's way of life and in that case might be not "a religion you go and venerate" (Gu Puzhong). Buddhism is constructed as compatible with contemporary issues, and is without hesitation considered as internationally relevant. It is assumed by all five interviewees as indigenously belonging to Chinese culture and as a positive heritage that contributes to the interviewees' self-esteem. The urban movement brings along a change in lifestyle. The interviewees recognise Buddhism as a tool for re-stabilising the moral codes and social structures. The codes themselves are, in all cases (especially Lin Yongfu and Li Zhiqiang), taken without further reflection as obvious and accepted as having been transmitted over the generations. The interviewees feel the need to preserve their values in the rapidly-changing urban space and construct "Buddhism" as a communicational space, which ensures that their codes are reasonable and thereby compulsory. To the extreme, the Buddhist field also offers the opportunity to resort to closed communities which offer high moral and behavioural stability (Cai Chenhao).

Summing up, Buddhist organisational resources offer citizens ways to socialise in the urbanising environment and reshape their social contacts, and are experienced as bettering social relations. The "Buddhist" discourse–in the form of a label, doctrine or social community–proves a helpful resource for situating oneself in the urban environment and seems to fit the urban climate of the area of Taipeh as it enhances and supports economic, social and private success. The historically-rooted roles of the lay Buddhists, like donors, remain available and the traditionally-oriented Buddhist communities fill niches. Movements resulting from Buddhist Modernism and forms of a Taiwanese "Engaged Buddhism" gather communities of followers. The diversification of consumption patterns is a result of the integrative dynamic within the Buddhist field, which is based on loose boundaries and missing organisational monopolies on the one hand and organisational and discursive threads that unite the field on the other. Low entry barriers make a "soft switch" to the Buddhist field possible for the general public as, commonly, the spread of religio-social behaviour is unopposed, Buddhist doctrine is formulated in a simple, applicable manner with discourse threads oscillating between karma, practice, and veneration, and positive attitudes towards business enable potential supporters to make a smooth transition into the Buddhist field. In addition, due to the lack of a missing obligatory formal initiation or set of knowledge to enter "Buddhism", it can be shown that a concrete mental or social change is not necessarily a prerequisite for entering the Buddhist field. The attractiveness of Buddhism wins through a general positive notion of "Buddhism" in Taiwanese society, so that Buddhism is applied as a tool for re-stabilising the moral codes and social structures.

The Statistical Decrease in the Number of Buddhist Believers

Keeping in mind the analysed attractiveness of Buddhism in urban spaces as well as the statistical findings that there is a greater percentage of Buddhist believers in the urban areas, as well as witnessing the growth of the urban regions in Taiwan, one would naturally assume that the total number of Buddhist followers, over the years, is at least not decreasing. The *Taiwan Social Change Survey* reveals contrary results:

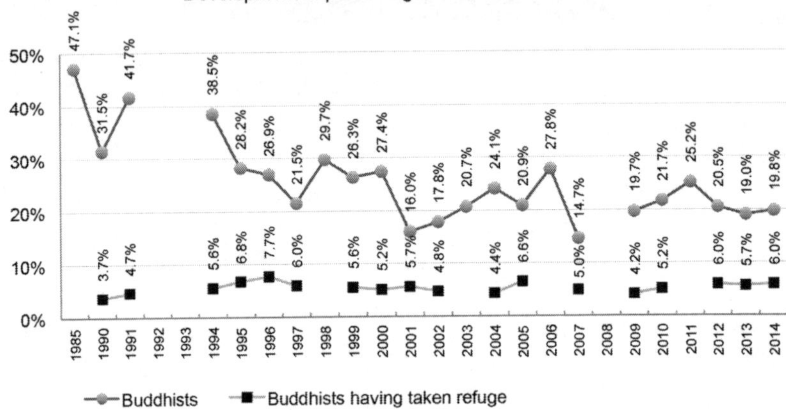

	1985.1	1990.1	1991.1	1992	1993	1994.2	1995.1	1996.1	1997.1
Buddhists	47.1%	31.5%	41.7%	–	–	38.5%	28.2%	26.9%	21.5%
	2030	797	1038	–	–	717	590	517	558
Buddhists taken refuge	–	3.7%	4.7%	–	–	5.6%	6.8%	7.7%	6.0%
	–	93	118	–	–	105	132	149	155
Total n	4307	2531	2488	–	–	1862	1948	1924	2596

	1998.2	1999.2	2000.1	2001.2	2002.1	2003.2	2004.2	2005.1	2006.2
Buddhists	29.7%	26.3%	27.4%	16.0%	17.8%	20.7%	24.1%	20.9%	27.8%
	534	507	538	328	355	418	453	449	548
Buddhists taken refuge	–	5.6%	5.2%	5.7%	4.8%	–	4.4%	6.6%	–
	–	108	102	116	96	–	83	141	–
Total n	1798	1925	1950	2052	1992	2016	1881	2146	1972

	2007.1	2008	2009.2	2010.1	2011.2	2012.1	2013.1	2014.2	
Buddhists	14.7%	–	19.7%	21.7%	25.2%	20.5%	19.0%	19.8%	
	300	–	380	412	554	438	381	288	
Buddhists taken refuge	5.0%	–	4.2%	5.2%	–	6.0%	5.7%	6.0%	
	101	–	81	98	–	129	115	116	
Total n	2400	–	1927	1895	2199	2134	2005	1875	

Figure 17 and Table 13: People believing in Buddhism and Buddhists having taken refuge–Percentages and frequencies for the period 1985–2014 (TSCS 1985-2014).

The percentage of Buddhist believers within the total population decreased from 1985 to 1997 by about 25.6%, from 47.1% to 21.5%. In 2007, only 14.7% of people claimed to be Buddhist. The fluctuation in the number of believers is massive. From one year to the next, the percentages can fall or rise by more than 10%. From 2006 to 2007, the number dropped by about 13.1% while, in the year before, it has risen by about 6.9%. Still, from 2009-2014, the percentage ceases to fluctuate, remaining relatively stable around 20%.

What can be concluded from this decrease and fluctuation? Is Buddhism as a religion decreasing in Taiwan and is it only a question of time before it disappears from the cities? What does it mean to be a "Buddhist", if more than 10% of the population can choose each year whether to consider themselves as such or not?

First, one must state that the study itself is reliable. The TSCS delivers results which, in the researcher's experience, in two parallel investigations of each year never exceeded an aberration of more than about 2%. The TSCS interviewers have been trained to recognise the potential doubts of the interviewees and try intentionally to provide similar stimuli. Of the five cases, Cai Chenhao and Gu Puzhong would probably never consider themselves as not Buddhist within any interview situation. Luo sees herself as being caught between "Daoism" and "Buddhism". She might answer differently in different years, while her karmic interpretation of her destiny can be supposed to remain constant. Also, Li Zhiqiang recognises times in his life when he engaged more with "Daoism". It depends on his social contacts and opportunities, whether he sides with one or the other. Lin Yongfu's notion of a "religious" or "Buddhist" belief is not central to him, but his emic terminology centres on "veneration" (*baibai*). Being aware of the doctrinal and practical aspects of Buddhism could imply for him a distance from it. Considering the intensifying communication means available in urban Taiwan, the presence of Buddhism, especially the Young Buddhist Monasteries in the media,[116] and the increased general educational level of the population, one could support the hypothesis of a growing awareness of Buddhism as a distinct doctrine and practice. This would make plausible a decrease up to a certain percentage of people, who claim to be Buddhist. A question from the TSCS of 1994–which to the author's knowledge regrettably has not been posed again since–sheds light on the depth of the doctrinal understanding leading to a religious commitment: in 1994, about a third of "Buddhists" admitted, that they "don't really understand" (*bu tai liaojie* 不太了解) the religion in which they believe. Only followers of denominational religions ("Bekenntnisreligionen") like Christianity or Yi Guan Dao were more likely to mention a deeper understanding of their religion.

[116] The Young Buddhist Monasteries even have, for example, their own TV channels and monks specialising in sūtra explanations participate in TV series.

v17	v22. How far do you understand the religion in which you believe? (對信仰的宗教瞭解得怎麼樣; u. = understanding)										
	No answer	Deep u.	U.	Some u.	Not really u.	Not u. at all	No belief	Don't know	Don't u. question	Don't want to answer	Total
Buddhist	0.4% (3)	2.9% (21)	8.4% (60)	51.5% (369)	30.7% (220)	4.2% (30)	0.0% (0)	1.0% (7)	0.1% (1)	0.8% (6)	100.0% (717)
Subgroup: Buddhists taken refuge	0.0% (0)	9.5% (10)	21.9% (23)	52.4% (55)	11.4% (12)	1.9% (2)	0.0% (0)	1.0% (1)	0.0% (0)	1.9% (2)	100.0% (105)
Daoist	0.6% (1)	4.1% (7)	5.9% (10)	47.3% (80)	33.1% (56)	4.7% (8)	0.0% (0)	2.4% (4)	0.0% (0)	1.8% (3)	100.0% (169)
Popular Religious	1.7% (10)	1.9% (11)	5.7% (33)	41.8% (241)	39.2% (226)	2.8% (16)	0.0% (0)	5.9% (34)	0.7% (4)	0.3% (2)	100.0% (577)
Yi Guan Dao	0.0% (0)	14.3% (7)	14.3% (7)	42.9% (21)	28.6% (14)	0.0% (0)	0.0% (0)	0.0% (0)	0.0% (0)	0.0% (0)	100.0% (49)
Muslim	0.0% (0)	0.0% (0)	100.0% (1)	0.0% (0)	0.0% (0)	0.0% (0)	0.0% (0)	0.0% (0)	0.0% (0)	0.0% (0)	100.0% (1)
Catholic	0.0% (0)	15.0% (3)	30.0% (6)	35.0% (7)	15.0% (3)	0.0% (0)	0.0% (0)	5.0% (1)	0.0% (0)	0.0% (0)	100.0% (20)
Protestant	0.0% (0)	12.7% (10)	15.2% (12)	49.4% (39)	15.2% (12)	5.1% (4)	0.0% (0)	1.3% (1)	0.0% (0)	1.3% (1)	100.0% (79)
No belief	0.0% (0)	0.0% (0)	0.0% (0)	0.0% (0)	0.0% (0)	0.0% (0)	100.0% (242)	0.0% (0)	0.0% (0)	0.0% (0)	100.0% (242)
Other	12.5% (1)	12.5% (1)	25.0% (2)	12.5% (1)	37.5% (3)	0.0% (0)	0.0% (0)	0.0% (0)	0.0% (0)	0.0% (0)	100.0% (8)
Total	0.8% (15)	3.2% (60)	7.0% (131)	40.7% (758)	28.7% (534)	3.1% (58)	13.0% (242)	2.5% (47)	0.3% (5)	0.6% (12)	100.0% (1862)

Table 14: Depth of understanding of one's own religion (TSCS 1994.2, v22 crossed with religious belonging, v17, percentage and frequency).

The grey area of potential believers is huge and contributes essentially to the high fluctuation. Buddhism cannot be seen as a strong identity marker in general. Historically, this is slight, as religious belonging was irrelevant in Taiwan prior to the Japanese colonial period (1895–1945). The creation and transmittance of the terminology has been outlined already (see chap. 1) and is reflected in the interviews: only Cai Chenhao and Gu Puzhong hold a differentiated notion of the terms "religion" and "Buddhism". Being the only member of the younger generation, Cai's search for a convincing way of life was triggered by the term "religion" itself, as he chose to study religious studies at university to become clearer about his life orientation. While Lin Yongfu and Li Zhiqiang assume without hesitation that their understanding of "religion" is certain, Luo Peirong is the only one who has experienced a personal search between Daoism and Buddhism as a recent terminological differentiation, which would lead her away from understanding the original practice (see also chap. 7.2, S7): When Buddhism was still not that "flourishing", she recognises, one spoke about "this or that god" and about "veneration", but not about different religions. Once Buddhism as a distinct religion entered the field, in her social perception, one started to differentiate between religions and Daoism became a separate one ("And only now, as there is Buddhism, do we separate between Buddhism and Daoism like that". *Er shi xianzai you fojiao, cai fen fojiao daojiao zhe yang zi* 而是現在有佛教才分佛教道教這樣子, Luo S7). She does not even try to argue, but simply states this change, showing that she had probably never encountered anyone who questioned this interpretation of the historical changes. The religious vocabulary of Lin Yongfu is identical to Luo's terminology when describing the "pre-Buddhist" period: "veneration" is seen for both as the central action through which communication with "gods" (and eventually "Buddhas") occurs. The propagated differentiation of the experienced unit of veneration into distinct religions, such as "Buddhism" and "Daoism", causes confusion when Luo tries to describe her belief during the interview. Through her statement, she reflects this consciously. The high fluctuation is therefore the statistical equivalent to the social fact that, for a large percentage of the Taiwanese population, being "Buddhist" and "religious" belong to a secondary category which is unconnected with their experienced reality of veneration. The rate of nearly 50% of believers in 1985 shows the generally positive notion of Buddhism in society by that time. People are even easily willing to identify with Buddhism when faced with choosing a religious belief. With the spread of Buddhism in Taiwan, one might assume that people complement their preliminary impression about Buddhism with concrete experiences of Buddhist communities and "Buddhists". This leads to a growing awareness and a decrease in the number of people who are willing blandly to call themselves Buddhist. It therefore would be a misinterpretation if one assumed that the statistical decrease in the percentage of Buddhist believers constituted a decrease in the spread of Buddhism in Taiwan. In contrast, while the percentages are dropping, the number of followers might even be growing.

Beyond the general decrease and stabilisation around 20%, one can ask what concrete incidences may have caused the extreme fluctuations. The Buddhist organisational institutions are young and are still to prove themselves. Single occurrences in the Taiwanese press have surely a certain impact on Taiwanese religious self-definition. For the Buddhist field, we know about several "scandals" that happened within the last two decades, which are also known to the interviewees. In 1996, there was a Young Buddhist Monastery, which ordained about 100 young people without notifying their parents. This led to high public feeling, with TV reports showing demonstrating parents in front of the monastery. "Buddhism" endangered the family ethos in a society where social life is traditionally dominated by family orientation. In the same year, an overseas branch of another Young Buddhist Monastery was involved in a financial scandal and, a couple of years later, the sexual integrity of the abbot of a third Young Buddhist Monastery was repeatedly questioned and discussed in the press.[117] This shows, on the one hand, the high, idealised ex-

[117] The scandals are not outlined in detail here, as they contribute nothing to the understanding of lay Buddhists' habitus and choices, but mainly feed a journalistic interest that relies on hardly provable facts. For further details, see the online archives of the

pectations of society with regard to the Buddhist monasteries, and, on the other, through the press-enforced scandals, how the idealised image of "Buddhism" easily becomes altered. In addition, the economic recession around the year 2000 and in 2009 might be, for donors like Li Zhiqiang, a reason for not engaging frequently in helping Buddhist organisations and concentrating on business affairs instead of religious activities.[118]

As a result, one can state that the huge fluctuation probably reflects the uncertainty about "being Buddhist" as an identity marker in Taiwan, while the fact that the general decrease in the number of Buddhists stabilised around 20% might be the result of a differentiated recognition of the Buddhist field which, besides its general positive notion, becomes clouded through concrete incidences.

What remains constant or might even be slightly increasing is the numbers of Buddhists who consider themselves as having taken refuge. It is the only criterion of a more intense or committed belief that has been measured constantly over the years and it shows a nucleus of perhaps around 5% of the population who consider themselves to be more intensely Buddhist. "Taking refuge" as a criterion for recognising a Buddhist believer can be traced back to the first centuries of Buddhism (Dutt 1945, 172). Still, if one considers the five cases assembled so far, despite Lin Yongfu, all of them have taken refuge, but none saw this as a pivotal life event. Lin does not speak of any initiation despite the carving of his Buddhist statue, which for him marks the beginning of his relationship with Buddhism. Gu Puzhong engages in a long search, Li Zhiqiang narrates the impression of his temple sojourn in his youth, Cai participated in a Buddhist youth group at school and, among other things, also takes refuge, and Luo oscillates consciously between two "religions". Taking refuge for the interviewees was not the moment of conversion which they would seek following a period of self-preparation, but the situation demanded at a certain moment the act of taking refuge. Taking refuge can be embedded in a process of spiritual reorientation, but is far more likely to take place occasionally on the initiative of a Buddhist organisation, which tries to bind its followers. The reasons for taking refuge can therefore also be merely situational ones or express the general support of a certain Buddhist master or organisation.

When attempting to measure the impact of Buddhist belief on people in Taiwan, one should therefore also consider that "Buddhism" is not always

---

major Chinese newspapers in Taiwan, and the author can also give further bibliographical hints.

118 The gross domestic product grew in general between 1985 and 2016, but decreased in 1998, 2001 and 2009, see http://www.tradingeconomics.com/taiwan/gdp, last accessed February 26, 2016.

connected with becoming part of a Buddhist community and separating oneself from other religious believers, but the notion of "Buddhism" diffuses into society and has to establish itself in people's argumentative patterns or practical habits. The success and attractiveness of Buddhism is therefore hardly traceable in statistical investigations, but reveals itself in the biographical narrations when it proves itself a part of life and an educational resource that is increasingly available. Here, it is plausible to speak of Conventional Buddhists not as a clearly distinct group of people, but as an integrative term, which tries to reveal the traces associated with Buddhism in society.

Setting out the Field of "Conventional Buddhists"

At the beginning of Part I, the term "Conventional Buddhists" resulted from a mere statistical definition: "Conventional" were believers, who chose within their Buddhist belief the–with more than 85% of all Buddhists–conventional, i.e. average and normal option, to "believe in/venerate Buddha". By making this choice, they failed to specify their belief further by locating themselves within the frame of a Buddhist school, like "Pure Land" or "Zen". Having presented in detail this selected group out of the broad spectrum of lay Buddhists who find themselves in this category, it is finally reasonable to ask: what unites them beyond their statistical common choice? Is it reasonable to talk about a group of average, "conventional" Buddhist believers?

The field analysed so far offers two extremes. The first extreme consists of Buddhists, who in their actual belief were virtually indistinguishable from popular religious believers–"popular religious Buddhists" would be a more appropriate label for them. Buddhism is sociologically to be seen as an artificial category which becomes obvious when one travels to the more remote areas of Taiwan. Within the vivid religious life of the old harbour cities, for example, Buddhist elements can be found, but Buddhism certainly does not make up a distinct organisational or believers' entity. A term closer to conventional believers is the already-established term "occasional" Buddhists. Holmes Welch, in his famous "Practice of Chinese Buddhism", speaks of the mass of "occasional" Buddhists and, only when becoming more specific about decided believers, talks of ("intelligent") "devotees" and "pure intellectuals".[119] At least in contrast to the latter, the concept of religious belief as a reflected orthodoxy that serves as a background and a clear bias for constructing "occasional" Buddhism as inferior to an intellectually reflected belief is visible. "Occasional" believers seem to follow an arbitrary practice of temple visits, and it is insinuated that their belief is not central to them, as they only con-

119 Welch 1967, 387ff. See also 375–377 and 389/390 for the range of Buddhists and biographical examples.

cern themselves with it on occasion. The case of Lin Yongfu showed precisely that his belief is the structuring moment for his whole social life. It is by no means just "occasional" to him. From an outer perspective, which would place the terminological separation between Buddhism and other religions first, it appears that Lin is merely by chance venerating a bodhisattva. Still, Lin is experiencing a religious unity in his actions, and seeing him as a religious patchworker is a misinterpretation due to a terminology which imposes an inappropriate dichotomy on the field. In concrete terms, one can assume that Lin certainly feels affection for those whom he venerates, and would never think of them as arbitrary choices from a variety of religions. The term "Conventional" Buddhist seems, to the author, therefore to be filled with fewer preconditions and less judgemental about the quality of the respective belief.

Still, no term is without connotations and the term "conventional" seems to allude to a historical continuity. Having analysed the five cases, one can actually see, on the one hand, the wide acceptance of an integrative belief that is close to popular religion but, on the other also, the concrete influence of the Buddhist historical movements, especially of Buddhist Modernism and Engaged Buddhism. This hints at the second characteristic of the field of Conventional Buddhists: not only "popular religious" oriented Buddhists, but also Buddhists with a historically-rooted doctrinal mission for society normally do not locate themselves within a Buddhist school–and they make up the main stream of Buddhism in Taiwan today.

Finally, the term "Conventional Buddhists" is misunderstood if one considers them as a clear distinct group who oppose the "Specifying Buddhists". As "Specifying Buddhists" in this concept would address all people who claim a Buddhist school affiliation, such a descriptive bifocal concept would impose an importance of school affiliation upon Taiwanese believers, which might be considerable for the case of Buddhism in Japan, but in Taiwan certainly would show a deformed model of the options of Buddhist self-construction. The second part of this analysis will not, therefore, try to differentiate the field of "Specifying Buddhists", but aims to elucidate forms of *intense* Buddhist belief and practice in contemporary Taiwan, which cannot primarily be analysed under the perspectives of popular religion and mainland Buddhist Modernism, but show options that lay people discover when exploiting "Buddhism" for biographical self-constructions and searching for answers to the challenges of urban life in the metropolitan areas of Taiwan.

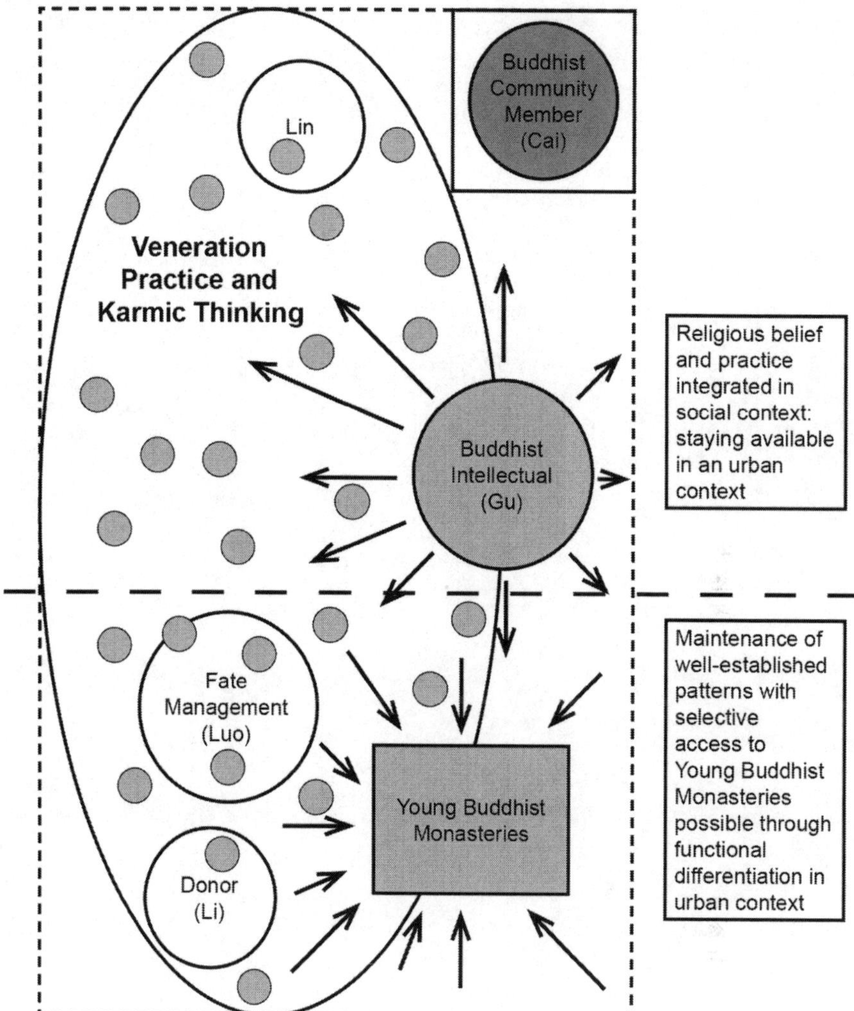

Figure 18: Part I–Access to conventional resources: "I believe in and venerate Buddha".

Part II
Intense Believers and Practitioners Exploring New Options for Living a Buddhist Lay Life

9 Introduction

In the urban climate of Taiwan, conventional Buddhist resources can make up the basic orientation of people's habitus, they prove themselves and transform with social change. Analysing the habitus formations of Buddhists in urban Taiwan, besides these conventional (popular religious or Buddhist Modernism-inspired) orientations, the analysis reveals newly emerging habitus formations which lay people discover when intensively exploiting "Buddhism" for biographical self-construction in search of answers to the challenges of urban life in the metropolitan areas. The evolving niches where Buddhism is applied are rapidly changing. Due to their highly-specific differentiation, it is impossible to cover the multitude of these concepts fully. Therefore, four cases have been chosen to form the core of Part II as examples of how "Buddhism" can serve, in a differentiated and specific way, intense forms of a Buddhist identity construction as a habitus resource in urban Taiwan. While the underlying patterns were revealed through a full case analysis, the aim of the second part is to demonstrate the possible width of variety of a Buddhist self-construction. Therefore, in contrast to Part I, in Part II, full case analyses are not presented, but are summed up as short portraits.

The urban environment allows people to invent and consume new forms of "Buddhist" resources. Programmatic young Buddhist movements (as we will see in the first case of Ma Fengling) can, for example, provide people from a lower educational background with a transformative knowledge that enables them to be socially active within their organisation and cross their own social boundaries. Three examples of Buddhists with a relatively high educational, financial, and employment status show how differently the resources connected with the label of "Buddhism" become engaged as formative concepts in urbanites' life mastery: Xu Wenhua undergoes a long process of identity search, employing Buddhist concepts, and ends up with a Buddhist vision as a life task. Zhang Yimin perceives Western Buddhist publications as providing him with the moral concepts necessary for his role as a father. Meng Fanyi leads a highly internationally-orientated and aestheticised life-style. A newly emerging Buddhist movement provides her with all-embracing life-concepts that pervade her life-style and hold together the width of her aspirations.

The choice of cases for Part I was firstly based on the criterion of whether people would consider themselves as "believing in/venerating Buddha" and the analysis concentrated on the general underlying patterns of habitus formation. As the focus of analysis in Part II is on the intense and specific forms of Buddhist belief, cases are chosen of people who show a more differentiated, while less pre-established, belief. A conscious school affiliation is (especially in Taiwan) not necessarily a prerequisite for a differentiated belief. The selection of cases in Part II is therefore not based on school affiliation. Nevertheless, the statistical subgroup of "Specifying Buddhists", i.e. Buddhists with a conscious school affiliation, is the group of intense and differentiating believers that reveals statistically the most extreme (compared with all other forms of intense belief) general characteristics of differentiated and intense Buddhist believers. Therefore, at the beginning, some statistically significant differences between "Specifying" and "Conventional Buddhists" will be outlined.

Significant for the social change present in contemporary Taiwan are the rising standards of education, especially for females, and higher incomes imbedded in a rapid industrial economic development which evokes discussion about a "new middle class". The socio-geographical development is the crucial background for a proper understanding of these recently-evolving options. That being the case, a short outline of the socio-geographical situation of Taiwan's urban development will introduce Part II, followed by the statistical profile of "Specifying Buddhists". The four cases will round that off, concretising the options of the arising intense Buddhist options related to belief in urban Taiwan.

10 The Socio-cultural Situation in Urban Taiwan

The Socio-economic Landscape of Taiwan: Urbanisation and the Northern Region

With regard to the niche that Buddhism fills in Taiwanese society, it is essential to understand the social context in which Buddhist organisations grow and Buddhist believers define themselves. To sketch a profile of the social change and urbanisation in Taiwan and the development towards Taiwanese Modernity, it might be useful to start with some basic geographical facts and statistical measures, to gain an impression of the social development that one can witness in contemporary Taiwan.

Taiwan is an island between the size of Belgium and the Netherlands. It is dominated by a mountain range, that covers the centre of the island, and by the economically vigorous, fertile plain of the west coast. During the last 50 years, Taiwan's export-oriented economy has witnessed enormous growth and Taiwan is counted among the four Asian Tiger Cub Economies. The Northern Region, with the capital Taipeh, is Taiwan's largest metropolitan area, followed by Kaohsiung in the southwest and Taichung on the mid-west coast. In 2004 (the year when the TSCS-survey on religion evaluated here was carried out), Taiwanese citizenship amounted to nearly 23 million people. The family was the dominant form of household in 2000, with about 15% being complex households and 55% nuclear family households.

The north of the island is the most densely-populated area, containing 44.1% of the population. More than 9000 people per square kilometer live in Taipeh. The population structure of the Northern Region shows (as typical for highly urbanised regions) a clear gourd-shaped structure. The majority of the population is aged between 15 and 50 years old. The rate of enrollment in education among 18-21 year-olds is rising in general and, in 2000, was the highest nationwide in Taipeh, at 70.8%. 30.8% of the migration population moved within the last five years within or to the North. The Northern Region has an increasing commuting rate, which is the highest in the country (41.1%). About 3 million people work in Taipeh itself. In 2000, 21.6% of them were commuting to their workplace, mostly from the areas around Taipeh like Taipeh County, Taoyuan County and Keelung City. Highly educated people are more likely to commute than others. The increasing local separation between occupational and private life could have an impact on the needs of the commuters when searching for leisure time activities and religious engagement.

Taiwanese modernity has, as its first pillar, rapid economic growth and urbanisation. This development has initiated a rise in income as well as leisure time. The high density of the population leads to socio-cultural specific subgroups with often highly-differentiated interests. Religious or Buddhist interests can find their niche within this setting.

As the second pillar of Taiwanese modernity can be counted the unique amalgamation of multiple cultural influences over the centuries. Taiwan's history is characterised by waves of immigration, by the Japanese colonial period (1895–1945) and the postwar coup by the Nationalist army, but also the far earlier attempts of Portuguese and Dutch merchants to conquer and colonise this "green" island, "illa Formosa", with its harbours, sugar industry, and strategically advantageous location. Its first inhabitants, the current aboriginal tribes, are probably of Austronesian origin, and brought with them languages unrelated to the Sino-Tibetan language family. These aborigines remain today a marginalised group in Taiwan, and have been over the centuries pushed back to the economically-less attractive mountain regions. They make up about 2% of the population today. Over the centuries, waves of economic refugees have come mostly from Fujian province across the Taiwan Strait, bringing with them their Fujianese dialect, so-called Taiwanese. They form about 70% of the total population, the largest language group in Taiwan. In addition to the Fujianese people, many Hakka-speaking people also came from the region of Guandong. Today, their ethnic group makes up to about 15% of the Taiwanese population. During the Japanese colonial period, not only did some Japanese migrate to Taiwan, but the control of the Japanese government also enforced the Japanisation of the Taiwanese inhabitants and their culture. This meant, on the one hand, the strong repression of the "indigenous" culture but, on the other, also established the basis for economic growth thereafter. The Japanese colonial period has to be seen as the first step towards modernity. Especially in organisational, governmental, and infrastructural terms, the Japanese enforced island-wide development. The Japanese people were expelled from Taiwan with the ending of the colonial period. With the Nationalists' army fleeing from the mainland, after the Second World War, Taiwan faced its hugest wave of immigrants ever. The Nationalist army and, with it, people from all over China settled in Taiwan, especially in the North of the island, and took control. These former mainlanders (the *waishengren* 外省人) and their descendants today make up about 12% of the population. The new-arrivals declared the "mandarin" dialect of Chinese to be the obligatory official language and built up a government and political administration. Taiwanese culture was harshly suppressed and, though a democratic constitution formed its base, de facto, Taiwan was under martial law until 1987. With the lifting of this, Taiwan became increasingly democratic, with freedom of association being granted in 1989. This amendment had a tremendous impact upon religious life, as the Buddhist monasteries and lay groups could register and become active as associations. As the analysis of the TSCS 2004.2 shows, the majority of lay Buddhists who converted to Buddhism recall their conversion date as not being prior to the 1990s.[120] Buddhist organisations were established easily in the following years and, through the new possibilities, people were able to establish a consciousness of formal belonging.

When considering contemporary culture in Taiwan, one can still witness, through its cultural and language diversity, the multilayered development of a country at the periphery. A country at the periphery it remains, even today. It has strong economic boundaries with Japan, and the international influence of Japan is obvious in daily life in terms of food, music, and fashion. America initially strongly supported Taiwan against mainland China but, in the 1970s, an increasing number of states came to recognise mainland China as a nation and Taiwan lost its UN seat to the advantage of China in 1974. Still, America is supportive of Taiwan and, in Taiwan, the cultural exchange with America has certainly had, besides the Japanese influence, a huge impact upon Taiwanese culture. With the growing economic connection with the mainland, nowadays, the cultural exchange with China is also increasing. Fewer than 350,000 people are ethnically and culturally non-Chinese foreigners in Taiwan. While "Westerners" are normally warmly welcomed, people from Indonesia mainly serve as blue collar workers or housemaids under often questionable circumstances.

Summing up, Taiwan can be characterised as a hybridising culture of immigrants (ethnically predominantly of Chinese descent), located in a periphery region, and being highly exposed to international influences. This situation shapes the social, cultural, and economic development of Taiwan in a unique way. Combined with a rising consciousness in Taiwan about its unique situation, it allows us to speak of a specific modernity taking place in this country–a Taiwanese modernity.

120 Selecting from the dataset the converted Buddhists and crossing them with v17a results in 100 converted Buddhists who cannot remember when this occurred, 41 who converted prior to 1990 (including those who have believed since childhood and so do not count as "convertees"), and 58 who converted between 1990 and 2004.

Stratification of Taiwan into Ten Regions

As already mentioned in the explanation of the sample, which was the base for the social change survey in 2004 about religion (TSCS 2004.2), the survey divides Taiwan into ten different regions following an analysis performed by Luo Qihong 羅啟宏 in 1993.[121] Through a stratification of Taiwan according to characteristics of the demographic data (industrial development, public facilities, fiscal status, and geographic environment), Luo pools the districts and cities of Taiwan into seven regions, which are named: (1) Newly Emerged Areas (*xinxing xiangzhen* 新興鄉鎮), (2) Mountain Areas (*shandi xiangzhen* 山地鄉鎮), (3) Industrial Areas (*gongshang shizhen* 工商市鎮), (4) Syndicated Areas (*zonghexing shizhen* 綜合性市鎮); (5) Hilly Areas (*podi xiangzhen* 坡地鄉鎮); (6) Remote Areas (*bianyuan xiangzhen* 偏遠鄉鎮); (7) Service Areas (*fuwuxing xiangzhen* 服務性鄉鎮). Three regions were added to the TSCS Survey due to the special situation of the capital: (8) Taipeh (*Taibei shi* 台北市); (9) the economically most vivid, highly developed region, Kaohsiung (*Gaoxiong shi* 高雄市); and (10) the cities under the direct jurisdiction of Taiwan (*shenghai shi* 省轄市), which form a separate area.

121 See Luo Qihong (1993). The stratifications have been adapted over the years by the TSCS team. In the 2014 survey, two new different sets of geographic stratification are tested. The survey of 2004 with the stratification following Luo remains decisive for this book, as it is closest in time to the interviews.

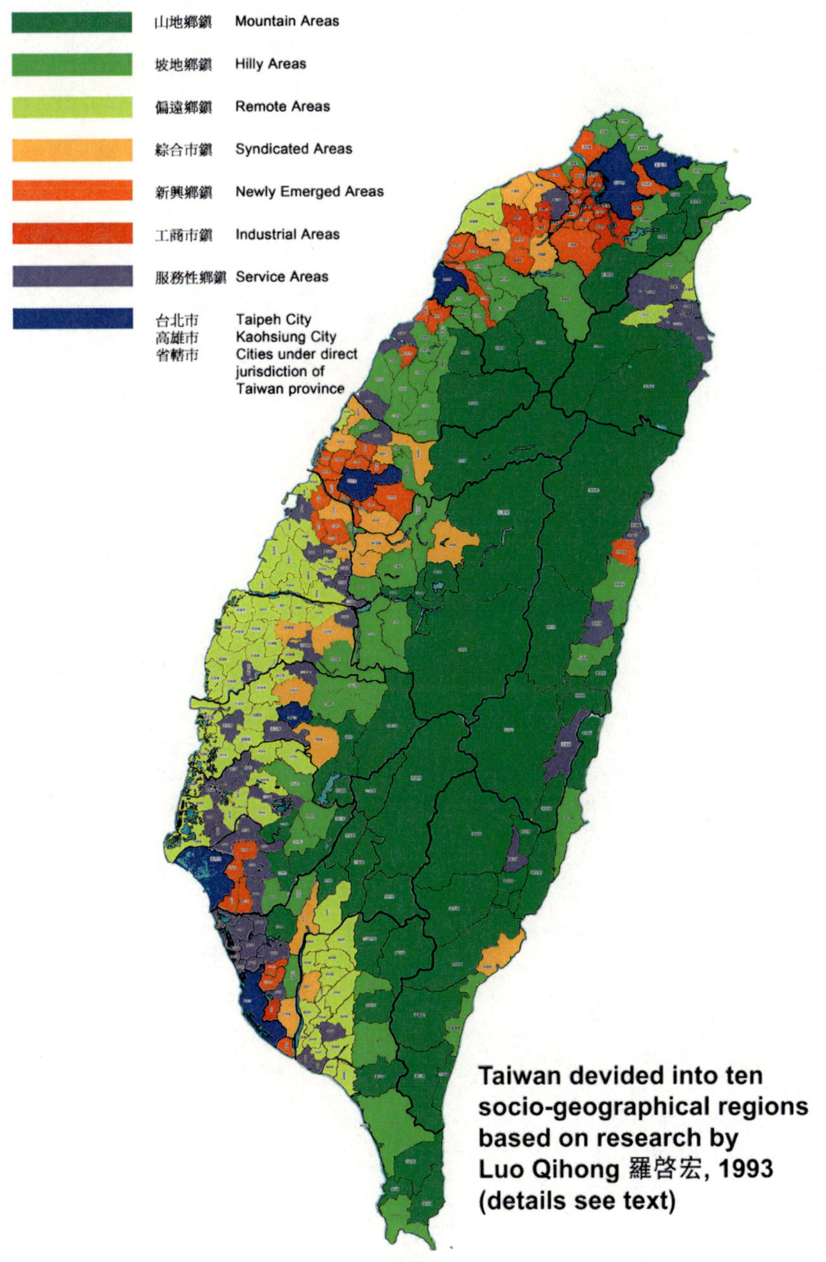

Figure 19: Map–Taiwan divided into ten socio-geographical regions based on research by Luo Qihong 羅啟宏, 1993.

11 Anticipated Tendencies among Intense Believers as Exemplified through a Statistical Investigation of School-affiliating "Specifying Buddhists"

The author's findings in the *Taiwan Social Change Survey* 2004.2 suggest that Buddhists, especially intense believers and practitioners, such as Specifying Buddhists, who regard themselves as belonging to a certain Buddhist school, are statistically more frequent in the urban areas (see chap. 6, fig. 6). Therefore a short outline of the TSCS 2004.2 with respect to the characteristics of Specifying Buddhists will be provided. [122] The sample population of the TSCS 2004.2 is very small for Specifying Buddhists: while 395 people out of 1,881 chose the general option "believe in/venerate Buddha", 18 people chose the Pure Land School, 12 the Zen School, three the Esoteric School, five thought of themselves as practising both Zen and Pure Land, four chose practicing exo- and esoteric teachings, none chose the Nichiren School, and three belonged to Sōka Gakkai. 13 Buddhists were unsure which option to choose. The total subgroup of 45 Specifying Buddhists is so meagre that the following statistical results can only be taken as giving preliminary tendencies and only a rough, tentative analysis of this subgroup is reasonable. The later qualitative case analysis will provide deeper insights into the statistical suppositions.

[122] In the following, the abbreviations CB and SB for Conventional and Specifying Buddhists are used. CB (Conventional Buddhist) := [v15b=30]. There are 395 CB in the sample. SB (Specifying Buddhist) := [v15b= 31–35.82]. There are 45 Specifying Buddhists in the sample. Total sample population n=1881. As most of the variables discussed in the following have been introduced in chap. 6, they can in the following tables be paraphrased and the original question in Chinese is not necessarily repeated.

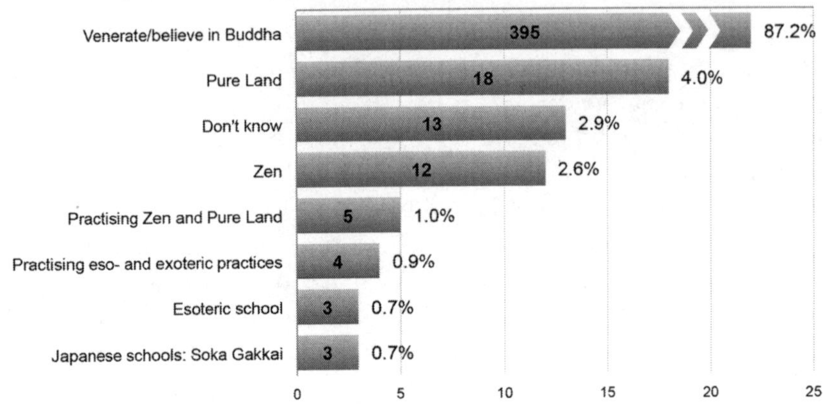

Figure 20: The group of "Conventional Buddhists", "uncertain" Buddhists, and the so-called "Specifying Buddhists", who consider themselves as belonging to a Buddhist school (TSCS 2004.2, v15b).

General Characteristics

Basically, one can state that there are more female than male Specifying Buddhists and they tend to be middle aged, between 30–50 years old. As already shown, they are likely to live in urban areas, with about 60.0% of the Specifying Buddhists living in cities. Most of them live in Taipeh, but they are not always born there, coming from Newly Emerging, Industrial or Syndicated Areas. The educational background of the Specifying Buddhists tends to be higher than the average. Two fifths have received a higher education. Also, in the case of high school education, a higher percentage of Specifying Buddhists has graduated from high school than the others. As they are better educated, so their English is slightly better. Specifying Buddhists are also more likely to come from a better educated family background. The Specifying Buddhists' sample population has studied various fields, especially the humanities and engineering. This observation echoes the fact that nearly every university has a couple of Buddhist clubs, which on the one hand reflects the proselitysing activities of Buddhist organisations and the intellectual interest in Buddhism among students, on the other hand. Although often working in industry or business, Specifying Buddhists are slightly more likely to be employed in the fields of transportation or communication, or in the service sector than Conventional Bud-

	Specifying Buddhists (n=45)	Conventional Buddhists (n=395)	Total (n=1881)
Gender: female (v1)	64.4% (29)	55.5% (219)	48.5% (912)
Ageclass: 30-49 (v ageclass)	55.6% (25)	38.7% (153)	39.4% (742)
Living in urban area (according to the three regions)	60.0% (27)	49.6% (196)	41.5% (781)
Living in Taipeh (v2: living place)	28.9% (13)	10.4% (41)	9.7% (182)
Place of birth: Newly Emerging Areas (v4)	17.8% (8)	9.6% (38)	12.6% (237)
Place of birth: Industrial Area (v4)	11.1% (5)	5.3% (21)	4.8% (90)
Place of birth: Syndicated Area (v4)	13.3% (6)	8.4% (33)	9.9% (187)
Having received higher education (v10c)	42.2% (19)	23.3% (92)	31.2% (586)
Having graduated from high school (v10a)	66.7% (30)	47.1% (186)	52.6% (990)
Situating one's English level above 5 points on a scale from 0 to 10 (v79d)	26.7% (12)	16.5% (65)	19.7% (370)
Employment in industry (製造業; v11a)	15.6% (7)	21.3% (84)	20.8% (392)
Employment in business (商業 ; v11a)	15.6% (7)	18.5% (73)	14.2% (268)
Employment in transportation or communication (運輸倉儲及通信業; v11a)	11.1% (5)	3.5% (14)	4.1% (77)
Employment in service sector (公共行政社會服務及個人服務業; v11a)	22.2% (10)	15.4% (61)	17.5% (330)
Occupation: professional worker (專業人員; v11b)	13.3% (6)	5.1% (20)	5.6 (106)
Occupation: technician or assistant professional worker (技術員及助理專業人員; v11b)	20.0% (9)	9.9% (39)	12.2% (230)
Occupation: houswife (家庭主婦; v11b)	20.0% (9)	17.7% (70)	14.9% (281)

Table 15: Selected characteristics of Specifying Buddhists in contrast to Conventional Buddhists and the whole sample (TSCS 2004.2, percentage and frequency).

dhists. Corresponding to their comparatively higher education and more urban living places, they are also more likely to be employed in jobs which require a university education. A fifth of them are housewives, which is above average.

Pronounced Characteristics

It is important to bear in mind that talking about "Specifying Buddhists" does not imply an intention to create a homogenous group of specifying believers, but rather to exemplify intense belief and show how, within the multitude of Buddhist believers, there is a core group which exhibits a strong dedication to Buddhism.

A statistical comparison between various groups of intense believers reveals not only that all forms of intense Buddhist belief are more frequent in urban areas (see Table 16), but also that intense believers behave in a parallel manner in their answering behaviour in other fields. School-Specifying Buddhists have been chosen as paradigmatic, as in the statistical comparison they present the most pronounced results. Other markers of an intense belief–which could also have been chosen to show similar tendencies of results–are, for example, conversion, ritual initiation such as taking refuge, spiritual or financial devotedness, closeness to Buddhist doctrine, a sincere search for truth, Buddhists following an individual spiritual practice or even Buddhists with a Buddhist organisational affiliation and the like.[123] None of these groups is "the pure real Buddhist group", but these categories show a tendency of belief, which characteristic helps to understand what is significant with regard to an intense Buddhist belief in Taiwan.

[123] Merely wearing Buddhist beads is not a strong marker for an intense belief: Specifying Buddhists just sometimes and only slightly more often wear Buddhist beads than Conventional Buddhists (v47 wearing Buddhist beads = yes: CB 78/395 19.7%; SB 12/45 26.7%; total 233/1881 12.4%).

	B	CB	SB	Converted B	Non-Converted B	Converted B, who specify	B with Individ. Spiritual Practice	Initiated B	Devout B	Total number of people
Remote Area	8.4% (38)	7.3% (29)	6.7% (3)	8.0% (8)	8.5% (30)	3.2% (1)	12.1% (18)	6.0% (5)	8.4% (21)	16.3% (307)
Developing Area	24.7% (112)	25.6% (101)	24.4% (11)	29.0% (29)	23.5% (83)	32.3% (10)	25.5% (38)	25.3% (21)	24.3% (61)	28.3% (532)
Urban Area	66.9% (303)	67.1% (265)	68.9% (31)	63.0 (63)	68.0% (240)	64.5% (20)	62.4% (93)	68.7% (57)	67.3% (169)	55.4% (1042)
Total	100.0% (453)	100.0% (395)	100.0% (45)	100.0% (100)	100.0% (353)	100.0% (31)	100.0% (149)	100.0% (83)	100.0% (251)	100.0% (1881)

Table 16: Different kinds of an intense Buddhist belief according to region (TSCS 2004.2, percentage and frequency).[124]

[124] Legend: B = Buddhists (v15b=30–35.39.82); CB = Conventional Buddhists (v15b=30); SB = Specifying Buddhists (v15b=31–35.82); Converted Buddhists (v15b=30–35.39.82 AND (v18=NOT 3 and NOT 10)); Converted Buddhists, who specify (v15b=31–35.82 AND (v18=NOT 3 and NOT 10)); Buddhists with Individual Spiritual Practice (v15b=30–35.39.82 AND v23h=0); Initiated Buddhist (*guiyi*, taken refuge: v15b=30–35.39.82 AND v20=1); Devout Buddhist (v15b=30–35.39.82 AND v22=1). Areas as shown on the map in Figure 30.

Already the overlapping groups of intense believers are of interest: intense belief is positively related to an awareness of being devoted. Specifying Buddhists see themselves as more devoted than Conventional Buddhists (v22 *qiancheng* 虔誠: SB 33/45, 73.3% vs. CB 213/395, 53.9%). Also, specifying school-belonging is positively related with the notion of undergoing a formal initiation and experiencing a conversion. Most of the Specifying Buddhists are aware of having undergone formal ritual initiation. In all cases, this is the traditionally acknowledged form of "taking refuge" (*guiyi* 皈依; v19 general initiation: SB 33/45, 73.3%; v20 taking refuge as ritual: SB 33/45, 73.3%), while Conventional Buddhists are rarely aware of any initiation (v19 general initiation: CB 58/395, 14.7%). Specifying Buddhists are not only sincere in their Buddhist practice and initiation, but also often experience a datable conversion and, in consequence, tend to distance themselves from the belief of their parents (v17 conversion yes: SB 31/45, 68,9%; CB 68/395, 17.2%). More than half of the Specifying Buddhists came to their belief within the last 20 years (v17a in 1985–2004: SB 28/45, 62.3%).[125] When questioned about what they believed in prior to their conversion (v18a), a third chose Buddhism, a quarter popular religion, and another quarter stated that they did not have any belief prior to their conversion (v18a: Buddhist 14/45, 31.1%; popular religion 11/45, 24.4%; Taoists 7/45, 15.6%; no belief 10/45, 22.2%). In connection with the migration to urban areas, it is hard to draw any firm conclusions but, for example, of the 13 Specifying Buddhists of the sample population who live in Taipeh, seven were not born there. Though not significant in number, it is remarkable that they either consider themselves as always having been Buddhists (4 people) and, if not, they converted to their current belief while already living in Taipeh (3 people). None converted prior to moving to Taipeh. Two thirds of the Specifying Buddhists born in Taipeh think of themselves as having converted (4 out of 6), while only two consider themselves as having always been Buddhist. The phenomenon of conversion therefore might be positively related to living in urban areas. In addition, an intense Buddhist belief can be connected to a life crisis: There is a slightly higher number of Specifying Buddhists compared with the others, who could not work due to injury or illness (v70): 28.9% of the Specifying Buddhists were unable to work for a year or longer (v70: SB 13/45, 28.9%, CB 92/395, 23.3% other 332/1441, 23.0%). There might be a biographical connection between their long periods of illness and their religious search. Due to their conscious conversion, it might also be that Specifying Buddhists tend more often to distance themselves from the non-Buddhist belief of their parents: While about 80%

125 Correspondingly, 64.4% (29/45) of the Specifying Buddhists state that they attended the initiation rite within the last 20 years (v21).

of the Conventional Buddhists claim that their parents are also Buddhists, less than 50% of the Specifying Buddhists do so. Specifying Buddhists more often state that their parents are popular religious, Taoists or do not belong to any religion, which hints at their more elaborate, narrower concept of Buddhism. This is in line with their answer to the question about why they believe in Buddhism. Only 22.2% of the Specifying Buddhists state to follow the belief of their parents (v29 following belief of parents = yes: CB 265/395, 67.1; SB 10/45, 22.2%; other 754/1441, 52.3%).

Belief of father	Conventional Buddhists (n=395)	Specifying Buddhists (n=45)	Belief of mother	Conventional Buddhists (n=395)	Specifying Buddhists (n=45)
No belief	3.5% (14)	8.9% (4)	No belief	1.3% (5)	4.4% (2)
Popular religion	4.6% (18)	20.0% (9)	Popular religion	4.3% (17)	13.3% (6)
Buddhism	79.5% (314)	31.1% (14)	Buddhism	84.6% (334)	46.7% (21)
Taoism	6.1% (24)	17.8% (8)	Taoism	3.8% (15)	15.6% (7)

Table 17: Parents' belief of Conventional Buddhists and Specifying Buddhists (TSCS 2004.2, v16a: belief of father; v16b: belief of mother, percentage and frequency).

As intense believers, Specifying Buddhists consider, far more than do Conventional Buddhists, their belief to be influential upon their life (v30.4 strong agreement: CB 132/395, 33.4%; SB 27/45, 60.0%; other 323/1441, 22.4%). Similar high percentages only the group of Christians delivers (43/71, 60.6%). This influence on life is reflected statistically in: a) the organisational affiliation, including financial support and voluntary work, b) individual spiritual practice, and c) commonly-held values.

a) Organisational Affiliation

More than a third of the Specifying Buddhists attend a Buddhist institution once a week or fortnight, while only about 15% of the Conventional Buddhists do so. (v31: "going once every week or fortnight": SB 17/45, 37.8%; CB 57/395, 14.5%). The Specifying Buddhists show a high engagement especially with the four Young Buddhist Monasteries: the highest participation rate among all Buddhist organisations belongs to the Buddhist social welfare organisation, Tzu Chi. Commonly estimated in Taiwan and known for placing less emphasis on Buddhist doctrinal explanations than on active social help, Tzu Chi is a Buddhist institution that is also spreading among Non-Buddhists: 9.1% of the whole sample population are involved in Tzu Chi. Also, the Specifying Buddhists score the highest together with their involvement in the internationally-known monastery, Foguang Shan (10 participate in both cases), while 15.2% of the Conventional Buddhists are affiliated with Tzu Chi (v26). Foguang Shan is far less widespread in the population in general (3.5%). Another Young Buddhist Monastery caring for a more intellectual, Japanese influenced image is also spread among Specifying Buddhists, Fagu Shan (7 participating Specifying Buddhists). Chungtai Shan, a Chan monastic-oriented monastery with a clear school affiliation, aiming to build up intense relationships with its followers and asking for a strict spiritual practice, attracts six of the 45 Specifying Buddhists. Even though, in this respect, this monastery is the most outspoken one of all of the aforementioned Buddhist organisations, the instability of religious belonging and concepts becomes obvious especially through nine people of other than Buddhist belonging (9/1441, 0.6%), who count themselves followers of this monastery.

v26	SB	CB	Other	Total
Tzu Chi	22.2% (10)	15.2% (60)	7.0% (101)	9.1% (171)
Foguang Shan	22.2% (10)	5.8% (23)	2.3% (33)	3.5% (66)
Fagu Shan	15.6% (7)	2.3% (9)	0.7 (10)	1.4% (26)
Chungtai Shan	13.3% (6)	1.3% (5)	0.6% (9)	1.1% (20)

Table 18: Specifying Buddhists' engagement with the four Young Buddhist Monasteries (TSCS 2004.2, v26, percentage and frequency, abbreviations please refer to table 16).

Donations to religious institutions are widespread among Specifying Buddhists. Three quarters of them donate money to religious groups. They tend to donate more than Conventional Buddhists. Of the 34 Specifying Buddhists who donate to religious organisations, nearly all of them, 33 people, donate to Buddhist organisations. Specifying Buddhists have a mostly exclusive and strong organisational financial affiliation. Only a few of them, in addition to their Buddhist donations, donate money to other non-Buddhist religious organisations: five donate money to popular religious institutions (v55.1), three to Taoist institutions (v55.4), and none to Christian, Muslim, or any other religious organisation (v55.5–v55.12). A third of the donors donate a fixed amount (11/33 people, v56.1).

v53-55.58–Selection	Specifying Buddhists (n=45)	Conventional Buddhists (n=395)	Total (n=1881)
Donation within the past year (v53)	75.6% (34)	59.5% (235)	54.6% (1027)
Donation under 1000 NT$ (v54)	8.9% (4) (as 34 SB donate, the remaining 30 SB donate more than 1000 NT$)	21.8% (86)	20.7% (390)
Donation to Buddhist organisation (v55.3)	73.3% (33)	50.1% (198)	27.7% (521)
Donation to non-religious organisation (v58)	44.4% (20)	25.3% (100)	23.8% (448)

Table 19: Donating behaviour of Specifying Buddhists in comparison with Conventional Buddhists (TSCS 2004.2, v53-55.58, percentage and frequency).

Regarding the intention in donating, more than half of the Specifying Buddhists say that they do it to "extinguish calamities, ask for luck and gain merit" and with the same frequency they see it as their spiritual practice of giving alms. Less frequently, they want to help in the "construction of religious buildings" or "repay society". Specifying Buddhists are not only financially engaged in the support of the Buddhist institutions, but also show a higher financial commitment to society. Nearly half of all Specifying Buddhists also spend money on non-religious organisations, while only a quarter of Conventional Buddhists do (v58: CB 100/395, 25.3%; SB 20/45, 44.4%; other 328/1441, 22.8%).

v57–Selection	Donating Specifying Buddhists (n=33)
To extinguish calamities, ask for luck and gain merit (消災祈福做功德; v57.1)	56.7% (19)
Spiritual practice of giving alms (佈施修行; v57.6)	56.7% (19)
Construction of religious buildings (建廟, 修廟; v57.7)	42.2% (14)
Repay society (回饋社會; v57.5)	36.4% (12)

Table 20: Intentions to donate among Specifying Buddhists (TSCS 2004.2, v57, percentage and frequency).

Their strong connection with their Buddhist organisation is expressed not only through membership and financial support, but a quarter of the Specifying Buddhists also engage in voluntary work (v60 or v61: SB 12/45, 26.7%) for at least a few hours per week and they also strongly engage in winning new members through introducing their friends to the organisation: A fifth of the Specifying Buddhists came into contact with their organisation through the zealous introduction of their friends (v.29 answer: through the zealous introduction of friends: CB 32/395, 8.1%; SB 9/45, 20.0%; other 59/1441, 4.1%).

b) Individual Spiritual Practice

The intensity with which Specifying Buddhists are engaging in their belief is expressed not only at an organisational level, but also has a direct effect upon their personal spiritual practice. Specifying Buddhists are far more likely to follow an individual spiritual practice:

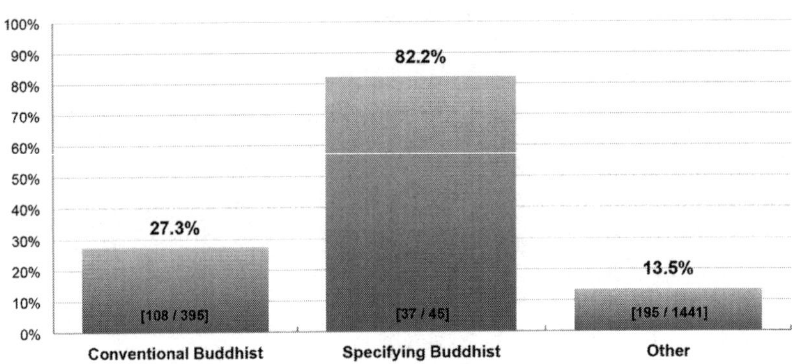

Figure 21: Conventional and Specifying Buddhists following an individual spiritual practice (data based on TSCS 2004.2).

This is not only the case for individual spiritual practice in general, but appears constantly also in various specific forms of individual Buddhist spiritual practice, such as meditation, name or mantra recitation, or the reading of sūtras:

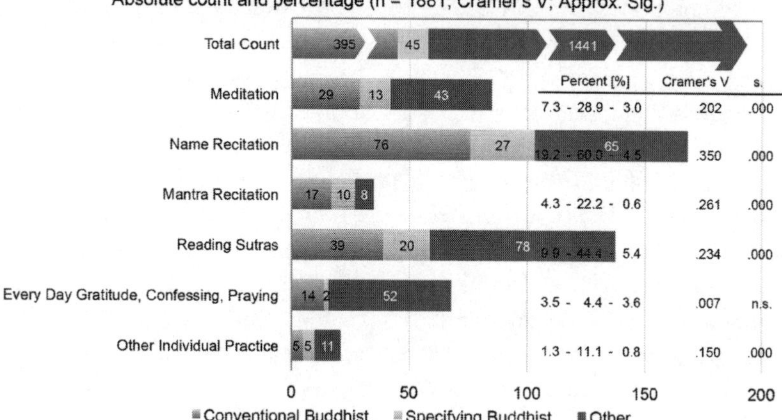

Figure 22: Various kinds of individual spiritual practice conducted by Conventional Buddhists and Specifying Buddhists (data based on TSCS 2004.2).

c) Spiritual and Doctrinal Orientation

As to be expected, Specifying Buddhists show a stronger belief in the core Buddhist ideas, such as, for example, "karma and rebirth": 42 of the 45 Specifying Buddhists believe at least somewhat in karma and rebirth. This is also reflected in their stronger belief that karmic luck has been decided as it has been built up both in previous lives as well as the present one. They believe more strongly also in the pejorative interpretations of karmic thinking, such as the idea that marrying the "wrong wife" is a consequence of a former life as is suffering for one's children.

v27–Selection	Specifying Buddhists (n=45)	Conventional Buddhists (n=395)	Total (n=1881)
At least somewhat believing in karma and rebirth	93.4% (42)	84.4% (333)	75.5% (1420)
Strong belief in karmic fate as decided in previous and present lives.	44.4% (20)	30.6% (121)	23.9% (449)
Strong belief in marrying the "wrong wife" as a consequence of a former life	35.6% (16)	27.1% (107)	20.8% (392)
Strong belief in suffering for one's children as own karmic consequence	35.6% (16)	22.5% (89)	19.5% (367)

Table 21: Belief in Buddhist ideas of Specifying Buddhists and Conventional Buddhists (TSCS 2004.2, v27, percentage and frequency).

This might have consequences for their own life conduct, as they also strongly agree that an individual's good or bad behaviour influences the luck of the following generation as well as his/her own next life. Specifying Buddhists are strongly aware of the spiritual influence of religion upon their life–two thirds of them think, that "religion gives life a direction". This sense of the meaning of life might relativise their opinion about the importance of obtaining wealth. Specifying Buddhists are, on a financial level, strongly bound to the institutions to which they donate, but that does not mean that they consider themselves less tolerant towards others' opinions. In contrast, they estimate slightly more "tolerance to other opinions" than the rest of the population. Even in the interview behaviour, the awareness of the value of positive social behaviour appears to be internalised: Specifying Buddhists are normally very willing to cooperate during an interview and make a reliable impression in their answering behaviour. They are less impatient during the interviews.

v28.30.74–Selection	Specifying Buddhists (n=45)	Conventional Buddhists (n=395)	Total (n=1881)
Strong agreement that an individual's good or bad behaviour influences the luck of the following generation (v28.3)	75.6% (34)	56.5% (223)	51.0% (959)
Strong agreement that an individual's good or bad behaviour influences his/ her own next life (v28.4)	75.6% (34)	48.4% (191)	41.4% (779)
Strong agreement that religion gives life a direction (給人人生的方向; v30.5);	66.7% (30)	25.3% (100)	20.4% (384)
4 points on scale from 0 to 4 for the importance of getting rich (v74.6)	28.9% (13)	42.0% (166)	42.2% (793)
4 points on scale from 0 to 4 for the importance of respecting other opinions (v74.5)	31.1% (14)	22.3% (88)	24.6% (463)

Table 22: Attitudes towards life of Specifying Buddhists versus Conventional Buddhists (TSCS 2004.2, v28.30.74, percentage and frequency).

var r4-r9–Selection	Specifying Buddhists (n=45)	Conventional Buddhists (n=395)	Total (n=1881)
The interviewee never refused to be interviewed (有無拒絕受訪? 從頭到尾均未表示拒絕; r4).	84.4%(38)	70.6% (279)	76.1% (1431)
The interviewee was never impatient (是否不耐煩? 從未表示不耐煩; r5).	84.4% (38)	69.9% (276)	76.2% (1433)
The interviewee was very cooperative (合作程度? 很合作; r8).	68.9% (31)	57.7% (228)	63.9%(1202)
The interviewee was very reliable (可靠程度? 很可靠; r9).	57.8% (26)	48.9% (193)	54.2% (1020)

Table 23: Behaviour of Conventional Buddhists versus Specifying Buddhists during the interview (TSCS 2004.2, var r4–r9, percentage and frequency).

Buddhist values are also reflected in the Specifying Buddhists' answers about their view of life. While (probably also due to their better organisational integration) they are less likely to feel lonely and might even feel less frequently insecure about life, they tend to view life as more bitter than Conventional Buddhists or even other people. The feeling that life is "empty" (also a variously interpreted but central idea in Buddhist philosophy) does not differ from that of other people and Conventional Buddhists.

v67-68–Selection	Specifying Buddhists (n=45)	Conventional Buddhists (n=395)	Total (n=1881)
Never or seldom feeling to be very lonely (v67.2)	80.0% (36)	72.4% (286)	74.2%(1395)
Seldom or never feeling that things are very unstable (v67.3)	64.4% (29)	56.0% (221)	57.5% (1082)
Thinking that human life is really very bitter and not very joyful (v68.2)	55.6% (25)	42.0% (166)	34.3% (646)
Believing human life is from its beginning always an empty place (v68.4)	37.8% (17)	39.7% (157)	34.0% (640)

Table 24: The emotional status of Specifying Buddhists versus Conventional Buddhists (TSCS 2004.2, v67-68, percentage and frequency).

Specifying Buddhists especially differ from Conventional Buddhists with regard to the intention that underlies their belief. While the most common answers about believers' choices (see Part I) such as the "search for peace" are less often mentioned among Specifying Buddhists, they are, in contrast, far more likely to search for truth. Half of the Specifying Buddhists are searching for the meaning of life and wisdom. Self-cultivation (*xiushen yangxing* 修身養性) is most important to them.

v29–Selection	Specifying Buddhists (n=45)	Conventional Buddhists (n=395)	Total (n=1881)
Searching for peace	28.9% (13)	44.1% (174)	37.3% (701)
Searching for truth	33.3% (15)	9.4% (37)	0.7% (134)
Understanding the meaning of life	51.1% (23)	14.9% (59)	0.9% (177)
Searching for wisdom	51.1% (23)	15.9% (63)	0.9% (176)
Self-cultivation: "yes"	62.2% (28)	32.9% (130)	20.5% (386)

Table 25: Reasons for believing in Buddhism of Specifying Buddhists versus Conventional Buddhists (TSCS 2004.2, v29, percentage and frequency).

The possible function of Buddhism in helping people through a life crisis (such as losing one's job–see above) fits the aims that Buddhists pursue through their belief and, in consequence, Specifying Buddhists are more likely to reduce their problems with the help of their religion. More than half of them agree that religion can help people to find a way out of their difficulties and they see more often the consoling function of religion.

v29.30–Selection	Specifying Buddhists (n=45)	Conventional Buddhists (n=395)	Total (n=1881)
Religion as helping to diminish troubles (v29)	40.0% (18)	17.7% (70)	13.5% (253)
Strong agreement that religion can help people in difficulties to find a solution (v30.1)	53.3% (24)	23.0% (91)	18.3% (344)
Strong agreement that religion can let people search consolation of heart and soul (v30.3)	77.8% (35)	41.0% (162)	32.7% (616)

Table 26: Psycho-social functions of Buddhism as seen by Specifying Buddhists and Conventional Buddhists (TSCS 2004.2, v29.30, percentage and frequency).

Primarily doctrinal questions are, in general, answered with stronger affirmation by Specifying Buddhists independently of whether these questions are addressing Buddhist or other doctrinal issues. Half of the Specifying Buddhists believe strongly in heaven and hell. The majority of all Taiwanese believe more or less intensely in heaven and hell. The belief in the existence of a soul after death is also commonly assumed in Taiwan (v27.4 total: 72.4%, 1361/1881), but also the Specifying Buddhists are more definite about this, although the term "soul" (*linghun* 靈魂) in the questionnaire can be replaced by the specific Buddhist term "*shenshi* 神識", "divine consciousness", by the interviewer, and is therefore situated at the core discussions of Buddhist philosophy on the soul and self (skt. *ātman*). Still, five out of the 45 Specifying Buddhists (11.1%) do not really believe in it. Specifying Buddhists believe strongly (at 22.2%) more than the average population (at 14,6%) in the existence of a highest god in the universe, but some Specifying Buddhists also strongly reject this assumption.

v27.15–Selection	Specifying Buddhists (n=45)	Conventional Buddhists (n=395)	Total (n=1881)
Believing strongly in heaven and hell (v27.2)	48.9% (22)	25.3% (100)	21.3% (400)
Believing in a more or less intense way in heaven and hell (v27.2)	82.1% (37)	69.1% (273)	64.7% (1217)
Believing not really in heaven and hell (v27.2)	11.1% (5)	23.3% (92)	23.1% (435)
Believing strongly in a highest god in the universe (v.27.1)	22.2% (10)	14.2% (56)	14.6% (275)
Believing not at all in a highest god in the universe (v27.1)	17.8% (8)	8.1% (32)	11.0% (158)
Venerating gods and ancestors (拜神, 拜祖先; v15a)	91.1% (41)	93.9% (371)	84.8% (1595)

Table 27: The attitudes of Specifying Buddhists versus Conventional Buddhists regarding doctrinal issues (TSCS 2004.2, v27.15, percentage and frequency).

Specifying Buddhists also more often strongly agree with the concept that there are positive and powerful influences of "energy" (*qi* 氣).

v27–Selection	Specifying Buddhists (n=45)	Conventional Buddhists (n=395)	Total (n=1881)
Strong belief that *qigong* can help people to manage illness (氣功可以幫助人治病, v27.11)	18.5% (73)	26.7% (12)	15.8% (298)
Strong belief that human *qi* can be strengthened through practice (人的氣可經由修練而加強, v27.12)	27.8% (110)	40.0% (18)	22.0% (414)
Strong belief that at a place of huge *qi*, trees, flowers and gras will grow very well, and the place will flourish all over (地氣盛的地方, 樹木花草會長得很好, 地方也都會興旺, v27.14)	29.9% (118)	40.0% (18)	24.7% (465)

Table 28: Belief of Specifying Buddhists versus Conventional Buddhists in the concept of *qi* (TSCS 2004.2, v27, percentage and frequency).

The traditional Chinese concepts of harmony, like micro- and macrocosmic relations or the necessity of balancing *yin* and *yang*, are more widespread among Specifying Buddhists.

v27–Selection	Specifying Buddhists (n=45)	Conventional Buddhists (n=395)	Total (n=1881)
Strong belief that one has to keep *yin* and *yang* balanced and in harmony, only then will the body and heart be healthy (要維持陰陽平衡與調和, 身心才會健康; v27.15)	34.4% (136)	48.9% (22)	31.4% (590)
Strong belief that every human is a small "magnetic field", the cosmos is the big "magnetic field". When humans fall ill, is it because the big and small magnetic fields are not coordinated (個人是小磁場, 宇宙是 大磁場, 人會生病是因為大小磁場沒有協調的緣故; v27.16)	14.7% (58)	26.7% (12)	13.1% (246)

Table 29: Cosmologically related beliefs of Specifying Buddhists versus Conventional Buddhists (TSCS 2004.2, v27, percentage and frequency).

In their veneration behaviour, Specifying Buddhists do not distance themselves from the most widespread attitude in Taiwan to venerate gods and ancestors.

Summing up, the subgroup of school-specifying believers was chosen, as it provides the most pronounced, but general parallel, results in comparison with other forms of intense Buddhist belief. Although the subgroup of Specifying Buddhists is relatively small, one can detect several tendencies through the evaluation of the TSCS 2004.2: one can state that an intense and differentiating Buddhist commitment exemplified through School-Specifying Buddhist believers hints at a tendency towards a group of mainly middle-aged, often female individuals from a well-educated background, living in urban areas. They see themselves generally as devoted and have undergone the initiation ritual of taking refuge. They often recall the actual date of their conversion and distance their new belief from that of their parents. It might be more common to undergo the process of conversion in urban areas. Specifying Buddhists are aware of the influence of their belief upon their life and experience it in an organisational, individual and doctrinal way: they are strongly affiliated with Buddhist organisations and the majority of Specifying Buddhists donate money, mainly to Buddhist organisations, but also to non-religious organisations. Their commitment is also expressed through their voluntary work within their Buddhist organisation, with which they often came into contact through the zealous introduction of their friends. Specifying Buddhists tend to follow a strong individual spiritual practice, like meditation, recitation or the reading of sūtras. They believe in the core Buddhist ideas, such as karma and rebirth, heaven and hell, but also more often in a highest god. They do not distance themselves from the traditional, widespread ancestor and gods veneration and approve of traditional Chinese concepts, such as "*qi*" or "*yin* and *yang*". It seems that Specifying Buddhists have often undergone a period of personal upheaval. They are less in search of practical aims through their belief, such as peace or wealth, but more engaged in a personal search for truth, the meaning of life, wisdom and especially self-cultivation through their belief, which they experience as consolation and as diminishing their troubles. Although they understand life as bitter in general, Specifying Buddhists tend to feel less lonely and less insecure about life. Intense Buddhist belief, one might assume, may be especially connected to private life-style and less to doctrinal consistency, providing as a resource for personal crisis management and proving itself through an individual spiritual practice in combination with participation in a Buddhist organisation.

12 Four Short Portraits of Intense and Differentiating New Forms of Belief

12.1 Case A: Ma Fengling–Organisational Representatives and Socially Engaged Buddhism[126]

*Ma: [...; 3.1:45] Finally, I saw a book about the biography of Bodhisattva Guanyin writing in depth about Bodhisattva Guanyin. Ha. When she became a princess, for saving the dharma and so forth... All that I remember is that she bore a lot of sorrow, etc. Then I read this book. Ha. I say, how happy! The whole/ whole/ whole evening I read and read without a break. A. Then there, at that time, finally I suddenly became aware of that (*huangran dawu *恍然大悟) me. Originally, when we are venerating this, we all say Mother Guanyin. Ha. Buddhist ancestor Guanyin. La. Only since then we knew: "Oh. Originally Bodhisattva Guanyin, she's helping them. It is not only/ only letting us ask/ ask what can I do, what can I do/ ask what can my family do? Originally, she wants to help the living beings/ help them. Reading that book, I finally really understood the original spirit of Buddhism that says it is helping them. Ha. Na. After reading that book a, just it was nearly mother's day. So I at that time/ because we at home all worship this bodhisattva la, the life (*shengming *生命) a. Then na I took incense and just started asking that the mothers under the whole sky should all be able to be peaceful and happy. Because I read this book, I learnt that: Ei, it is under the whole sky. It is not just for single people. And: At that time, in fact, when I read this book I was about 30 years old [laughs] [3.3:29].*[127]

Biographical Sketch

Ma Fengling (female, 55 years old) was introduced to the researcher as an official representative of a Buddhist social welfare organisation that is so well-known in Taiwan that any attempt at anonymisation would be pointless: According to the *Taiwan Social Change Survey*, 12.6% of the Taiwanese popu-

---

126 The following two cases are the focus of Guggenmos (2014).

127 Ma: [...] [3.1:51] 後來我是看到一本 觀世音菩薩傳記 專門寫觀世音菩薩 � 她在 當公主的時候 她為了要求法 等等 所記得受很多的苦等等 然後我看了那一本 喃 我說好高興 整/ 整/ 整晚上一直看一直看啊 然後那裡 那時候 才讓我恍然大悟 原來在我們拜的這個 我們都講 觀世 媽 喃 觀音佛祖 啦 我們才知道 哦 原來觀世音菩薩 她是利益她的 不是只有 只讓我們求 求我能怎麼樣 求我怎麼樣 求我家人怎麼樣 原來是要利益眾生 利他 看了那一本 我才真正的了解 原來佛教的精神 是講究利他 喃 那 我看了那一本書之後啊 剛好就是母親節 來到 所以我那時候 因為我們家都有 供奉 那個 菩薩啦生命啊 然後 那我拿去香來 我就開始祈求 然後讓普天下的媽媽 都能夠平安快樂 因為就是看這本書 然後學習到 欸, 是普天下 不是只有為了一個一個 還有 那時候 其實 看這本書的時候已經是三十歲左右的 [laughs] [3.3:29]

lation participated in 1999 in Tzu Chi, and 42.3% of the population knew of friends or relatives who did so. Meeting for a detailed interview at a branch of the organisation in an industrial suburb of Taipeh county, Ma models herself as an exemplary follower of the organisation.

She was born in a suburb of Taiwan, adopted by relatives, attended primary school and afterwards worked in the textile industry. Married at the age of 19 to a husband with a small family company selling magnetic tools, she raised her children and saw herself as a housewife. By the time of the interview, her children had grown up. She now spends her days volunteering at the organisation and also got her husband, whom she portrays as a reformed alcoholic, involved in it. In recounting her biography, she reveals herself to be a well-versed testimony teller, who at the end of the interview asks for the record to use further within her organisation. Having been involved in her organisation for over 20 years, she is deeply familiar with its structure and supervises the processes within it. Although she has no higher education, her organisation values her because of her managerial and practical skills and celebrates her, even publishing her biography as the embodiment of its social vision. Ma's biographical narration should be understood within this context: she has intensely internalised the vision of the organisation, identifies with it and reshapes her entire biographical narration according to it.

"Traditional" and "New" Buddhism

Several stereotypes can be identified in her narration: the change Ma experiences through the organisation is displayed through the dichotomy between the "old" and "new", between "tradition" and her organisation, between her parents' generation as exemplified by the religious behaviour of her mother and her own life orientation. This transformation culminates in her narration of conversion, presented at the beginning of this short portrait: while reading a book, Ma suddenly understands (*huangran dawu* 恍然大悟) the character of a bodhisattva, which brings her to a transformed understanding of veneration: veneration should not only beg for a certain goal limited to single people, but include "all sentient beings". Also, the function of the bodhisattva in the temple context, as someone who is *asked* for help, is reshaped, placing the emphasis not on the action of "asking" (*qiqiu* 祈求), but also on the helping attitude of the bodhisattva. This motif of care is present at the doctrinal level, connected to a new understanding of Buddhism and the role of a bodhisattva. The bodhisattva role is also implemented at all levels, as realised by the adored leader of the organisation and as a prototype and ideal for every member of it. Ma also tries to perform the ideal of help and care in her own life, so that the bodhisattva serves as a role model to "serve all sentient beings" (*liyi zhongsheng* 利益眾生) throughout her life. Her focus shifts from veneration behaviour and passive listening to religious doctrine (alluded to through the traditional beginning of Buddhist sūtras "*rushi wo wen* 如是我問", "This is what I heard") to taking action (alluded to by altering this formulation into "*rushi wo xing* 如是我行", "This is how I act") within her own life.

She finds easy but clear language in which to express this change in her own belief as now being a "spirituality of taking action". This transformation is expressed in the patterns of family life: the organisation is like an extended family and she herself plays her role as a caring, loving mother with the help of the organisation and the example of its master out in society up to a global context, when she is sent by her organisation to Sri Lanka to help the victims of the Tsunami in 2004.

"Traditional Buddhism"	**"New Buddhism"**
Guanyin within traditional veneration: • not bodhisattva, but "mother" and "Buddhist ancestor" (Guanshi Ma 觀世媽 / Guanyin Fozu 觀音佛祖) • veneration as *qiqiu* 祈求: asking for spiritual succour in private matters (one's relatives and personal matters): *erzi / nü'er ping'an* 兒子/女兒平安, *shiqing shunli* 事情順利)	*New perception of Bodhisattva Guanyin through reading and the organisation:* • finding the "original spirit" of Buddhism (*yuanlai fojiao de jingshen* 原來佛教的精神) • veneration as asking for the sake of all sentient beings (*liyi zhongsheng* 利益眾生) • to take over the helping attitude of the bodhisattva in one's own life
Characterised by: a) "This is, what I heard" (*rushi wo wen* 如是我聞) • mechanised devotion • available for a few • centred on monasteries and rites • not changing one's personal life • parasitic self-preservation b) "leaving the world" (*chushi* 出世) • conflict between family and Buddhism: endangering family, parasites of society c) Other-worldly aim: The "Western Paradise" d) Karma as being used for facing others without mercy	Characterised by: a) "This is, how I act" (*rushi wo xing* 如是我行) • constructed as "new Buddhist school" • socially applicable (*shenghuo hua* 生活化) • affecting the everyday culture of the family • affecting society: value creation for simple people b) "entering the world" (*rushi* 入世) • lays having their own function besides the monastic order—can better engage in society. c) This-worldly aim: being a bodhisattva among people d) Reinterpreting the karmic thought as orientedtowardsfutureandemphasising gratitude

Figure 23: The dichotomy between "traditional" and "new" Buddhism in the view of Ma Fengling.

Enlarging her role as a housewife to society, Ma Fengling continues to operate within the expectations of traditional Taiwanese society. One could even say that she is attempting to embody the perfect mother, with the attributes of benevolence, love, compassion, and care. Robert Weller and Julia Huang conducted extensive field observations of Tzu Chi followers since 1992 and Ma Fengling fits a number of their analysed stereotypes: not only are the majority of Tzu Chi followers women, but also the details respond to the biographical patterns. An example of this is the fact that Ma brought her husband into the organisation: Huang never "encounter[ed] a case in which a husband joined first and then brought in his wife" (Huang 2009, 171). Also, the focus on action as providing solutions to family life and social problems appears widespread. Still, Ma's low educational background might not be representative: The followers of Tzu Chi stem, according to the field work of Weller and Huang, to a large degree from a comparatively well educated middle class of women who witness a lost sense of community in the urban market economy. Although they are faced with an increase in their unstructured leisure time, they find restrained options of action at home. While their husbands are easily lost in their search for social life with alcohol problems, the family experiences, in general, new economic wealth (Huang and Weller 1998). The aforementioned new social role of Ma Fengling, which fits the traditional expectations of domestic life and filiality, is particularly in accordance with the differentiation of Huang and Weller:[128] "*Ciji* suceeds in combining a very traditional idea of womanhood with a very modern sphere of action in the world" (Huang and Weller 1998, 390) and "*Ciji*'s unique appeal to women in Taiwan stems from its universalisation of women's family concerns" (Huang and Weller 1998, 389). Family values and roles are extended to the wider society and, historically, the function of the formerly widespread "vegetarian halls", Zhaitangs 齋堂, is continued (Huang and Weller 1998, 386).

Social Activation

Looking back upon her life before she joined the organisation, Ma Fengling constructs it in the light of being socially-disadvantaged. It is only through the organisation that she is enabled to compensate for her lack of education and have an active social life under the motto of "helping others". Her narration stresses this restricted starting position: her unfortunate upbringing and educational unfulfilled longings are accompanied by a situation in her private life, which shall be identified as typical for the general sociocultural

[128] Besides Huang and Weller, Elise DeVido analysed this connection between the roles of motherhood, bodhisattvas and the respective organisation: Zai (2005) and DeVido (2006).

situation of Taiwanese "average"-people, marked by "superstition", irrational fate management and the perception of Buddhists as parasites of society, endangering family life. Through contrasting her common but unfortunate starting position with her transformation through the community and its master, she tries through her own biography not only to legitimise her own transformation but also to involve others in the dynamic of conversion. Unfolding her reshaped biography to the interviewer cannot follow the aim of converting the listener, but is narrated in the light of praising the organisation and its master, as they are represented as having helped a whole socially-disadvantaged class of people in Taiwan to transform themselves for the betterment of their own situation, their families as well as society:

> [14.0:29] Indeed it is like/ We are like that/ Such an average [*pingyong* 平庸] family housewife a/ Where does she have such a [sc. karmic] luck? One could say whatever big master, big master–A big enterpriser only could achieve such a [laughs] deal ne. But our master [different expression] a increases our [sc. karmic] luck. Changes us mediocre people like this to be able to achieve such a classy, classy achievement a [14.1:04].[129]

Ma experiences the interest of the organisation and its master in her as an undeserved honour, breaking with her expectations of the social hierarchy. She is grateful for the respect and degree of involvement which she achieves in her organisation, as she understands it–probably supported by the meta-narratives of the organisation–as treatment that is suitable for a higher social class than herself. Ma–stemming from a small family business–would see the higher social class as represented by successful businessmen. Her perception of the social stratification is shaped by economically-oriented concepts. Still, Ma does not remain restricted to her economical orientation, but is able to formulate (following the pattern of transformation through the organisation) that she obtained an education through the organisation which goes beyond a cognitive knowledge which she describes as a "*Herzensbildung*" (*xinling shang de jiaoyu* 心靈上的教育; education in respect to the heart):

> Ma: [20.4:35] At home, right. When I had children, I still dreamt that I would study. Continuously, until I entered the Buddhist door, I only satisfied one of my thirsts for knowledge. In fact, I received here education.
> Interviewer: Right. So do you have here a formal kind of class, or/?
> Ma: No. Also, there is, of course, a class la. Says, here it is also training classes a and so forth. Advanced classes. Of course, also. But the most real ha, should be just the education of the heart through our master [21.0:11].[130]

---

129 [14.0:29] 尤其是像 我們這樣 這麼平庸的家庭主婦阿 哪有這種福報 能講 甚麼大法師 大法師 大的企業家才能夠得到這樣的 [laughs] 待遇呢 可是我們上人阿 讓我們的福報增長 變成我們這樣平庸的人 可以得到 這樣 上等上等的接待阿 [14.1:04]

130 Ma: [20.4:35] 在家裡 對 我生了孩子 還會作夢 我在讀書 一直到我進入佛門 我才滿足我的求知慾一 其實在這裡就是在受教育 Interviewer: 對 所以你們這裡也有

Ma's self-perception		
Part of "traditional" society • Mother and wife with a basic education only • Married off at an early age to an alcoholic • Popular religious background and conventional religiosity • Image of Buddhists as parasites and family destroyers	 Conflict  Results in development:	Personal skills and interests • Self-confident, dominant • Charity-oriented and socially engaged • Practically-talented • Spiritually-interested • Intellectual longing
Process of searching for a meaning/solution: She unites spiritual interest and practical orientation into a spirituality of "acting". → Compensation for her lack of education → Positive transformation of the family She opens up to herself a new, but traditional and family-recognised, field of action and secures economic stability.		

Figure 24: New life conduct as the transformed continuation of a traditional frame of action–Buddhists as helpers and designers of the family and society.

The actual impact of Ma's organisation upon social change in Taiwan cannot be traced back through an interview which has been functionalised and is even given in the situational context of the organisation itself. Still, the interview makes a statement that is intended to solve, in an exemplary way, the collision of a female facing traditional society. As a self-confident, practical, spiritually-interested person, Ma had a poor education, early marriage, poverty and a religious background that is shaped by conventional veneration behaviour and a negative image of the Buddhist monastic order as parasitic and family-destroying. In her search for the meaning of life, Ma was able to reinterpret popular religious veneration and alter her impression of Buddhism with the help of her organisation. This leads to a process in which she can combine her personal interests, like her spiritual search and her practical, managerial skills, with the expectations of society regarding the role as a caring mother. With the help of the organisation, she can not only combine her own longings with the traditional expectations, but even receives praise for fulfilling and exceeding the traditional expectations: her family experiences a positive transforma-

真正 的一種課 還是 Ma: 不是 當然課也有啦 說是在培訓課程阿等等 進修的課程 當然也 但是最 實際的哈 應該就是上人給我們的 心靈上的教育 [21.0:11]

tion, her marriage gains in quality and she can even engage actively in social life in her extended role as a caring mother. The anthropologist, Ting Jenchieh, spoke of the case of the organisational pendant of Ma's view upon life as a "somatic realisation" of socially-acknowledged moral values, and marked it as an alternate traditionality, which does not conflict with society's expectations (Ting 1997 and 2006).

Ma Fengling's narration in the context of this book is interesting, especially as she sees herself as an ideal follower of a Young Buddhist Monastery, propagating a form of Buddhism known in Taiwan to be situated "among the people" (*renjian fojiao* 人間佛教, also named "Engaged Buddhism"). Similar to her narration, there have been other interviews that were very similar to that discussed. They mostly developed out of official interview requests to the Young Buddhist Monasteries and organisations in Taiwan in search of lay Buddhists. These people were chosen by the organisations because they are seen as their "ideal followers" and thus reflect "the voice of their masters". The interviewees feel generally honoured at being invited and understand the task of narrating their own biography as a quest to display the splendour of the organisation through the positive performative effects it has had upon their own lives. The narrations are clearly presented under the influence of the situation. They might have been quite different had the same people related them outside the organisational context on another occasion. Similar in pattern, they are suitable for identifying the aims of the Young Buddhist Monasteries and organisations regarding the impact that they wish to have upon their followers. While they share common features, like having at their centre a single person, a master, highly-recognised, identified with and venerated by the followers, they consciously also propagate, under the slogan of a socially Engaged Buddhism, a change within the general perception of Buddhism.

12.2 Case B: Xu Wenhua–The Making of a Modern Buddhist Activist[131]

Xu: [1.1:35; directly starting after the initial question, how she came into contact with Buddhism; low voice, fast and relaxed] I am because my mum fell ill. Na, therefore, at that time, I/ I did not know, what to do. Because/ a/ it was always constantly my mum was ill. [...] At home, everything was done by my mum. [...] Therefore she/ she just hoped, that we'd learn/ study well. [...] The doctor of this hospital said:

131 This case was presented at the Chun Chiu Conference "Plurality & Representation" in Oregon, April 2008. For detailed, inspiring comments, I am indebted to Hung-Yok Ip, Ng Zhiru, and Charles Brewer Jones.

*No chance. Because "cancer", final. Na, if we are doing that. Na. Therefore [I/ we] at that time just did not know, what to do. […] I have a relative, my cousin. She accepted Buddhism earlier. Then she just/ But we lived in different places. Because we were in Taibei, she in Taizhong. Na, she especially brought her teacher from Taizhong, too. Her teacher is a lay [*zaijia ren *在家人] like us. She asked him. Then [they] came. Then [they] let my mum see him. Of course [he] said to us: "Recite some easy mantras. Then you can help her". Then he said as well: "I can also recite some mantras". La, a, right. Na, just because of that. But of course there was no chance. Just she knew this. Just she left this world. M. Then after she left, right at that moment, I was very sad. Na, but just because of my cousin. Na, I searched myself for some Buddhist books and read them. La. Then I just read this couple of Buddhist books. Then it helped me to overcome this bitter/ That matter. Therefore since that time it began. [inhales sharply; resumes in a slightly higher voice] Na, there is still one/ in Taiwan, in general, one says: After a human has left the world, within 49 days, if one can go [lit. eat] vegetarian, na, this is very helpful for the person, who left the world. Therefore I just, I just did it like that. Then I said to my father: Ok, I'll go [lit. eat] vegetarian for this time. When 49 days were over, then, I just said to my father [laughs]: I/ I don't want to eat mixed again, ok. I'll continue to eat vegetarian. Ok. This way. Then [I] began to come into contact with Buddhism. It was right like that. My mum fell ill. This is the story. [1.4:27]*[132]

Biographical Sketch

Xu Wenhua 徐雯華 (female, age about 40) was, like Ma Fengling, introduced to the interviewer in the context of a Young Buddhist Monastery, but not as its representative. She is a single, who lives in the Northern Region and works as an English teacher in a renowned high school. Simultaneously, she studies at a Buddhist college and was, at the time of the interview, writing up

132 Xu: [1.1:35; directly starting after a question, low voice, fast and relaxed] 我是因為我媽媽生病　那　所以我/　我那個時候不曉得怎麼辦　因為　阿　一直都是我媽媽生病[...]我們家裡我媽媽都是在作. […] 所以她/ 她就是希望我們好好讀書 [...] 那個醫院的醫生就是說 沒有辦法. 因為cancer 最後的. 那是不是我們做. 那. 所以那個時候 就不曉得怎麼辦.[...] 我有一個 親戚 我的表姊 她先接受得佛教. 然後 她就/ 可是我們住在不一樣的地方 因為我們在台北 她在台中 那她特別從台中把她的老師也帶來 她老師是一個跟我們一樣在家人 叫他 然後就來 然後 讓我媽媽 看到他 當然他會跟我們說 唸一些簡單的咒 然後可以幫助她 然後也說 我也可以唸一些咒 嚇阿 對 那就因為這樣子的關係 可是 當然沒有辦法 就她知道這件事情 她就是離開這個世界 m 然後 離開之後就是那個時候 心理很難過 那可是就是因為我表姊的關係 那我自己找一些佛教的書來看 嚇 然後 就是 看這些佛教的書 然後幫助度過那一段痛苦的 那一事情 所以從那個時候開始 [inhales sharply; resumes in a slightly higher voice] 那還有一個 在台灣一般會說　人過世之後　四十九天之內　如果能夠吃素的話　那對過世的人是很有幫助　所以我就是 就是這樣 然後跟我爸爸說 好, 我這一段時間吃素吧 然後四十九天到的時候 我就跟我爸爸說 [laughs] 我我不要再吃葷好 我繼續吃素 好了 這樣子 然後開始跟佛教的接觸 就是這樣子 我媽媽生病 故事這樣 [1.4:27]

her M.A. thesis. The interview was conducted in the library of the Buddhist college, out of earshot of anybody. Still, the library atmosphere led to her lowering her voice. Xu Wenhua speaks very fast, chats with ease, and constantly laughs during the interview. She shows habitual uncertainty and an urgent interest in presenting her partly tragic, non-standard biography as communicable and acceptable to the interviewer by initiating a quasi-intimate atmosphere.

With Xu, one witnesses an approach to Buddhism which permeates her whole self-definition. Due to the early death of her mother, she had experienced a traumatic childhood. In the context of coping with her bereavement, she learnt about Buddhism. Through name and mantra recitation, reading Buddhist books as well as becoming vegetarian, she tried adopting ritual, intellectual and daily life approaches towards Buddhism during her youth in order to cope with the gap left by her mother's death and her pain and questions about life arising from this context. At the end of her interview, when asked about her final motivation for becoming a Buddhist, she still recognises herself as being influenced by this childhood experience:

> [15.1:21] Interviewer: Why finally are you so interested in Buddhism? It seems, it is a very natural part of your life, but what is that final reason? [15.1:32; 10 seconds silence until 15.1:42]
> Xu: [very low voice] I don't want to have pain.
> Interviewer: M.
> Xu: Like that. Na, why is it Buddhism? Because/ Because when [sc. I/it] was most painful, Buddhism helped me. Very/ very easy it is just like this. [15.2:04]
> Interviewer: Thank you [both uncertain laughing; Interviewer thanks her for the interview, exchange of email addresses; end of interview; end of record: 15.3:59].[133]

In the narration, the painful, traumatic experience of her youth and her task of coping with it remain the formative topic for her throughout her life and determine the role that Buddhism plays within it. The ritual, intellectual, and daily life role of "Buddhism" permeates her self-perception and self-shaping: The ritual approach is primarily non-cognitive and matches her longing to do something "good" for her mother. Through reading "Buddhist books", she aims to develop a cognitive understanding of her situation by gaining intellectual independence, while also later in life, for all her Buddhist studies, remains central since they "have to do with her life" (In the context of her Mādhyamika studies: [7.1:04] *Zhiyao gen wo shenghuo you guan*

[133] [15.01:21] Interviewer: 你到底對佛教為甚麼是這麼那麼有興趣的 好像是很自然你生活的一部分 但是最後的那個原因是甚麼? [15.1:32; 10 seconds silence until 15.1:42] Xu: [very low voice] 我不想要有痛苦 Interviewer: ㄇ Xu: 這樣 那為甚麼會是佛教? 因為/ 因為最痛苦的時候 佛教幫了我 很/ 很簡單 就是這樣. [15.2:4] Interviewer: 謝謝你 [both uncertain laughing; Interviewer thanks her for the interview, the exchange of email addresses; end of interview; end of record: 15.3:59]

de wo hui hen kuaile 只要跟我生活有關的我會很快樂). Vegetarianism she experiences positively as fostering a positive attitude towards herself among others and serving as an identity marker which integrates Buddhism as an outward sign into her daily social life.

Besides the three layered approach to Buddhism in the initial passage of the interview, quoted at the beginning, it is interesting to note that Xu situates herself mentally in the Taiwanese context while developing referring, but still autonomous, concepts: She practises "of course" the mantras at her mother's deathbed, but does not anticipate the commonly assumed effect of actual healing. She follows the common practice of 49 days of vegetarianism, but finds her own way to continue it. She knows about her cultural Taiwanese background, but distances herself from it and reflects on it. In her later life, a gradual process can be seen, which continues this pattern of a balancing adaptation between the expectancies of her environment and her own interests.

A Biographical Development in Three Phases

Xu Wenhua shows a strong filial obligation towards her parents. Her mother's wishes she prolongs beyond her death, caring for her through recitations and carrying out her wish to study until late into adulthood. Only at the time of the interview, when asked about her plans for the future, does Xu state that she does not intend to change much, but is considering stopping studying. While, in her early childhood, Buddhism helped her to cope with the loss of her mother (Fig. 25), her interest in Buddhism brings her, later in life, into conflict with her father and society, who do not understand her desire to lead a monastic life (Fig. 26). Following her behavioural pattern of longing for situational harmony, she does not take sides in this confrontation, but finds a specific solution that fits her circumstances, putting her visions of a Buddhist life into practice while adapting herself to the role of a lay, as she feels obliged to do due to her father. This leads her to a self-definition as being actively involved as an intellectual lay Buddhist in society, with the aim of spreading Buddhism through translations of Buddhist texts as well as through teaching Buddhist English. She loses sight of the monastic order during this process (Fig. 27).

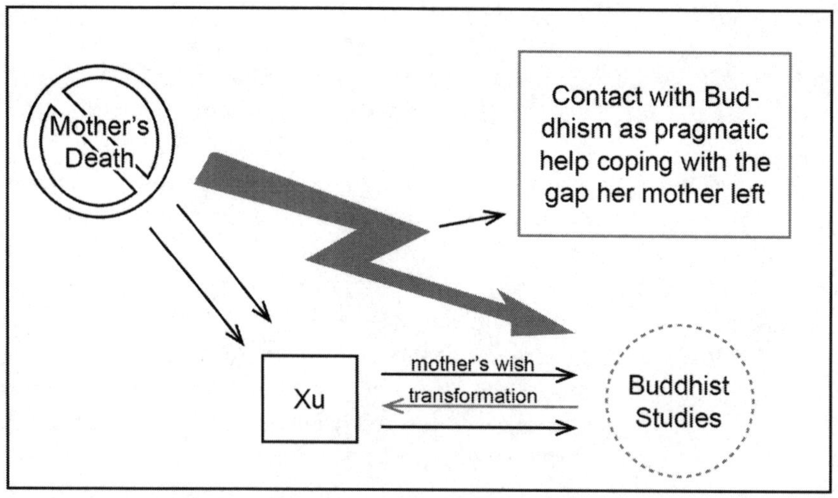

Figure 25: Buddhism's role in coping with life and pain.

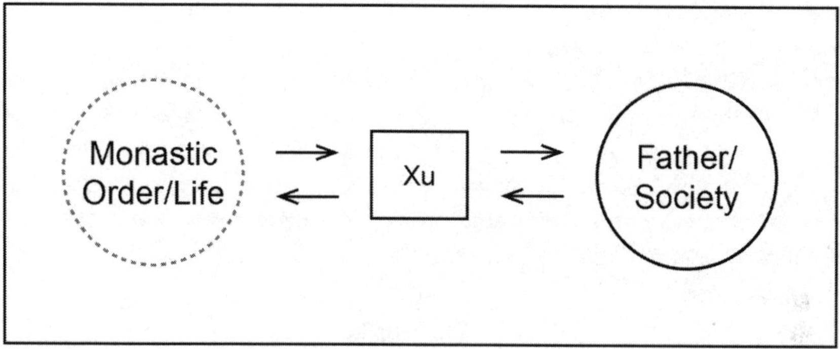

Figure 26: The challenge of the monastic order brings Xu Wenhua into conflict with society.

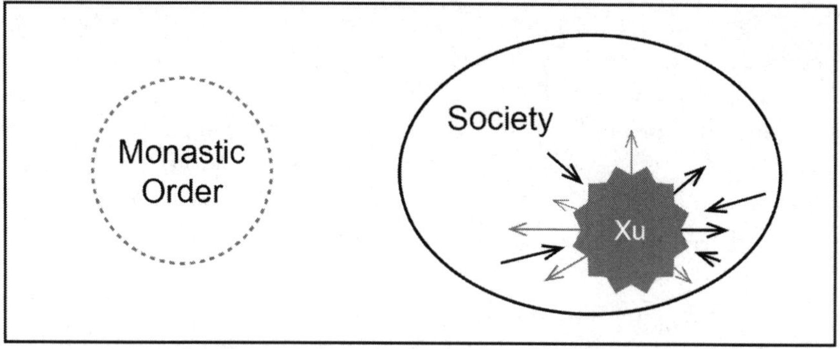

Figure 27: Interacting and spreading Buddhism as a lay Buddhist in society.

Analysing Xu Wenhua's narration, she constructs Buddhism as helping her to cope with her pain. This she elaborates through commonly-acknowledged patterns, stating the calming effect of Buddhist practice. She specifies this tranquillising function of Buddhism in connection with her current practices. The morning recitation, which she does whenever possible, "relaxes her mind" (*xinli bijiao qingsong* 心裡比較輕鬆; [7.3:38]). The statement is casual, non-specific, and nearly trivial. Spiritual practice serves a function for her, which is seen in the pragmatic light of the positive effect that one can experience (*tihui* 體會) in daily life–they calm one down. Neither a transcendent aim (reaching enlightenment, entering the Western Paradise, etc.) is mentioned throughout the interview, nor did philosophical recognition (the search for truth, life-concepts) play a role for her when choosing her activities. Practical experience and applicability stand central to the interviewee, as coping with the loss of her mother and her life situation remains her main aim.

Besides the prevalent tranquillising effect, a screen through the interview for the functions of Buddhism in the interviewee's life reveal four key expressions–"*jiuuuu*", "*gandong*", "*qiguai*", "*fahui*"–that open up the perspective on four additional semantic fields in which Buddhism plays a role in the life of Xu:

Xu Wenhua describes how at least every three of four weeks suddenly sentences out of a text she recites regularly arise and disperse upcoming emotional heat. This cooling down in distinct situations through suddenly upcoming sūtra sentences Xu onomatopoetically illustrates with a long sigh: a sentence arises and "jiuuuuu"–she would calm down:

> [9.2:12] For example, when eating and I encounter other people scolding me, suddenly a sentence out of this sūtra might jump out. Then it is just/ for example/ in case you scold me. Then I get excited. This sūtra comes up. Then just jiuuuu [she depicts a floating movement downwards with her right hand]. Just like this. Therefore, perhaps there lies the meaning, why I like to recite sūtras so much. [9.2:35][134]

During the recitation of sūtras, Xu mentions that she likes to imagine that "Buddha is talking to her" through the texts (*Wo hen xihuan shi juede fotuo haoxiang gen wo zai jianghua* 我很喜歡是覺得 佛陀好想跟我在講話). Her spirituality here includes a personal relationship, in which she feels directly addressed. The recitation is not perceived as her own action, but transforms into an action of the founder of the teaching himself. Linked to the effect of single sentences appearing in daily life, this hints at a general tenor in Xu's

134 [9.2:12] 譬如說 在吃飯 的時候 會碰到別人 罵我一句的時候 突然那個經裡面的句子可能會跑出來 然後 就是 譬如說 罵我 我就有火 那個經出來 我就 jiuuuu [she depicts a floating movement downwards with her right hand] 就這樣 所以我可能是 為甚麼喜歡念經的意思在這裡 [9.2:35]

life: she feels that she is guided and is gaining orientation in daily life through her Buddhist practice. The general tranquillising effect is to be seen also as a consequence of spiritual practice.

Another linguistic marker of a distinct function of Buddhism appears, when Xu refers to a sudden deep understanding of Buddhist doctrinal matters: even in her youth, Xu describes how, through reading "Buddhist books", she suddenly was very "touched" by them (*gandong* 感動). This is due to the lucid argumentation of the books; they answer her questions ("How to venerate correctly?", "Where is my mother now?"). This sense of being deeply touched she feels later in life when studying Buddhism and suddenly understanding that, in essence, it cannot be separated into schools or branches (*mei you paibie* 沒有派別), but that her longing to differentiate between Buddhist schools conceals the basic teachings of Buddhism. The verb "*gandong*" features in the interview, when Xu wants to express that she could suddenly connect Buddhist doctrine with her daily life. The content of this connection is based intellectually, but stays unspecified, as in the case of her childhood and seems less easy communicable than, for example, the effect of "calming down".

Besides the semantic patterns of "*jiuuu*" and "*gandong*", Xu from time to time implies the word "*qiguai* 奇怪" (strange) to mark incidences in her life, where she experienced something unexpectedly positive happening due to her Buddhist belief. By marking these incidences as "strange", she avoids describing herself as believing in miracles happening due to Buddhism, but leaves the possibility of such a phenomenon open, wondering with her conversation partner about the "strange" things happening when living the life of a Buddhist: she feels that it is "strange" and even "wonderful" (*qimiao* 奇妙) that, while reciting, sudden feelings arise (*ganjue chulai* 感覺出來). Besides her spiritual and intellectual experiences, she mentions that, unexpectedly, her vegetarianism marked her out as special and obviously also especially trustworthy. When it became known at her school, the father of one of her students offered her a room to stay in, which she interprets as the "strange" positive social effect of being a Buddhist. Xu does not regard the positive incidences that occur in daily life due to being a Buddhist in her narration–in contrast to Luo Peirong especially–as proof of her belief, but as an enjoyable side effect that she alludes to playfully and which interpretation might hint at a deeper dimension without claiming it openly.

Still, Xu's belief shows a dimension that is not directly related to her intellectual habitus and her chatty distancing from rationally less easily justifiable happenings: at almost the end of the interview, Xu mentions in passing that she participated in a recitation (*fahui* 法會) to improve her father's liver count. Also, at the beginning of her mother's illness, she explained that the recitation of mantras was expected naturally to assist with this, although the illness finally won. For her, there seems to be a direct influence of recitation upon the body of someone else, even if this person is not physically present during it. This issue seems to be self-evident and not a major aspect of her belief, as she does not expand on it. There is no conflict to be seen between her distinct intellectual standards and her belief in the power of rituals and recitations through distant healing. At the same time, Xu strongly opposes any "superstitious" veneration behavior, like other interviewees, which she recognises in her parents' generation and opts for the psychological effects of veneration instead:

> [14.0:00] One should not be that superstitious a. One should not/ this is just/ one should not say/ I go/ I go and pray (*bai*), then certainly it just becomes peaceful. A. [laughs] I in fact, think, praying will bring peace [which means] that it leads the heart to be peaceful; in reality, it is in the heart peaceful/ If it is really peaceful, this one should not say, that would be better. A. [14.0:25][135]

The Making of a Future Engaged Buddhist?

Xu Wenhua is undergoing a long personal development process, in which she is gaining a profound Buddhist education. She has, over the years, been coping with her personal situation through studying and practising Buddhism. Initially, she shows no interest in transmitting her knowledge to society. Only on becoming a teacher did she conceive the idea of improving her English with the aim of promoting Buddhism to foreigners, and so enrolled in an English graduate school:

> [4.0:09] But at this time, I was quite interested in Buddhism. Because I think it/ Buddhist things can help me to solve the biggest questions and problems in my life. Na. A. I would like to say, from childhood onwards, I studied such a lot. Why in/ ei/ Like that, it also couldn't help me. But Buddhism can. So I'm quite interested in Buddhism. Na, so later. I think Buddhism is so good. Like that introducing it to foreigners [laughs] Just, I only can [speak] English. But my English isn't very good. [4.0:55][136]

Her interest in Buddhism is based on her conviction that it has proven, in contrast to all of her other studies, a profound help in her life. As her con-

---

135 [14.0:00] 不要那麼迷信阿 不要 就是說 不要想說 我去/ 我去拜了 然後就一定會平安啦 [laughs] 我其實覺得 拜會平安 心會讓平安的 真的是在心裡平安的 外在會不會真的平安 其實不要講 就比較好一點阿 [14.0:25]

136 [4.0:09] 可是那個時候我是對佛教比較有興趣了 因為我覺得他/ 佛教的東西可以幫助我解決生活最大的問題跟困難 那 阿 我想說 我從小到大 我唸了那麼多書 為甚麼在/ 欸/ 這樣的話也沒有辦法幫我 可是佛教可以 所以對佛教比較有興趣的 那所以後來我覺得佛教這麼好 這麼給介紹給外國人 [laughs] 當我只會英文 可是我這個英文不太好 [4.0:55]

viction about Buddhism grows, Xu feels the need to pass on the essential knowledge she has gained. At the time of the interview, she was teaching Buddhist English at a university in Taipeh and has formulated her aim for her future development:

> [14.2:51] I think my current life now won't change very much. I'll follow my current life pattern. One is, that I might not continue a/ no/ I won't continue to study/ just to use/ independently if it is about Buddhism or not just deeply continuing to study, maybe not. Ei. I might more use the way of translation and go for Buddhist/ m otherwise, it is just the situation of Buddhism. Otherwise, just translate Buddhist sūtras/ Buddhist sūtras or Buddhism/ when quite good reasonable things were said. Right. I want to do more like this. Right. [14.3:35][137]

She was about to change her life by moving away from "studying" to translating Buddhist texts, sūtras as well as other Buddhist explanations in order to help to spread internationally what helped her essentially to master life.

Witnessing this development, one might see, through Xu's life phases, how a lay Buddhist engagement in the modern world takes shape step by step. Xu's engagement is a secondary consequence of her intense personal development.

She sought to distinguish herself from her social environment even during her youth, marking herself as a vegetarian. In narrating her eating behaviour, she adds casually: "I'm someone more strange[/unusual]" (*Wo shi bijiao qiyi de fenzi* 我是比較奇異的分子. [3.0:00]). She likes this distinction in general, although does not use it to mark herself out from others as outstanding, but prefers a harmonising solution: when directly asked whether she sees herself as a special Buddhist, she answers: "We're all special" [11.1:00]. Xu experiences herself as special and is self-confident about distinguishing which Buddhist knowledge interests her–it is only this knowledge that links to her own life. Buddhist doctrine, she is convinced, therefore should also be formulated in such a way that it is practically applicable and can serve as a general wisdom for life even beyond religious boundaries. Here, she provides an example of her Christian sister, who would teach her son in daily life a sentence that has been formulated into a catchphrase by a famous Buddhist contemporary abbot: "*Xuyao de bu duo–xiangyao de tai duo* 需要的不多–想要的太多"–"One doesn't need much–one wants too much". She comments on this, saying:

137 [14.2:51] 我想我目前的生活 現在不會改變太多 我去按照我目前這個生活型態 有一個是我可能不會 在繼續 阿/ 不是/ 我不會在繼續去唸 就是用/ 不管跟佛教有關還是沒有關 就深造繼續唸書可能不會 欸 我比佼可能 用翻譯的形式去佛教的/ ㄇ 要不然就是佛教現在的狀況 要不然就是把佛經的 佛經要不然就是佛教 有講過比較好的道理 做翻譯 對 我想做比佼這樣 對 [14.3:35]

> [13.2:45] Na, this sentence becomes a thing [which] a Christian/ he also can accept. Na, using this thing to educate his children. I think, like this, it's very good. I think, Buddhism is best like this. Making its things how one can know/ Someone not being a–It can also become part of his/ his habit. I think it's very good. [13.3:04][138]

Combining everything she has learnt about Buddhism with her own life experience enables Xu to distinguish between how she constructs Buddhism in her life. In the third part of the interview, which makes the interviewee an expert in the field, a higher level of reflection and consciousness about the individual's role within society is demanded. The interviewee here considers the questions at length and arrives at detailed answers partly by scientific arguments and partly by illustrating her thoughts, giving examples from her own life-experience. These reflections show that she has not only studied Buddhism, but also has a comparatively well-developed level of self-reflection. Buddhism serves for her the function of a personal search for meaning and an intellectual self-display becomes an integral part of her life-composition.

In addition to her habitus of intellectuality, Xu's views and practices are in constant flux, as she searches and explores various Buddhist approaches. For example, in the context of explaining her daily practice, she states that, currently, she would not include meditation practice in her morning recitation, but that she discovered meditation through her studies at the Buddhist college. Although unable to integrate it into her own current practice, she is curious about it and sees the potential for developing her own practice further: "But I think, after some time, it could also be that I change. It could also be that I change" (*Keshi wo juede guole yiduan shijian, keneng ye hui huan, keneng ye hui huan.* 可是我覺得過了一段時間 可能也會換 可能也會換 [10.4:30]).

When asked about the difference between monastics and lay people [6.0:00] and the future of Buddhism in Taiwan [14.4:40], Xu appears to see herself as being on a path towards living a quasi-monastic life in a secular environment: when asked how far the idiom, oft quoted by Engaged Buddhists, "going into the world" (*rushi* 入世) is to be understood, she states that, for her, entering the world (*rushi*) and withdrawing from it (*chushi* 出世) belong together. While therefore in a monastic existence, especially in Taiwan, one would be able to combine the two to a high degree of perfection, she still realises that profound Buddhist practice can today also be performed by lay people perfectly. As an example, she mentions being a teacher–which could be herself in future–who, married or unmarried, once

138 [13.2:45] 那這一句話 變成說 一個基督徒 他也可以接受的東西 那用這一個東西來教育他的孩子 我覺得這樣很好 我覺得佛教最好是這樣子 把它的東西怎麼樣能夠知道不是 佛教徒 它也可以變成他的/ 他的習慣 的一部分 我覺得很好 [13.3:04]

retired and no longer having to look after grown up children, would have lots of time for practice, while having an income.

Due to a tragic event in her childhood, Xu came into contact with Buddhism as a resource for helping her to cope with her pain. In her search for life orientation, she develops her understanding of Buddhism over the years profoundly, always linking it back to its applicability within her life. After years of studying, Xu combines her language skills with her Buddhist conviction into a mission in which she wants to spread internationally what has proven for herself to be Buddhist help to cope with life. Her concept of Buddhism comprises general wisdom for daily life, ritual elements, intellectual studies, recitations of long-distance healing effects upon relatives, and vegetarianism as an identity marker in social life. Although Xu does not become programmatic and does not invent her own agenda, she holds a different opinion on a wide range of Buddhist topics. As a translator, she selects texts which have proven helpful in her own life as worth spreading internationally. As a single female with an excellent education and sizeable income, Xu is able to imagine her life in the future consistently, recasting her traumatic childhood experience as a standard trigger for a Buddhist life and extensive studies into a coherent story-line. Through the case of Xu, one can witness the birth of a possible future lay Buddhist engaging in society. This might be relevant for a reflection on the characteristics of an Engaged Buddhism in Taiwan (see chap. 12.6).

12.3 Ma Fengling and Xu Wenhua in Contrast

Ma Fengling and Xu Wenhua both have a strong organisational affiliation to the Young Buddhist Monasteries. Their organisational affiliation is strikingly stronger than those of Luo Peirong or Li Zhiqiang. Luo abandoned her affiliation and drifted back into popular religion, Li Zhiqiang estimates his free contributions to the monastery at his convenience. In contrast, Ma Fengling spends her daily life within her organisation and Xu lives half of the week in the Buddhist college of the Young Buddhist Monastery, participating in its activities. As Specifying Buddhists, Ma Fengling and Xu Wenhua not only display a high degree of organisational affiliation, including voluntary work and probably even financial support, but also both follow a personal spiritual practice. "Buddhism" certainly gives their life a direction and Buddhism for Xu has, without doubt, a consoling function.

In concrete terms, Ma experiences Buddhism through a Buddhist social welfare organisation, while Xu is far less socially-engaged. During the interview, we see her Buddhist identity developing in a multi-layered process that leads her to an intellectually explainable Buddhist self-definition as being on a mission to spread the Buddhist doctrine to an English-speaking public internationally.

One can actually witness two diverging functions that Buddhism fulfils in the self-construction of both cases: Ma, on the one hand, is very explicit about the primarily pragmatic focus of her Buddhist belief. Buddhist teaching, as she formulates it and actively tries to live it, is connected with taking over the caring attitude of a bodhisattva in her own life, to serve sentient beings (*liyi zhongsheng* 利益眾生). The concept of Buddhism, she perceives, helps her to overcome the gap between herself and the tradition, to which she has to adapt. This takes place for her in two social fields–that of her family, where Buddhism helps her to re-organise her traditional life without questioning it as such, and also in society, where her organisation opens up a new horizon of action to her, within which she can apply her pragmatic abilities. For Xu, "Buddhism" has accompanied her through all the hardships of her life and transformed itself into a resource, until she was finally able to make her daily life a direct expression of her developed "Buddhist" belief. Primarily, Buddhism proves valuable to her, because she feels that it helps her to overcome her painful experiences. It tranquillises her mind, but also leads her to an intellectual understanding of life's purpose. Despite the functions which she recognises consciously on her own, one also witnesses in her narration that she believes that inexplicable positive changes have happened in her life through "Buddhism"–all of a sudden or induced through rituals. Looking at her habitus during the interview, presenting herself as a "Buddhist" also serves the aim of an intellectual self-representation.

While the interviewees apply "Buddhism" differently in their lives, they share in common the recognition of a gap between their own understanding of "Buddhism" and that of their parents' generation. They both define their belief by distancing themselves from their personally experienced history and establishing their own belief through constant contrasts. This indicates a change in the social perception of Buddhism in Taiwan. The commonality with which the interviewees employ their argument hints at a common narrative: both of the interviewees describe a belief in the previous generation as a mechanistic request for spiritual succour (*qiqiu* 祈求). They mark this approach as an "outer" one, contrasting it with their "inner-worldly" or "personal" way of living as Buddhists.

For Ma, distancing herself from her parents' generation leads to active engagement, to concrete social actions. She expresses this by applying the slogan of her organisation to replace the traditional, "This is, what I heard" (*Ru shi wo wen* 如是我聞), a common opening for sūtras, with the action-demanding formulation, "This is, how I act" (*Ru shi wo xing* 如是我行). This prevents mechanised devotion and the parasitic attitude of self-preservation with which Buddhism was, according to her personal impression, connected previously. Her new attitude includes also the questioning of the primacy of the monastics. For Xu, the turn seems more an internalisation of her request for peace. Obtaining inner tranquillity, she claims, is the aim of spiritual practice, not the outer effects that mechanistic belief is asking for, as veneration does not lead to outer peace but tranquillises the mind.

Ma has few educational, financial, and social resources for undertaking a long process of identity search on her own. The organisation she engages with delivers an acceptable concept to her, which she can fully identify with, and which reshapes her social life, and legitimises her social activities through "Buddhism"–a religious background of socially highly-recognised authority. As a consequence, she has become enormously active within the framework of her own organisation, without initiating any further movements on her own. Ma is in search less of identity development than the "right group", which takes over the task of self-positioning for her in a way that she can accept intuitively. German biographical social research would call the pattern underlying this behaviour a "stellvertretendes Lebensdeutungsmuster" ("pattern of substitutive life interpretation"): her organisation provides her with a role and interpretation pattern to which she adapts herself.

Xu's non-standard biographical identity development confronts the researcher with a processual approach to Buddhism that might be described, within the context of recent identity conceptualisations, as a "lifelong process of aesthetic and symbolic self-positioning" (Eickelpasch). Her narration about the psychological internalisation of Buddhist belief can be interpreted, on the one hand, as her personal fate-management while, on the other–as she, in a personal, eclectic way, employs educational, economic and social means and facilities that have become accessible to the middle classes only recently–it might be seen as a more self-healing and inward-looking response to modernity. The popularity of a Buddhism that serves the needs of the urban generation might be plausible in this context.

Xu's concept of Buddhism is closely linked to her own biographical development but, in coping with her personal problems, she finally reformulates her understanding of Buddhism as a message to the international Buddhist world. Once Xu had made her personal search, she seems, apart from the paths of any organisation, to get a *new distributor and diffuser* of Buddhist belief. Wei-Hsian Chi analysed the contemporary social change in the religious sphere of Taiwan as being due to the increasing involvement of lay people in active roles as decision makers (see Chi 2005): former "consumers" become "producers". In this respect, Xu defines her Buddhist agenda "productively" by herself, while Ma experiences a deep change and becomes in her daily life very "productive", but remains a "consumer" in the sense of adopting her organisation's rhetoric and programmes.

Social Engagement and Transnational Agents

As pointed out earlier, both interviewees hold, in their either more consuming or producing ways, a concept of themselves as not only Taiwanese or Chinese, but also with respect to a global horizon ("Welthorizont", Ulrich Beck).

Ma Fengling corresponds, through her social engagement, with one of the main characteristics that are communicated internationally under the label "(Socially) Engaged Buddhism" or, within Taiwan, propagated through the Chinese pendant "*renjian fojiao* 人間佛教". Without doubt, the current Buddhist agenda in Taiwan is focused on charitable work. Almost every Buddhist organisation supports a variety of social or environmental activities and runs its own kindergartens, orphanages, schools, universities, nursing homes and hospitals. In fact, Buddhists contribute significantly through their activities to Taiwan's social welfare system. This phenomenon has its roots in the early days of the Buddhist modernist movement: "Social engagement" and engagement in "worldly affairs" have already been described by Heinz Bechert as the main changes in Sri Lankan Buddhism around 1900–a phenomenon that he calls "Protestant Buddhism", as the movement was imitating the missionary efforts and characteristics, while protesting against these, with the aim of creating an indigenous movement that was equivalent to the Christian organisations (see also chap. 1).

Social engagement and the involvement of lay people have certainly contributed to the generally changed notion of Buddhism in Taiwan today. The biographical narration of Ma Fengling shows how such an agenda finds her appraisal by identifying fully with it. While the social dimension of contemporary Buddhism might not be the only rhetoric of the Engaged Buddhist institutions, cases like Ma prove that it greatly enhances the attractiveness of Buddhism in Taiwan. Ma Fengling is enabled literally to travel abroad (to Sri Lanka) with her organisation while continuing to act in the enlarged frame of the traditional role of motherhood. Xu Wenhua develops an agenda that intends to foster an interchange between international Buddhism and Buddhism in Taiwan through her Buddhist English-Chinese translational skills. Xu is absorbed by the question of how to overcome her pain and make sense of her situation. Living in the Northern Region, she is exposed to an internationally influenced society. Decisive for Xu in defining herself as a "Buddhist" is the promising outlook that it might deliver a consistent belief compatible with the "modern", transculturally valid, urban life. Her gradually emerging doctrinal set not only delivers her orientation, but she even experiences it as a motivating force which enables her to construct her own life agenda in coherence with the organisational limits, but also in accordance with her own interests and knowledge.[139]

Social engagement via Buddhist communities can be important for Buddhists, as in the case of Ma. *De facto*, the task of social welfare is a generic part of nearly every Buddhist contemporary institution in Taiwan. The case of Xu shows how social engagement is not the driving force for all lay people to commit themselves to Buddhism, but that a premise for flourishing urban religious groups might be their response to the transnational milieu of their participants, so that these can use the offers creatively for their own longing to build up a consistent definition of their individual role within society. "Buddhism", in that case, is attractive, as it gives dynamic space to the negotiation of rivalling resources. In an increasingly transnational context, a "Buddhist" self-construction can contribute to subjective well-being, ensuring social or ideological cohesion, and can be experienced by the believer as a tool for successful self-imagining. Xu–educated, and defining herself within an urban and transnational milieu–finally becomes involved with a Buddhist organisation, because it serves as a vehicle for overcoming her life's pain, while simultaneously realising her own dreams and concepts, under the label of engaging in the "spread of Buddhism".

12.4 Case C: Zhang Yimin–Cultural Buddhist and Family Father

*Zhang: [14.2:29; regarding the question of whether Buddhism has changed over the last hundred years in Taiwan] I think it nevertheless has. So I think that that essence (*benzhi 本質*) which it has has not changed la. But the style of appearance has changed. Right a. So I think, you see, in the* Diamond Sūtra *it is said/ So before the Buddhist patriarchs it was said: "All conditioned dharmas are like a dream, an illusion, a bubble, a shadow". Isn't it written like that in the sūtras. So conditioned dharmas means that it has a style, times will change. So now one talks about the Buddha's dharma. But one talks about the Buddha's dharma/ lots of Buddhist books, but one will not use classical texts from ancient times. It will change now into a different language to be expressed. One uses average modern Chinese, or examples, or/ In fact, many Americans write about this Buddha's dharma. Buddhist books they write very well. [laughs] Because they are very easy to read and understand. A method of being very adapted to life. Na, this China has also the Chan [i.e. Zen] school. Na, when it comes to the West, it is still the same. The method through which it gets expressed is not the same. […] I think when Americans write Buddhist books, they still more/ still quite more "touch" that essence. Because, as I just said, these Chinese/ Interviewer:*

139 The implications of Buddhism as a vehicle of internationalisation upon the attractiveness of denoting oneself a Buddhist have been outlined in Guggenmos (2014).

Although originally it is Chinese Buddhism. Zhang: Right. Chinese truth because it too much sticks to the single characters/ or sometimes sticks too much to discussing cause and effects. That/ That/ Whatever godly power/ These gods and Buddhas/ that/ right a. Na, I say, when Westerners explain these things, they are a bit quite more adapted to life. Sometimes they will tell it more quickly. [14.4:34][140]

Biographical Sketch

Zhang Yimin 張奕民 (male, age about 40) is married and having two young children. He works during the week as a computer hardware salesman in the capital, returning home to Kaohsiung at weekends. He gives the impression of being a dynamic, open-minded man. On a walk with his family in the mountains, the interviewer learnt that Zhang was enthusiastic about certain Buddhist publications and appeared closely-acquainted with Chan Buddhist vocabulary. Asked for an interview, he spontaneously agreed. The interview took place in his living room, with his children and wife coming in from time to time. The family atmosphere is certainly present, but in general the interview takes place out of earshot of others. Zhang does not seem disturbed by his environment, and the interview situation is relaxed.

From the very beginning of the interview, Zhang describes his encounter with Buddhism as an intellectual journey, starting in his youth. During his childhood, he grew up with Chan Buddhist stories at home, like that of Bodhidharma (approx. 440–528)–coming to China and telling, when asked, to Emperor Liang Wudi that temple constructions do not bring merit–or the well-known story of two monks helping a young woman to cross a river.[141] While he did not read these stories to gain analytical insights, he still estimated them as containing some "life philosophy" (*rensheng de zhili* 人生的哲理). His second memory of Buddhism marks it as something that "Chinese intellectuals can accept" (*zhongguo de zhishi fenzi [nenggou] jieshou* 中國的知識份子[能夠]接受). Following his high school teacher, he understands the Song dynasty poet Sushi

140 Zhang: [14.2:29] 我覺得還是有. 所以我覺得說 那有 本質沒變啦 但是表現的型式有變 對阿 所以我覺得說 你看 金剛經 裡面它說/ 所以佛祖之前有講 一切有為法 如夢幻泡影 它不是經文這樣寫. 所以有為法是說既有一個型式 時代會改變 所以現在講 佛法 但是講佛法/ 很多佛法的書 但是不會用古老經文 他現在會轉換不同的語言來表示 用白話 或是 用例子 或是 其實上很多美國人寫到那個佛法 佛教的書寫得很好 [laughs] 因為他們有很淺顯 很生活化 的方式 那這個在中國也有禪宗 那到西方還是一樣 他現在表達的方式不一樣 [...] 我覺得美國人寫得 佛教的書 還比較/ 還比較更 touch 到那個本質. 因為就是我講中國的/ Interviewer: 雖然本來是中國佛教 Zhang: 對 中國真理因太拘泥文字/ 或是有時候太拘泥因果論 那個/ 那個/ 甚麼神力/ 那個神佛/ 那個/ 對阿 那我說西方人 在解釋 這一些東西方面 有一點 比較 更生活化一點 有時候 他們會走先講出去 [14.4:34]

141 The first story is explained in McRae 2003, 22. The second goes back to a famous autobiographical record of the Sōtō Buddhist monk, Hara Tanzan 原坦山 (1819-1892), see Reps 1958, 33-34.

蘇軾 (1037–1101) as someone who developed his thought through fictitious dialogues with Buddha. For Zhang, it is important to note that Buddhism is "not only a religious thing" (*bu zhi shi zongjiao de dongxi* 不只是宗教的東西), but has a philosophical character. This definition of Buddhism he later enlarges on several times. In his intellectual screening through his life, he remembers next coming into contact with works by the Indian spiritual leader, known as "Osho" (Chandra Mohan Jain; 1931–1990), from which he recalls having learnt the wisdom that the world will not change because of oneself, but change in the world only happens when one's own heart changes (*Shijie bu hui yin ni er gaibian, hui yin ni de xin de gaibian er gaibian* 世界不會因你而改變會因你的心的改變而改變, [3.02:44]). Later in his life, the *Platform Sūtra of the Sixth Patriarch* (*Liuzu tan jing* 六祖壇經) and the *Diamond Sūtra* play a role. With ease Zhang paraphrases during his narration classical Zen masters: "Fundamentally there is not a single thing–Where could any dust be attracted?" (*Benlai wu yi wu. He chu re chen'ai.* 本來無一物 何處惹塵埃, see for example Taishō vol.48, no. 2008, p.349a8). Still, only after he read "The Diamond Cutter" (Roach 2000) in Chinese does he report gaining a deeper understanding of "nothingness" and "emptiness" (*wu* 無; *kong* 空). The explanations of the *Diamond Sūtra* by an American teacher who is trained in Tibetan Buddhism he finds easier to understand. Enlarging on the non-self (*wuwo* 無我) and impermanence (*wuchang* 無常), Zhang is able to display plastically the idea of impermanence as misinterpreted especially by the traditional Chinese argumentation patterns in a pessimistic way, leading to flee society, and corrects this view: impermanence would involve expressing an awareness of the impermanent and preliminary nature of reality. The appearance (*xianxiang* 現象) and real nature of things have to be separated from each other. Also, the principle of the non-self he is able to interpret through his new readings as leading to objectivity and discouraging people from clinging to their own views as well as leading to a compassionate view of others.

Reference to Daily Life

By enlarging fluently on doctrinal topics, interpreting Buddhist topoi, quoting from Buddhist sūtras, exactly remembering titles, and naturally applying and integrating Buddhist vocabulary, Zhang Yimin reveals himself to be an intellectual, to whom Buddhist doctrine is an integral part of his thinking, while he in general structures his narration well and displays international awareness, using Japanese sayings and mixing English expressions into his explanations. Reading American publications on Buddhism and comics on Buddhist doctrine (*Heart Sūtra*), he is open to change, including new sources of knowledge. The intellectual approach stays prevalent for him, but his narration wins its dynamic through his constant reference frame to his own life experience. The style of a biographical interview corresponds with this understanding that intellectuality and Buddhist knowledge have to prove in life.

Remembering his early youth, Zhang Yimin states that, when he read Chan Buddhist stories, he did not connect them to any deeper reflection. Still, he feels that their philosophical wisdom lead him to ask about the purpose and meaning of life (*rensheng de mudi* 人生的目的; *rensheng de yiyi* 人生的意義, [3.0:00]). Still, these questions and the reading of Buddhist texts, he admits, did not bear fruit until he read the American Buddhist's publication, and he also needed life experience (*rensheng de lilian, suiyue de cengchang* 人生的歷練 歲月的增長, [3.3:20]). Through Zhang's life shaping decisions, one can see this balance between intellectual claims and private life. Buddhism, as Zhang explains, is for him the path to happiness (*likudele* 離苦得樂). His ideals are centred on his family life. Caring for his wife and children, his work serves the purpose of earning money and is intended to secure subsistence, while the well-being of his family and the quality time spent with them are central. Together with his wife, he shares an interest in a spiritual search and the intellectual habitus of both leads to mutual enrichment, which even can be seen during the interview when Zhang recommends a book that his wife has read. Buddhism in this context of a spiritual search serves as a tool for mind control and helps to achieve a stable heart ("[14.0:13] A peaceful heart. Or just don't pay attention to how the world outside is. Then you can maintain that state of the heart." 心靈平靜 還是不管外在的環境怎麼樣 你就可以保持 那一種心境). Although this change of mind and behaviour is seen as difficult, Zhang states that it leads to happiness:

> [15.3:40] You're not allowed to stop at the level of thought. You have to change your behaviour. Na, that is very difficult. For example: Somebody scolds you. You will get angry. But Buddhism says: A. You can control your thoughts. At that moment, when you are getting angry, you don't get angry. Na, you still can change your thought. Na, that is just very difficult. So talking about spiritual growth, that point is very, very difficult. That is not: A. You are today understanding knowledge. A. So it/ Why does Buddhism/ So it/ So Buddhism tells you not to stick to the letter. Na. Not to stick to the letter. That is a bit like going into the fire spellbound. But one can say/ But you can–not sticking to the letter– say: He believes in a high realm, means: It is your behaviour, not your language. Many people can by language talk about this realm. But they can't do it. But the Buddhist realm says: […, slurred] One can reach this realm. What is this realm? It is just/ You can/ Your insufficient self can leave bitterness and reach happiness. You can liberate the sentient beings to leave bitterness and reach happiness. [16.0:18][142]

142 [15.3:40] 你不能停在思想的層次 你要改變到你的行為 那這樣就很難 譬如說 有人罵你 你會生氣 可是佛教講說 阿 你可以控制你的思想 在你快生氣的那一段 你就 不會 生氣 那還可以轉換你的想法 那這個就很難 所以講的是心靈的成長 那這一點是非常非常不容易 這個不是說 阿 你今天是個知識上理解 阿 所以他 佛教為甚麼 所以他 所以佛法他講不立文字 那 不立 文字 是有一點 走火入魔 可是會講說 可是你可以不

Although Zhang favours an intellectual approach, already in the previous quotation it became obvious that the "change of mind" requests a "change in behaviour" which is not easy to fulfil. It fits into this context that Zhang seems to nourish a longing to meditate. Experiences of bodily practices he traces back to his youth. When asked about his upbringing, he remembers his father meditating and gaining a state of tranquillity, which would "let you hear your inner voice". Zhang recognises the tranquillising effect of his father's meditation, but also stresses that his father tried meditation by himself without any professional instruction to overcome his illness. The bodily help Zhang acknowledged, but puts Buddhism above it on a spiritual level (*xinling de cengci* 心靈的層次). Zhang shows a longing to start meditation–possibly seeing himself as following his father, but professionalising his approach–and even asks the interviewer for advice in search of a good monastery to practise meditation on a course.

Zhang feels attracted to monastic life, but stresses that meditation practice would be only a process, not the aim. A "real monk" would lead others towards a "change of their mind", to a realisation that would have an influence upon their language conduct, their behaviour, and their speech (*yanxing* 言行, *xingwei* 行為). Liberating living beings (*pudu zhongsheng* 普渡眾生) would be the aim of the monastic life. Monks he sees as the traditional Chinese pendant of the Western priest or psychologist.

A Definition of Buddhism

The change of mind implies realising that there is nothing such as losing (*shibai* 失敗) or being successful (*chenggong* 成功) in life. Buddhism is therefore in Zhang Yimin's eyes a tool for changing one's life. As he recognised in his youth, Buddhism stays for him closely connected to a standard of being able to prove itself and to be able to bear serious consideration. Buddhist thinking implies a reflection of the method (*fangfa* 方法) itself. It would not give an answer, but one would have to prove one's own way and penetrate one's thoughts (see also above, [3.1:00]). In that sense, he does not understand Buddhism as "religious" and throughout the interview distances himself from the term "religion" when talking about "real Buddhism" or its "essence" (*benzhi*). Buddhism does not exist in any shape, but anything that would enable people to leave bitterness and attain happiness would be Buddhism:

立文字檔說 他認為很高的境界就在說 是你的行為 不是你的言語 很多人言語講到那個境界 但是作不到 但是佛教的境界說 [..., slurred] 可以到那個境界 那他境界就是甚麼就是 你可以 可以不只自己 可以離苦得樂 你可以渡化眾生 離苦得樂 [16.0:18]

> [7.0:45] Because I think the main point is how you apply these things a. Just like you say what influence it has upon your life. [sc. That, I] am more interested in. [laughs] Just does it really influence your life, whatever, heart. So I/ I think, in fact, if one looks at it like that, it does not necessarily have to be Buddhism. For example, a book or a thought or an exchange by all who are interested in this topic, I'm interested in them all. Just like I recently saw a book belonging to my wife [...] Talking about real Buddhism, in fact, it really has to do some things. So, including Taiwanese people saying that also, a. Buddhism at whatever stage, it has less of a religious character. If one looks at it from this angle, for example, because for example: Christians say, some of their teaching can also control, it also helps to leave bitterness and attain happiness. Na, like this, it's all the same. If everybody's aim is the same, it is good. Independently, if you are Muslim, Christian, just if you enable people to leave bitterness and attain happiness, that is all, that is all Buddhism. A. Right. So Buddhism is not an existence in a certain shape. [8.0:00][143]

Throughout the interview, Zhang is trying to relate to the identification pattern of "Buddhism". As his interests lie in a practically applicable life wisdom, he either therefore defines Buddhism as a concept that is not bound to any concrete religious doctrinal and practical content–called "real" Buddhism–or is uncertain whether to consider himself a Buddhist. Still, while doubting that he is a Buddhist compared with other imagined Buddhists, he dialectically questions their counting themselves Buddhists according to his understanding of Buddhism as a way of investigating the meaning of life leading to happiness:

> [10.0:00] Looking at myself: I basically do not count myself as a Buddhist. I am interested in Buddhism. So I do not go to venerate. I do not go especially. But I think/ But I think: The Buddhists of today are exactly also not certainly understanding the Buddha's dharma.[144]

143 [7.0:45] 因為我覺得重點是在於你怎麼在運用這些東西阿 就像你講他對你的生活帶來甚麼樣的影響 比較有興趣 [laughs] 就是說他會不會真的去影響你的生活甚麼心 所以我 我覺得說 其實作這樣來看也不一定要是佛法 假如一本書或者一種想法 或者一種大家的交流 是對於這一種議題有 有接近 我都會有興趣 就像我最近看我老婆的一本書那個甚麼 [...] 真正的佛教來講 其實他是真正的要做一些事情 所以 包括台灣人也講阿 佛教某一程度 他比較沒有宗教色彩 以這一種角度來看 譬如說 因為譬如說基督教來講 他一些教義他可控制 他也離苦得樂 那這樣都是一樣 大家目的一樣就好了不管你是回教阿 基督教 只有你是勸人 離苦得樂 那都是 這一些都是佛法 阿 對不對所以佛法不是某莫一種形式 的存在 [8.0:00]

144 [10.0:00] 對我來看 我根本不算是一個佛教徒 對佛法有興趣 所以我不會去拜拜我不會去特別 可是我覺得說 但是我覺得說 現在的佛教徒剛好也不一定了解佛法

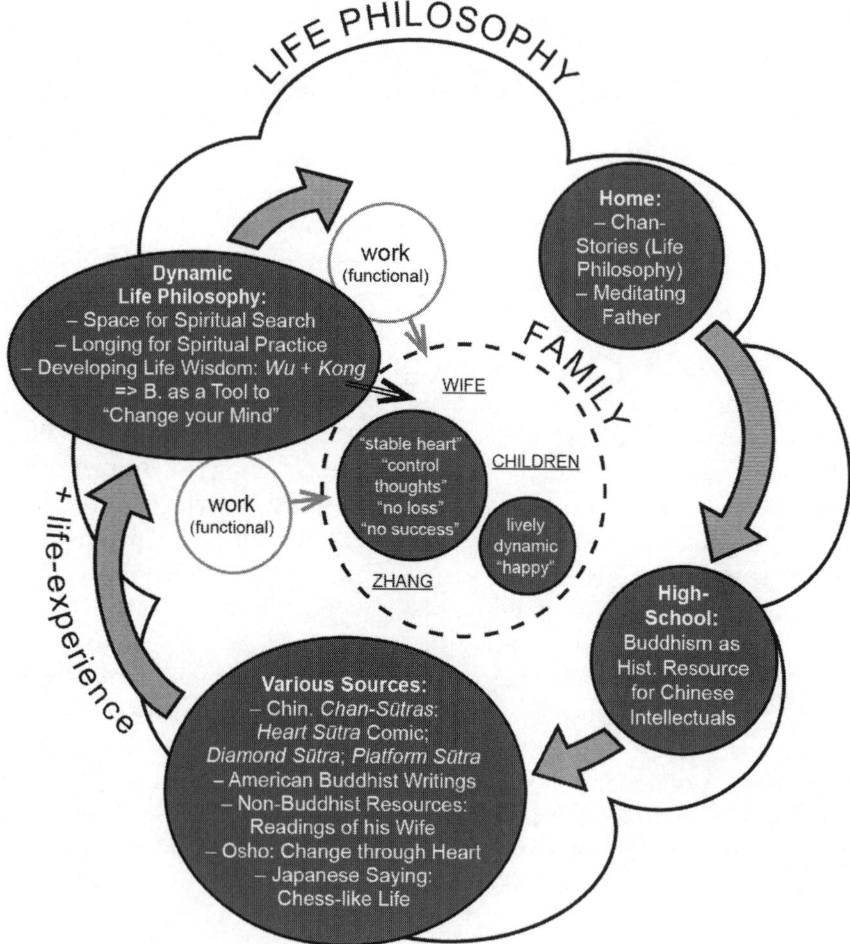

Figure 28: Zhang Yimin–Buddhism as a cultural resource to "change one's mind".

Conclusion

Summing up, Zhang Yimin is a Buddhist neither in consequence of a personal tragedy nor does he need a hobby, but Buddhist-influenced thinking is an integral part of his world view and life shape. Zhang adopts a processual definition of Buddhism that is characterised by a pragmatic, open, positive-minded and dynamic approach. He cultivates his independent intellectuality that stands in direct relation to his daily life on the one hand, but can be formulated without problem on the other. Zhang communicates the basic principles of his life guidance with the help of Buddhist doctrinal patterns with ease and does not show any desire to create a representative story. Self-confidently, he approaches new resources with curiosity. His intellectuality is based proudly on the roots of

Chinese intellectualism stretching back over centuries–like through the reference to the poet Su Shi–but does not show connections to a conservative traditionality. Even American Buddhist resources he accesses as a valuable, refreshing way of expressing Chinese Buddhist ideas. Zhang is mainly acquainted with the Chan Buddhist tradition, but cultivates a discovering spirit.

Although a diachron reading of the case of Zhang could bring to light further interesting differentiations of this case, for the purpose of outlining the width of the field of intense Buddhist believers and practitioners, Zhang's case hints at the existing possibility of defining oneself as a "cultural Buddhist"–a Buddhist, who is inspired by Buddhist ideas and practices, but not limited to it nor organisationally bound. His habitus reveals a smooth compatibility with contemporary urban family life in Taiwan while maintaining an awareness of ongoing Chinese tradition of Buddhist inspired intellectualism. Chan Buddhist doctrine as well as bodily practices are seen by Zhang as a concept of delivering a habitus and a method of developing life concepts and conduct, leading to satisfaction. These concepts are, in the case of Zhang, perceived via his family tradition and education and have been enriched in the course of his life through the reading of Buddhist publications. It helps our understanding of the demarcations of the Buddhist field to note that Zhang does not follow any organisationally bound practice nor commit to certain rituals. His longing for practice and self-cultivation does not exclude training in the context of a Buddhist organisation or monastery, but his belief is certainly not centred around any institutional belief. Zhang, in contrast, independently develops his belief in addition to a more narrow concept of religion as a life wisdom, which is in its method and intentions inspired by Buddhism, but in its concrete shape determined by cultural and interreligious openness.

12.5 Case D: Meng Fanyi–Elite Aestheticisation and Life Design

Meng: [6.3:20] In fact, it's very difficult to describe through language ei. You'll just feel very hm very natural. There [i.e. in the Buddhist group she attends], these people, you know, are all the same like you, diligent, are all practising, are all/ are constantly examining themselves. Then, everybody has similar correct views. I think, there it is very natural. A. I don't feel restricted. Also, one also doesn't need to say a lot, because this is common knowledge. Really that kind of/ How does one call that/ hm How does one call that/ Buddha "twists the flower and smiles". That kind of/ That kind of feeling that "heart spreads to heart". Because everybody has experienced together so many things, heard so many classes of the teacher, then participated in so many of these processes of spreading the teaching. I think these all are/ How to say/ They already became a tacit understanding. When everybody is connected to each other, there will be some other kind of different/ I think, it is a very comfortable method, one does not have to think ex-

tra about anything. O. If one follows somebody, how shall one connect with each other/ I have to pay attention to whatever language behaviour/ what I want to say. When you meet normal people outside, you just have to think: A, how tired! Being together with these people, is really, I think/ everybody is just/ just very open/ very/ very/ I cannot say very pure, but everybody knows, one has to examine oneself, so for me it is a more natural environment [7.0:20].[145]

Biographical Sketch

Meng Fanyi 孟凡依 (female, nearly 40) is at the time of the interview married, and caring for her young child. She is committed to a small, recently-established Buddhist lay organisation, participating in its offers, attending its lessons and visiting its temple on a weekly basis. She has been participating in the group for about ten years and the teachings and practices of the group have become second nature to her. On the one hand, she makes a very spontaneous, dynamic impression, welcoming the interviewer and introducing her to the community. On the other hand, Meng seems to care about all aspects of her environment. The interview at her home was perfectly arranged: an elderly woman was looking after the child, and in her flat–quietly situated in the mountains near the capital–she awaited the interviewer with light music, incense, tea and nibbles. Her Chinese is not mixed with Taiwanese and she speaks quickly, describing situations in a broad vocabulary and applying with ease the doctrines of her organisation.

Meng's awareness and informedness is backed by her education. Born into an intellectual family, with her father's family being mainland Chinese, Meng experienced in her childhood her parents' critical attitude towards any kind of "religious" behaviour, including "Buddhism" and "popular religion". In her home, there was no "veneration" (*baibai*) or ancestor tablets. Her mother thought of Buddhism as a form of superstitious popular religion. Her father also did not value Buddhism, but followed the principle of "becoming a good human" (*zuo haoren* 做好人), for which one would not need to learn Buddhism:

---

145 Meng: [6.3:20] 其實很難用語言描述欸 就是你會覺得非常的 hm 非常的自在 在那邊這一些人 你知道 都是跟你 一樣在努力 都是在修行 都是在 在不斷的自我實踐 然後大家有相同正確的觀念 我覺得在那邊很自在 阿 不會覺得有隔閡 也 很多話 也不需要講 因為這是有共識 真的那一種 那叫甚麼 hm 那叫甚麼 佛陀捻花微笑 那一種 心傳心的那一種感覺 因為大家一起都經歷過這麼多事情 聽過這麼多導師的上課 然後參與過這麼多的 這個弘法的過程 我覺得這一些都是 怎麼說 已經便成了一個默契了 大家在一起相處的時候 就會另外一種不同的 我覺得很舒服的方式 不需要去特別考慮到 哦 跟著一個人要怎麼相處 我要注意甚麼言行 要說甚麼話 你在外面碰到一般的人 就必須覺得 阿 好累 跟這一些人在一起 真的就是我覺得 大家 就就 很開放 很 很 我不能說很純淨 但是 大家都知道 要 自我反省 所以對我來說 是比較自在的一個環境 [7.0:20]

> [4.0:00; ... approx.: Because my family considered religion unnecessary] Because it was like that, I thought "Why would one need to believe? My father can also become a human [*zuo ren* 做人]". Whatever they said, I also said. a. For him, going to learn Buddhism was just like encouraging people to be good. A. Just wanting to do good things. A good heart has good rewards. A. For him, this was becoming a human, a correct view. A. How to become a human, he thought, this he all knows. A. For that, one does not need to go and learn Buddhism. For them, it was like that.[146]

Her parents considered themselves intellectuals (*zhishi fenzi* 知識份子). This intellectual approach Meng continued in her studies at university by enrolling in Eastern philosophy. Later in her biographical narration, she stresses the sensitivity of Chinese people about controlling one's body with the help of *qi* 氣, energy. Now, when she goes to France or Germany, she witnesses people using their "force/power" (*li* 力) more than harmonising their energies. Her contact with religious organisations date back to her attending a Catholic high school. Especially at university, she came into close contact with Catholic nuns and priests, who helped her with her essential problems (confusion about life, *shengming de kunhuo* 生命的困惑). Through this encounter, she remembers that questions about the meaning and power (*yiyi* 意義, *liliang* 力量) of religion gained importance for her. Still, she never entered the church. Only when she changed university and encountered a Buddhist monk from Sri Lanka, who frequently had deep conversations with her in very simple English, did she get a feeling for the direction in life that she would have to pursue (*shengming de yige fangxiang, wo bixu yao qu zhuiqiu de* 生命的一個方向 我必須要去追求的 [2.2:00]). She was unable to connect with common Buddhist monastics, as she perceived and continues to perceive monastic life as unrelated to her own (*lingwai de yizhong shenghuo* 另外的一種生活 [2.2:30]). When the monk left after a year, she was alone and at the same time interested in practicing *qi*, searching for a course in *Qigong* 氣功. At that time, some friends introduced her to her present community, which unites bodily practices employing the concept of *qi* and Buddhist teachings. She attended weekly classes until her teacher wanted her to stop–an event that puzzles her even today–and afterwards went to France to study design. Overseas, she re-discovered her cultural roots anew, practising calligraphy, painting, classical Chinese music and meditation and feeling "very Eastern" (*ba ziji gao de hen dongfang de ganjue* 把 自己搞的很東方的感覺 [3.4:45]). Back in Taiwan, she rejoined her community, participating in classes from the beginning, and has reached a high level of class by the time of the interview. Her life rhythm is dynamic, with frequent stays abroad and,

[146] Meng: [4.0:00; ...] 因為這樣我一直覺得 為甚麼需要去信仰 我爸爸也會作人 他們講甚麼我都會講阿 對他來說 去學佛阿就是 勸人為善阿 就是要做善事 好心有好報阿 對他來說 這是作人一個正確的觀念 阿 怎麼樣做人他覺得 這個他都知道阿 這不需要去學佛阿 對他們來說.

at the same time, she is strictly bound through the regular offers of her Buddhist community, the doctrine and practice of which seem to be her dominant hobby and guiding principle in life.

A "Natural" Environment

Meng Fanyi's organisation answers a double need for her: she feels "naturally" socialised through her Buddhist group and experiences the group as "naturally" compatible with what she calls "modern society". "Heart spreads to heart" in a barrier (*gehe* 隔閡)-free communication. Meng feels "natural" and "free" in the context of her group (*zizai* 自在). The "tacit understanding" (*moqi* 默契) in her group results from the constant exchange of personal experiences, on the one hand, and from listening and obeying the teachings of the master of the group on the other. This balance between expressing one's own experiences and being guided by the teacher, Meng describes as a dynamic, which "lets you develop" and "search for your own way" (*rang ni fazhan, zhao ziji de lu* 讓你發展 找自己的路 [17.1:20]). The community's principle seems to consist of the individual experiences of its members and is inspired by its teacher's sensitivity regarding tackling the unspoken questions of his listeners:

> [6.4:32] But class/ each time I go to class I feel as if I go again/ go again to recharge [laughing]. Having no energy. Or, no matter if it is the mood of the brain or the body, I also go there. Everybody is meditating together, practising together. That monastery is quite pure. Especially the teacher. When he "opens the light" [*kaiguang* 開光, normally the initiation ceremony of a statue, but in this context the opening of higher insight; EMG] also everybody will open the light. Everybody [has] value. So every time I go to the lesson, I will think my spirit seems to be very well [laughs]. Very calm. When I then hear [him] talking about some Buddha's dharma, I think, you know, I just feel very calm, then I can suddenly/ I can go for introspection. Because the teacher, when he is teaching, it is all in connection with the current karmic connections. Current just includes the people in the current place. Then the things that happened this week. Or the things that happened recently. So, very strange, every time you hear the things you say, it is like he is talking about me ei. How come that the things he says are just the things I think about, the problems I'm worrying about, right. The teacher just will/ just will have some answers. Afterwards, when you go and listen in the class, there will be introspection about human life. This is just for me also a very important/ It is not: This is at home. Of course, at home you have to put it into practice yourself. But you still have to have one/ one/ you know, one [who] has more/ more power/ has more power/ or [let us] say hm one more clear aim, like that, which is guiding you. […; 6.1:20][147]

[147] [6.4:32] 可是上課 每次去上課感覺 好想再去 再充電一下 [laughing] 沒電了 或者不管是頭腦 或者身體上的心境也是去那邊 大家一起打坐 一起共修 那個道場比較清靜 甚至是導師 他會開光的時候 也是每個人都開光 都價值 所以每次去上課 我會去覺得

The sensitivity of the teacher to questions about the mastery of daily life is responding to the needs of Meng Fanyi, to whom introspection (*fansheng ziji* 反省自己) is central. Longing for sustained socialisation, she integrates into her group as she feels socialised without being restricted. Meng is convinced of that integration as the groups prove to be dynamic (*huopo* 活潑) and undergoing constant, frequent change (*duobian* 多變). This flexibility is not only due to the personal input of its members, but even to its master, who sees himself also as being on a spiritual discovery, trying new "dharma doors" (*famen* 法門). Meng feels at home in her group, can be herself, and feels more energetic, "recharged" (*chongdian* 充電), like a battery, after participating in classes and activities. Without comparing her group with others, as it is "natural" for her to participate in her community and without knowing much about other Buddhist groups (her knowledge she spontaneously bases on watching sūtra explanations on television), Meng perceives her group as being the "most free" and most "perfect" (*zui ziyou* 最自由, *yuanman* 圓滿).

A Culmination of "Modern Society"

Her enthusiasm about the perfection of her group Meng Fanyi attributes, besides the idea that she would feel "naturally" at home in her community–being socialised on a profound level of existence while preserving her individuality–also to the fact that her community would perfectly fit into the needs of contemporary times (*xianzai de shidai* 現在的時代). Three characteristics are mentioned by her repeatedly: first, her community's teaching would be scientifically based; second, they would initiate the participant into a deep esoteric bodily knowledge; and, third, they would deliver a concept that permeates the whole life of the participant.

The experiential dimension fits the independent intellectual character of Meng. Her community would hold the principle of "really practicing something and through that really proving it" (*shixiu shizheng* 實修實證). Counting the number of recitations of one of Buddha's names, Meng has noticed that, on certain numbers, she would react bodily, like by diarrhoea or catching a cold. The teachings of her group therefore would always be based on "objective" (*keguan* 客觀) experiences that one could also reproduce by oneself.

好像精神很好 [laughs] 非常的寧靜 然後聽到在講到一些佛法的時候 覺得你知道 就是感覺自己很安靜 然後可以沉澱 可以反省自己 因為導師 他在講課的時候 都是針對當時的因緣 當時 就是包含 在當場的一些人 然後這個禮拜發生的事情 或是最近發生的事情 所以很奇怪 每次你聽到你講的事情 好像 他在講我欸 怎麼他講的事情 就是我在想的事情 我在困擾的問題 對 導師就會 就會有一些答案出來 然後你去聽課的時候就會有人生的反省 就對我來說 這還是很重要的 不是說這是在家裡 當然在家裡 是你要自己去實踐 但是你還是需要一個 一個 你知道 一個更 更力的 更有力的 或者是說 hm 一個更明確的目標 這樣子 引導你 [6.1:20]

The knowledge of her teacher is transmitted to the participants of the group according to their stage of spiritual development and transmits an increasingly esoteric bodily knowledge. The members of her group are not allowed to pass on their knowledge to others, as they are told that this could be harmful to others. A direct result of this knowledge is the fact that Meng tries to live in "harmony" with her body, avoiding for example cold food or certain movements. While the effect of her behaviour seems to lead her to take care of her own body in an esoteric informed attitude of responsibility, avoiding harmful behaviour (*suiyuan baozheng* 隨緣保證), it seems also be driven by a certain curiosity about mysterious happenings. She is interested in following her teacher to overcome the normal limits of the body, being enabled to "open the light" (*kaiguang* 開光), control sicknesses (*zhibing* 治病), or communicate with gods (*shentong* 神通). As in intellectual matters, Meng likes to be deeply informed and the idea of possessing knowledge that makes her special in society might be attractive to her. Highly specialised on the one side, the teachings of her group are on the other side not finalised. Her teacher sees himself as being on a spiritual search. It is characteristic that the group understands itself as comprising all other teachings (*yuanrong wanxiang* 圓融萬象) and combining them into a highest, arcane knowledge. The initiated follower is able to judge other doctrines and Meng is clearly pleased during the interview about watching other religious communities and being able to discover their deficiencies. The community seems to transmit an expertise that enables its followers to decide independently about the value and limits of other competing organisations.

The teachings of the group are experienced by Meng Fanyi as applicable in daily life (see above), as helping her self-cultivation, and guiding her according to the rules of her community to be "compassionate" (*cibei* 慈悲), observe "equality" (*pingdeng* 平等), "liberating sentient beings" (*pudu zhongsheng* 普渡眾生), or "doing something for people without looking at oneself" (*wuwo weiren* 無我為人). While such principles depend on the capacities of a single person and can be fullfilled to various degrees–unlike the traditional monastic rules–they even sound quite "abstract" (*chouxiang* 抽象) to her. In addition to trying to put into practice the principles she learns in her community, Meng also follows a regular spiritual practice of meditation and name recitation. For the name recitation, Meng's group does not use the, common in Taiwan, invocation of Bodhisattva Amithābha, but one of the rarely known invocations of Buddha, describing him as "natural"–in line with the overall approach of the group itself.[148] Reciting the name when sitting, tired, on the underground, Meng feels calmer (*anjing xialai* 安靜下來), entering a stable state (*ruding* 入定) and awakes refreshed, full of energy

[148] The name is omitted here, as through doing so this group could be identified.

(*buchong liliang* 補充力量), at exactly the right station. She is so used to name recitation that she does not feel disturbed when performing it but very relaxed and that parallels other activities, like talking or walking. Also, Meng is deeply acquainted with meditation and can describe in detail how to observe one's mind and meditate in a "natural" manner. Once a year, in August, she also goes on a longer retreat.

Meng Fanyi showed the interviewer the facilities of her Buddhist group and it turned out that her own approach of putting life "on stage" in all its dimensions–like the setting of the interview itself–parallels the self-presentation of the master of the group, who sees himself as not only an innovative Buddhist leader, but also as a productive artist, exhibiting his work all over the world, as a composer and musician recording CDs, and even as a perfume seller, successfully heading a company and chemist shop. While the financial concept of the Buddhist group seems discordant with the regular expectations of a Buddhist organisation, the idea of self-cultivation is meant not only to be a form of observing one's own conduct, but also implies an outlook on an all-comprising life-design. Daily life is enlarged with an aesthetic dimension that seems to transform life itself into art. Meng might feel that her background in philosophy and design parallels well the life concept of her teacher, that comprises daily life in a creative way in all its dimensions, including art, creativity, self-cultivation, and bodily practices as a "natural" way of staying dynamic and aiming at constant further development.

Life-Design and Elite Aestheticisation

Meng Fanyi fills her life, through immersing herself in a dynamic, recently established and small Buddhist group, with an aesthetic concept that transforms daily happenings into a composition of multidimensional life mastery. The doctrines and practices of the group Meng applies to all aspects of her life, identifying with both the group and its teacher. The integration of Meng as a highly intellectually-active person is possible through the dynamic and processual structure of the group. Meng can integrate into this group passively, consuming its teachings and enjoying at the same time describing herself as a "lazy" (*landuo* 懶惰) person, who does "not like to think", but who feels well guided by her teacher. She does not feel restricted by the teaching, but feels that it is "natural", and she cultivates throughout the interview a habitus, which is not closed up in itself, but explicitly enjoys a conduct that is not totally determined and structured ("I like to jump"; "You can put my narration in order".). The intellectual is pleasantly entertained by the all-comprising offer of the life design of her group and adapts her whole life-style to it: "Every day, every minute, every second" (*meitian meifen meimiao* 每天每分每秒), when "walking, residing, sitting or sleeping" (*xing zhu zuo wo* 行住坐臥), she observes her habits and tries to apply the teachings of her group. Great efforts are possible, because she is convinced–unlike her parents–that the question of religion, where the meaning of this world and one's life would be, is closely connected and expressed in one's daily life. Where this life of "examining herself" (*fansheng ziji*) leads her, she is not sure, but feels that she is on a journey of discovery, while finding support from her group and guidance from her teacher:

> Na, now, of course, I am myself not that clear. I feel my feelings are all blurred, very hazy, very dizzy. But there is an inner feeling that lets me get closer without break. This/ Or after ten years have passed, I can still tell it to you. [20.1:03; end of interview] [149]

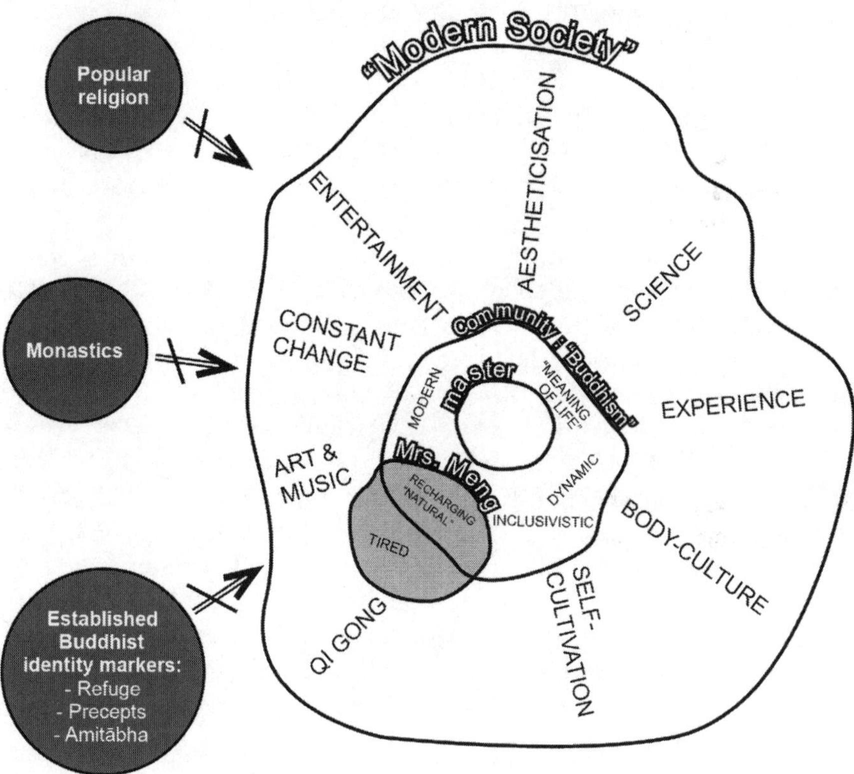

Figure 29: Meng Fanyi–Life-design and elite aestheticisation.

149 那目前 當然 自己還不是那麼清楚 我覺得感覺都是迷迷糊糊 很朦朧 很模糊的 但是有一種內在的感動 會讓你不斷的前進 這個或是還過十年以後還可以告訴你 [20.1:03]

Buddhist doctrine is, in her life and the construction of the group and its teacher, applied to the needs of contemporary Taiwanese society. Established Buddhist identity markers are being transformed. Instead of taking the three refuges, the group members take–after an initial study phase–five refuges, also taking refuge in their "own character" (*zixing* 自性) and the teacher. That makes sense, given that around these two poles the balance and dynamic of the group evolve. Also, the five precepts of lay Buddhists are reinterpreted by the group. Vegetarianism would be "absurd" (*huangmiu* 荒謬). When eating meat, one should be aware that one is taking the life of someone else. One should be "thankful to the food that it has given its body" to support one's life, to be able to practise and one should reward it and use it to liberate living beings. Eating meat would not be connected with the idea of killing. In contrast, alcohol is said by the group to have bad effects upon the body after a certain degree of practice and is therefore discouraged. Still, all rules have to be adapted to one's abilities and are seen as an ideal; in any case, everyone is regarded as being different.

The group is clearly oriented towards lay practitioners and Meng shows little awareness of other Buddhist groups or Buddhist historical developments within Taiwan or China. Particularly the monastic life would demand too much in terms of leaving modern civilisation and would be a totally different life, but also would not enable the practitioner to prove his transformed attitude in daily life and "free sentient beings" (*duhua zhongsheng* 渡化眾生). By embracing "modern times", the community and Meng are displaying an approach towards daily life that transforms it through intellectual insights, daily practice, and constant self-observation. This approach encompasses a differentiated body culture and a multidimensional, aestheticised transformation of daily life. It promises to be compatible with experientially provable science while being a dynamic, developing and entertaining teaching. Answering the needs of contemporary Taiwanese urban citizens, the relation of this group towards the established Buddhist institutions and doctrines loses its relevance.

12.6 Is it "Engaged Buddhism"?

The four presented cases have been chosen as they exemplify intense and specifying forms of Buddhist belief. Interestingly, each of them, regarding their constructions of the function that Buddhism plays in their lives, falls back upon resources, which only recently are at Taiwanese Buddhists' disposal–Buddhist social charity work on a large and international scale; profound Buddhist college education for lay people; American Buddhists' translations; and independently evolving unorthodox Buddhist movements. While Buddhist translations might be the result of a flourishing book market, charity work, colleges and weekly seminars all rely upon the engagement of the Young Buddhist Monasteries or New Buddhist Movements (for definitions, see abbreviations) which have started to mushroom all over the island since freedom of association was granted in the late 1980s. Especially the Young Buddhist Monasteries are known for propagating a socially "Engaged Buddhism". One of the author's initial questions when embarking on this research was how far the organisationally propagated slogan, "Buddhism among the people" (*renjian fojiao* 人間佛教), really reaches those addressed and becomes an integral part of their biographical self-imagining (see chap.1). It might be therefore consequential to ask how far the propagated slogans and their biographical counterparts match each other and whether the results of the analyses help to shape the Buddhist self-construction beyond or in correspondence with the concepts of Engaged Buddhism.[150]

Internationally, it is *en vogue* to make "Engaged Buddhism" a topic of academic discussion, describing one of the major changes in Buddhism reaching back until the end of the 19th century.[151] As already shown in the short historical sketch that traced the motivation of Cai and Gu (see chap. 8.2), it is clear, that Engaged Buddhism in Taiwan today is, to a certain degree, inspired by Buddhist Modernism active in Mainland China during the Republican Period. The movement in China itself stood in interaction with its predecessor in Sri Lanka. Internationally, the Theravāda embarking on a reformation of the Buddhist community was influential, especially in the English-speaking world. As mentioned before, Heinz Bechert analysed it by applying the term "Protestant Buddhism".

---

150 For more detailed information on the following outline of Engaged Buddhism, its international and Taiwanese meaning, Young Buddhist Monasteries and New Buddhist Movements, please refer to Guggenmos (2006) and (2012). In the following, I partly quote from these two articles while more details can be found there.

151 The *Journal of Buddhist Ethics* hosted an online conference in 2000 on the topic of "Socially Engaged Buddhism." Christopher S. Queen initiated this discussion, was responsible for the conference and helped to publish four edited volumes: Queen and King (1996), Williams and Queen (1999), Queen (2000a), Queen, Prebish, and Keown (2003). The discussion started with a collection of work of socially Engaged Buddhist leaders: Eppsteiner (1988), Kotler (1996). The discussion was continued through a conference in Oregon entitled "Buddhist Activism in China and Beyond" (April 2008, Oregon State University), which resulted in a special issue of the "Journal of Global Buddhism", Vol. 10, 2009: Buddhist Activism and Chinese Modernity. For studies on Engaged Buddhism see also Kraft (2000), Queen, Christopher S. (1996b), esp. 4–13. Bingenheimer (2003), DeVido (2005), Schak and Hsiao (2005), Bingenheimer (2004). A recent approach analysed the phenomenon of Engaged Buddhism in the light of the secularisation thesis (Lai and Main 2013).

The term "Engaged Buddhism" underwent a different historical development, but merged and was identified internationally especially with the Theravāda phenomenon. The Chinese Buddhist reformatory movement was internationally present through the monk Taixu 太虛, who supported a reformation of the Buddhist order, reemphasising its value for human life. Taixu did this under the slogan of a *rensheng* 人生- or *renjian fojiao* 人間佛教, *Buddhism in human life* or *among the people*. His work was translated into Vietnamese and the monk Thích Nhất Hạnh (*1926), when opening his monastery in French exile, translated it, employing the term "engagé", which has a slightly more socially active connotation in French. When the Anglo-American discourse analysed the change in Buddhism in the 20th century, the movement was labelled "Socially Engaged Buddhism". As the movement itself was internationally–despite its name–more inspired by its Theravāda roots, collected volumes assembling the works of Engaged Buddhists today refer rarely to Taiwan. Even where they do, they mention the explicitly socially active group of Tzu Chi (see further below and Huang 2003). Besides figures like Anagarika Dharmapala (1864–1933) and Colonel Olcott (1832–1907) for the Sri Lankan movement or more recent figures like the founder of the Sarvodaya Shramadana movement A.T. Ariyaratne (*1931), Bhimrao Ramji Ambedkar (1891–1956) is often mentioned as a second figure in the chain of new departures: as the fourteenth child of an Indian family of the lowest caste, who had the chance to study at Columbia University (New York), he campaigned vehemently for the Buddhist reorientation of the so-called "Untouchables" on his return home. This line up can be continued. In Thailand, for example, the monks Buddhadasa (1906–1993) and Sulak Sivaraska (1933–) are amongst the "Engaged Buddhists", but also Thích Nhất Hạnh or the 14th Dalai Lama Tenzin Gyatso (*1935). With some argumentation also, those organisations were included which conduct themselves exclusively with regard to other religious traditions, such as for example the Japanese lay movement, Sōka Gakkai 創価学会, under the heading "Engaged Buddhism". Thematically, all of these groupings appear to feed from the same source which contains the typical topics of modern social criticism: peace work, environmental protection, human rights, gender issues, democracy, health care, educational offers, emergency aid and social work, which are an expression of social engagement and political activism and often carry strong moral and ethical values.

In seeking clear definitions of the term, one gains an insight into a complex, lively discussion, that mainly concerns itself with the self-discovery of a modern Buddhism which is predominantly focused on America and the departure of Theravāda Buddhism. As a result, Engaged Buddhism appears constantly to require an updated description and to be a search term with positive connotations or a collective motion, which is less concerned with contrasting definitions to the outside world, but focuses instead on a pragmatic synopsis of the already present Buddhist views. It claims a fundamental change within Buddhism in its encounter with the modern and Western world, which partially even leads to the wish to establish a "fourth vehicle" next to Hīnayāna, Mahāyāna, and Vajrayāna Buddhism.[152] When picking up the term as descriptive from an academic point of view, one has simultaneously to be aware of its operational usage by "Engaged Buddhists".

One of the most often revisited definitions is that tested by Christopher Queen in his first volume entitled Engaged Buddhism. Queen understands the term Engaged Buddhism as a liberation movement which he relates to–amongst others–"personal, doctrinal and institutional dimensions" (Queen and King 1996, 6) initially. 1) These movements rally around a new kind of leader, around Asians who received a grounded education in the West and have successfully overcome extreme difficulties in their own life. 2) Referring to historical roots, these leaders offer a new interpretation of Buddhist teachings, the intent of which is not solely liberation in the afterlife, but represents more a *mundane awakening*. Queen describes this new and worldly orientation as the main distinctive feature of socially Engaged Buddhism. It aims to establish the teachings in the present world, making it compatible with the modern spirit. This often includes ecumenical and inter-religious openness. 3) The movements are held together by a collectively, socially, economically and politically explosive vision of a new society, which is based on peace, justice and freedom. The creation of a just and peaceful society via Buddhist means is, according to Queen, the common characteristic of the present-day Buddhist liberation movements.

Looking at Taiwan from an organisational perspective, the rhetoric of the Young Buddhist Monasteries are, in some sense, similar and match the requested identity markers of an "Engaged Buddhist" movement: all of the Young Buddhist Monasteries emerged around a charismatic monk or nun. Mostly inspired by mainland visions of a Buddhist renewal, they started after their arrival in Taiwan to establish Buddhist monasteries. Doctrinally, they emphasise the social engagement of the organisation in society. They maintain charitable foundations, establish kindergartens, hospitals, and universities, and organise activities that are often based on the help of lay Buddhist volunteers.

---

152 See Queen (2000b), 22–26, and Queen (2003), 22–25. Stating that the approach of Engaged Buddhism is new within Buddhist history has of course caused informed criticism, which shows the predecessors of this development. Concerning the critics, see, for example, Queen, Prebish, and Keown (2003), 251–344, and especially Yarnall (2003).

In the case of Tzu Chi 慈濟 (Fojiao Ciji Gongdehui 佛教慈濟功德會–The Buddhist Compassion Relief Tzu Chi Association), for example, a Buddhist charitable foundation, founded in 1966, this *mundane awakening* certainly applies most revealingly through a focus on social practice. Buddhist teachings make up the basis of the social engagement and the organisation is focused less on the dissemination of these than on social commitment. Essential to this are the abbess Zhengyan's 證嚴 (*1937) teaching, which she gives regularly and which is propagated via their own television channel. The nun Zhengyan is without doubt a famous leader, whose family background did not suggest this path in life. Significantly, in Taiwan, she is often compared to Mother Teresa due to her undisputed integrity. Zhengyan was born into a poor family. Her suffering made a deep impression on her which guided her and her followers to help the poor and sick and build–with the aid of small donations received throughout the years–a huge relief organisation run by more than a million volunteers. After the foundation of Tzu Chi in 1966, she built a hospital as well as a nursing and medical college on the relatively poor East coast of Taiwan in 1984. Educational, social and cultural programmes are also offered. The organisation has been operating at an international level since 1985, and today has branches in 30 countries. At the same time, Tzu Chi is increasingly involved with work in areas affected by war, flooding or drought, providing general material and medicinal but also spiritual aid, since for Tzu Chi physical and spiritual well-being belong together. In accordance with Queen's third definition feature, the followers of Tzu Chi want to create a "Tzu Chi World", a world of charity and compassion through charitable work, medical help, education and cultural activities. Tzu Chi transmits a strict behavioural code. One could entertain the hypothesis that Tzu Chi is trying to establish a new behavioural etiquette in Taiwanese social life.

Foguang Shan 佛光山, the second largest and also already by the 60s well-established Buddhist monastery, with its cultural, educational and charitable activities and institutions, strives, with regard to content, the realisation of a "Pure Land" on earth. With this, the monastic order appears to fulfil Queen's second and third criteria for a new interpretation of Buddhist teachings and the collective cohesion through the vision of a new society. Referring back to the reformer Taixu, Foguang Shan seeks an encounter with society. Laymen are granted a central role in the Foguang Shan movement. With an emphasis on *humanistic Buddhism* (Chin. equally *renjian fojiao* 人間佛教), the abbot Hsing Yun (Xingyun 星雲, *1927) favours the "middle way" in Buddhist practice, which does not lose itself in the worldly, nor completely shut itself within asceticism. Modern progress has a positive connotation with the path to a realisation of the "Pure Land": with the help of Buddhism, the future is going to be an ethically oriented society. *Humanistic Buddhism* "is living life, making life happier and family life more joyful, and adding harmony to human relations, the mind, and the spirit" (Hsing Yun 2003). This is why the Buddha's Light International Association, which is affiliated to Foguang Shan, states in its maxim: "May kindness, compassion, joy, and equanimity pervade all Dharma realms. May all beings benefit from our blessings and friendship. May our ethical practice of Chan and Pure Land help us to realise equality and patience. May we undertake the Great Vows with humility and gratitude" (ibid.).

Fagu Shan 法鼓山, only founded in the 80s, is in its Mahāyāna Buddhist orientation intellectually very reflected and resorts to several Buddhist schools (Tiantai 天台, Huayan 華嚴, Chan 禪, Weishi 唯識) and meditation techniques (*huatou* 話頭-, *mozhao* 默照-techniques), without disregarding the functional interpretation of the modern world. The goal of Fagu Shan is to build a "Pure Land" amongst people and to save above all–besides the natural, living and social environment–the "spiritual environment" (*xinling huanbao* 心靈環保), which was a slogan developed by Shengyan 聖嚴 (1929–2009) in 1992. Fagu Shan convinces in particular through the academic quality of its Chung-Hwa Institute of Buddhist Studies (Zhonghua Foxue Yanjiusuo 中華佛學研究所) which is by all means comparable to Western standards. This institute also operates, amongst other things, the digitisation of the Taishō Tripiṭaka and makes it freely available on the internet. In the case of Fagu Shan, socially Engaged Buddhism comes across as very self-contained. Its clear social vision and implementation through the community of followers are signs of an Engaged Buddhism, according to Queen.

Another large and widely known monastery, the Zhongtai Shan 中台山, claims to represent a socially engaged Buddhsim propagating Chan Buddhism in society by relating it to its modern needs. It thereby distinguishes itself from the other monastic orders by the fact that charitable or cultural activities, such as, for example, the construction of schools, are part of its programme, but are not explicitly at its centre. With statements such as "Tzu Chi performs good deeds, Zhongtai undertands life and death",[153] Zhongtai Shan propagates the permeation of everyday life with the Chan practice and finds itself in deliberate contrast to the previously described monastic orders based on socially Engaged Buddhism. Zhongtai Shan, therefore, differs from the three hitherto described monastic orders due to its traditionality, exclusiveness and use of the Chan practice. Just like the other monasteries, Zhongtai Shan is characterised by a relatively large number of laymen–10,000 followers are thought to have taken refuge with the master–yet, for example, a specific reference to the reformers, such as Taixu and Yinshun, is not central to the movement.

---

153 "*Ciji zuo gongde, Zhongtai liao shengsi* 慈濟作功德, 中台了生死", see Kan 2004, 428.

Although four large monastic organisations have been mentioned already, this does not of course mean that the full landscape of Taiwanese Buddhism has been exhausted. Contemplating the full range of Buddhism in Taiwan today, one can first of all find alongside the aforementioned monasteries a multitude of smaller, sometimes traditional, temples and monasteries, which are often found in remote locations and do not see their character as primarily socially orientated. Although they account for a considerable part of the *saṃgha* in Taiwan, they are less likely to be considered during an examination of socially Engaged Buddhism. On the other hand, the Young Buddhist Monasteries have prevailed in the parlance of Taiwan due to their social dedication, their strong inclusion of laymen and, as a result, their popularity.

Taiwan is witnessing strong development especially in the field of independently organised lay organisations. Buddhist lay organisations are so numerous in Taiwan that only a partially more detailed account is possible. The first departure towards a social commitment in the spirit of Taixu was exhibited by the Lotus Community in Taizhong (Taizhong Lianshe 台中蓮社), which remains well-known across Taiwan (Kan 2004, 242–277). As early as 1951, the scholar Li Bingnan 李炳南 (1890–1986)–following his escape from the mainland–founded a community in Taizhong which dedicated itself to the study of Confucian and Buddhist scriptures, the practice of name recitation according to the school of the "Pure Land" and its commitment to society. The community grew to be quite strong in the past, but appears to have lost some of its magnetism following the death of its founder, particularly among young people. Conceptually, it realises much of the ideal–developed at the beginning of the Buddhism reform–of a lay following which is oriented on the *saṃgha*, but organisationally independent, and which puts Buddhist teachings in a direct relationship with one's present life, making it its transforming centre. An on-site remembrance hall, dedicated to the reformer Taixu, reinforces this orientation towards a socially Engaged Buddhism.

Two more examples suggest that pure lay organisations, which are not associated with a monastery, are considerably more unstable in their structure than monastic formations. The fragility of structure, or rather the transformation process towards a monastic order, can be seen in the case of Modern Chan (Xiandai Chan 現代禪) and the New Rain Association (Xinyu She 新雨社).

The former disappeared abruptly from Taiwan's social scene after the death of its leader Li Yuansong 李元松 (1957–2003)–suddenly there were no longer a website, publications and position statements, nor any way to contact the organisation. The group was a young establishment (1988), gathering around their leader who was inspired by the ideas of Yinshun and consequently also of Taixu. The intellectually orientated group attracted attention by building their own housing development to try to link their meditative practice with an "empirical" and rationally responsible Buddhism (see Bingenheimer 2004, 120–124). The community of Modern Chan definitely had a strong social vision which fed on Buddhism. It thereby concentrated on the implementation of its communal life and less on socio-political activity which is the characteristic impetus for Engaged Buddhism.

The second community, Xinyu She, still exists today, but has undergone considerable change. In America, it had a small precursor community which was founded in 1987, bore the name the Society for Buddhist Renaissance and committed itself to the Theravāda tradition. In 1991, after his return to Taiwan, Zhang Citian 張慈田 (1952–2009), who was involved with the society at that time, began to disseminate the community throughout the island. This only succeeded in part, and the groups soon fell apart. The initiator became ordained in the Theravāda tradition and bore the name Bhikku Mingfa 明法. He established a monastery in Jiayi under the name Fayu Daochang 法雨道場 which continues to exist after his sudden death in 2009. Besides Theravāda Buddhism, the movement is also inspired by the ideas of Yinshun of a return to a pristine Buddhist tradition. It furthermore sees its meditative practice as one which needs to be experienced "amongst people" and addresses the problems of society, so that the "Pure Land" can become a reality.[154]

Fayu Daochang's reference to the Theravāda tradition shows that societal pluralism in Taiwan is accompanied by an international opening of Buddhism, which encompasses not only the southern Buddhist traditions alongside the Mahāyāna Chinese ones, but also those of Tibetan and Japanese Buddhism. Especially the young Japanese lay movements are increasingly present in Taiwan. For example, both Sōka Gakkai 創価学会 and Shinnyo-En 真如苑 have opened branches in Taiwan. The influx of Tibetan-orientated communities is particularly strong, similar to what has been observed internationally. An increasing number of monasteries and communities are influenced by Tibetan Buddhism or were founded by Tibetan monks (see Xiao 2002). As a result, even those societies which actually practise the Pure Land tradition–albeit in a very independent way–sometimes feel obliged critically to engage with Tibetan Buddhism and to delineate it from their own tradition.

In recent years, ecological awareness has begun to unfold further in Taiwan and is being increasingly discovered by those Buddhist communities which refer to themselves as socially engaged. Fuzhi 福智–by today's standards, a relatively small community with 20,000 followers–began astonishingly early and forcefully with this. Fuzhi was allegedly founded in 1987 by

154 A detailed description of the relationship of this organisation with Yinshun's *renjian fojiao* (see below) and his work is provided by Yang 2000, 275-312.

the monk Richang 日常 (1929–2004) and is in its Buddhist reference strongly shaped by Tibetan Buddhism. Apart from their engagement in the movement for "life education"–a new subject introduced into Taiwan's school curriculum–it created its own foundation which verifies organic food products and markets them through its own shops. Thematically, this group falls clearly within the scope of Engaged Buddhism. Its leader, however, is less at the community's centre as is the case of other Buddhist movements in Taiwan–in favour of a stronger concentration on the goals that are to be implemented. Despite this, Richang offers his followers his own interpretation of Tibetan teachings. Even without covering the socio-political sector, the community pursues a clear vision in the education and ecological sector and, as a result, sets itself apart from other Taiwanese Buddhist movements.

The last group to be mentioned here is a community called Zhengjue Tongxiu Hui 正覺同修會 which was founded in 1997 by Xiao Pingshi 蕭平實 (*1944 in Taiwan). This community is an example of Buddhist movements which have been initiated by a lay person. They are serving especially the needs of people who, after a day of challenging office life, search for spirituality and a world view that comprises their daily experience and puts it into a meaningful perspective. They tend to link this search with bodily practices that serve the function of balancing the pressure of a job with tranquillising techniques. Xiao Pingshi is propagating name recitation in combination with slow-motion prostrations. This practice he enriches with lessons, in which he enlarges on his understanding of Buddhism and interprets the Buddhist sūtras. While this community partly aggressively missionarises against other Buddhist organisations, it shows fewer social activities in comparison with, for example, the established Young Buddhist Monasteries.

How strongly Buddhism in Taiwan is undergoing a creative change not only becomes clear from the monastic and lay communities, but also from the rapidly increasing number of educational seminars and Buddhist institutes (*foxueyuan* 佛學院). These play a part in the theoretical discourse on socially Engaged Buddhism, but also comment on concrete–for example, gender-specific–topics. Thus, several institutes advocate vehemently the abolishment of the "eight rules of respect" (*bajingfa* 八敬法) for nuns with regard to monks or the re-establishment of nunneries in Southern Buddhism. An eloquent and publicity-savvy spokesperson for the equality of nunneries in Taiwan is the popular founder of the Buddhist institute Hongshi Xueyuan 弘誓學院, the nun Zhaohui 昭慧 (*1957). In part provocative, these activists enrich the overall picture of Taiwanese Buddhism by giving it a component of oppositional inner-Buddhist explosiveness.

This overview of Taiwanese Buddhism which mostly labels itself as socially engaged shows thus a great bandwidth of very young movements throughout, which more or less satisfy Queen's three defining criteria. Tzu Chi most strikingly conforms to these criteria of a leading figure, newly defined teachings and a collective vision–Taiwan's "Mother Theresa" best matches the picture of Engaged Buddhism which arose from a "Protestant Buddhism" and therefore caters for a Christian ideal. However, all of the movements discussed here strive towards a *relecture* of Buddhist teachings which is relevant to the present and the world, compatible with modern life, historically verifiable and with ecumenical and global dimensions. The difference to Queen's definition of the Buddhist *liberation movements* appears above all to relate to his third defining characteristic; although the groups are of benefit to and visible within society, they only rarely dabble in an oppositional and sociopolitically explosive implementation of their visions. Instead, they stress the reciprocal relationship between social engagement and spiritual practice.

A glance at the thematic bandwidth shows that Buddhism in Taiwan is similarly orientated to Engaged Buddhism. Topics such as charity services and emergency aid (particularly in Tzu Chi), education (all discussed monasteries, Taizhong lianshe), environmental/health (Fuzhi) and gender issues (Zhaohui) also play a part in Taiwan. However, more confrontational topics, such as the question of human rights, democracy, peace work or a politically oppositional virulent movement, are not a primary aspect of the overall picture of Taiwanese Buddhism. Even politically active monasteries–such as, for example, Foguang Shan and Zhongtai Shan[155]–appear harmless compared to the strongly politicised Buddhism in places such as Sri Lanka. This is not due to speculations over the Taiwanese conflict mentality, but is more a direct consequence of its historical nature:

Engaged Buddhism in Taiwan–Historical Characteristics

Engaged Buddhism, as systematically propagated through the monastic institutions, evolved in Taiwan only after World War II and the subsequent arrival of the Nationalist Army. About 100 monks came to Taiwan as refugees. Often educated in elite monasteries on the mainland, they were acquainted with the reformist Buddhist ideas. Starting in Taiwan their own monasteries, they needed the support of either the population or the government. The Taiwanese population was not always welcoming to the newly arrived monks and in consequence the monastic community developed under the protection of

[155] Some of the monasteries took sides in the elections or even presented an–unsuccessful–presidential candidate. Such an action led to public criticism and therefore the monasteries today seem to be less openly politically active.

the ruling Nationalists. Buddhism in this context certainly did not see itself as a liberation movement. Political criticism and "activism" were rarely on the agenda of the Young Buddhist Monasteries. A major difference in comparison with the situation for example in Sri Lanka is also the role of "Western" countries. Although Taiwan was often under foreign rule, the Western colonial period in Taiwan was only brief. After the Japanese colonial period (1895–1945), Taiwan was protected by the United States, which prevented any takeover of the island on the mainlander's side. Buddhism therefore could never get an identification movement for an anti-western development, fostering its own Asiatic-Taiwanese self-construction. Buddhism in Taiwan after World War II was, from the very beginning, connected internationally, establishing branches with overseas Chinese all over the world. Engaged Buddhism in Taiwan developed its own profile as it is far less "protesting", but the Buddhist movements see themselves more in a socially constructive role, shaping people's perception of Buddhism in general and their recognition of Buddhism as actively engaging in social life in particular. Contemporary Buddhism in Taiwan therefore does not primarily exhibit the direction of an Engaged Buddhism in the sense of pursuing the socio-politically relevant visions of a new society, propagating any kind of "Buddhist Activism".

Are the Interviewees "Engaged Buddhists"?

Still the question remains of how the rhetoric of the presented Buddhist organisations affects the life of lay people. An indicator of a changed self-perception can be the relationship of Taiwanese lay Buddhists with the monastic community. The question of how the interviewees see the difference between lay people and monastics and how far they can imagine getting part of the *saṃgha* themselves was asked in each of the interviews. The reflection on Part I (chap. 8.2) revealed that the first five presented cases were not deeply affected by the possibly changed role of the lay Buddhist community: Luo Peirong and Lin Yongfu did not see the relevance of a renewed understanding of the monastic order. Cai Chenhao made a conscious choice to become a lay Buddhist–the desire to better his social relations prevailed–and admired in accordance with the traditional expectations the members of the monastic orders as the "real practitioners". Also, Li Zhiqiang, who himself tried to enter the monastic community, stated that, as a lay person, one would remain a "person from society". At the same time, he points out the positive role of Buddhism for business and family life in reassuring his moral standards. Gu Puzhong somehow joins in with the rhetoric about the advantage of becoming a monastic as "karmic luck" and describes himself as one of those ordinary people, who "bit by bit" and "slowly", take the Buddhist path.

Gu is, at the same time, the only one who is blurring the boundaries between lay people and monastics, stressing that one would have to become a monastic in one's heart, not with one's body. Whoever therefore has the qualities of a monastic could also live this life of a monastic as a lay.

The rhetoric patterns of the first part–the habitual understatement of lay people like Cai Chenhao, Li Zhiqiang or Gu Puzhong–is partly subliminal in the second part. Intense forms of lay Buddhist belief extend to talking of monasticism as a lifestyle which seems an absurd demand in modern times (Meng Fanyi). Monastic life is simply not feasible for her, because it firstly is seen as a practice belonging to a different life that is unconnected to the contemporary life-style and secondly is portrayed as a misunderstanding of Buddhism: Buddhism is a practice that permeates daily life. Buddhist practice is designed as a form of life management, which loses meaning once it is no longer practised in daily life. Zhang Yimin is, at this point, close to Meng Fanyi: although he holds a silent sympathy for the life of a monastic, he stresses repeatedly that monastic life also would be misunderstood, if it were not lived, in the Buddhist spirit, to "liberate all sentient beings". Monks and nuns therefore have the task of teaching in society what it means to "change one's mind". Zhang entertains the hypothesis that the Chinese monks would be the historical pendants of priests and psychologists in the West. Xu Wenhua sincerely struggled between remaining a lay or becoming a monastic. Finally, she chooses a lay life, but sees herself as open in future to adopting a quasi-monastic life-style: adapting to a monastic community she feels to be impossible at her age and, with a similar humility to the other interviewees, states that her ego would be too strong for such a commitment. Still, Xu has reflected on the interdependency between secluding herself from social life and entering it. She thinks that, with enough financial means and leisure time, as, for example, a retired teacher would possess, it would be possible to live a life close to the monastic one. The special value of the monastic order seems in her eyes under threat through this development.

Ma, Xu, and Zhang share the idea that society is anxious about people becoming monastics. Ma struggled with her husband to be allowed to listen to a sūtra explanation. Xu would have to oppose her father to join a monastic community and Zhang, as soon as he shows interest in a monastic life, elicits an immediate, mocking comment from his wife. Ma consciously reflects upon this social perception of the danger of becoming a monk or nun and repeats her organisation's re-interpretation of the monastic-lay relationship: the monastics would today use lay people to propagate the teaching in places and situations that are inaccessible to monastics.

In concluding, one could say that especially intense Buddhist believers and practitioners like those discussed here tend to have a positive notion of the role of a lay. The imagery they hold of the monastic order is either emphasising the necessary social engagement or denying that monastic life is appropriate in contemporary society at all. Lay people also discover their own abilities and search orientation in a quasi-monastic life. They are confidently trying to live up to Buddhist teachings by putting it into practice in their life. Engaged Buddhism seems therefore present not only through the propagation of the social engagement and active involvement of lay people in the Young Buddhist Monasteries, but also leads to a confident self-definition of intense Buddhist believers and practitioners.

The topic of monastic social engagement, expressed as "entering" the world (*rushi* 入世) in contrast to "leaving it" (*chushi* 出世), is explicitly known to Ma Fengling, Zhang Yimin and Gu Puzhong, and also Xu Wenhua reacts upon it, seeing the entering and leaving of society in a mutual dynamic. Still, the act of "entering" society imprints an interpretation pattern on the field which reflects a common language trope of Taiwanese Buddhism, but might be less helpful for tracing the success of Buddhism in urban Taiwan. The central dynamic of the Buddhist identification pattern is not based on a dichotomy where a defined Buddhist doctrine is being applied in a secular life, but "Buddhism" proves a performative resource among others–one might recall the initial sequence of this book by quoting a lay Buddhist inspired by "Buddhism and travelling". "Buddhism" is an integral part of people's life, which is not necessarily always recognised as a separate resource. It is applied dynamically, transforms people's life-style and is, especially among intense Buddhist believers and practitioners, experienced as giving guidance and delivering the meaning of life. For a comparatively small group of people, "Buddhism" gets a highly successful tool for daily life-mastery, which can dissolve from historical continuity or, the awareness of monastics and lay people as the transmitters of Buddhism (Meng Fanyi).

Buddhism in contemporary Taiwan is therefore not only successful because of the vigorous promotion of Engaged Buddhists, but a shift in the notion of the monastic order in Taiwan can be seen in the interviews. The fear that any contact with the monastic community might lead to becoming a monastic becomes less prevalent in a society where the dynamic of the Young Buddhist Monasteries is based on the active engagement of their lay followers. The promotion of an Engaged Buddhism reshapes the reflection about the act of veneration or the interpretation of karma. These changes in the general perception of Buddhism in Taiwanese society are certainly to be counted among the preconditions for the positive identification of lay adherents to the Buddhist community. Still, much of the attractiveness of "Buddhism" as a social, doctrinal and organisational resource is not based on the frequently narrated argumentation patterns of a reinterpretation of the Buddhist doctrine and the monastic order's behaviour towards lay people. "Buddhism" in the lives of intense lay believers goes far beyond the propagated attitudes towards society or the monastic order through the so-called "Engaged Buddhist" movements. Lay Buddhists in contemporary Taiwan experience Buddhism beyond organisational borders as a highly flexible resource that they can bring into accordance with their social experiences and with discussion threads prevalent in their urban lives. Buddhism is being employed in lay Buddhist believers' life as a transformative resource when coping with daily challenges. Therefore it might be less important to find an academically elaborated descriptive term for the phenomenon of an "Engaged Buddhism"–may it be Socially Engaged Buddhism, Protestant Buddhism, Humanistic Buddhism, *Renjian Fojiao*, or "Buddhist Activism", but to look beyond the patterns of narrations for the dynamic interplay between resources of social life tagged as "Buddhist" and the needs of urban citizens in contemporary Taiwan. A reflection of the interplay between Buddhist and religious resources and imaginations and the urban environment is therefore necessary.

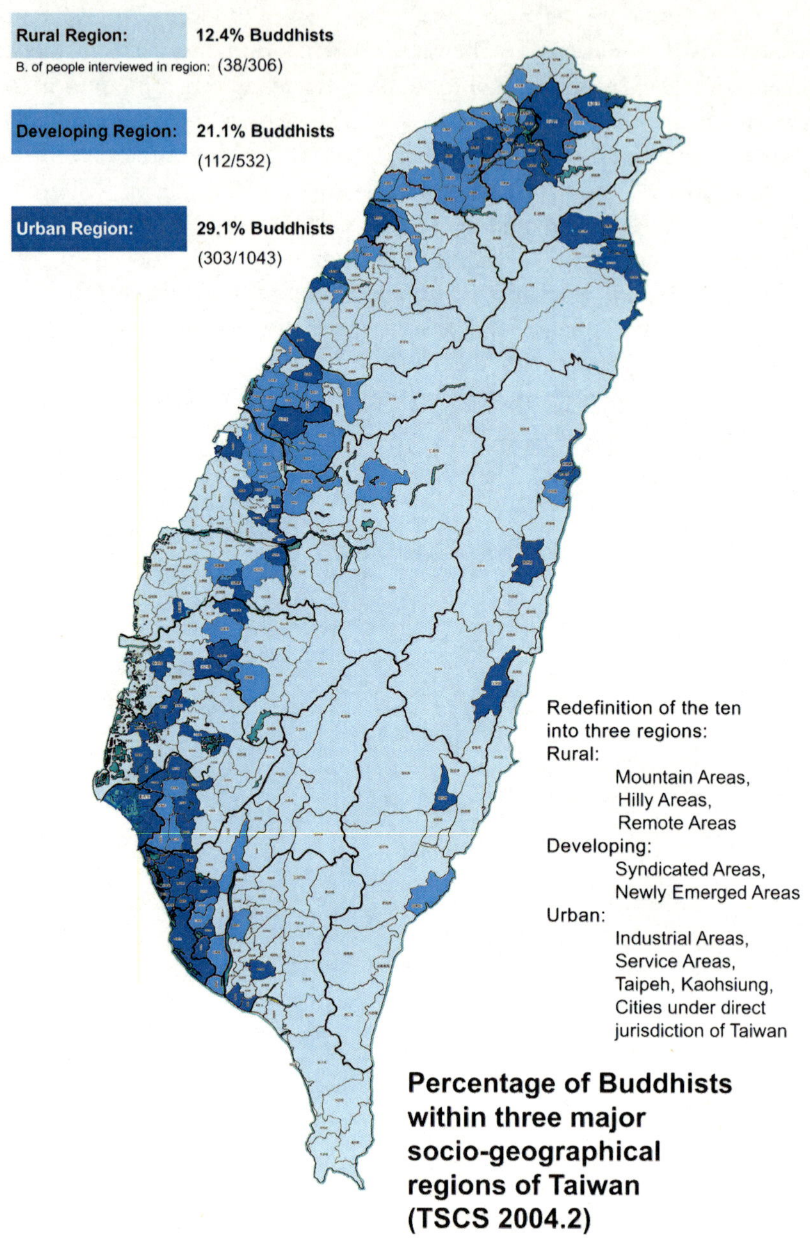

Figure 30: Map–Percentage of Buddhists within the three major socio-geographical regions of Taiwan (TSCS 2004.2).

Reflections
The Profile of Buddhism as a Habitus-Resource– On the Attractiveness of Denoting Oneself a Buddhist in the Urban Spaces of Taiwan

13 Religion in the City

Stating that Buddhism is more attractive in the cities than in the remote areas of Taiwan contrasts with the general sociologically reflected experience that institutionalised Christianity is under threat in the cities. Due to the strong change in the religious and especially Christian communities that are trying to remain or establish themselves in the urban regions of Europe or America, the longstanding academic reflection about the relationship between religion and the city flourishes even today, especially in the United States.

The topic of the relationship between "religion" and the "city" is as old as the reflection about social change in the rapidly-growing industrialised cities, which means that it dates back to the above discussion about urbanisation, beginning in Weberian times. From the very beginning, these reflections were closely connected to the European and American observation of the Christian churches that their Sunday worshippers do not regularly attend services when living in the cities. The deep anxiety of the Church fearing its decline has led to a multitude of studies,[155] especially in the humanities, from Max Weber and his "disenchantment of the world" ("Entzauberung der Welt") to Karl Marx, Sigmund Freud and Émile Durkheim, and up until the seventies' discussions under the headline of secularisation. Urbanisation, modernisation, and secularisation were, for decades, seen as virtually synonyms.

Samuel Kincheloe, together with Arthur Holt, were among the early researchers coping with the topic of "Religion in the City". Both affiliated with the Chicago Theological Seminary and inspired by the Chicago School of Urban Sociology, they set up in the late 1920s a seminar on "Research Methods for the Study of the Church in the City"[156] to investigate the geographical, historical, anthropological, and sociological perspectives of religious life in Chicago. Among others, social-psychological considerations shed light on, for example, "types of religious persons in the city" (Kincheloe 1965a, 65), pondering the sense of constructing "ideal types" to produce structural insights.

The first scare about the loss of faith gradually became differentiated, however. Thomas Luckmann in the sixties started to write about "invisible religion" ("unsichtbare Religion", Luckmann 1963), arguing that a decrease

---

155 Frequent studies about Sunday participation as well as a precise registry of its members are common, for example, in Germany, during pastoral theology ("Pastoraltheologie") seminars within theological faculties and the declining membership numbers have currently visible consequences as churches are sold and parishes combined.

156 Kincheloe offers an extensive overview of the development through two retrospective lectures, printed in the *Review of Religious Research:* Kincheloe (1965a and 1965b).

in church attendance is not necessarily accompanied by a decline in religious belief in general. The religious field goes far beyond what is easily quantifiable by the handy statistics of institutions and especially the church. A decade later, Hugh McLeod in a review essay about the development of the research field "Religion in the City" (McLeod 1978), reviewed the development and the fight of the church to avoid failure in the city. He is also aware of the fact that it is organised religion which is in decline: "It is true [...] of the majority of larger Western cities during the last two centuries that participation in organized religion as far as the adult population is concerned has been fairly low, with seldom more than a quarter, and often much less, attending services in any given week" (McLeod 1978, 10). As a consequence, he wants to widen the spectrum of research from church religiosity to fortune-tellers, magic practices, folk-doctors and spiritualists (McLeod 1978, 16), bearing in mind the multiplication of subcultures through differentiation in the cities.

He criticises the one-sided dichotomy between urban and rural areas 25 years before the publication of Champion and Hugo (Champion and Hugo 2004) by differentiating the countryside as not necessarily religious: "It can be said, however, that in many countries the extremes of religious observance and non-observance are found in the countryside, with the town somewhere in the middle, but below the rural average" (McLeod 1978, 10). Still the "modern" city remains coarsely carved as "rational, mobile, industrial, cosmopolitan, [and] secular" (McLeod 1978, 7).

While, already with McLeod's essay, the first traces are visible that might question the secularisation hypothesis, in the following years, the debate challenging any link between urbanisation with regard to modernity and secularisation became so intense that, in 1996, Callum G. Brown sums up: "If the rest of social history has been retreating from social science models and rules, the urban history of religion stands out as a notable exception. [...] One of the reasons why social science model-building is still so prevalent in this field is that most of the practitioners have been for the last two decades committed to debunking a model: the model created by the theory of secularization" (Brown 1996, 372). Already early criticised by Mary Douglas and others,[157] Rodney Stark and Peter Beyer were among the strong voices that rejected the secularisation theory. Peter Beyer admits: "I think what I and most other sociologists of religion write in the 1960s about secularisation was a mistake. Our underlying argument was that secularisation and modernity go hand in hand. With greater modernisation comes greater secularisation. It

157 Beyer (1997), here 978. Quoted in the article "Secularization, R.I.P" of Rodney Stark (1999), which provides a helpful overview of the debate including Douglas (1982).

isn't a crazy theory. There was some evidence for it. But I think it's basically wrong. Most of the world today is certainly not secular. It's very religious".

By now, it is widely-acknowledged that modernity does not automatically accompany "secularisation" in any plain sense, though aspects of it such as the decline in religious authority have been partly successfully defended.[158] More recent publications tend to display the diversity of religious life in the urban areas. Urban historians rediscover the topic and single studies approach it with primarily descriptive intentions.[159] Current large-scale projects that seek new theoretical frameworks try to avoid any premature theorising by focusing on "Religious Diversity" (project "Urban Aspirations" in Shanghai, Singapore, Mumbai, and Seoul, Max Planck Institute for the Study of Religious and Ethnic Diversity, Göttingen; director: Peter van der Veer, see chap. 17). The study of single cities and their religious landscape is *en vogue*. The ongoing HERA-project "Iconic Religion" works on the presence of religion in Berlin, Amsterdam and London (Volkhard Krech, Kim Knott, Birgit Meyer).[160] In America, there have been at least three recent major studies concentrating on religious movements in cities.

Robert A. Orsi (Orsi 1999a) collected a variety of works covering different cities in America, pointing out the specific development of many American cities being characterised by ethnic diversity and migration. With this basis of ethnic diversity, American cities also develop further into "world cities", being shaped by the accelerated transmission of information and transportation. Religion evolves in this climate as one form of urban culture, in which for example the images and narratives about other groups are important for the groups' own self-construction. As an "intimate commingling of lives and narratives" (Orsi 1999b, 56) can be analysed, religious groups seem often to offer a "mode of assimilation of children in their parents' habitus" (Orsi 1999b, 56). Two years later, the study of religious groups in New York (Carnes and Karpathakis 2001) states basically the same function of religious communities: often ethnically bound, they try to "sustain [the members'] ancestral identity and that of their children" against an American society that is often perceived as "immoral" (Carnes 2001, 10.12). Carnes in addition points out the psychological functions of religious groups as providing "familial warmth and accep-

158 See Mark Chaves and the debate on neosecularisation (Chaves 1994). There have been numerous publications also intending to sum up the vast debate. Daniel V.A. Olson (2000) lists selected articles in his book "The Secularization Debate". More recent publications include Martin (2005) and Pecora (2006).

159 See the special issue of the Journal of Urban History in 2002 (Vol. 28, No. 4, May) devoted to the topic "Religion and the City." Other single studies, for example, include contributions from the "L.A. School" (see above): Engh (1997).

160 HERA-research project "Iconic Religion: How Imaginaries of Religious Encounter Structure Urban Space" (2013–2016, Ruhr University Bochum, FU Berlin, Lancaster University, Utrecht University).

tance" (Carnes 2001, 17). While Orsi as well as Carnes and Karpathakis both present broad detailed panoramas of selected groups and regions, they draw few broader conclusions. The volume "Faith in the City" edited by Lowell W. Livezey (Livezey 2000a, including an introduction by Livezey and an epilogue by R. Stephen Warner) is the result of the "Religion in Urban America Program" with which the topic of "Religion in the City" returned to the Chicago School in 1992. Situated–explicitly stating its secular approach–in the Department of Sociology at the University of Chicago, the publication is the profound result of the work of a research group whose geographical approach defines religious communities through investigations in concrete neighbourhoods rather than public registries. An optimal sounding research setting enabled the team to undertake joint field research and avoid distributing the topics and locations among the team members. The contributions of the book show how religious congregations and institutions respond to "the opportunities and pressures of urban change" (Livezey 2000b, 20). This response Livezey sees as distinct from the classical role of churches in the social welfare sector in benefiting the underprivileged. While remaining a "significant form of religious engagement", the fields of social engagement are gradually being taken over by the government and are "not the central dynamic of urban religion" (Livezey 2000b, 20). Only a fraction of religious contribution to urban life is located in the social service sector. In his epilogue, Warner picks up the thesis that the religious groups are not mainly "activist cadres dedicated to social change" (Warner 2000, 298), and concludes that, with regard to contributions, religious organisations concentrate more on their "intergenerational and interpersonal solidarity" (Warner 2000, 302) and are "primarily concerned with themselves" (Warner 2000, 303). While migration, class, and ethnic questions play a structuring role for many communities, "throughout this book, we read of religious institutions made up of people of every color and creed that invite their members to get acquainted with one another, provide safe havens for members' (and neighbors') children, promote family values, facilitate homeownership, attempt to channel behavior in constructive directions and discourage indulgence in temptations, promote concern for others who themselves are expected to hew to the standards of the group, nurture positive identifications when negative ones are so near at hand, offer moral support and a psychological shield against a perceivedly hostile society, and promote spiritual growth where pressures of the job are experienced as soul-deadening" (Warner 2000, 298).

14 Religion, Immigration, and Conversion in Taipeh

These findings are presented here in such detail, because they shed light on the characteristic differences that mark the situating of "Buddhism" as a religious resource in Taipeh. The first eye-catching difference between the debates in America or Europe and those in Taiwan is that, in Taiwan, there has not been a united institution like the church determining and defining the religious life of Taiwanese people. The impact of the rapid social change upon religious life and institutions is therefore not experienced as the loss of influence of a single dominating group that claims to be the backbone of the fundamentals of social life securing the orientation and moral behaviour of the entire society. In this context, it is important to note that Buddhism in Taiwan is experienced as a resource which does not tend to build upon a long-established local tradition. The local tradition is connected with what is commonly called popular religion. Popular religious temples serve, particularly in the countryside, a strong social function. Although recognised as similar to each other by believers, popular religious temples are locally bound and diverse. Because of that, they cannot react with similar univocal strength to social changes like, for example, the Christian churches can.

Urban regeneration projects in Taiwan have recognised increasingly the role of local temple communities in mobilising social life. They state that the traditional culture is important for the "spatial fabric" of urban development. In their article about "Culture-led Urban Regeneration and Community Mobilization", Cheng-Yi Lin and Woan-Chiao Hsing analyse a cluster of social resources provided by the Bao-an Temple Area in Taipeh (Lin and Hsing 2009). As "the temple's square is the public space for local inhabitants to encounter their neighbourhood" (Lin and Hsing 2009, 1323), it provides networks based on kinship, cultural and educational activities, transmits local knowledge systems, norms, religious narratives, and cultural heritage, and is recognised as a public space that contributes to a symbolic identity of religious and local culture (Lin and Hsing 2009, tab. 1 on p.1329 and p.1324). The attention which is now paid to the local traditional resources in urban planning reflects that the rapid urbanisation, especially in the Northern Region, has paid little attention to preserving temple life so far.

Secularisation in the form of the loss of the popular religious traditions is a commonly-held opinion in Taiwan. This is reflected in the interviews: similar to the classic lamentations about the decreasing church membership in Europe and America, the younger generation in Taiwan is often said to distance themselves from popular religion. In Xu Wenhua's case, she described how she and her siblings were reluctant to accompany their parents to the temple at new year, and how her mother would normally go and venerate "[b]ecause we young people don't really like this kind of/ Right a". ("可是只有我媽媽會在拜因為 我們年輕人比較不喜歡這一種 對阿", Xu [9.4:05]). That his grandchildren are growing up following this tradition filled Lin Yongfu with pride. There is a notion that temple practice is becoming less common among young people and in the major cities in Taiwan. Certainly, the temples are not structuring the daily life in Taipeh to the same extent as they are in the villages in Taiwan. They tend not to dominate geographically and fixed office times might make it less likely for some people to pass a temple regularly. These results are statistically hard to verify. Still, in 1999, 87% of the sample population went to a temple to pray (1675/1925; TSCS 1999.2, v15). The 1990 and 2004 surveys provide comparable data in respect to fortune-telling. Here, one can find a slight decrease: the "traditional" practices of fortune-telling are in general less frequent in 2004 than in 1990 (1990: 31.7%; 2004: 26.8%), but in 2004 more than 10% of the sample population were going online for fortune-telling (2004: 13.1%).[161] The traditionally established religiosity is searching for new ways to express itself, while through the institutionally missing univocality, a protest movement about how best to investigate and counter this development is mostly absent.

The second eye-catching difference besides the lack of a single dominating religious institution in the religious sphere is the fact that, although migration and ethnicity play a role in Taiwan, the problem situates itself very differently than in America. Among people denoting themselves Buddhists, ethnic identity plays a marginal role. Taiwan has seen several waves of immigration (see above), but the three main population groups besides aborigines and recent worker immigrants especially from Indonesia speak Chinese dialectic variants–Fujianese/Taiwanese, Hakka, and Mandarin. The young generation in the cities communicates in Mandarin and is often not even aware that their families stem from different ethnical backgrounds. None of the interviewees mentioned the ethnic question in relation to their Buddhist belief. Gu Puzhong might be more inspired by the mainland experience of his grandmother, while Ma Fengling might be bound to her Taipeh local origin. Certainly, as one can see from the short historical outline, there was a generation of Buddhist immigrants, lay people and monks alike, who were inspired by the Buddhist reformist efforts on the mainland or the Buddhist

161 Results of TSCS 1990.2: Do you engage in fortune-telling (*suanming* 算命)? Answer: Yes 802/2531 (31.7%); No 1729/2531 (68.3%). Results of TSCS 2004.2: v40: Did you go to someone in the past to have you fortune told? Answer: Yes 505/1881 (26.8%); No 1376/1881 (73.2%); v38: Did you go online in the past to have your fortune told? 過去有沒有在網路上算過命？Answer: Yes 247/1881 (13.1%), No 1634/1881 (86.9%).

culture they experienced there. The first generation of immigrants certainly inspired the Buddhist movement in Taiwan through founding monasteries, lay communities (group of Cai Chenhao), or publishing houses (Gu Puzhong), etc., but the current belief in and practice of Buddhism in Taiwan is at least not consciously dominated by ethnic questions. In the American megacities, the question of ethnicity is not one of dialectical differences, but of migrants' groups who stem from vastly different cultural background and feel that their lifestyle and self-concept at threat. Aims like preserving one's ancestral identity and passing on the culture to the next generation, practical aspirations like facilitating homeownership and in general a focus on intergenerational and interpersonal solidarity are therefore logical consequences in the American context.

While, in Europe and America, the loss of members of the major Christian churches has caused a stir, there is at the same time a vivid interest in questions about the entry into a religious community and the motivation for such. Research on "conversion" covers a whole research field in America and Europe. Conversion within the context of migration has even been researched a) under a gender focus for Taiwanese immigrants in Southern California and–even more relevant to the hypothesis presented here–b) centring on the conversion to Protestantism in urban Taiwan.

a) Interestingly, the cases presented in this book show partial parallels to the observations made by Carolyn Chen on Taiwanese immigrant women who convert to Buddhism or Christianity in Southern California (Chen 2005). Women, through religious conversion, often try to build up their own independence and authority. They become able to distance themselves from ideals experienced as traditionally Confucian or Taiwanese, like obedience and dependence on male relatives, and see the chance to "individuate from traditional kinship structures" (Chen 2005, 346). She sums up: "Through religious conversion, women carve out spaces of independence and authority for themselves, albeit never at the cost of threatening the nuclear family" (Chen 2005, 336). For the cases presented, one can also state that especially female urbanites are integrated through entering a Buddhist community into new social fields, which helps them to cope better with their daily tasks and family life. Ma clearly sees a new field of social welfare practice opening up to her through her participation in the organisation. The case of Ma is so mainstream that even the trope of the husband's conversion under the persistent influence of his wife features equally in Ma's story and Chen's analysis (Chen 2005, 350). Voluntary work might play a huge role in establishing their own space of action for Taiwanese women in Taiwan and America alike. Ma sublimates her task of caring for her children within the Buddhist community once her children have grown up; Luo tries, by joining a Buddhist peer group to escape family stress; Xu Wenhua follows a more complex structure in her biography but is finally able to find via Buddhism her own agenda; and Meng Fanyi uses the Buddhist community to aestheticise her own life as an intellectual, artist and mother under the flag of Buddhism. Still, the phenomenon itself might not be that women-specific, as Cai Chenhao also carves out, through his Buddhist engagement, his own space in relation to his family. It seems more due to the situation of obviously a majority of Taiwanese women that they, on the one hand, especially in the role of the mother, fall mainly under the social pressure from the family while, on the other hand, cannot build up a balance with that through embracing an occupational career. It therefore seems more likely, that they are in special need of a space in addition to family life, which is estimated by society as making a valid contribution to social life–similar to job-life. Certainly, this hypothesis requires further verification, and an additional gender focus goes beyond the scope of this study.

b) The topic of religious conversion in combination with immigration has even been studied in the direct context of Taiwan. Hsing-Kuang Chao describes the "Conversion to Protestantism among Urban Immigrants in Taiwan" (Chao 2006).[162]

Converts are often introduced to groups via personal bonds. They like to experience within the group on the one hand a cultural continuity–especially as it maintains their ancestral practices and their intergenerational family-bonds and social support–while on the other hand outstanding religious experiences convince them of their specific group. These miracles, comprising glossolalia, instant healing, and exorcism, often respond to their immediate needs. Outwardly, the institutional factor also, of course, plays a role, as well-organised institutions are more likely to attract and retain converts. In addition, Chao recognised, that "the interviews showed that no one converted to either congregation because of the moral teaching or doctrine regarding eternal life" (Chao 2006, 200). The last argument fails to reflect on socially-acknowledged reasons in certain interview situations and possible further motivations.

The idea of converting to obtain "social support" through the new community is not new. J.B. Holt in 1940 put forward the hypothesis that immigrants experience a cultural "shock", wherefore they tend towards sectarian-

162 While delivering excellent results, Chen and Chao's articles share the same approach: in searching for reasons for conversion, they take the explicit reasons stated by the interviewees as the accurate description of the factual conversion process and do not reflect on other, not necessarly explicitly articulated, motivations. The interviewees' statements are often applications of commonly spread narrative patterns. In consequence, the outcomes of Chen's studies show remarkable parallels to Ma Fengling's narration–a narration which has clearly seen standardising re-shapement.

ism: "[T]he immigrant seeks security and social adequacy by turning to emotionalism and escape activities" (Holt 1940, 747 in Nelsen and Witt 1972, 380). In contrast, Kilian states more than ten years later that, in general, the opposite would be true, and immigrants from the countryside would not join religious groups, as "the city church did not perform the social function of community integration for them that the rural church did, and they tended to develop a 'vacation attitude' toward church participation" (Kilian 1953, 67). Nelsen and Witt summed up this discussion in 1972, suggesting through quantitative testing that neither of these extremes can really be proven, but that immigrants undergo a "gradual resocialization to the urban setting" (Nelsen and Witt 1972, 381).

While the last sentence might always be safe to say, in the case of Taipeh, one can state, that people coming to the metropolitan area on the one hand might maintain their connections with their hometown and its temples and/or search for new possibilities in the city. Here, they might look for communities which provide some social bonds and provide cultural continuity. Interestingly, in none of the selected interviews as well as those not discussed here, a migrational background in the form of searching for orientation in the city plays a role, implicitly or explicitly, in the conversion process. Only Meng Fanyi reports feeling especially "Eastern" when she lived in Paris. One could conclude that the interviewees did not feel strongly alienated. Their orientation towards "Buddhism" was normally a process that took years–they tended to grow up already with a feeling of being "Buddhist" or sensing a Buddhist heritage. They discover Buddhism anew and shape as well as experience it as a helpful resource in their daily life.

In denoting oneself a Buddhist, as discussed, certainly also personal bonds played a role not only in the participation of the Protestant converts (Chao 2006) but also for the interviewees in the Buddhist communities presented. None of them got to know their group via impersonal contact, like a flyer, newspaper or the internet. Luo Peirong, Li Zhiqiang, Ma Fengling, Xu Wenhua, and Meng Fanyi were introduced via friends. Cai Chenhao's school teacher was involved in his later community. Gu Puzhong, Lin Yongfu, and Zhang Yimin grew up with "Buddhist" (but different) sources and Zhang finally does not belong to any group or have any friends there–which might also be a reason for his non-participation. All of the interviewees' social life was closely connected to their Buddhist self-construction. Problems with cultural continuity are rarely uttered by the interviewees, although the analyses showed that especially Luo has great problems combining her family tradition with the habits of her Buddhist groups. Cai highlights the improvement of his close family relations through his practice, but draws a clear line between the habits of his community and those outside. Gu had to undergo a long process before he could see himself in continuity with his grandmother. Xu is clearly distanced through her practice from the more popular religious behaviour of her parents' generation and Zhang and Meng appear highly creative in re-defining Buddhist resources. In the concrete biographies, matters of cultural continuity are therefore negotiated, while the argument itself seems to be much less established than the classic narrative topos in the context of conversion to Christianity that it would be a foreign religion opposing ancestral services.

The argument of miracles as a motivation for sticking to a certain religious practice seemed dominant in Chao's analysis and also in our cases one can see more or less commonly presented arguments about miracles centring around physical healing or well-being: a belief in miracles breaking the laws of nature was strongest in Luo's case, but also Cai (fragrant bodies), Gu (healing), and Meng (bodily reactions to recitation) used miracles to strengthen the convincing character of their Buddhist community. It is remarkable that miracles are never narrated without being transformed into a cause that shall convince others of their respective community. Stories of miracles–which could be further differentiated through more detailed research–are obviously a well-recognised argument in Taiwanese society. The usage of such an argument is not necessarily linked to a person's belief in it, but it may be a situation chosen where one sees oneself forced to justify one's decision while at the same time being unwilling to discuss it further. Gu–having lived ten years in Canada–is far more careful with this argument than for example Luo. Although Gu appears convinced of the argument itself, it seems he has learnt that, during discussions with "Westerners" (as he combines the interviewer and his Canadian experiences), a story of a miracle is not such a positively received "showstopper" as it is in Taiwan.

Summing up, one can conclude that the situation in the American megacities, characterised by migration and ethnic diversity, faced with the recent economic polarisation, spatial dislocation and a lack of public authority (Livezey 2000b, 9), does not parallel the situation of Taiwanese urbanites. No all-embracing religious institution is losing power and fearing "secularisation". Within the new image of religious and cultural diversity, it is not simply the fact that there are more Buddhists in the cities which delivers insights, but especially the panorama displayed with the help of the interviews that shows how "Buddhism" is constructed and experienced in urban Taiwan.

The attractiveness of the Buddhist groups does not rely mainly–as obviously the case in major American cities with a high percentage of immigrants–on the desire to uphold the family tradition and rescue the children from their immoral environment. Still, for the selected interviewees in Taiwan, Buddhism offers a commonly-assumed moral code and secures ethical behaviour in business and family life. As for other Taiwanese immigrants, social support, cultural continuity narratives, psychological help, spaces of (female) independence, and miraculous narratives play a role in Buddhists' choices for their commitment, but starting from the cases themselves, other differential categories stand central.

With the phenomenon of religion in American cities there exists one further commonality: Social engagement via Buddhist communities can be important for Buddhists like Ma Fengling but, although the task of social welfare is a generic part of nearly every Buddhist contemporary institution, the analysis of the biographies showed, that social work is–as Livezey stated for America–also in Taiwan "not the central dynamic of urban religion" (Livezey 2000b, 20). As in the "world city" of Chicago, Buddhists as long as they participate in Buddhist organisations are highly engaged in the interpersonal solidarity of the group and less likely to be socially or politically active. Going beyond the research on urban religion reviewed so far, the usage of Buddhism as a resource for urban Taiwanese self-construction shall in the following be summarised based on the cases themselves.

15 Influence of Urban Conditions on the Engagement of Interviewees in Buddhist Groups

"Buddhism" features in manifold ways in the biographies of Taiwanese urbanites. The narrative biographical interviews reveal some of the imaginaries underlying a Buddhist self-construction and show a multiplicity of potential factors ("Plausibilitäten") that might explain the higher number of Buddhists in urban areas. The analysis shows that the general conditions for organisational movements are advantageous in cities and that the Buddhist organisations know how to use these resources. They also show that a self-definition as a Buddhist is supported by several characteristics specific to the social construction of "Buddhism" in Taiwan.

Urban conditions can be of advantage for any organisational movement. This is not specific to "Buddhism", but simply valid as higher mobility, greater density and proximity, developed mass-media and high informational exchange, the existence of leisure-time and the awareness of it as a time that requires structuring, and a high educational standard can have positive effects on the growth and development of movements and organisations.

In their "Buddhist" engagement, the interviewees often rely either on their high mobility within or when departing from an urban region or profit from the advantage of their proximity to Buddhist institutions and the possibility of being able to find more like-minded people for frequent meetings because of the high density of the population. High spatial mobility is accompanied by increased informational exchange.

While also, in the rest of their daily life, the interviewees make use of mobility and proximity, partly being frequently abroad, Luo, Li, Ma, and Meng all contribute to or participate in Buddhist groups, which are nearby or accessible via public transportation. For Luo and Ma, proximity seems important–their groups have bases within the same districts–while for Li and Meng it is more important to find within the Northern Region a group that fits their specific needs–personal abbot friendship and a highly-aestheticised life-style design. In contrast, Lin, Cai, and Xu are not afraid to travel considerable distances to reach their specific organisation. Lin travels regularly throughout Taiwan, Cai visits his group in central Taiwan often while studying in Taipeh, and Xu is constantly travelling between her father's home, her job, and the Buddhist college, which are all located in the Northern Region. Also Gu is flexible within the Northern Region: from his

	Mobility	Density/ Proximity	Mass-media / Informational Exchange	Leisure-time and Awareness of it	Educational Level	"Buddhism" as
Lin Yong-fu	*regular temple visit in South Taiwan*	job as taxidriver relying on it	–	no sign	low, but *integrated in temple life*; watching his grandchildren and the "new time": curios and open-minded	*temple life and basic life philosophy*
Luo Pei-rong	–	*Buddhist peer-group participation possible because of proximity*	*group contact via friends, reading of works of group, books of Buddhist group*	yes, no special awareness	low, but *Buddhist education through group*	*temporary group participation*
Cai Chenhao	here and back from university to Buddhist community	–	*Buddhist publications as his job sector*	Buddhism combined with job: Buddhism as vocation	university education, Buddhist education	*being part of a group*
Li Zhi-qiang	from South to North and international	*found a fitting Buddhist group in the North*	–	no clear border as employer, Buddhism as karmic task and social prestige	university education	*temple and group*
Gu Pu-zhong	flexible in the Northern Region, international mobility normal	*good for his Buddhist activism, publishing house within MRT region*	*Budhhist publishing possible through developed market*	retired; before: Buddhism combined with job	university education, Buddhist college	*all-embracing intellectual life-concept*
Ma Fengling	through Buddhist group in Taiwan and international mobility	*Buddhist group participation possible because of proximity*	*Buddhist books of group*	yes, but no special awareness	low, but Buddhist education through group	*group participation*
Xu Wen-hua	switching between job – father – Buddhist college	–	*tries to get into this sector through Buddhism*	Buddhism combined with job: Buddhism as vocation	university education, Buddhist college	*life-concept & group*
Zhang Yimin	weekend in South Taiwan, during week in North	*no personal contact to Buddhist group, just knowing that "a meditation group is down here"*	*Buddhist internat. bookmarket and newspapers*	few, but aware	university education	*life-concept*
Meng Fanyi	2 months abroad per year	*exclusive Buddhist group within MRT region*	*Buddhist books of group*	yes, job and leisure time as life-design concept	university education	*group & life-concept*

Table 30: Buddhist engagement as relying on general characteristics of urban Taiwan (italics: Buddhist engagement is resorting to these resources; italics and underlined: Buddhist engagement is delivering this resource; normal: not specific for *Buddhist* engagement).

home, he must travel across Taipeh to reach his Buddhist publishing house. His Buddhist activities rely on a broad audience, which profits from the population density of the region.

The interviewees often come into contact with Buddhist groups through their social networks. In addition to this face-to-face informational exchange, in particular, the participants in the Buddhist groups report reading the publications of the group diligently. Luo takes the reading of the abbot's publications very serious as personal life instruction, Ma mentions to read the leader's biography and aphorisms to make use of them also in her daily life, and Meng reads whatever her group publishes. Zhang replaces his non-participation in any Buddhist group with extensive reading, especially of translations by American Buddhists, and pays attention whenever a Buddhist book is reviewed in a newspaper. His concept of Buddhism is highly dependent on the increased informational flow, which is provided by the dynamic of the urban region. Cai, Gu, and Xu try all three to enter the market of information with a Buddhist message. Cai is concentrated on his own community's publications, Gu tries to spread his own understanding of Buddhism, and Xu thinks that through translations she can help Buddhist teaching to spread throughout the world.

These later three are, through the mass-media, trying to combine their conviction about "Buddhism" with their job, and through that their leisure-time and career are becoming inseparable. Also, Meng puts all of her life spaces under a Buddhist perspective. The main difference is that she is not engaged in making Buddhism a message for others. Zhang is the only one who employs his lack of free time as a reason for not engaging in Buddhist activities more deeply, despite his reading. Lin does not show any sign of separating his job from his leisure time. Luo and Ma, as housewives, have plenty of time, for Li, Buddhism is an additional engagement beyond his career, but linked to it. The engagement in "Buddhism" is therefore not necessarily seen as a hobby. "Buddhist" activities can be reduced to a hobby, but it also is possible to integrate them successfully into one's work life or even make it part of a integrative outlook upon life.

The interviewees often participate in the Buddhist communities' educational offerings. In cases of low formal education, like Luo and Ma, they receive a Buddhist education through their community through which they can be enabled–like Ma–to compensate for their low educational background. Despite adherents with low education, also young and old people with a high education, often university based, can successfully combine their Buddhist self-concept with their intellectual self- and world-understanding. Here, a specific profile of "Buddhism" as a social and intellectual resource comes into play, which needs further investigation.

Summing up, participating in the open streams of information, lay Buddhists enter the market and sometimes even start to promote independently their concept of Buddhism as a mission in society. Besides increased mobility, the density, proximity, intensified informational exchange, and rising educational standards also contribute to the spread of Buddhism. Buddhist organisations, on the one hand, profit from the higher educational level of their followers and help them present "Buddhism" as a modernity- (and "science-")compatible and "up-to-date" belief. On the other hand, the interviewees often take part in educational offers by the Buddhist communities. Individuals with a low formal education might receive a Buddhist education through their community through which they may be enabled to compensate for their low educational background. Urban life–and this is also reflected in the interviews–brings with it an awareness of leisure time, which must be actively structured. While this space can be filled with "Buddhist" activities, some interviewees also integrate their Buddhist vision successfully into their work life or even make it part of their integrative outlook upon life.

16 The Specific Profile of "Buddhism" as a Resource and Option in Urban Taiwan

Beyond the advantageous conditions for organisational movements, the analysis of how "Buddhism" as a cultural resource, a label, and concept is employed shows the potential factors that might explain the special attractiveness of "Buddhism" within Taiwan's urban climate.

The reflection upon the first five presented cases revealed several potential factors that contribute to the attractiveness of Buddhism in the cities.

Firstly, the contemporary perception of Buddhism in society is embedded in the Chinese cultural heritage, without having a concrete, long-standing history in Taiwan itself. Today's large Buddhist monasteries were founded despite Tzu Chi by mainland refugee monks no earlier than the 1960s. Buddhism in Taiwan has become, over the centuries, integrated into popular belief. In the second half of the 20th century, the Buddhist reformers from the mainland saw an opportunity to create a fresh start in Taiwan by emphasising a socially Engaged Buddhism. A Buddhist revival with restorative hopes, as one can partly witness at present on the mainland (Ji and Goossaert 2011), finds therefore no base in Taiwan. Tradition in Taiwan is perceived in a delocalised mode.

Besides the unique historio-geographical situation that Buddhism faces in Taiwan, "Buddhism" in the population was, and continues to be, given an intellectual and "traditionally" elite connotation that promises the adherent an attractive prospect of possible upwards social mobility. As a result of the positive associations linked to Buddhism, self-denoting Buddhists use the label "Buddhism" to stabilise their own moral convictions and family traditions in an increasingly cosmopolitan context. The stabilising function is complemented by the amalgamation with the current discussion threads. Within this dichotomy, Buddhism is discovered and recreated as one's own "tradition". To the attractiveness of Buddhism is added also the fact that the established roles of the donors smoothly integrate into the capitalist society. The generally capitalism-friendly disposal of the Buddhist organisations shapes the role of the donors without a deeper doctrinal knowledge as a positive identification pattern.

Intense Buddhist believers and practitioners reveal especially how "Buddhism" is employed creatively to position themselves in the fluidity of Taiwanese modernity–either independently or through integrating with organisations that label themselves "Buddhist". That adds to the previously analysed reasons for the attractiveness of a conventional Buddhist self-denotification and the perspective that a "Buddhist" self-construction is experienced as a tool for successful self-imagining and contributes to subjective well-being, ensuring social or ideological cohesion. The compatibility of Buddhists with a scientifically up-to-date world view is of crucial relevance in this context. In addition, in the urban climate especially, movements flourish that not only actualise the dialectic between traditional values and the current topics of society, but also serve the interests of self-cultivation, lifestyle practices and light forms of self-legitimation and sense-delivery. Central to this context is the construction of Buddhism as a tool serving the needs of the contemporary office generation regarding bodily practices, recreation and leisure-time management. Current sociological reflections try to capture the major discussion threads of contemporary society, and especially the debate on a bodily culture and embodied practices in its relation to Buddhism, as seen in the case of Meng, would certainly be worth extra investigation. Social change suggests a "somatic turn" (Hancock 2000) in contemporary society up to a recognition of it as a "somatic society" (Turner 1984), leading through dietary practices, exercise and cosmetic culture to an aestheticisation of daily life (Juvin 2005). The "Buddhist" community of Meng is serving the whole spectrum for a rediscovery of the body and would definitely be worth its own analysis.

While explaining the attractiveness of Buddhism can at this point only give a rough idea about how it is being constructed as a tool for matching the discussion threads of Taiwanese modernity, two foci will be outlined in more detail. Firstly, by now, the perspective can be sharpened on the phenomenon that the Buddhist field is characterised by low entrance barriers that enable people flexibly and selectively to employ Buddhist resources. Secondly, it is also part of Taiwanese modernity to become increasingly involved in transnational cultural flows. Life in Taipeh, as possibly in any metropolitan area around the world, is under the influence of cosmopolitan scripts that drive the aspirations and actual lives of its citizens (see below). "Buddhist" imaginaries–as can be illustrated by most of the interviews–establish themselves successfully in this cosmopolitan context, which leads to the perception of "Buddhism" as an emergent form of association, contributing to a transnational, deterritorialised identity formation. In combination with the light historical positive reminiscence and usage as a value stabiliser, "Buddhist" identification patterns have been established as a new method of cultural reproduction in the interplay between a creative preservation of tradition and the integration of new resources. The Buddhist identification pattern seems to suit the skills that are advantageous to its members who live in the constant cultural flux of the metropolitan areas.

Low Entrance Barriers and Soft Switching

The low entrance barriers and the possibility of switching softly in and out of the field make "Buddhism" an easily, without further obligation, employed resource. For the interviewees, it is out of question, that the resource "Buddhism" is not necessarily *institutionally* bound. Lin Yongfu, the taxi driver, when chatting with the researcher, practises situational shifting: he changes smoothly into being a Buddhist when he recognises that this might help him to have a pleasant conversation. Luo Peirong has adapted her beliefs over the years to her family situation. She has had periods in her life where she was more explicitly Buddhist and learnt about Buddhism as a distinct religion, but now she finally sees "Buddhism" in her life as inseparable from what she calls "Daoism"–a belief based on miraculous helping powers and a retributionary veneration pattern. Gu Puzhong is a mostly institutionally-independent Buddhist, with a developed belief, while being highly doctrinally-informed. Ma Fengling in contrast sees no necessity for becoming deeply involved in doctrinal matters and sees herself as a sincere Buddhist as she identifies with a social welfare organisation which claims to be "Buddhist". Zhang Yimin can explain the long-established basic Buddhist principles and applies these in his daily life, but is unsure whether he can be called a Buddhist, while Meng constructs herself as deeply devoted to Buddhism, attending a highly syncretistic, but nominally "Buddhist" community.

The label "Buddhism" seems to be a vehicle of integrative power, soaking up people and organisations with various backgrounds and interests. Neither a reflection of "conversion" nor a discussion about "invisible religion" has evolved from the phenomenon of "Buddhism" in Taiwan. "Buddhists" do not necessarily perceive themselves as part of a variety of religions, but "Buddhism" as a resource could be located somewhere between "*Lebensweisheit*" (worldly wisdom), spirituality, monastic respect, and the concrete Buddhist organisations. For believers and practitioners, this integrative power is regarded as enabling them to slide in and out of the field, according to their own interests and social contexts. Although the possibility of sliding into and the low entrance barriers to the field are not clear to all of the interviewees, their freedom is reflected in the interviewees' narrations and contributes to the attractiveness of Buddhism.

The high *fluctuation* in this field, as shown also in the longitudinal statistical studies, is caused by people assessing themselves over time as Buddhists or not. Li Zhiqiang stresses that the attractiveness of Buddhism for him as a manager lies also in its flexibility in allowing him to adapt his monetary or organisational contribution to a Buddhist monastery continuously, thus saving him from any long-term obligations. When his business is doing well and even leaves him some free time, he likes to support the monastery–

financially or through his own efforts–but he certainly would not like to enter into any long-term obligations. Flexibility means for Zhang Yimin intellectual eclecticism, making "Buddhism" a helpful tool for children's education. Lin Yongfu does not seem to experience a lot of criticism for denoting himself a Buddhist either. Popular religious elements are not insistently rejected by most higher ranking Buddhist institutions, which play a role in shaping the social discourse about the access to the Buddhist field.

Historically speaking, in the years after World War II, the Buddhist Association of the Republic of China (BAROC) successfully controlled the ordination of monks and nuns. The Buddhist field was organisationally bound to the BAROC's imagination of orthodoxy but, since the lifting of martial law and democratisation in the late 1980s, the freedom of association led to a multitude of registered Buddhist communities, which claim affiliation without being effectively controlled regarding their content by any association or institution. Upcoming new interests, such as ecology, education, human rights or social welfare, easily become integrated into the agenda of the Buddhist organisations. In addition, lay people were never the focus even of the BAROC. It is practically impossible to be excluded as a lay Buddhist from an imaginative "Buddhist" community.

Buddhist involvement has several ritual dimensions for expressing a degree of commitment and involvement. Zhang doubts whether he sees himself as a Buddhist, but none of the interviewees shows signs of excluding him- or herself with their experience from the Buddhist community. While, certainly, the monasteries and Buddhist institutions argue over their legitimacy and inner hierarchy, lay Buddhists are sometimes aware of the question of whether to count the popular religious field as Buddhist or not, but never related their personal multitude of religious experiences as excluding them from their Buddhist community. The hypothetical "concentric structure" (Paul Harrison, see chap. 1) of the field, with its low entrance barriers, seems to be experienced as an adhesive power, which integrates believers with various tasks and orientations under the umbrella term "Buddhist".

Buddhist Aspirations in a Transnational Context

The international dimensions of the organisational spread of Taiwanese Buddhism around the world are well-documented.[163] Far less attention has been paid to the question of how far the international activities and argumentative patterns affect the actual biographical self-construction of Buddhist lay peo-

[163] The organisational dimensions of single international and Taiwan-wide Buddhist organisations have been well studied, see ann. 4, chap. 1.

ple.[164] The interviews show that, in the experience of Taiwanese urbanites, Buddhism is perceived as a resource, opening up a global perspective. The interviewees refer to "Buddhism", for example, as a parallel category to "travelling". Both, Buddhist belief as well as travel, Kong Shuqing explains, are, for her, complementary resources for coping with life through developing an optimistic basic attitude. Travel puts her personal problems into perspective, while the idea of retribution helps her to understand that any negative events are limited by the law of karma. For Meng Fanyi, Buddhism serves as a background concept for an aestheticised lifestyle, which frames her perception of the world that has to comprise French, German, and Taiwanese elements. Gu Puzhong, in contrast, constructs Buddhism as an indigenously Eastern source of knowledge, that serves as the base for a positive Eastern self-construction and aims to restore Asian self-confidence against the odds of falling behind in terms of economic, technological or cultural development. In the case of Xu Wenhua, exactly the same concept is transformed into a Buddhist mission to the West that motivates her to professionalise her English skills. An international active business manager, Li Zhiqiang feels that he has a moral base at home through Buddhism. "Buddhism", in his view, provides him with rules for running a successful business–cheating has bad karmic effects and will not lead to sustainable success. As he spends most of his time abroad, he also obtains a sense of inner-Taiwanese social recognition through his donations. In contrast to regarding "Buddhism" as an "Eastern" resource of wisdom for life-management, Zhang Yimin perceives Buddhism through a Western lens. Cleansed of its local Chinese flavour with its traditional Chinese expressions, he prefers to read Chinese translations of American Buddhists' works. This, he is convinced, provides him with concepts that support an up-to-date, Buddhism-inspired way of life that is also valid in a modern family context. Luo Peirong is the only one of the interviewees who does not show any international awareness and is caught up in her family situation. The other two interviewees, also from a lower educational background, are successful in finding ways to internationalise "Buddhism". Lin, the taxi driver, is–as mentioned before–shifting to Buddhism, as he recognises it as a tool that will enable him to make connections internationally. While the international motive lies more hidden within him, it serves as a tool for Buddhist proselytisation for Ma Fengling. She portrays herself as being highly moved that she, who would normally not expect to be able to travel abroad due to her inability to speak English and her poor elementary school education, was literally enabled by her organisation to visit Sri Lanka and help in the aftermath of the Indian Ocean tsunami in December 2004. She felt appreciated and taken seriously, and emphasises that she did not return to Taiwan soon because she was not

164 The following considerations are reflected upon in more detail in Guggenmos (2014).

really able to help, but because she was needed back home. Her message to the auditor is clear and promoted by her organisation: 'Average, poorly-educated people like me are enabled to play an active role in social life in Taiwan and even internationally. Participating in our organisation is an advantage for everyone, as people who are normally low in the social hierarchy are highly valued and can enlarge their activity radius even internationally and flourish.' One reclusive Buddhist community member takes his international awareness a stage further. Having obtained an education covering the religious traditions of the world, he now feels freed from the lack of confidence that unites especially Luo, Li, Gu, Ma, and Xu, and able to decide consciously on withdrawing from international engagement in order to confine himself to his Buddhist community.

Concluding, one could venture to say that the attractiveness of Buddhism in urban Taiwan is firstly not to be explained through the rhetoric of the Engaged Buddhist players of the field. In accordance with the observation of Lowell Livezey, "social action"–comparable to the range of activities in which Ma Fengling is involved–can be described as influential in contemporary Buddhism but "is not the central dynamic of urban religion" (Livezey 2000b, 20). The attractiveness of Buddhism in urban Taiwan and the difference between urban and remote regions with regard to the percentage of Buddhist believers is a central observation as far as it hints at the dynamic interplay between "Buddhist" resources and the current social developments and characteristics of Taiwanese modernity, which–as can be proven by the statistical outcomes (education, income, leisure time management)–seems to be experienced as more intense in the urban regions of Taiwan even if the urban-rural dichotomy is blurring and the image of urban areas is being replaced by the model of megalopolitan regions.

Summing up, concerning the attraction of "Buddhist" resources in urban Taiwan, one can therefore state that they give dynamic space to the negotiation of rival resources, contribute to subjective well-being, ensure social or ideological cohesion, and can be experienced by the self-denoting Buddhist as a tool for successful self-imagining, combining the notion of an elite and intellectual self-understanding, a science compatible world view while serving as a means of stabilising the moral codes and social structures and contributing to economic and private success. The possible eclectic application of Buddhist resources and a smooth transition into the Buddhist field make "Buddhism" a doctrinal and social integrative dynamic movement that responds to the discursive threads of Taiwanese modernity. Buddhist patterns of self-construction successfully reflect the transnational milieu of their participants, so that these can creatively apply Buddhist resources to fulfil their own longing for a consistent definition of their individual role within society.

17 Lay Buddhists in Contemporary China and Taiwan

One might finally ask how far the situation presented here is specific to the case of Taiwan. Field research in mainland China has been hindered for a long time by political circumstances. It is only recently that one has seen the first studies of a religious revival on the mainland. Two larger studies have been conducted, directly related to the development of lay Buddhism. The first study by Alison Denton Jones (2010) focuses on lay Buddhists in the urban context of Nanjing and analyses the public narratives, organisations and players in the field of Nanjing Buddhism, as well as the reception and deployment of Buddhist narratives by lay people (Jones 2010, 15). The second study by Gareth Fisher (2014) is an in-depth analysis of Buddhist life in the outer courtyard of the Temple of Universal Rescue (Guangji Si 廣濟寺) in Peking–an in-between space of postmodern characteristics (ibid., 18) already belonging to the monastery and therefore not part of the secular public space, but also out of the focus of the monastics' attention. This "island of religiosity" (ibid., 204) is revealed as a kind of 'Hyde Park Corner' (ibid., 8), in which people stroll by, listen to others preaching, or shape their own creative discourses on the political and religious master narratives. The whole interactions and narrations reflect how people experience and process life-challenges and what Fisher calls "moral breakdowns" (ibid., 3). These are induced by a rapidly developing Chinese modernity that accompanies the urbanisation process and social change, including the increasingly unstable social relations, the pressure of success and the loss of job security while at the same time a general shift of the communist agenda towards a capitalism friendly society is taking place.

Religious politics in mainland China have led to the official recognition of five religions, among them (besides Daoism, Islam, Protestantism and Catholicism) Buddhism.[165] These are equipped with representative official bureaus that are united in the Bureau of Religious Affairs (State Administration for Religious Affairs, Guojia Zongjiao Shiwuju 國家宗教事務局), founded in 1954. The bureaus serve as a link and continuity between religious life and the political agenda of the communist state. Communities that intend to belong to one of the five official religions must register with their respective bureaus. Recognised institutions perform regular services for the believers' community under the supervision of the state. Forms of licit religious life

[165] For a first overview about religion and religious politics in mainland China, see Clart (2014).

make up what the sociologist Yang Fenggang calls the "red market" which is accompanied by a "gray market" (Yang 2006). The gray zone refers to all kinds of religious activities that are not officially recognised but tolerated by the state. Traditionally, in Late Imperial China, exclusive religious belonging was expected from religious specialists, while the average citizen would choose religious services according to their varying needs. In communist China, the attribution of the neologisms "religion" and "superstition" (see chap. 1) were directly linked to the harsh political consequences and triggered the need for religious institutionalisation and formal belonging. Non-recognised religious activities were discouraged, banned and persecuted as "superstitious". This was accompanied by the building up of a strong narrative of "militant atheism" (Jones 2010, 4) that remains present in the narrations of Beijing and Nanjing lay Buddhists although the communist philosophy of which the atheistic view is an integral part is increasingly out of the focus while capitalism-oriented, economic growth and the building of a strong, competitive nation remain central. In general, all kinds of religious traditions in a broad sense fill this vacuum and movements can gain a huge dynamic. Conversions to Christianity have attracted the attention of missionary organisations for years.[166] Mantic techniques and prognostication are again visible in urban life and the rediscovery and growth of these techniques, central to popular religious belief over the centuries, is reflected for example in the publishing market (Lackner 2011). The practice of *qigong* 氣功 was already in the 1980s common on the mainland and supported by politicians. One spoke of "Qigong fever" even, until it became associated with the Falun Gong movement. They were and remain harshly prosecuted as they developed into a large movement that was able to assemble and instrumentalise their large crowds of followers with ease (Palmer 2007). There is a rising search for a positive outlook on life, for concepts that go beyond materialistic and utilitarian orientations. Movements of this kind are sometimes called "feverish" (*re* 熱) in mainland China. One for example also speaks of a "fever of happiness", the "happiness craze" as the sociologist Li Zhang (*xingfu re* 幸福熱) names it: "A new form of urban aspiration is emerging among China's middle-class professionals in the midst of rapid and often disorienting socioeconomic transformations: namely, an intense interest in and fervent pursuit of personal happiness in the name of science and well-being" (Zhang 2015, 315). A "science of happiness" evolves, addressing a growing clientele which describes its affective life experiences with adjectives like "restless" or "anxious" (*fuzao* 浮躁, *jiaolü* 焦慮; see Zhang 2015, 318). Recent Buddhological research shows how far Tibetan Buddhism is re-

166 See the regular "News Update" that appears in the journal *Religions & Christianity in Today's China* and for a state-of-the-field report Wenzel-Teuber (2014).

discovered by Han Chinese citizens and leads to a new and vital spread of Tibetan religious knowledge (Smyer Yü 2012).

In comparison with mainland China, the socio-religious movements in Taiwan are less commonly designated as "feverish". While under martial law, the government strictly controlled religious life, freedom of association was granted in 1987, prompting the emergence of numerous religious communities all over the island. As there is no divide between the officially recognised traditions in contrast to a gray market or illicit religious life, the percentage of people denoting themselves as Buddhist is at least ten times higher. There is no reliable statistical data for the mainland available[167]–and already for the case of Taiwan it has been shown that it makes limited sense only to ask for people's identification with a neologism (see chap. 1). In the statistical survey of the religious experience of the mainland in 2005 jointly conducted by the Religious Experience Research Centre at the University of Wales, Lampeter, and the Ian Ramsey Centre at the University of Oxford, 5.3% of the respondents claimed to have a religion, while 2.6% claimed to be Buddhist (Yao 2007, 178). In contrast, in Taiwan in 2004, 79.3% (1491/1881) of the population saw themselves as having a religious belief and 24.1% of the population saw themselves as Buddhist (see chap. 5). This huge difference is connected to the fact that, on the mainland, seeing oneself as a Buddhist might place one at the margins of society, and could even be a stigma. This connotation is in general not associated with a Buddhist belonging in Taiwan.

Becoming a Buddhist seems to ask for a stronger decision in China and can at times even be intentionally hidden by the convert (Fisher 2014, 92f.). Occasional belonging seems rarely to be the case in mainland China. The Buddhist identity is less easily communicable. Neither Fisher nor Jones report believers occasionally referring to themselves as Buddhist. Softly sliding into the field and the general notion of the Buddhist field as having a general positive value is linked to Taiwanese society. In mainland China, Buddhist followers often even seem to be unaware of the real names of their co-practitioners, but are only aware of their dharma names (Jones 2010, 253). Horizontal relationships are less often created among disciples: "(m)ost people do not know each other and do not get to know each other much [...]" (Jones 2010, 213). This implies a totally different role for the researcher in Taiwan: while interviews in Taiwan by the author were recorded and could therefore be transcribed and analysed in detail, the suspicion on the part of the interviewees as well as the official institutions about the aims of the researcher hindered the audiotaping as well as restricted access to research material on the mainland (Jones 2010, 16ff., esp. 18).

167 See for an overview about recent statistics with regard to religion on the mainland Guggenmos (2015).

Also, internationality is much less a topic for the believers described by Fisher and Jones.[168] The peculiarity of mainland internationality seems to be that it is one-directional. Buddhist publications–that are distributed for free at certain officially recognised sites only–might be of international origin–from Taiwan, the United States, or Singapore, for example, but there are no Chinese Buddhist publications that are successfully spreading outside mainland China (Fisher 2014, 147). On the mainland, the most widespread Buddhist publications are the publications of Master Jingkong, originally from Taiwan, who now lives in Australia. His introductory work "Understanding Buddhism" is a frequent point of reference.[169] His publications are also well known and widespread throughout Taiwan. The overseas Chinese community is present in mainland China through their publications. These are of greater importance than in Taiwan. While freely distributed material is available easily all over Taiwan, the demand for such publications is modest. Buddhist institutions in Taiwan in general have branches all over the island, if not internationally. Believers read their organisations' publications, but they are also in direct contact with believers from other places. On the mainland, Buddhist institutions cannot build up branches and offices across the country or even internationally, but are restricted to one location only. Therefore, the freely distributed output of Buddhist publications might help believers to catch up with a larger imagined community of Buddhists.

The fact that organisations cannot spread their branches across mainland China freely has lead to a Buddhist field where the institutions less specifically address lay Buddhists' interests and needs. The inner differentiation of the organisational field shows a smaller variety on the mainland as translocal alliances and networks among religious organisations are forbidden. Jones notes: "Taiwanese Buddhist organisations are developing distinct 'branches' like environmentalism, charity, traditional Chan, or intellectualism [...]. Temples in Nanjing do not seem to have established clear 'brands' or foci, and the major temples all basically offered or housed the same sorts of activities and groups" (Jones 2010, 77). Buddhist producers offer "only one package, the 'traditional devotee'" (Jones 2010, 178).

In contrast, mainland Buddhist *believers* follow a broader variation of orientations, although the diversity in Taiwan might be much more developed. The methodologies of Jones and Fisher follow quite different paths from Structural Hermeneutics applied in this book, thereby making a direct com-

168 Jones notes that her interviewees "did not seem to see Buddhism as a global imagined community. Few seemed to feel any connection to Buddhists in other countries or even to ethnically Tibetan lay Buddhists within the PRC" (Jones 2010, 284).

169 *Renshi Fojiao* 認識佛教; Fisher 2014, 147; also Jones 2010, 223: "Jing Kong is far and away the single most important producer of teachings about Buddhism, especially at the introductory level, in Nanjing Buddhism."

parison impossible. Fisher's cases are, of course, all in some way linked to the temple's courtyard that he focuses on and any practitioners that fall outside this scheme will not be represented in his sample. Jones' definition of being a lay Buddhist is narrower. In choosing her interviewees, she also applies contrastive criteria, but these are linked to other categories.[170] Still, some of the outcomes of both researches shall be presented here in relation to the Taiwanese situation:

In her analysis, Jones identifies two main orientations within the four modes of practicing Buddhism that she developed from the material–intellectual, self-transformative, compassion-oriented, pragmatic (Jones 2010, 190–194): traditional devotees with a more ritualistic orientation and scholars with a more rationalistic orientation. While traditional devotees tend to describe their mode of becoming Buddhist more as an adoption of a natural, orthodox and legal belief that is part of traditional culture (Jones 2010, 122f.), rational scholars of Buddhism would represent a minority of lay Buddhists, highly educated and predominantly male, who describe becoming a Buddhist in the modes of converts and seekers. They are more likely to be involved in meditational practices, be less ritualistically-orientated and more likely to be in contact with esoteric (Tibetan) Buddhism, as these would be the best educated teachers. In between these two modes, Jones identifies a "'messy middle'" of "'non-traditional eclectics'" (Jones 2010, 192)–younger, well-educated, not yet retired, often white-collar professionals. Reading through the cases, Jones mediates the impression that self-positioning within a society that once promoted atheism and is now focusing on maximising economic growth is a major point of departure for lay Buddhist engagement: "the Maoist campaigns to destroy traditional Chinese values, coupled with the wide-spread discrediting of communist ideology, have left Chinese people with few cultural resources for establishing self worth other than by displaying economic success through conspicious consumption" (Jones 2010, 204). Within the given limits, people explore the Buddhist options of answering this need for establishing self worth: conspicuous benevolence, displaying high culture, being a good person, performing competence, and being a good citizen are the five strategies that Jones derives from the material (Jones 2010, 206–209). The main difference between mainland China and Taiwan seems to be that the dominant metanarrative of coping with an atheistic ideology is characteristic for mainland China, while in the case of Taiwan the options of living a Bud-

170 Jones aims at the highest variation regarding gender, age, education, Buddhist organisation and Buddhist practices (Jones 2010, 19–20). The author also intended to get as close as possible to people from all kinds of background, but the decisive criterion for holding an interview was based on how far it is different from the hypothesis developed in the run of the other interviews' analyses.

dhist lay life are much broader and more homogenously developed. Taiwanese self-denoted Buddhists play with ease with various roles and patterns of Buddhist identification. They profit from their delocalised mode, where no major restorative hopes of the once established Buddhist schools and traditions are self-suggestive and no comparison with historically sectarian movements like the White Lotus Sect (ter Haar 1992) is causing excitement.

Fisher in his analysis of the interactions in the outer courtyard of the Temple of Universal Rescue comes to "key symbols" (Ortner; see Fisher 2015, 20) as identifiable central tropes in the practitioners' own description of their experiences and identities as Buddhists. The trope of finding inner tranquillity and balance (*pingheng* 平衡; Fisher, chap. II) is certainly common also in Taiwan as it is the shared heritage of the Pure Land and Chan Buddhist traditions. The division between these two major directions is emic to the field. Fisher describes Pure Land followers as holding an anticipatory mode, focusing on a better rebirth in their next life. At least for the case of Taiwan, one can state that the effects of name recitation are explored in inventive ways especially by highly educated and young people in Taiwan, although there is also the general notion of elderly people performing mechanistic recitations without major intellectual involvement. The publisher Gu is deeply engaged in name recitation, for example. The mode of "synthesis" to resolve "external contradictions through internal psychological adjustments" (Fisher 2014, 73)–hinting at meditational techniques and the way of Chan Buddhism–is also in Taiwan in the public notion more connected to younger people and intellectual ambitions. Still, screening through the cases presented would not suggest making these two approaches characteristic for two kinds of Buddhist followers. The biographies are mostly not only much more complex, but the decision "meditation or recitation" does not play a central role in the narrated belief development.

Karmic connections are assumed to share a common rhetoric in Taiwan: while 75.5% of the general population believed in Karmic retribution and rebirth (TSCS 2004.2, v27.5), 88,4% of those involved in the above mentioned study on religious experience on the mainland believed that "the good will be rewarded and the bad will be punished" (Tsai 2013, 295). The talking of *yuanfen*, karmic connections, is ubiquitous in Taiwan, but less so is explicit reference to *foyuan*, to which Fisher refers (Fisher 2014, chap. III). Buddhists try to enter a new moral code related to karmic thinking rather than rely on interpersonal relationships (*guanxi* 關係)–this seems to be peculiar for the case of mainland China. Established in the post-Mao period Buddhist thinking on "cause and effect" (*yinguo* 因果) as a "substitute teleology" (Fisher 2014, 126) that helps to overcome mainland Chinas moral decline (Fisher 2014, 62), neither features in the narratives of the interviewees nor reflects the situation in Taiwanese society. While Chinese urban spaces also focus less on "moral breakdowns" in comparison with the outer courtyard analysed by Fisher, Buddhists in Taiwan certainly turn to Buddhist sources in order to cope with difficulties in their lives–one might recall the outstanding case of Luo Peirong, but in general the analysis leads more to personal biographical issues that might be connected to the frame of an open, democratic, capitalism- and achievement-oriented society than to communism-forced structural social problems. The pressure of *guanxi*-related corruption is obviously much less prominent. Still, whether in China or Taiwan, people perceive the question of how they became Buddhists as making sense. One can of course refer to the fact that defining oneself as a lay Buddhist as a conscious choice is new. As Jones writes: "I believe this greater inclination towards formal religious involvement stems from the expansion of formal education in China by the communist state and in particular from the adoption of a formal model of religion as a modern ideal" (Jones 2010, 154). Therefore, for Jones, "[T]he necessity of converting to Buddhism from a conflicting worldview, and the adoption of Buddhism as a rationalized, coherent worldview, are both novel developments in the history of lay Buddhism in China" (Jones 2010, 153). Becoming a Buddhist is historically seen as a new option rather than an inherited belief over generations, as Buddhist belonging itself is a young differential category. It is interesting to note that the formalisation of religious belonging is occurring on both sides of the Taiwan Strait. The forced process of secularisation in its communist shape on the mainland and the more open and complex development toward a modern democracy in Taiwan that both might be seen in connection with the revised secularisation thesis by José Casanova result in conscious choices by people to denote themselves as belonging to a certain religion.[171]

In addition, it might also be characteristic of Engaged Buddhist movements in particular to smoothly integrate into a secularised society: Jessica Main and Rongdao Lai describe socially Engaged Buddhism as a continuing reformation process of 20th century East Asian Buddhism and parallel it to the ongoing secularisation processes. Engaged Buddhism can, in Lai and Main's words, even be described as the "mirror image of secularization" (Lai and Main 2013, 4). Picking up the revised secularisation hypothesis of Casanova, Lai and Main analyse the social engagement of Engaged Buddhists itself as liberating and soteriologically relevant. Buddhist engagement in consequence does not have to be socially recognisable as "Buddhist". In consequence, Engaged Buddhists do not necessarily perceive the secularisation

171 Casanova (1994) suggested a modified secularisation thesis characterised by 1) the structural differentiation of secular spheres such as politics, economy, and science from the religious sphere, 2) the overall decline of religious practices and beliefs, and 3) the privatisation of religion.

process as a threat for religious life: they found ways to escape any marginalising privatisation.

Mainland China and Taiwan are both part of a process of secularisation that is intensely present in urban spaces across the two hugely differing political systems. This might finally lead to specific biographical developments in religious belonging that remain conscious to urbanites and are reflected in the interviews.

Research on religion in urban spaces is back on the agenda in a recent huge research project at the Max-Planck-Institute in Göttingen, Germany. The director, Peter van der Veer, of the Institute for the Study of Religious and Ethnic Diversity has launched several research projects on the role of religion in urban spaces, resulting in the "Handbook of Religion and the Asian City" (2015). Van der Veer converged the broad pan-Asian projects by outlining a concept of spirituality, which he defines as a modern phenomenon (van der Veer 2009, 1097). Through comparing Indian and Chinese megacities, van der Veer finds "a similar appropriation of spiritual traditions to cater for the newly emerging middle classes". "These newly manufactured spiritualities", he concludes, "have a tenuous relationship with textual traditions, guarded by centers of learning and spiritual masters. They are creative in their response to new opportunities and anxieties produced by globalization and are, as such, comparable to Pentecostal and charismatic varieties of Christianity" (van der Veer 2009, 1117). This search for spirituality, that at times results in consciously moulding one's way of becoming a Buddhist, appears particularly intense in Taiwan as well as in mainland China. Future research will benefit from analysing the impact of urbanisation and secularisation on the development of lay Buddhism by a comparative perspective including other regions such as Japan, Theravāda Buddhist countries or even "Western" Buddhist developments.

Conclusion

18 On Being a Lay Buddhist in Contemporary Taiwan

Lay Buddhist self-construction in contemporary Taiwan is attractive, especially in the urban areas. This book takes as its starting point a statistical investigation into Taiwanese Buddhist belief with the help of the *Taiwan Social Change Survey* (TSCS 2004.2). The findings of the analysis suggest that more people denote themselves Buddhists in the urban regions of Taiwan than in its remote or developing areas. This being so, an array of nine biographical narrative interviews with urban citizens of Taiwan who claim to be lay Buddhists was analysed, applying the method of Structural Hermeneutics developed by U. Oevermann. The analysis concentrated on two foci:

In the first part of the book, in-depth analyses of Buddhists who in the survey would not have specified their belief further were analysed under the aspect of identifying the underlying conventional narrative patterns that shed light on the social perception of Buddhism.

Karmic tropes were frequently employed in the conversations and their usage was identified, unlike other usages of this trope within Asia, as creating situational harmony, serving as a means of protecting one's privacy and fostering smooth group integration. Besides its predictive or explanatory functions, it served as a highly flexible integrative script of communication. The belief of the lay Buddhists also emphasised social harmony, respect for authority and family values. The topic of veneration (*baibai*) was approached in different ways by the interviewees and showed that either Buddhists integrate popular religious veneration behaviour smoothly with their Buddhist belief, distance themselves from it, or find ways to argue for a continuation of veneration through re-interpreting the act itself, from asking personally for spiritual succor to emphasising veneration for the sake of "all sentient beings". Buddhism is also applied in the interviews to sustain a moral code ritually or cognitively, which is rooted in the social discourse and which values are not based upon primarily religious orientations. This code appears to centre around social well-being, health, business success, and a peaceful, unproblematic family life. A strongly-established narrational pattern describing the effect of Buddhist recitation or meditation practice in daily life lies in the description of its positive transformation of social life through its tranquillising effects.

In evaluating the interviews of Part I and trying to explain the higher percentage of Buddhists in cities, a number of motivations could be identified that lead to a self-denotation as a Buddhist in urban Taiwan: Buddhist organisational resources offer citizens ways to socialise in an urban environment, reshape their social contacts and experience better social relationships. The

"Buddhist" discourse–in the form of a label, doctrine or social community–proves a helpful resource for situating oneself in the urban environment and seems to fit the urban climate of Taipeh, as it enhances and supports economic, social and private success. The historically-rooted roles of lay Buddhists, like donors and Buddhist intellectuals ("cultural Buddhists"), remain available, and the traditionally-oriented Buddhist communities fill niches. Movements resulting from Buddhist Modernism and forms of a Taiwanese Engaged Buddhism gather communities of followers. The diversification of consumption patterns is a result of the integrative dynamic within the Buddhist field, which is based on loose boundaries and missing organisational monopolies on the one hand and organisational and discursive threads that unite the field on the other. Low entry barriers make a "soft switch" to the Buddhist field possible for the general public, as the widespread religio-social behaviour is not opposed, Buddhist doctrine is formulated in a simple, applicable manner with discourse threads oscillating between karma, practice, and veneration, and positive attitudes towards business, which enable potential supporters to make a smooth transit into the Buddhist field. In addition, with a missing obligatory formal initiation or set of knowledge to enter "Buddhism", it can be shown that a concrete mental or social change is not necessarily a prerequisite for entering the Buddhist field. The attractiveness of Buddhism wins through a general positive notion of Buddhist self-denotification in Taiwanese society, so that Buddhism is applied as a tool for re-stabilising moral codes and social structures.

In the first part of this book, the emphasis was on the conventional patterns of Buddhist belief, which revealed that the field of self-denoting Buddhists is often blurred with that of popular religious practitioners. In Part II, the focus shifted from the underlying conventional patterns to habitus formations, which intensively exploit "Buddhism" for biographical self-construction in search of answers to the challenges posed by urban life in the metropolitan areas. Four cases were presented in the form of short portraits to demonstrate the possible width of the field regarding the question of how "Buddhism" can serve–unlike in the conventionally-established patterns–in a differentiated and specific way intense forms of Buddhist identity construction.

Buddhist believers and practitioners inspired by the reformatory efforts during the Republican Era on the Mainland were presented. Their Buddhist self-imagining was shaped by their seclusion from the field of popular religious belonging and by designing Buddhism as a tool for a positive Eastern self-reconstruction. In contemporary Taiwan, the image of Buddhism in public is shaped especially by the Young Buddhist Monasteries which know how to engage huge numbers of followers in their activities. Ma Fengling was chosen to exemplify the transformation of her whole social environment and life concept by identifying with a Young Buddhist Monastery that was engaged in charity work. The framework of her institution led her to restate her own biography and reshape her role in society, enlarging the caring role of a mother to become a helping bodhisattva for those in need of social help. The Buddhist engagement enabled Ma to match her personal expectations of life with the traditional expectations of society, without compromising her belief. Xu Wenhua, in contrast, reflected the option of lay Buddhist belief that is not organisationally-induced. She had the financial, educational and leisure-time resources to embark on a long spiritual journey, based on coping with the bereavement of her mother's death in her early youth. This intensive personal search lead her finally to develop her own concept of living a quasi-monastic lay life in society while trying to reach out, through translation activities, to society by spreading Buddhism internationally. Xu was in the end becoming organisationally independently active in society. The self-concept of Zhang Yimin revealed similar independence. Zhang fell back upon non-organisational resources–his home, where Chan Buddhist stories and meditation were present, and his teacher, who made him aware of Buddhism as a long-established source of Chinese intellectual inspiration. Zhang demonstrated the dynamic self-concept of a cultural Buddhist who is confidently approaching new resources by developing his world view and Buddhist concept further, including international resources. Meng Fanyi finally integrated totally into a New Buddhist Movement which satisfied her longing to give shape to a multidimensional and processual life-design and aestheticisation. Her group cultivated a processual, dynamic approach, balancing the guidance of its master with the individual experience of its members. Meng thankfully embraced this offer and enjoyed the flexibility, dynamic, and personal approach of the group, without having to shape the concept as a whole.

The cases presented revealed that the Buddhist identification pattern seems to suit the skills that are advantageous to members living in the constant cultural flux of the metropolitan areas. Discussions on "Engaged Buddhism" and "Buddhist Activism" make clear that Taiwan is embedded in an international Buddhist development that started in the late 19th century. While, in contrast to other East Asian countries, "Engaged Buddhism" in Taiwan is far less politically engaged and less anti-colonial aggressive than in other countries, only the analysis of lay Buddhist biographical narratives revealed what makes it attractive to denote oneself a "Buddhist" in the urban climate of Taiwan. The driving inspiration for such a self-definition might also be fostered by slogans from the Young Buddhist Monasteries and other movements, but the field of Buddhist resources is revealed to be far broader. Lay Buddhists can construct Buddhism as a highly flexible script of integrative power and as a means of coping with contemporary society, enhancing economic, social, and personal success and well-being. A strong experiential dimension close to empirical provability in accordance with the natural sciences is easily integrated into this concept of Buddhism. Lay Buddhists thematise the body in correspondance with to a growing bodily awareness in urban Taiwan. Buddhism serves the longing for the development of a body-culture in a society which is increasingly aware of the possibilities and capable of shaping the body according to one's own wishes. The bodily self-cultivation allowed practitioners to merge the aesthetical and ethical ideals of life conduct into an all-embracing life-design that was united via a concept of Buddhism as the "method" and "principle" that shall enable people to judge any upcoming issue.

The driving force and major reason for the attraction of denoting oneself a lay Buddhist in contemporary Taiwan is therefore to be found at the core of the social dynamic of the transforming society. Buddhism is constructed as securing orientation in an increasing width of possibilities. At the same time, it coheres with the major discussion threads that arise in highly populated areas with a high educational rate and good income: self-aestheticisation, leisure-time management, entertainment, body-shaping and bodily practices, conscious life-construction, up to an international awareness, are all integrated into Buddhist discussion threads and creatively interpreted by the followers themselves. A further study of the thriving phenomenon of "Buddhism" in urban Taiwan would therefore request deeper studies of the specific profile of Taiwanese modernity and of the notion of global interconnectedness and the transnational flows within it, and explore the relationship of lay Buddhists with distinct topics like, for example, the role of body culture, life-design and aestheticisation in contemporary Taiwanese urban society.

Introducing a comparative perspective including Taiwanese and mainland Chinese Buddhism, this book finally opens up a comparative perspective. In the two cases, the political setting differs drastically. In consequence, the percentage of people denoting themselves as Buddhist is at least ten times higher in Taiwan than on the mainland. On the mainland, seeing oneself as a Buddhist might place one at the margins of society, and imply stigmatisation. Becoming a Buddhist seems to ask for a stronger decision in China and occasional belonging is no convenient option. In contrast to Taiwan, for mainland believers internationality is much less a topic and consists mainly of the perception of Buddhist publications from outside of China. Translocal alliances and networks among religious organisations are forbidden, Buddhist organisations cannot spread their branches freely and therefore the inner differentiation of the Buddhist organisational field shows a smaller variety. The main difference to Taiwan seems to be that the dominant metanarrative of coping with an atheistic ideology is characteristic for mainland China, while in the case of Taiwan the options of living a Buddhist lay life are much broader: Taiwanese self-denoted Buddhists play with ease with various roles and patterns of Buddhist identification. They profit from their delocalised mode, where no major restorative hopes of the once established Buddhist schools and traditions are self-suggestive and association with persecuted sectarian movements is a possible threat.

Narrations of lay Buddhists in mainland China and Taiwan share several patterns: The trope of finding inner tranquillity and balance is common. The talking of *yuanfen*, karmic connections, is ubiquitous in Taiwan, while explicit reference to Buddhist karmic connections, *foyuan*, seems to prevail on the mainland. On the mainland, Buddhists try to enter a new moral code related to karmic thinking rather than rely on interpersonal relationships when entering the Buddhist community. Interestingly, in the post-Mao period Buddhist concepts of cause and effect seem to serve as a "substitute teleology" (Fisher) – a development that has no parallel in Taiwan. The moral and religious vacuum is politically induced on the communist mainland and Buddhist movements try to fill the niches that result from this vacuum. In Taiwan secularisation and urbanisation processes as well as the challenges of a capitalism- and achievement-oriented society are more prevalent in the process of shaping the adaptation of Buddhism.

It is interesting to note that the formalisation of religious belonging is occurring on both sides of the Taiwan Strait. Mainland China and Taiwan are both part of a process of secularisation that is intensely present in urban spaces across the two hugely differing political systems. This finally leads to specific biographical developments in religious belonging that reflect in the interviews. Future research on the impact of urbanisation and modernisation processes upon religious and Buddhist movements will benefit from opening up the perspective to the whole of East Asia up to including Theravāda Buddhist countries or "Western" Buddhist movements.

Bibliography

Andrade, Tonio. 2008. *How Taiwan Became Chinese: Dutch, Spanish, and Han Colonization in the Seventeenth Century.* New York: Columbia University Press.

Austin, John Longshaw. 1962. *How To Do Things With Words. The William James Lectures delivered at Harvard University in 1955*, edited by J.O. Urmson. London: Oxford University Press.

Barrett, Timothy H., and Francesca Tarocco. 2006. "Dongya zongjiao jiemi: Yige Xin de puxi 东亚宗教揭密：一个新的谱系" [East Asian Religion Unmasked: A New Genealogy]. *Dangdai Zongjiao Yanjiu* 当代宗教研究 [Contemporary Religious Studies] 4: 37–43.

Barrett, Timothy H., and Francesca Tarocco. 2012. "Terminology and Religious Identity: Buddhism and the Genealogy of the Term 'Zongjiao'." In *Dynamics in the History of Religions between Asia and Europe: Encounters, Notions, and Comparative Perspectives*, edited by Volkhard Krech and Marion Steinicke. Leiden: Brill. 307–319.

Bechert, Heinz. 1966–1973. *Buddhismus, Staat und Gesellschaft in den Ländern des Theravada-Buddhismus.* 3 vols. Frankfurt and Wiesbaden: Metzner and Harrassowitz.

Bechert, Heinz. 1995. "Buddhist Revival in East and West." In *The World of Buddhism*, edited by Heinz Bechert and Richard Gombrich. London: Thames and Hudson. 273–285.

Becker-Lenz, Roland, Andreas Franzmann, Axel Jansen and Matthias Jung, eds. 2016. *Die Methodenschule der Objektiven Hermeneutik: Eine Bestandsaufnahme.* Wiesbaden: Springer.

Bertaux, Daniel, and Martin Kohli. 1984. "The Life Story Approach: A Continental View." *Annual Review of Sociology* 10: 215–237.

Beyer, Peter. 1997. "Epistemological modesty: An interview with Peter Berger." *Christian Century* 114: 972–975.

Bhambra, Gurminder K. 2007. *Rethinking Modernity: Postcolonialism and the Sociological Imagination.* New York: Palgrave.

Bielefeldt, Carl. 2005. "Practice." In *Critical Terms for the Study of Buddhism*, edited by Donald S. Lopez Jr.. Chicago: The University of Chicago Press. 229–244.

BIOS. 2007. *Zeitschrift für Biographieforschung, oral history und Lebensverlaufsanalysen* 20, 1/2007.

Bingenheimer, Marcus. 2003. "Chinese Buddhism Unbound–Rebuilding and Redefining Chinese Buddhism on Taiwan." In *Buddhism in Global Perspective*, edited by Kalpakam Sankarnarayan. Mumbai: Somaiya Publications. 122–146.

Bingenheimer, Marcus. 2004. *Der Mönchsgelehrte Yinshun (*1906) und seine Bedeutung für den chinesisch-taiwanischen Buddhismus im 20. Jahrhundert.* Heidelberg: Edition Forum.

Bohnsack, Ralf. 1999. *Rekonstruktive Sozialforschung: Einführung in Methodologie und Praxis qualitativer Forschung.* Opladen: Leske+Budrich.

Bourdieu, Pierre. 1967. "Postface." In *Architecture gothique et pensée scolastique. Traduction et postface de Pierre Bourdieu,* Erwin Panofsky. Paris: Éditions de Minuit. 133–167.

Bourdieu, Pierre. 1974. "Der Habitus als Vermittlung zwischen Struktur und Praxis." In *Zur Soziologie der symbolischen Formen,* Pierre Bourdieu. Frankfurt: Suhrkamp. 125–158.

Bourdieu, Pierre. 1979. "L'habitus et l'espace des styles de vie." In *La distinction. Critique sociale du judgement,* Pierre Bourdieu. Paris: Éditions de Minuit. 189–248.

Bourdieu, Pierre. 1980. "Structures, habitus, pratiques." In *Le sens pratique,* Pierre Bourdieu. Paris: Éditions de Minuit. 87-109.

Bourdieu, Pierre. 1990. *The Logic of Practice.* Stanford: Stanford University Press.

Bourdieu, Pierre. 1992. "Habitus, illusio et rationalité." In *Réponses pour une anthropologie réflexive,* Pierre Bourdieu. Paris: Éditions du Seuil. 91–115.

Brown, Callum. 1996. "Religion in the City: A Review Essay." *Urban History* 23: 372–379.

Broy, Nikolas. 2014. "Die religiöse Praxis der Zhaijiao ('Vegetarische Sekten') in Taiwan." Ph.D. diss., Universität Leipzig.

Buswell, Robert E. Jr. and Donald S. Lopez Jr., eds. 2014. *The Princeton Dictionnary of Buddhism,* Princeton: Princeton University Press.

Cai, Yongmei 蔡勇美, and Zhang Yinghua 章英華, eds. 1997. *Taiwan de dushi shehui* 台灣的都市社會 *[The Urban Society of Taiwan],* Taipeh: Juliu Tushu Gongsi 巨流圖書公司.

Campany, Robert Ford. 2003. "On the Very Idea of Religions (In the Modern West and in Early Medieval China)." *History of Religions* 42(4): 287–319.

Carnes, Tony, and Anna Karpathakis, eds. 2001. *New York Glory: Religions in the City.* New York: New York University Press.

Carnes, Tony. 2001. "Religions in the City – An Overview." In *New York Glory: Religions in the City,* edited by Tony Carnes and Anna Karpathakis. New York: New York University Press. 3–25.

Champion, Tony and Graeme Hugo. 2004. "Introduction: Moving Beyond the Urban-Rural Dichotomy." In *New Foms of Urbanization: Beyond the Urban-Rural Dichotomy,* edited by Tony Champion and Hugo Graeme. Aldershot: Ashgate. 3–24.

Chandler, Stuart. 2004. *Establishing a Pure Land on Earth: The Foguang Buddhist Perspective on Modernization and Globalization.* Honolulu: University of Hawai'i Press.

Chandler, Stuart. 2005. "Spreading Buddha's Light: The Internationalization of Foguang Shan." In *Buddhist Missionaries in the Era of Globalization*, edited by Linda Learman. Honolulu: University of Hawai'i Press. 162–184.

Chao, Hsing-Kuang. 2006. "Conversion to Protestantism among Urban Immigrants in Taiwan." *Sociology of Religion* 67(2): 193–204.

Casanova, José. 1994. *Public Religions in the Modern World.* Chicago: University of Chicago Press.

Chau, Adam Yuet, ed. 2011. *Religion in Contemporary China: Revitalization and innovation.* London: Routledge.

Chaves, Mark. 1994. "Secularization as Declining Religious Authority." *Social Forces* 72(3): 749–774.

Chen, Carolyn. 2005. "A Self of One's Own: Taiwanese Immigrant Women and Religious Conversion." *Gender and Society* 19(3): 336–357.

Chi, Wei-Hsian. 2005. "Wandel der Sozialform des Religiösen in Taiwan." Ph.D. diss., Universität Bielefeld.

Clart, Philip. 2014. "Religionen und Religionspolitik in China: Historische Grundlagen und aktuelle Perspektiven." In *Länderbericht China*, edited by Doris Fischer and Christoph Müller-Hofstede. Bonn: Bundeszentrale für Politische Bildung. 607–640.

Corbin, Juliet, and Anselm Strauss. 2008. *Basics of Qualitative Research: Techniques and Procedures for Developing Grounded Theory.* 3rd ed. London: Sage.

Day, Lincoln H., and Ma Xia, eds. 1994. *Migration and Urbanization in China.* New York: Sharpe.

DDB (*Digital Dictionary of Buddhism*), edited by Charles Muller. Accessed Dec 31, 2009, and Feb 15, 2016. http://buddhism-dict.net/ddb/.

Dean, Michael. 2005. "Los Angeles and the Chicago School: Invitation to a Debate." In *The Urban Sociology Reader*, edited by Jan Lin and Christopher Mele. Abingdon: Routledge. 106-116.

DeVido, Elise Anne. 2005. "Mapping the Trajectories of Engaged Buddhism in Taiwan and Southeast Asia." *The Ricci Bulletin* 2005: 31–62.

DeVido, Elise Anne. 2006. "The Women of Ciji." *eRenlai*, Feb 25, 2006, 7 p. Accessed March 16, 2016. http://www.erenlai.com/media/downloads/Ciji.pdf.

Diesinger, Gunter. 1984. *Vom General zum Gott: Kuan Yü (gest. 220 n. Chr.) und seine „posthume Karriere".* Frankfurt a. Main: Haag & Herchen.

Douay, Nicholas. 2008. "From Urban Corridor to Megalopolis: The 'Metropolization' of Taiwan." Paper presented at the Fifth Conference of the European Association of Taiwan Studies, Prague, April 18–20, 2008. Accessed March 16, 2016. http://www.soas.ac.uk/taiwanstudies/eats/eats2008/file43175.pdf.

Douglas, Mary. 1982. "The Effects of Modernisation on Religious Change." In *Religion and America: Spirituality in a secular age*, edited by Mary Douglas and S.M. Tipton. Boston: Beacon Press. 25–43.

Dutt, Nalinaksha. 1945. "Place of Laity in Early Buddhism." *The Indian Historical Quarterly* 21(3): 163–183.

Eickelpasch, Rolf, and Claudia Rademacher. 2004. *Identität*. Bielefeld: transcript.

Encyclopedia of Buddhism. 2004, edited by Robert E. Buswell, Jr.. New York: Macmillan Reference USA.

Engh, Michael E. 1997. "'A Multiplicity and Diversity of Faiths': Religion's Impact on Los Angeles and the Urban West, 1890–1940." *The Western Historical Quarterly* 28(4): 463–492.

Eppsteiner, Fred, ed. 1988. *The Path of Compassion: Writings on Socially Engaged Buddhism*. Berkeley: Parallax.

FBD (*Foguang Buddhist Dictionary. Foguang dacidian* 佛光大辭典). 2000, edited by Foguang Shan Zongwu Weiyuan Hui 佛光山宗務委員會. Kaohsiung: Foguang Shan.

Feige, Andreas, Bernhard Dressler, Wolfgang Lukatis, and Albrecht Schöll. 2000. *'Religion' bei ReligionslehrerInnen. Religionspädagogische Zielvorstellungen und religiöses Selbstverständnis in empirisch-soziologischen Zugängen. Ein Forschungsprojekt des Instituts für Sozialwissenschaften der TUZ Braunschweig im Forschungsverbund mit dem Religionspädagogischen Institut Loccum, Pastoralsoziologischen Institut der EFH-Hannover, Comenius-Institut Münster*. Münster: LIT.

Fischer-Schreiber, Ingrid, Franz-Karl Eberhard, and Michael S. Diener, eds. 1991. *The Shambala Dictionary of Buddhism and Zen*. Boston: Shambala.

Fisher, Gareth. 2014. *From Comrades to Bodhisattvas: Moral Dimensions of Lay Buddhist Practice in Contemporary China*. Honolulu: University of Hawai'i Press.

Fisher, Gareth. 2015. "The Flexibility of Religion. Buddhist Temples as Multiaspirational Sites in Contemporary Beijing." In *Handbook of Religion and the Asian City: Aspiration and Urbanization in the Twenty-First Century*, edited by Peter van der Veer. Oakland: University of California Press. 299–314

Flick, Uwe. 2002. "Qualitative research–state of the art." *Social Science Information* 41(1): 5–24.

Freiberger, Oliver. 2000. *Der Orden in der Lehre. Zur religiösen Deutung des Saṅgha im frühen Buddhismus*. Wiesbaden: Harrassowitz.

Gebhardt, Uta. 1988. "Qualitative sociology in the Federal Republic of Germany." *Qualitative Sociology* 11(1–2): 29–43.

Giddens, Anthony. 1986. *The Constitution of Society*. Cambridge: Polity.

Goldfuß, Gabriele. 2001. *Vers un bouddhisme du XXe siècle: Yang Wenhui (1837–1911), reformateur laïque et imprimeur.* Paris: Institute des Hautes Études Chinoises.

Gombrich, Richard. 1971. *Buddhist Precept and Practice: Traditional Buddhism in the Rural Highlands of Ceylon*. Oxford: Clarendon Press.

Gombrich, Richard. 1975. "Buddhist Karma and Social Control." *Comparative Studies in Society and History* 17(2): 212–220.

Goodell, Eric Stephen. 2012. "Taixu's (1890–1947) Creation of Humanistic Buddhism." Ph.D. diss., University of Virginia.

Goossaert, Vincent. 2005. "The Concept of Religion in China and the West." *Diogenes* 52(13): 13–20.

Goossaert, Vincent, and David Palmer. 2011. *The Religious Question in Modern China.* Chicago: The University of Chicago Press.

Gottmann, J. 1961. *Megalopolis: The Urbanized Northeastern Seaboard of the United States.* New York: Twentieth-Century Fund.

Gottmann, J. 1987. *Megalopolis Revisited: 25 Years Later.* College Park: The University of Maryland Institute for Urban Studies.

Grand dictionnaire Ricci de la langue chinoise. 2001. Préparé par les instituts Ricci de Paris et Taipei, 8 vols. Paris: Desclée de Brouwer, Paris: Institut Ricci, Taipeh: Institut Ricci.

Guggenmos, Esther-Maria. 2006. "'Engaged Buddhism' in Taiwan? Zum Profil eines gesellschaftlich engagierten Gegenwartsbuddhismus." *China heute* 25(3): 105–116.

Guggenmos, Esther-Maria. 2012. "Engaged Buddhism in Taiwan." In *Buddhism in East Asia*, edited by Anita Sharma. Delhi: Vidyanidhi. 232–253.

Guggenmos, Esther-Maria. 2014. "'Mrs. Ma' and 'Ms. Xu'–On the Attractiveness of Denoting Oneself a 'Buddhist' in the Increasingly Transnational Milieu of Urban Taiwan." In *Globalization and the Making of Religious Modernity in China: Transnational religions, Local Agents, and the Study of Religion, 1800–Present*, edited by Thomas Jansen, Thoralf Klein, and Christian Meyer. Leiden: Brill. 156–181.

Guggenmos, Esther-Maria. 2015. Review of *Religious Experience in Contemporary Taiwan and China* edited by Yen-zen Tsai (Taipeh: Chengchi University Press, 2013). Accessed March 24, 2016. http://chinet.cz/reviews/religion/religious-experience-in-contemporary-taiwan-and-china/.

Guggenmos, Esther-Maria. In preparation. *Auf dem Weg zu einem globalisierten Regionalbuddhismus.*

Guldin, Gregory Eliyu. 1997. *Farewell to Peasant China: Rural Urbanization and Social Change in the Late Twentieth Century*. New York: Sharpe.

Günzel, Marcus. 1998. *Die Taiwan-Erfahrung des chinesischen Saṅgha: Zur Entwicklung des buddhistischen Mönchs- und Nonnenordens in der Republik China nach 1949*. Göttingen: Seminar für Indologie und Buddhismuskunde.

Guterman, Stanley S. 1969. "In Defense of Wirth's 'Urbanism as a Way of Life'." *The American Journal of Sociology* 74 (5): 492–499.

Hammerstrom, Erik. 2015. *The Science of Chinese Buddhism: Early Twentieth-Century Engagements*, New York: Columbia University Press.

Hancock, Philip, and others, eds. 2000. *The Body, Culture and Society. An Introduction*. Philadelphia: Open University Press.

Harding, John, ed. 2012. *Studying Buddhism in Practice*. Abingdon: Routledge.

Harrison, Paul. 1995. "Searching for the Origins of the Mahāyāna: What Are We Looking For." *The Eastern Buddhist* 28: 48–69.

He, Bingyu 何丙郁 (Ho Peng Yoke). 1988. *Cong li, qu, shu guandian lun Ziping tuimingfa* 從理氣數觀點輪子平推命法 *[Looking at the Ziping Method of fate-calculation from the standpoint of the principles of 'li', 'qi', and 'shu']*. Xianggang 香港: Xianggang Daxue Chuban She 香港大學出版社.

Hill, R. C., and J.-W. Kim. 2000. "Global cities and developmental states: New York, Tokyo and Seoul." *Urban Studies* 37(12): 2167–2195.

Hitzler, Ronald, and Anne Honer. 1997. *Sozialwissenschaftliche Hermeneutik*. Stuttgart: UTB.

Ho, Peng Yoke. 2003. *Chinese Mathematical Astrology. Reaching out to the stars*. New York: Routledge.

Hoheisel, Karl. 1990. "Do ut des." In *Handwörterbuch religionswissenschaftlicher Grundbegriffe*, edited by Hubert Cancik, Burkhard Gladigow, and Matthias Laubscher, vol. 2. Stuttgart: Kohlhammer. 228–230.

Holt, J. B. 1940. "Holiness Religion: Cultural Shock and Social Reorganization." *American Sociological Review* 5: 740–747.

Hsiao, Hsin-Huang Michael. 2002. "Coexistence and Synthesis: Cultural Globalization and Localization in Contemporary Taiwan." In *Many Globalizations: Cultural Diversity in the Contemporary World*, edited by Peter L. Berger and Samuel P. Huntington. New York: Oxford University Press. 48–67.

Hsiao, Hsin-Huang Michael, ed. 2006. *The Changing Faces of the Middle Classes in Asia-Pacific*. Taipeh: Center for Asia-Pacific Studies, Academia Sinica.

Hsing Yun, Venerable Master. 2003. *Humanistic Buddhism: A Blueprint for Life*. Hacienda Heights: Buddha's Light Publishing.

Huang, Julia. 2003. "The Buddhist Tzu-Chi Foundation of Taiwan." In *Action Dharma: New Studies in Engaged Buddhism*, edited by Christopher S. Queen, Charles Prebish, and Damien Keown. London: Routledge Curzon. 134–151.

Huang, C. Julia. 2005. "The Compassion Relief Diaspora." In *Buddhist Missionaries in the Era of Globalization*, edited by Linda Learman. Honolulu: University of Hawai'i Press. 185–209.

Huang, C. Julia. 2009. *Charisma and Compassion. Cheng Yen and the Buddhist Tzu Chi Movement.* Boston: Harvard University Press.

Hugo, Graeme, and Tony Champion. 2004. "Conclusions and Recommendation." In *New Forms of Urbanization: Beyond the Urban-Rural Dichotomy*, edited by Tony Champion and Graeme Hugo. Aldershot: Ashgate. 365–384.

Huang, Chien-Yu Julia, and Robert Weller. 1998. "Merit and Mothering: Women and Social Welfare in Taiwanese Buddhism." *The Journal of Asian Studies* 57(2): 379-396.

Ip, Hung-yok. 2009. "Buddhist Activism and Chinese Modernity." *Journal of Global Buddhism* 10: 145-192.

Ji, Zhe, and Vincent Goossaert, eds. 2011. *Les implications sociales du renouveau Buddhique en Chine / Social implications of Buddhist revival in China.* Special Issue: *Social Compass* 58(4).

Jindra, Ines W., and Michael Jindra. 2003. "Structural ('Objective') Hermeneutics and the Sociology of Religion." *Research in the Social Scientific Study of Religion* 14: 253–276.

Jones, Alison Denton. 2010. "A Modern Religion? The State, The People and the Remaking of Buddhism in Urban China Today." Ph.D. diss., Harvard University.

Jones, Charles Brewer. 1997. "Stages in Religious Life of Lay Buddhists in Taiwan." *Journal of the International Association of Buddhist Studies* 20.1: 113–119.

Jones, Charles Brewer. 1999. *Buddhism in Taiwan. Religion and the State, 1669–1990.* Honolulu: University of Hawai'i Press.

Juvin, Hervé. 2005. *L'avènement du corps.* Paris: Gallimard.

Kan Zhengzong 闞正宗. 2004. *Zhongdu Taiwan fojiao. Zhanhou Taiwan fojiao* 重讀台灣佛教. 戰後台灣佛教 *[Reading intensively Taiwanese Buddhism. Postwar Taiwanese Buddhism]*, vol. 2. Xizhi 汐止: Daqian 大千.

Kapaló, James A. 2013. "Folk Religion in Discourse and Practice." *Journal of Ethnology and Folkloristics* 7(1): 3–18.

Kelle, Udo. 2007. *Die Integration qualitativer und quantitativer Methoden in der empirischen Sozialforschung: Theoretische Grundlagen und methodologische Konzepte.* Wiesbaden: VS Verlag für Sozialwissenschaften.

Keown, Damien. 2003. *Oxford Dictionary of Buddhism.* Oxford: Oxford University Press.

Keyes, Charles F., and E. Valentine Daniel. 1983. *Karma. An Anthropological Inquiry.* Berkeley: University of California Press.

Kilian, L.M. 1953. "The Adjustment of Southern White Migrants to Northern Urban Norms." *Social Forces* 32: 66–69.

Kincheloe, Samuel C. 1965a. "The Theoretical Perspectives for the Sociological Study of Religion in the City: (Lecture I) Ecological and Anthropological Perspectives: In Special Reference to the Growth and Distribution of Religious Institutions and People in Metropolitan Areas." *Review of Religious Research* 6(2): 63–76.

Kincheloe, Samuel C. 1965b. "The Sociological Study of Religion in the City: The Perspective of Social Interaction (Lecture II)." *Review of Religious Research* 6(2): 77–81.

Kluge, Susann, and Udo Kelle, ed. 2001. *Methodeninnovation in der Lebenslaufforschung. Integration qualitativer und quantitativer Verfahren in der Lebenslauf- und Biographieforschung*. Weinheim: Juventa.

Kotler, Arnold, ed. 1996. *Engaged Buddhist Reader*. Berkeley: Parallax.

Kraft, Kenneth. 2000. "New Voices in Engaged Buddhist Studies." In *Engaged Buddhism in the West*, edited by Christopher S. Queen. Boston: Wisdom Publications. 485-511.

Krais, Beate, and Gunter Gebauer. 2002. *Habitus*. Bielefeld: Transcript.

Lackner, Michael. 2011. "Die Renaissance divinatorischer Techniken in der VR China – ein neues Modul chinesischer kutlureller Identität?" In *China, Japan und das Andere. Ostasiatische Identitäten im Zeitalter des Transkulturellen*, edited by Stephan Köhn and Michael Schimmelpfennig. Wiesbaden: Harrassowitz. 239–263. Eng. trsl. available at http://www.ikgf.fau.de/content/articles/Michael_Lackner_-_The_Renaissance_of_Divinatory_Techniques_in_the_Peoples_Republic_20111214.pdf, accessed March 24, 2016.

Lai, Lei Kuan Rongdao. 2013. "Praying for the Republic: Buddhist Education, Student-Monks, and Citizenship in Modern China (1911–1949)." Ph.D. diss., McGill University.

Lai, Rongdao, and Jessica L. Main. 2013. "Feature: Socially Engaged Buddhism. Introduction: Reformulating 'Socially Engaged Buddhism' as an Analytical Category." *The Eastern Buddhist* 44(2): 1–34.

Lamnek, Siegfried. 1995. *Qualitative Sozialforschung: Lehrbuch*. Weinheim: Beltz Psychologie Verlagsunion.

Lau, D.C., trsl. 1970. *Mencius*. London: Penguin.

Learman, Linda, ed. 2005. *Buddhist Missionaries in the Era of Globalization*, Honolulu: University of Hawai'i Press.

Legge, James, trsl. 1861. *The Chinese Classics, vol. 1*. London: Trübner & Co. Reprint. Taipeh: SMC 1998.

Lin, Cheng-Yi, and Hsing Woan-Chiao. 2009. "Culture-led Urban Regeneration and Community Mobilization: The Case of the Taipei Bao-an Temple Area, Taiwan." *Urban Studies* 46(7): 1317–1342.

Lin, Jan, and Christopher Mele, eds. 2005. *The Urban Sociology Reader*. Abingdon: Routledge.

Lin, Meirong 林美容. 2007. “Taiwan Guanyin xinyang de zhuyao xingtai 台湾观音信仰的主要形态 –Jianlun minjian fojiao yu minjian xinyang de guanxi 兼论民间佛教与民间信仰的关系” [The outstanding features of Guanyin belief in Taiwan: Discussing simultaneously the relation between popular Buddhism and popular belief]. In *Minjian fojiao yanjiu* 民间佛教研究, edited by Tan Weilun 谭伟伦. Beijing: *Zhonghua Shuju* 中华书局. 15–31.

Liu, Haiyan 刘海燕. 2004. *Cong minjian dao jingdian: Guan Yu xingxiang yu Guan Yu chongbai de shengcheng yanbian shilun* 从民间到经典: 关羽形象与关羽崇拜的生成演变史论 *[From folk to classics: A theory of the history of the generation and development of the figure of Guan Yu and Guan Yu worship]*. Shanghai: Shanghai Sanlian Shudian 上海三联书店.

Livezey, Lowell W., ed. 2000a. *Public Religion and Urban Transformation: Faith in the City*. New York: New York University Press.

Livezey, Lowell W. 2000b. “Introduction: The New Context of Urban Religion.” In *Public Religion and Urban Transformation: Faith in the City*, edited by Lowell W. Livezey. New York: New York University Press. 3–25.

Lo, Shih-Wei. 1996. “Figures of Displacement: Modes of Urbanity in Taipei 1740–1995.” Ph.D. diss., Katholieke Universiteit Leuven.

Lucius-Hoene, Gabriele, and Arnulf Deppermann. 2002. *Rekonstruktion narrativer Identität: Ein Arbeitsbuch zur Analyse narrativer Interviews*. Wiesbaden: VS Verlag für Sozialwissenschaften.

Luckmann, Thomas. 1963. *Das Problem der Religion in der modernen Gesellschaft: Institution, Person und Weltanschauung*. Freiburg: Romback 1963. (Eng. trsl.: Luckmann, Thomas. 1967. *The Invisible Religion: The Problem of Religion in Modern Society*. London: Macmillan.)

Luo, Qihong 羅啟宏. 1993. “Taiwan Sheng junheng difang fazhan zhi yanjiu 台灣省均衡地方發展之研究” *[Research on the balanced regional development of Taiwan Province]*. Ph.D. diss., Chinese Cultural University 中國文化大學.

Lutz, Helma, Bettina Dausien, Bettina Völter, and Gabriele Rosenthal. 2009. *Biographieforschung im Diskurs*. 2nd ed. Wiesbaden: VS Verlag.

Mann, S. 2007. “Understanding Farm Succession by the Objective Hermeneutics Method.” *Sociologia Ruralis* 47(4): 369–383.

Manthorpe, Jonathan. 2005. *Forbidden Nation: A History of Taiwan*. New York: Palgrave Macmillan.

Martin, David. 2005. *On Secularization*. Aldershot: Ashgate.

Masini, Frederico. 1993. “The Formation of Modern Chinese Lexicon and Its Evolution Toward a National Language: The Period from 1840 to 1898.”

Monograph Series of the Journal of Chinese Linguistics 6. Berkeley: University of California Press.

Mathews' Chinese-English Dictionary. 1975. 13th ed. Cambridge: Harvard University Press.

McLeod, Hugh. 1978. "Religion in the City." *Urban History Yearbook* 1978: 7–22.

McNair, Amy. 2007. *Donors of Longmen: Faith, Politics, and Patronage in Medieval Chinese Buddhist Sculpture.* Honolulu: University of Hawai'i Press.

McRae, John R. 2003. *Seeing Through Zen. Encounter, Transformation, and Genealogy in Chinese Chan Buddhism*. Berkeley: University of California Press.

Meja, Volker, Dieter Misgeld, and Nico Steht, ed. 1987. *Modern German Sociology.* New York: Columbia University Press.

MFQWJ. 2006: *Minguo fojiao qikan wenxian jicheng* 民國佛教期刊文獻集成 *[Complete Collection of Republican-Era Buddhist Periodical Literature]*, edited by Huang Xianian 黃夏年 and Li Yangyuan 李陽泉, 209 vols. Beijing: Quanguo Tushuguan Wenxian Suowei Fuzhi Zhongxin 全國圖書館文獻縮微複製中心.

MFQWJB. 2007: *Minguo fojiao qikan wenxian jicheng bubian* 民國佛教期刊文獻集成補編 *[Supplement to the Complete Collection of Republican-Era Buddhist Periodical Literature]*, edited by Huang Xianian 黃夏年 and Li Yangyuan 李陽泉, 86 vols. Beijing: Quanguo Tushuguan Wenxian Suowei Fuzhi Zhongxin 全國圖書館文獻縮微複製中心.

Mitchell, Robert Edward. 1972. *Levels of Emotional Strain in Southeast Asian Cities: A Study of Individual Responses to the Stresses of Urbanization and Industrialization. A Project of the Urban Family Life Survey*, July 1969. Taipeh: The Orient Cultural Service.

Mögling, Wilmar, trsl. 1994. *Die Kunst der Staatsführung: Die Schriften des chinesischen Meisters Han Fei.* Köln: Komet.

Müller, Gotelind. 1993. *Buddhismus und Moderne: Ouyang Jingwu, Taixu und das Ringen um ein zeitgemäßes Selbstverständnis im chinesischen Buddhismus des frühen 20. Jahrhunderts*. Stuttgart: Steiner.

Nedostup, Rebecca. 2009. *Superstitious Regimes: Religion and the Politics of Chinese Modernity*. Cambridge: Harvard University Press.

Nelsen, Hart M., and Hugh P. Witt. 1972. "Religion and the Migrant in the City: A Test of Holt's Cultural Shock Thesis." *Social Forces* 50(3): 379–384.

Oberlaender, Franklin A. 1997. "My God, They Just Have Other Interests." *The Oral History Review* 24(1): 23–53.

Obeyesekere, Gananath. 1968. "Theodicy, Sin and Salvation in a Sociology of Buddhism." In *Dialectic in Practical Religion*, edited by E.R. Leach. Cambridge: Cambridge University Press. 7–40.

Obeyesekere, Gananath, and Richard Gombrich. 1988. *Buddhism Transformed: Religious Change in Sri Lanka*. Princeton: Princeton University Press.

Oevermann, Ulrich, Tilman Allert, Elisabeth Konau, and Jürgen Krambeck. 1979. "Die Methodologie einer 'objektiven Hermeneutik' und ihre allgemeine forschungslogische Bedeutung in den Sozialwissenschaften." In *Interpretative Verfahren in den Sozial- und Textwissenschaften*, edited by Hans-Georg Soeffner. Stuttgart: Metzler. 352–434.

Oevermann, Ulrich. 1981. "Fallrekonstruktion und Strukturgeneralisierung als Beitrag der objektiven Hermeneutik zur soziologisch-strukturtheoretischen Analyse." Accessed Jan 6, 2016. http://publikationen.ub.uni-frankfurt.de/frontdoor/index/index/docId/4955.

Oevermann, Ulrich. 2000. "Die Methode der Fallrekonstruktion in der Grundlagenforschung sowie der klinischen und pädagogischen Praxis." In *Die Fallrekonstruktion–Sinnverstehen in der sozialwissenschaftlichen Forschung*, edited by K. Kraimer. Frankfurt: Suhrkamp. 58–157.

Oevermann, Ulrich. 2001. "Die Struktur sozialer Deutungsmuster–Versuch einer Aktualisierung." *Sozialer Sinn* 2001(1): 35–81.

Oevermann, Ulrich. 2002. "Klinische Soziologie auf der Basis der Methodologie der objektiven Hermeneutik–Manifest der objektiv hermeneutischen Sozialforschung." Accessed Jan 6, 2016. http://www.ihsk.de/publikationen/Ulrich_Oevermann-Manifest_der_objektiv_hermeneutischen_Sozialforschung.pdf.

Oevermann, Ulrich. 2004. "Objektivität des Protokolls und Subjektivität als Forschungsgegenstand." *Zeitschrift für qualitative Bildungs-, Beratungs- und Sozialforschung* 2004(2): 311–336.

O'Flaherty, Wendy. 1980. *Karma and Rebirth in Classical Indian Tradition*. Berkeley: University of California Press.

Olson, Daniel V.A. 2000. *The Secularization Debate*. London: Rowman & Littlefield.

Orsi, Robert A., ed. 1999a. *Gods of the City. Religion and the American Urban Landscape*. Bloomington: Indiana University Press.

Orsi, Robert A. 1999b. "Introduction: Crossing the City Line." In *Gods of the City: Religion and the American Urban Landscape*, edited by Robert A. Orsi. Bloomington: Indiana University Press. 1–78.

Pecora, Vincent P. 2006. *Secularization and Cultural Criticism*. Chicago: Chicago University Press.

Palmer, David A. 2007. *Qigong Fever: Body, Science, and Utopia in China*. New York: Columbia University Press.

Panofsky, Erwin. 1967. *Architecture gothique et pensée scolastique. Traduction et postface de Pierre Bourdieu*. Paris: Éditions de Minuit.

Park, Robert E., Ernest W. Burgess, and Roderick D. McKenzie. 1928. *The City*. Chicago: University of Chicago Press.

Pittman, Don A. 2001. *Toward a Modern Chinese Buddhism: Taixu's Reforms.* Honolulu: University of Hawai'i Press.

Pye, Michael. 1996. "Aum Shinrikyō. Can Religious Studies Cope?" *Religion* 26: 261–270.

Queen, Christopher S., and Sallie King, eds. 1996a. *Engaged Buddhism: Buddhist Liberation Movements in Asia.* New York: State University of New York Press.

Queen, Christopher S. 1996b. "Introduction: The Shapes and Sources of Engaged Buddhism." In *Engaged Buddhism: Buddhist Liberation Movements in Asia*, edited by Christopher S. Queen and Sallie King. New York: State University of New York Press. 1–44.

Queen, Christopher S., ed. 2000a. *Engaged Buddhism in the West.* Boston: Wisdom Publications.

Queen, Christopher S. 2000b. "Introduction: A New Buddhism." In *Engaged Buddhism in the West*, edited by Christopher S. Queen. Boston: Wisdom Publications. 1–31.

Queen, Christopher S. 2003. "Introduction. From altruism to activism." In *Action Dharma: New Studies in Engaged Buddhism*, edited by Christopher S. Queen, Charles Prebish, and Damien Keown. London: RoutledgeCurzon.1–35.

Queen, Christopher S., Charles Prebish, and Damien Keown, eds. 2003. *Action Dharma: New Studies in Engaged Buddhism.* London: RoutledgeCurzon.

Qiu, Baoxing. 2007. *Harmony and Innovation: Problems, Danger and Solutions in Dealing with Rapid Urbanization in China.* Milano: L'Arcaedizioni.

Reader, Ian, and George J. Tanabe. 1998. *Practically Religious: Worldly Benefits and the Common Religion of Japan.* Honolulu: Hawai'i University Press.

Reckwitz, Andreas. 1997. "Kulturtheorie, Systemtheorie und das sozialtheoretische Muster der Innen-Außen-Differenz." *Zeitschrift für Soziologie* 26: 317–336.

Reichertz, Jo. 2004. "Objective Hermeneutics and Hermeneutic Sociology of Knowledge." In *A Companion to Qualitative Research*, edited by Uwe Flick, Ernst von Kardoff, and Ines Steinke. London: Sage. 290–295.

Rhys Davids, T.W., and J.E. Carpenter, eds. 1890–1911. *Dīghanikāya.* 3 vols. London: Henry Frowde.

Ritzinger, Justin R. 2010. "Anarchy in the Pure Land: Tradition, Modernity, and the Reinvention of the Cult of Maitreya in Republican China." Ph.D. diss., Harvard University.

Roach, Geshe Michael. 2000. *The Diamond Cutter: The Buddha on Strategies for Managing Your Business and Your Life.* New York: Doubleday. (Chinese translation: Luo'ou Maike 羅區・麥可. 2001. *Dang heshang yudao zuanshi–Yige foxue boshi ruhe zai shangchang shang shijian fofa* 當和尚遇到鑽石: 一個佛學博士如何在商場上實踐佛法. Taipeh: *Maotouying* 貓頭鷹.)

Samuels, Jeffrey. 1999. "Views of Householders and Lay Disciples in the Sutta Piṭaka: A Reconsideration of the Lay/Monastic Opposition." *Religion* 29: 231–241.

Schak, David, and Michael Hsin-Huang Hsiao. 2005. "Taiwan's Socially Engaged Buddhist Groups." *China Perspectives* 59: 43–59.

Schopen, Gregory. 1997. *Bones, Stones, and Buddhist Monks: Collected Papers on the Archaeology, Epigraphy, and Texts of Monastic Buddhism in India.* Honolulu: University of Hawai'i Press.

Schütze, Fritz. 1983. "Biographieforschung und narratives Interview." *Neue Praxis. Kritische Zeitschrift Für Sozialarbeit Und Sozialpädagogik* 13: 283–293.

Schütze, Fritz. 1984. "Kognitive Figuren des autobiographischen Stegreiferzählens." In *Biographie und soziale Wirklichkeit: Neue Beiträge und Forschungsperspektiven*, edited by M. Kohli and G. Robert. Stuttgart: Metzler. 78–117.

Seiwert, Hubert. 2003. *Popular Religious Movements and Heterodox Sects in Chinese History*. Leiden: Brill.

Shahar, Meir. 1998. *Crazy Ji: Chinese Religion and Popular Literature.* Cambridge: Harvard University Press.

Sharf, Robert H. 2002. *Coming to terms with Chinese Buddhism: A Reading of the Treasure Store Treatise.* Honolulu: University of Haiwai'i Press.

Slote, Walter H., and George A. De Vos. 1998. *Confucianism and the Family.* Albany: State University of New York.

Smyer Yü, Dan. 2012. *The Spread of Tibetan Buddhism in China: Charisma, Money, Enlightenment.* Oxon: Routledge.

Sparham, Gareth. 2004. "Saṅgha." In *Encyclopedia of Buddhism*, vol. 2. 740–744.

Speare, Alden Jr., Paul K.C. Liu, and Ching-lung Tsay. 1988. *Urbanization and Development. The Rural Urban Transition in Taiwan*. Boulder: Westview.

Stark, Rodney. 1999. "Secularization, R.I.P." *Sociology of Religion* 60(3): 249–273.

Stevenson, Daniel B. 2001. "Text, Image, and Transformation in the History of the 'Shuilu fahui', the Buddhist Rite for Deliverance of Creatures of Water and Land." In *Latter Days of the Law: Images of Chinese Buddhism 850–1850. Cultural Intersections in Later Chinese Buddhism*, edited by M. Weidner. Honolulu: University of Hawai'i Press. 30–72.

Taiwan Sōtokufu 台灣總督府, and Keijirō Marui 丸井圭治郎. 1919. *Taiwan shūkyō chōsa hōkokusho: dai 1-kan* 台灣宗教調查報告書（第一卷）*[Report on the survey of religion in Taiwan]*. Reprint, Taipeh: Jieyou Chubanshe 捷幼出版社, 1993.

Tarocco, Francesca. 2007. *The Cultural Practices of Modern Chinese Buddhism: Attuning the Dharma.* London: Routledge.

Tarocco, Francesca. 2008. "The Making of 'Religion' in Modern China." In *Religion, Language and Power*, edited by N. Green and Mary Searle-Chateerjie. London: Routledge. 42–56.

ter Haar, Barend. 1992. *The White Lotus Teachings in Chinese Religious History*. Honolulu: University of Hawai'i Press.

Ting, Jen-chieh (Ding Renjie 丁仁傑). 1997. "Helping Behavior in Social Contexts: A Case Study of the Tzu-Chi Association in Taiwan." Ph.D. diss., University of Wisconsin–Madison.

Ting, Jen-chieh. 2006. "A Typological Discussion of Civil Engagement: The Case of the Buddhist Tzu-Chi Association in Taiwan." Paper presented at the AAS Annual Meeting, Panel 200: Dynamics of Civil Society in East Asia, April 9, 2006.

TLS (*Thesaurus Linguae Sericae. An Historical and Comparative Encyclopaedia of Chinese Conceptual Schemes*), edited by Christoph Harbsmeier and Jiang Shaoyu 蔣紹愚. Accessed April 1, 2009, and Jan 21, 2016. http://tls.uni-hd.de.

Travagnin, Stefania. 2009. "The Mādhyamika Dimension of Yinshun. A Restatement of the School of Nāgārjuna in Twentieth-Century Chinese Buddhism." Ph.D. diss., SOAS University of London.

Tung, An-Chi, Chen Chaonan, and Liu Paul Ke-Chih. 2006. "The Emergence of the Neo-Extended Family in Contemporary Taiwan." *Journal of Population Studies* 32: 123–152.

Turner, Bryan S. 1984. *The Body and Society: Explorations in Social Theory*. New York: Blackwell.

Unger, Ulrich. 2000. *Grundbegriffe der altchinesischen Philosophie. Ein Wörterbuch für die Klassische Periode*. Darmstadt: WBG.

van der Veer, Peter. 2002. "Religion in South Asia." *Annual Review of Anthropology* 31: 173–187.

van der Veer, Peter, ed. 2015. *Handbook of Religion and the Asian City: Aspiration and Urbanization in the Twenty-First Century*. Oakland: University of California Press.

Wang, Chia-Huang. 2003. "Taipei as a Global City: A Theoretical and Empirical Examination." *Urban Studies* 40(2): 309–334.

Wang, Jianchuan 王見川. 1996. *Taiwan de zhaijiao yu zhaitang* 台灣的齋教與齋堂 *[The Vegetarian Religion and Vegetarian Halls of Taiwan]*. Taipeh: Nantian Shuju 南天書局.

Wang, Jianchuan 王見川, and Li Shiwei 李世偉. 2004. *Taiwan de simiao yu zhaitang* 台灣的寺廟與齋堂 *[Temple and Vegetarian Halls of Taiwan]*. Luzhou 蘆洲: Boyang Wenhua 博揚文化.

Warner, R. Stephen. 2000. “Epilogue: Building Religious Communities at the Turn of the Century.” In *Public Religion and Urban Transformation. Faith in the City*, edited by Lowell W. Livezey. New York: New York University Press. 295–307.

Welch, Holmes. 1967. *The Buddhist Revival in China. 1900–1950.* Cambridge: Harvard University Press.

Wenzel-Teuber, Katharina. 2013. “Statistical Update on Religions and Churches in the People’s Republic of China.” *Religions & Christianity in Today’s China* 4(2): 17–39.

Wernet, Andreas. 2000. *Einführung in die Interpretationstechnik der Objektiven Hermeneutik.* Wiesbaden: VS Verlag für Sozialwissenschaften.

Wernet, Andreas. 2014. “Hermeneutics and Objective Hermeneutics.” In *The Sage Handbook of Qualitative Data Analysis*, edited by Uwe Flick. London: Sage. 234–246.

Williams, Duncan Ryūken, and Christopher S. Queen, eds. 1999. *American Buddhism: Methods and Findings in Recent Scholarship*. London: Routledge Curzon.

Winston, Diane. 1999. *Red Hot and Righteous: The Urban Religion of the Salvation Army*. Cambridge: Harvard University Press.

Wirth, Louis. 1938. “Urbanism as a Way of Life.” *The American Journal of Sociology* 44(1): 1–24.

Wohlrab-Sahr, Monika. 1998. “Symbolische Transformation krisenhafter Erfahrung. Über Form und Funktion von Konversionen zum Islam in Deutschland und den Vereinigten Staaten von Amerika.” Habil. thesis, FU Berlin.

Wohlrab-Sahr, Monika. 1999. “Conversion to Islam between Syncretism and Symbolic Battle.” *Social Compass* 46: 351–362.

Wohlrab-Sahr, Monika. 2006. “Symbolizing Distance: Conversion to Islam in Germany and the United States.” In *Women Embracing Islam: Gender and Conversion in the West*, edited by Karin van Nieuwkerk. Austin: University of Texas Press. 71–92.

Xiao, Jinsong 蕭金松 (Hsiao, Chin-Sung). 2002. “Taiwan zangchuan fojiao fazhan guankui 台灣藏傳佛教發展管窺” [A Personal Look at the Development of Tibetan Buddhism in Taiwan]. *Faguang Xuetan* 法光學壇 6: 102–116.

Yang, Fenggang. 2006. “The Red, Black, and Gray Markets of Religion in China.” *The Sociological Quarterly* 47: 93–122.

Yang, Huinan 楊惠南. 2000. "Cong Yinshun de renjian fojiao tantao Xinyu She yu Xiandai Chan de zongjiao fazhan 從印順的人間佛教探討新雨社與現代禪的宗教發展" [Discussing from Yinshun's 'Buddhism among the people' the religious development of the New Rain Society and Modern Chan]. *Foxue Yanjiu Zhongxin Xuebao* 佛學研究中心學報 5: 275-312.

Yao, Xinzhong. 2007. "Religious Belief and Practice in Urban China 1995–2005." *Journal of Contemporary Religion* 22(2): 169–185.

Yarnall, Thomas Freeman. 2003. "Engaged Buddhism: New and Improved!(?) Made in the U.S.A. of Asian Materials." In *Action Dharma: New Studies in Engaged Buddhism*, edited by Christopher S. Queen, Charles Prebish, and Damien Keown. London: RoutledgeCurzon. 286–344.

Yoder, Don. 1974. "Toward a Definition of Folk Religion." *Western Folklore* 33(1): 2–15.

Yü, Chün-fang. 2001. *Kuan-yin: The Chinese Transformation of Avalokiteśvara*. New York: Columbia University Press.

Zai, Ailian 載愛蓮 (Elise Anne DeVido). 2005. "Nüxing zai Ciji 女性在慈濟" [Women in Tzu Chi]. *Renlai Lunbian Yuekan* 人籟論辨月刊, May 2005: 42-51.

Zhang, Kunzhen 張崑振. 2003. *Taiwan de lao Zhaitang* 台灣的老齋堂 [The old Vegetarian Halls of Taiwan]. Xindian 新店: Yuanzu Wenhua 遠足文化.

Zhang, Maogui 張茂貴, and Lin Benxuan 林本炫. 1992. "Zongjiao de shehui yixiang. Yi ge zhishi shehuixue de keti 宗教的社會意像 一個知識社會學的課題" [The Social Imaginations of Religion: A Research Problem for Sociology of Knowledge]. Zhongyang Yanjiuyuan Minzu Yanjiusuo Jikan 中央研究院民族研究所集刊 74: 95–123.

Zhonghua minguo bashi nian Taiwan Diqu: Zongjiao tuanti diaocha baogao 中華民國八十年台灣地區: 宗教團體調查報告 *[Year 80 of the Republic of China, region of Taiwan: Report on the Survey of Religious Associations]*. 1992. Taipeh: Neizheng Bu Tongji Chu 內政部統計處.

Zhonghua minguo bashiyi nian Taiwan Diqu: Zongjiao tuanti diaocha baogao 中華民國八十一年台灣地區: 宗教團體調查報告 *[Year 81 of the Republic of China, region of Taiwan: Report on the Survey of Religious Associations]*. 1993. Taipeh: Neizheng Bu Tongji Chu 內政部統計處.

*Zhonghua minguo bashi'er nian Taiwan Diqu: Zongjiao tuanti diaocha baogao*中華民國八十二年台灣地區: 宗教團體調查報告 *[Year 82 of the Republic of China, region of Taiwan: Report on the Survey of Religious Associations]*. 1995. Taipeh: *Neizheng Bu Tongji Chu*內政部統計處.

Zhang, Li. 2015. "Cultivating Happiness. Psychotherapy, Spirituality, and Well-Being in a Transforming Urban China." In *Handbook of Religion and the Asian City: Aspiration and Urbanization in the Twenty-First Century*, edited by Peter van der Veer. Oakland: University of California Press. 315–332.

Zhang, Yinghua 章英華, and Zhuan, Yingzhi 傅仰止, eds. 2007. *Xingzheng Yuan Guojia Kexue Weiyuan Zhuanti Yanjiu Jihua Zhixing Chengguo Baogao. Taiwan Shehui Bianqian Jiben Diaocha Jihua. Di si qi di wu ci Diaocha Jihua Zhixing Baogao.* 行政院國家科學委員會專題研究計畫執行成果報告. 台灣社會變遷基本調查計畫. 第四期第五次調查計畫執行報告 *[Report on the results of the achievements for the monographic study agenda of the Administrative Yuan's governmental scientific committee. Agenda of the Social Change Survey in Taiwan. Report on the achievements of the survey agenda, 4th round, 5th time]*. Taipeh: Zhongyang Yanjiu Yuan Shehuixue Yanjiusuo 中央研究院社會學研究所.

Abstract

Buddhists are more frequent in urban than in rural Taiwan–this statistical discovery of the present volume leads to an investigation into the motivations of people who denote themselves as Buddhist. Nine biographical narrative interviews stand central in an analysis following *Structural Hermeneutics*–a sociological method applied for the first time in an Asian context.

Guggenmos analyses why it can be attractive for an urban citizen to consider him- or herself a lay Buddhist. She surveys underlying conventional orientations as well as modes to intensively exploit Buddhism for a modernity compatible self-construction. Are Buddhist identification patterns advantageous to members living under constant cultural fluctuation? The Buddhist religious field reveals an integrative dynamic. Buddhists in Taiwan construct Buddhism as a highly flexible script with a strong experiential dimension. Self-aesthetisation, leisure-time management, entertainment, body-shaping and bodily practices, conscious life-construction, up to an international awareness, are creatively applied. Historical developments, organisational resources, Buddhist discourses like that on "Engaged Buddhism", as well as reflections on the role of religion in cities deliver helpful background information. A comparative approach to Mainland China rounds off this picture.

The book provides a comprehensive overview about lay Buddhist orientations in Taiwan and describes how the driving force and the major reason for the attraction of denoting oneself a lay Buddhist in contemporary Taiwan is to be found at the core of the social dynamic in the transforming society.

Esther-Maria Guggenmos is Deputy Chair of Sinology at the University Erlangen-Nuremberg. Trained in Sinology and Religious Studies her research focus lies in the field of Chinese Buddhist cultural history and transmission processes including contemporary developments.

BEITRÄGE ZUR KULTURWISSENSCHAFTLICHEN SÜD- UND OSTASIENFORSCHUNG

ISSN 2195-0962

Herausgegeben von
Eva De Clercq | Bart Dessein | Franziska Ehmcke
Ann Heirman | Andreas Niehaus

1 | Weber, Chantal M.
Kulturhistorische Netzwerkanalyse.
Am Beispiel des japanischen Tee-Meisters Kanamori Sôwa
2011. 267 S. Kt. € 38,00
ISBN 978-3-89913-863-4

2 | Ehmcke, Franziska –
Müller, Martin (Hrsg.)
Reisen im Zwischenraum – Zur Interkulturalität von Kulturwissenschaft.
Festschrift für Helmolt Vittinghoff zum 65. Geburtstag
2012. 241 S. Fb. € 39,00
ISBN 978-3-89913-928-0

3 | Theile, Nina
Der *on'yōji* Abe no Seimei und die *oni*.
Genese einer literarischen Figur
2013. 318 S. 6 Abb. Kt. € 42,00
ISBN 978-3-89913-964-8

4 | Frings, Alexander
Feldforschung der Internierung.
Zeitgenössische Sozial- und Kulturwissenschaft und japano-amerikanische Loyalität (1942-45)
2013. 283 S. Kt. € 38,00
ISBN 978-3-95650-017-6

5 | Wittkamp, Robert F.
Altjapanische Erinnerungsdichtung:
Landschaft, Schrift und kulturelles Gedächtnis im *Man'yōshū* (萬葉集)
Band 1: Prolegomenon: Landschaft im Werden der Waka-Dichtung – Band 2: Schriftspiele und Erinnerungsdichtung
2014. 279/500 S. 2 Bde. Fb. € 98,00
ISBN 978-3-95650-009-1

6 | Schiedges, Olaf
Die Raumordnung in ausgewählten Romanen des japanischen Schriftstellers Murakami Haruki
2016. 355 S. Kt. € 45,00
ISBN 978-3-95650-222-4

7 | Guggenmos, Esther-Maria
"I believe in Buddhism and Travelling".
Denoting Oneself a Lay Buddhist in Contemporary Urban Taiwan
2017. XXVIII/365 S. Kt. € 55,00
ISBN 978-3-95650-216-3

ERGON-VERLAG · WÜRZBURG